MIKE ASHLEY is an author and editor of over sixty books, including many Mammoth titles. He worked for over thirty years in local government but is now a full-time writer and researcher specializing in ancient history, historical fiction and fantasy, crime and science fiction. He lives in Kent with his wife and over 20,000 books.

Praise for *British Monarchs*

'Mike Ashley doesn't skimp on dates.'

Independent on Sunday

'. . . destined to be probably the most complete and authoritative record.'

Books Magazine

Other titles in this series

A Brief History of The Boxer Rebellion
Diana Preston

A Brief History of The Druids
Peter Berresford Ellis

A Brief History of Fighting Ships
David Davies

A Brief History of The Great Moghuls
Bamber Gascoigne

A Brief History of The Royal Flying Corps in World War I
Ralph Barker

A Brief History of Science
Thomas Crump

A Brief History of The Tudor Age
Jasper Ridley

A BRIEF HISTORY OF

BRITISH KINGS & QUEENS

MIKE ASHLEY

CARROLL & GRAF PUBLISHERS
New York

Carroll & Graf Publishers
An imprint of Avalon Publishing Group, Inc
161 William Street
16th Floor
NY 10038–2607
www.carrollandgraf.com

First Carroll & Graf edition, 2002

First published in the UK as *British Monarchs*
by Robinson Publishing 1998

Published as *The Mammoth Book of British Kings & Queens*
by Robinson Publishing 1999

This revised and abridged edition published in the UK by Robinson,
an imprint of Constable & Robinson Ltd, 2002

ISBN 0–7867–1104–3

Library of Congress Cataloging-in-Publication
Data is available on file

Printed and bound in the EU

CONTENTS

PREFACE

I have long been fascinated by the kings and queens who have ruled these British Isles. I don't mean simply the forty-three from William the Conqueror to our present Elizabeth II, only twelve of whom have ruled a 'united' kingdom, but all of them, almost a thousand, stretching back over two thousand years.

Many of them we know little about, yet they all contributed to the development (not all of it beneficial) of these islands, and many of them interweave in a complex and fascinating way. You can picture it almost like the many tributaries of the mighty river Amazon. Hundreds of these small streams and rivulets starting high up in the Andes and other mountainous regions of South America, filter down, combine and gradually create bigger and bigger rivers until they all flow into the Amazon, the greatest river of them all.

So too the many chieftains and petty tribal kings of England, each of whom ruled their territories, fought with others over theirs, gradually merging some territory, perhaps dividing others, but all steadily coming together over a period of some seventeen hundred years until the United Kingdom emerged in the eighteenth century. The British royal family is one of the oldest in the world. Queen Elizabeth II can trace her ancestry back with certainty for fifteen hundred years and with a degree of accuracy another five hundred. Very few of the world's remaining royal families can do that.

That has been my fascination. Over the years I have gathered data on all of these rulers and, in 1998, I was at last able to bring this together in my book *British Monarchs*, subsequently issued in paperback as *The Mammoth Book of British Kings & Queens*. That was a rather mighty tome – all 840 or so tightly printed pages – but it achieved what I wanted to do, capturing all the data available on those thousand kings.

However, the picture is so vast and complex that it helps to have a simpler version, one that tells the story from start to finish without too many diversions and backwaters and tributaries. With the considerable help of Elfreda Powell, this *Brief History* does just that. You will be able to follow through the story of the many rulers of Britain from the earliest times down to the present day and see how the United Kingdom came about and what part each ruler played.

Today the British monarchy has but a symbolic, ceremonial role, whose crucial power is one of restraint. This, of course, was not always so. Our first kings were absolute rulers and warriors. Over the centuries the concept of kingship has changed drastically, often turbulently, as our warring kingdoms evolved, conquered and eventually coalesced.

Fighting and slaughter were not confined to neighbouring tribes and kingdoms, or to kings and their ambitious relatives, but wave after wave of invaders – Celts, Romans, Saxons, Angles, Danes, Vikings, Normans – raided our shores, causing havoc and devastation, until the Normans imposed their strict rule and created order. The main part of this book concentrates on that magnificent procession of strong, weak, benign and bloodthirsty kings and queens whose ambitions, or lack of them, made this kingdom what it is today. The book is also full of charts and lists to help take you through these complex tributaries to the one mighty river of today.

Whether one is a devout royalist or a staunch republican one cannot but be intrigued and fascinated by the process that caused this evolution and by the thousand or so known kings or queens who have ruled part or all of Britain. This book tells that story.

– *Mike Ashley*

Kingdom Against Kingdom:

Early Britain

THE CELTS (700BC–AD43)

The islands that form Great Britain have been occupied by man since the end of the last Ice Age, when a social structure began to emerge that brought with it the need for more powerful and organized leaders. It seems that communities inevitably fall into hierarchies and need a dominant figure to lead, someone whom they can respect and elevate to a higher level – almost to one of godhead. We have no record of what these people were like in Britain's earliest times, however. Whether they were men who had distinguished themselves through brute strength or cunning, or whether they possessed certain outstanding mystical qualities to become leaders of their nomadic tribes, we do not know. But their role would have been primarily to defend their territory and help their kinsmen to subsist through the changing seasons by hunting and gleaning.

There have been kings and chieftains in Britain for at least 3,000 years, probably much longer. At first they lived in tiny agrarian communities commanding high ground, in a land of forests and swamps, pasture and moors, the population of the whole country not exceeding about 20,000. Historians vary on dates, but around the eighth century BC the first wave of Celts arrived from mainland Europe, and probably finally settled in Ireland and the Isle of Man; the second wave came in the fifth century BC and, with their superior knowledge of iron to make weapons and farm tools, and their horses and knowledge of the wheel, they soon established a significant tribal structure with themselves as the dominant aristocracy.

In about 75BC and over the next hundred years, there were fresh invasions of Celts from Gaul, who fought with swords and spears and, using chariots were highly mobile. These were the Belgae who settled in what is now Kent, the Atrebates in Hampshire and Sussex, and the Parisii in Yorkshire; while other Celtic tribes, their sworn enemies, were the Trinovantes in Essex, the Iceni in Norfolk, the Dobunni in the Cotswolds, the Dumnonii in Cornwall, the Silures and Ordovices in Wales and the Marches, and the Brigantes of Yorkshire, all independent of one another. In northern Britain (now Scotland) were the Picts. With this steady influx of Celts the population rose to around 250,000.

When the Greek navigator Pytheas visited Britain in the fourth century BC and sailed around the island, he noted that it was a country of many kings. Pytheas visited the tin mines of Cornwall where there was a thriving trade with Greece and the Middle East. Britain was known to the Greeks as the Tin, or Pretanic, Isles, from whence the name Britain comes.

We know little of these kingdoms' individual leaders before the Romans recorded them. Celtic tradition, however, has kept alive many of the names of Irish kings and there are also many stories about the Irish settlement of parts of Britain. One such tells us that around the year 330BC Fergus, the son of Feradach, a descendant of Conn of A Hundred Battles, high king of Ireland, settled in the western highlands of Argyll. There is a legend, variously dated, that Cruithne, the ancestor of the Picts, settled in northern Britain from Ireland and from his sons sprang the seven provinces of Pictland. Setting aside the likelihood of such legends there is little doubt that there was much relationship between the

Celts of Britain and of Ireland throughout the pre-Roman era, and that this continued beyond the Roman conquest.

Legend also tells us of a British king, Beli Mawr (Mawr means 'the Great'), father of Llud, mentioned in the twelfth-century *History of the Kings of Britain,* written by Geoffrey of Monmouth, who, again, relies on legend rather than fact (he also claims that the first king of Britain was Brutus, great grandson of the Trojan prince Aeneas!). Llud's name still survives in Ludgate in the City of London.

The earliest known historical British king is Caswallon or Cassivelaunos who flourished between 60 and 48BC. He ruled the Catuvellauni tribe who dominated the lands to the north of the Thames, and most of what is now Bedfordshire, Hertfordshire, Berkshire and Oxfordshire and into Wiltshire. His stronghold was at Wheathamstead. We know nothing of Caswallon's background other than that he was allegedly the son of Beli and brother of Lud. He was evidently a powerful warrior able to establish himself as the high king of the British tribes as, before Caesar's invasion of Britain in 55BC, Caswallon had already attacked the tribe of the Trinovantes in Essex and killed their king. Other, smaller tribes looked to Caswallon as their overlord, and, more importantly, protector, as Caesar prepared for his invasion.

Julius Caesar's first foray into Britain was something of a disaster. In 59BC he had decided to rout the troublesome Belgae from Gaul and many had fled to join their kinsmen in Kent. Caesar assembled a fleet of a hundred ships and an army of 10,000 infantry and cavalry and set sail for the Kentish Coast. While the infantry had problems finding a suitable landing place, the cavalry who followed were forced to return to harbour in a violent storm and a number of transport ships 'were shattered, having lost their cables, anchors and the remainder of their tackle,' near what is now Deal, and 'were unusable, which . . . threw the whole army into great consternation', Caesar recorded. After a few minor skirmishes Caesar ordered a retreat to Gaul. Even his second campaign a year later was not decisive. It is said that Caswallon had an army of over 4,000 charioteers (although that seems a wild exaggeration), let alone infantry. But, in the end, they were no match for the Romans.

After a series of battles and sorties, the British were forced into an encampment guarded by stakes along the north side of the Thames. Realizing the strength of the Roman army, Caswallon negotiated with Caesar, who exacted tributes and hostages, and returned to Gaul, where he feared another uprising. The fact that Caesar was unable to conquer Britain outright says something for the power and determination of the British tribes and of Caswallon as leader. The Romans saw it slightly differently: 'Caesar . . . did indeed intimidate the natives by a victory and secure a grip on the coast. But he may fairly be said to have merely drawn attention to the island: it was not his to bequeath,' Tacitus commented.

It would be almost ninety years before the Romans returned.

In the interim, another king: Cunobelin, or Cymbeline as Shakespeare called him, became one of the most powerful kings of the ancient British. He is said to have been the grandson of Caswallon and his stronghold was situated at what is now St Albans. He first invaded the kingdom of the Trinovantes and captured their headquarters near the mouth of the River Colne at Camulodunam (now Colchester) in AD10. The chief of that tribe was forced to flee and eventually he sought the protection of Emperor Augustus in Rome. Camulodunam was a collection of scattered huts stretching over several hundred acres and fortified by a system of dykes. It was, at the time, the largest settlement in Britain. Cunobelin now decided to use Camulodunam as his base, and with the river's outlet in the North Sea, he was thus able to conduct an expanding trade with Europe of cattle, corn, hides, iron, silver and slaves, in return for jars of southern wine, delicate jewellery, glassware and pottery.

By AD20 Cunobelin controlled a kingdom stretching from the north bank of the Thames over all the south-east. His power became a growing concern for the Roman Emperors, Augustus, Tiberius and Caligula, all of whom considered campaigns against him, but had to use all their military power to contain hostile tribes in Germany. Ever more ambitious, he continued to extend his territory, attacking the Atrebates and marching through what is now Sussex, Hampshire and Dorset, finally capturing the iron age fort of Maiden Castle. Cunobelin may be seen as the last great pre-Roman British king. He ruled his kingdom with a strong hand, but when he died in AD40 his kingdom collapsed.

Cunobelin had managed to remain on reasonably friendly terms with the Romans; his heir and successor, Caratacus (Caradoc), however, would have to contend with the mighty Roman invading army.

THE ROMAN OCCUPATION (43–410)

'Britain yields gold, silver, and other metals, to make it worth conquering' wrote the first-century Roman writer Tacitus, but warned: 'We are dealing with barbarians'.
(The word Celt, coming from the Greek word *Keltoi*, means precisely that – barbarians).

It finally fell to Emperor Claudius, in AD43, to organize the invasion, with Aulus Plautius leading the Roman army. This time they came with 40,000 men and landed on the Kent coast. They marched inland and engaged Caratacus and his army in the Battle of the Medway. Caratacus and his men were defeated and fled northwards to his father's former stronghold at Camulodunam. The Roman army pursued them, forging northwards until they reached a Celtic ford across the Thames, where 'it empties into the sea and at floodtime forms a lake', wrote Caius Dio. They crossed the river by raft, while their German contingent was obliged to swim. From there they pressed on but by the time they reached Camulodunam, Caratacus had fled westwards, into the lands of the Dobunni, around Gloucestershire, where he would initially build his defences and would continue a guerrilla warfare that would last for another ten years.

Claudius, meanwhile, remained for sixteen days on the island, during which he received the homage of eleven chieftains from the south-east, and a bridge-head was built at that Celtic ford, Llyn-Din, the hill by the pool, which would become Londinium, a strategically important site for the new Roman occupiers: easily reached by trading ships from Europe, but far enough inland from marauding sea raiders, and on a river that led into the heart of the country.

Claudius would never return to Britain, and would die eleven years later, possibly from poisoning. But from Rome he estab-lished the first governorship of Britain by Plautius, and Plautius's successor in AD47 would force Caratacus further westward, where he gained the support of the Silures and Ordovices in south and Central Wales. Caratacus amassed forces of over 15,000 but his brother and children were taken as hostages. He fled to the land of the Brigantes, but their queen Cartimandua betrayed him and handed him over to the Romans. He and his family were taken to Rome in chains. Since his reputation was well known, Claudius displayed them as evidence of his own power and authority. Caratacus was saved from execution by a stirring speech he made and Claudius pardoned him. But far from returning to his homeland, he remained living in comfort in Rome and probably died around AD54, though his brother Arviragus is believed to have returned to Britain as a Christian King of the Silures.

It would take the Romans a further thirty years or so before they conquered most of Britain, whose total population now amounted to around no more than 400,000. But the Romans pressed on. 'Their [the Britons'] strength is in their infantry,' Tacitus noted, adding that some of the tribes also fought from chariots, with the nobleman driving, and his dependants fighting in his defence. 'Once they owed obedience to kings; now they are distracted between the warring factions of rival chiefs. Indeed nothing has helped us more in fighting against their very powerful nations than their inability to co-operate . . . thus fighting in separate groups, all are conquered.' Added to which the climate was wretched, with frequent rains and mist, he went on to say.

Among the first of the British kings to co-operate with the Romans was Cogidubnus, whom the Romans rewarded for his 'unswerving loyalty' by giving him the kingdom of the Regnii in Sussex, spreading to Hampshire and Kent. He became increasingly wealthy and powerful, ultimately becoming a Roman legate –'an example of the long-established Roman custom of employing even kings to make others slaves', Tacitus tells us.

He established a magnificent palace at Fishbourne, near Chichester. He was the first of the British-Romano elite and it is almost certain that many of the British nobility subsequently followed his example. They were not offered kingdoms but became magistrates of the cities.

However, not all the tribal chieftains and kings were quelled. Some – like those in Cornwall and for many decades in Wales and the land of the Picts – stood firm, and continued their resistance. The most famous of these was, of course, Boudica, queen of the Iceni in the east, and wife of the client king Prasutagus. But she was only initially successful. Under the arrangement of his office, Prasutagus's territories had passed to Rome after his death. The Romans, who had made of Camulodunum one of their main camps, took this rather too literally and began pillaging the surrounding countryside. When Boudica objected she was flogged and her two teenage daughters raped. This was the final outrage for the Iceni who, in AD60, rose up in revolt, led by Boudica riding her legendary chariot. The neighbouring Trinovantes joined forces with them, for much of their land, like that of the Iceni, had been sequestered for the endowment of retired Roman officers. It was the culmination of ever-growing resentment of the colonizing Romans' 'greed and self-indulgence', Tacitus tells us. ' The whole island rose under the leadership of Boudica, a lady of royal descent – for Britons make no distinction of sex in their appointment of commanders.'

He goes on to tell us how they hunted down the Roman troops in their scattered outposts, stormed their forts, assaulted 'the colony itself' (Colchester), which they viewed as 'the citadel of their servitude' . . . 'there was no form of savage cruelty that the angry victors refrained from'. (At that time the Romans were busy erecting a temple there, in honour of Claudius whom they had recently deified.) After Colchester, they turned on Verulamium (St Albans), then Londinium, massacring and burning as they went. Then they advanced on the main Roman army, newly returned from Wales. But even though the British must have outnumbered the Romans by ten to one the lack of organization amongst the British was no match for hardened Roman discipline, and, after a day of intense fighting, the British were defeated. The Roman governor exacted terrible revenge, so much so that his own troops mutinied, and order could only be restored when Emperor Nero decided on a change of governor.

One account tells us that Boudica poisoned herself; others that she simply fell ill and died.

For the next few hundred years, Britain remained a colony of Rome and was subjected to a series of governors. We know from early geographers and historians, such as Ptolemy and Pliny the Elder, that in the first century AD there were still some thirty tribes in Britain and fifteen to twenty more in Ireland. Although their rulers are not named, each of these tribes would have had a war-leader and a chief priest, and, depending on the size of their territory, may have had sub-kings, or co-rulers who governed as a council of kings. Although the Romans conquered the tribes in the territory we now call England, they had little impact on the Celts of Wales, Cornwall or the land of the Picts. It is quite likely that the rulers of the Silures, Demetae and Ordovices in Wales, and the Caledonii of northern Britain continued to rule through-out the period of Roman occupation but we know almost nothing about them.

The Romans established their own communities or *civitates*, based largely upon the former British tribes. Although they brought in their own Roman administrators for these towns, they also married into the local nobility, and it is probable that descendants of the former tribal chiefs served as senior government officials with a Roman *civitas*. Early on the Romans established some client-kings, as we have seen, but this practice did not survive. By the time of the governor Julius Agricola, in AD78, the hierarchy of military, judicial and civic administration was established. Although none of these posts held the authority of king, and were not hereditary, they did have considerable power. The senior post – that of governor – was appointed directly by the emperor and had the rank of senator. Most of these administrators came from Italy, but in later years they may have originated from elsewhere in the Roman Empire. The only governor likely to have been of British origin was Marcus Statius Priscus, who governed 160–1 and is believed to have been born in Colchester.

Roman emperors seldom came to Britain: of those who did by far the best known is Hadrian. As the adopted son of Emperor Trajan, he succeeded him in 117, and was the first Roman emperor to visit Britain after it had been conquered by Claudius nearly eighty years before. He was a strong military tactician, the first to take the Empire's defences seriously and spent ten years touring its frontiers. He spent the summer of 122 in Britain, during which time he ordered the construction of Hadrian's Wall to demarcate the extent of Roman territory and to keep out the aggressive Picts. It was seventy-three and a half miles long, and took four years to build. A century later it was extended by the powerful emperor Severus (193–211) the first emperor to die in Britain (at York).

Hadrian's Wall marked the Roman Empire's farthest northern limit – its southernmost limits included the whole of the North African coast. The Empire extended in the east as far as Persia and the Black Sea and in the west to Spain and the Atlantic, stretching right across Europe. In its prime the Roman Empire boasted 500,000 army officers and men. The officers were Roman citizens, but the men came from all parts of the Empire's colonies: Gaul, Spain, the Rhineland, Switzerland, North Africa, Asia Minor, Thrace and Britain itself.

Being leader of the Roman Empire was a precarious privilege: of all those who ruled Britain during its 350 years of colonization, few died naturally in their beds and the majority met a sticky end – thirty-three were murdered, nine were killed in battle, four committed suicide. Nevertheless, in the latter days of the Roman Empire, it became increasingly common for soldiers or provinces to put forward their own candidates for emperor, sometimes declaring them in opposition to the existing ruler. Britain became notorious for this. The first person to do so was the governor of Britain Clodius Albinus who failed, and Severus was declared emperor. Albinus nonetheless amassed a following of troops discontented with their treatment by Rome, and announced himself emperor in 193. Four years later Severus met him in battle in Gaul, defeated and killed him.

Carausius – who came from the region of Holland – was a man of lowly birth, who had risen to become commander of the Channel fleet. When Emperor Maximian discovered that he was in league with the very Frankish and Saxon pirates he was supposed to be suppressing, he ordered his arrest. Where-upon Carausius moved to Britain, bringing his fleet with him, and declared himself Emperor of Britain in 286. He succeeded in ruling from London for the next six years, only to be murdered by his 'treasurer' Allectus, who became another self-styled Emperor of Britain, until he in turn was killed in battle by Constantius Chlorus, who recovered Britain for Rome in 296.

By the fourth century Britain was gaining a form of quasi-independence and an increasing number of emperors were de-clared in Britain. The most famous was Constantine The Great (306–37), who came from the region of Bulgaria. He was not only responsible for making Christianity the official religion of the Empire, but he also briefly visited Britain and implemented administrative reforms, initiated by Diocletian. He divided Brit-ain into four provinces: Britannia Prima (Wales and the west); Britannia Secunda (the North); Flavia Caesariensis (the midlands and Norfolk), and Maxima Caesariensis (the south), with four regional capitals: Cirencester, York, Lincoln and London. By the close of this century there was a cluster of British-made emperors, and one of them, Magnus Maximus, has passed into Welsh tradition as being descended from the kings of the Silures in Gwent.

But Britain was now coming under attack. The Picts raided in the north, the Irish from the west, and the Saxons and Franks in the south-east (where they actually landed in 367, and lay siege to London). Rome sent more troops, including many German auxiliaries to restore order both there and on the northern border. Further raids followed.

Then, within a generation of Maximus' death in 388 Britain was no longer part of the Roman Empire. Britain and the rest of the Roman frontier was coming under increasing threat from the Germanic tribes who, in 410, crossed the Rhine and invaded. The British wrote to the emperor Honorius for help, but Honorius had his hands full, protecting Rome itself. He wrote back telling the British to look after themselves. This was not a formal expulsion from the Empire. It just meant that Rome could no longer help. Then, the *Anglo-Saxon Chronicle* tells us, 'the Romans assembled all the gold-hoards which were in Britain and hid some in the earth so that no one afterwards could find them, and took some with them into Gaul'. However, many of the Romans would remain, along with some semblance of Roman administration, though after 410 Roman rule and Roman law no longer applied in Britain.

THE DARK AGES (410–802)

The release from Roman authority had the same effect 1,600 years ago as the end of Communism in the Soviet Union and in Yugoslavia. Tribalism and local cultures which had for so long been repressed and restrained by Roman rule erupted. Warfare spread right across Britain. For the most part it was a clash between those who sought to defend and maintain the Roman *status quo*, fighting invasions from the Picts to the north, the Irish to the west and the Germanic tribes from the east. But there was also internal fighting between tribes who sought to gain power over old tribal territories and, where possible, conquer neighbouring lands which might be richer. The period between 410 and 450 saw an almost complete breakdown of social order, particularly in the north. 'Here a dispirited British garrison stationed on the fortifications pined in terror night and day, while from beyond the wall the enemy constantly harassed them with hooked weapons, dragging the cowardly defenders down . . . and dashing them to the ground. At length the Britons . . . fled in disorder, pursued by their foes. The slaughter was more ghastly than ever before, and the wretched citizens were torn in pieces by their enemies. They were driven from their homesteads and farms, and sought to save themselves from starvation by robbery and violence against one another . . . until there was no food left in the whole land except whatever could be obtained by hunting,' Bede tells us. And with famine also came plague. The sixth-century historian Gildas in the first history of Britain paints a grim picture too.

During this first forty years certain chieftains became war leaders to defend their lands and conquer enemies. These were regarded as kings by their countrymen, though they did not have quite the mystical status of the kings in the pre-Roman era. The best known was Coel, the old King Cole of the nursery rhyme. He was a real king who sought to maintain order against the Picts in the northern territories. His own 'kingdom' may have extended as far as York in the east, perhaps to a line between the Humber and Mersey, and north to the Antonine Wall running between the Forth and the Clyde. He seems to have dominated this territory for about twenty years (c410–30) and one legend tells us that he died fighting the Irish near Ayr.

Others from this period in the north were Ceretic who ruled from Dumbarton and Cunedda who seems to have been a war leader in the area of the Votadini in Lothian before he migrated to north Wales. Although these kings had certain territories within which they operated they did not have kingdoms in the sense we understand them today. They were leaders of their people, not rulers of land. Thus Cunedda was king of the Votadini, meaning that tribe, not the land associated with it.

The kingship of southern Britain is more confusing. Some remnant of Roman administration continued, based around Glevum (Gloucester) and Verulamium (St Albans). The best known of the southern kings was Vortigern (c425–c466; c471–c480), though in fact the name merely means 'High King'. It's possible that his real name was Vitalinus, though this may have been his father's name. We know far more of him from legend than from history, but it seems that for over twenty years Vortigern led the organization and defence of Britain against

Saxon, Pict and Scottish (Irish) raiders. He solved the problem of the Roman imperial government's inability to send reinforcements by hiring Saxon mercenaries under the leadership of Hengist and Horsa to fight the Picts: strategies that proved successful. In return they were awarded the Island of Thanet (a bad move that finally led to the Saxon invasion of Britain). Later tradition has it that Vortigern became infatuated with Hengist's daughter Rowena and was given her in marriage in exchange for more land. But be that as it may, as Vortigern grew older his power diminished and finally civil war broke out. Vortigern was driven into Powys by Ambrosius Aurelianus, an equally vague character believed to be descended from an aristocratic Roman family, most likely that of Magnus Maximus. Ambrosius battled valiantly against Vortigern and against the Saxons and his success has caused some to believe that he may be one of the individuals who inspired the legend of Arthur. Ambrosius' descendants were believed to continue to rule in south Wales for several generations. And Arthur is closely associated with Wales and the West Country.

Although the legends of Arthur later acquired all the trappings of medieval chivalry (in the tales of Mallory, Wace, Geoffrey of Monmouth, The Mabinogion, Layamon and Marie de France), can the association of his name with so many places in local lore be entirely fictitious? In Cornwall, there are Arthur's Hall (the remains of a Dark Age long house) and Arthur's Seat (a rocky crag) on Bodmin Moor, with the River Camel close by, as well as Dozmary Pool associated with his sword Excalibur, and there is also Tintagel, the legendary birthplace of Arthur, to which Uther Pendragon laid siege, killing the castle's owner Gorlois and forcibly marrying Ygerne. Later Ygerne gave her son Arthur over to the care of Merlin. In Somerset, as well as Cadbury Hill (supposedly the seat of Camelot) the seventeenth-century historian William Camden claimed to have copied a grave ornament of King Arthur at Glastonbury Abbey, inscribed with:

HIC IACET SEPVLTVS. IHCLITVS. REX ARTVRIVS. IH
IHSVLA. AVALOHIA

Many, of course, claim that this was a forgery. And where is it
now?

In Wales, Caerleon has Arthurian associations, while Badbury
Rings in Dorset is one of the suggested sites of the Battle of Badon
in which Arthur supposedly slaughtered over 160 enemy single-
handed.

However, there is a snag, for if Arthur were a real sixth-century
king, why does Gildas make no mention of him in his first history
of Britain, *De Excidio Britanniae,* written in 540? Indeed there is
no mention of Arthur until Nennius's *Historia Brittonum* written
in the ninth century, and in two other ninth-century works: a
Welsh poem called *Verses on the Graves of Heroes* and the
Annales Cambriae. Here we are told that in 516 Arthur fought
in the Battle of Badon for three days and three nights and the
Britons were victors. In 537 Arthur and Medraut both fell in
battle at Camlann. Nennius calls Arthur a *dux bellorum* or leader
in battle, not a king in his own right, and lists twelve battles that
Arthur waged against the Saxons. Gildas mentions the battle of
Badon (but, as we have seen, not Arthur) and dates the battle at
500. So all we can safely, and somewhat prosaically, conclude is
that a battle leader called Arthur lived at about the year 500 and
during this period succeeded in rallying the kings of Britain
against the invading Saxons and soundly defeating them at
Badon. For the next twenty years there was a period of relative
calm, before he was killed in a second wave of fighting.

A near contemporary of Arthur and certainly a successor as
one of the High Kings, or 'pendragon' is Maelgwyn Hir ('Hir'
means tall, while 'gwyn' means fair). He flourished between 534
and 549 and was a powerful and tyrannical ruler. Maelgwyn's
life was turbulent. He is recorded as killing his uncle as a youth.
Once established in Gwynedd, he underwent a brief period of
repentance and became a monk, before resuming his evil ways.
Having married, his passions soon turned to his nephew's wife.

So he murdered his own wife and his nephew in order to assuage his heart's desire. There is also reason to believe that he married a Pictish princess. He established a rich and powerful court at Deganwy, to which he attracted many bards, whom he ensured wrote copiously of his triumphs and achievements. He was recognized as both a great patron of the arts and as a lawgiver, though some of this was probably his own propaganda. By the time of his death, Maelgwyn was firmly established as the primary ruler of the British. He died, most probably, of cholera which was then sweeping Europe. One of Maelgwyn's sons Brude was chosen by the Picts to be their leader in 554, and it was he who accepted Christianity under Columba.

The period from 450 to 550 is nonetheless known as the age of Arthur. Whoever he was, he symbolizes the oppressive nature of the period when Britain was riven with warfare and strife until one master war-chief struck back so decisively that peace and prosperity returned for the first time in nearly a century. No wonder that chieftain became such a hero of legend.

There were many other heroes and villains from this period: ranging from Urien and Peredur to the treacherous Morcant.

The Picts were Celtic, like the other tribes, but seem to owe their origins to an earlier Irish migration around the third century BC. The Picts had established an inheritance based on matrilinear succession and the Pictish princesses were much honoured, since only they could confer kingship. There were many Pictish chieftains across the Scottish glens and highlands and the Isles. There is evidence to suggest each individual island or group of smaller islands was ruled by its own chief, but insufficient names survive to make any coherent sense. Certainly the larger Hebridean islands (Skye and Lewis) had their own chiefs who were originally Picts but later were displaced by the Irish, and later still by the Norse, and similarly the Orkneys whose chiefs were ousted by the Norse. One Irish settlement changed the name of Pictland. This was the Northern Irish kingdom of Dál Riata who, as we have seen, came across to Argyll and Kintyre from as long ago as the third century. These settlers were called 'Scotii' and their name gradually became applied to the whole of Pictland. Aedan mac Gabhran who ruled them from 574 to 608 was the first known king of the Dál Riata to be anointed and one of the most powerful rulers in sixth-century Britain. While 140 years later Angus would be the first king to rule both Picts and Dál Riata together. Constantine too would rule both kingdoms from 811–20.

The major surviving British kingdoms were in Wales. Although the Romans had infiltrated southern Wales they never conquered north Wales and it is certain that kings of the Ordovices continued to rule there, though we do not know their names. By the end of the Roman domination in Britain Irish settlers were invading Wales. One tradition has it that the British under Cunedda came south from Gododdin to fight the Irish, and they settled in North Wales. Cunedda established the kingdom of Gwynedd, which became the strongest of all the Welsh kingdoms. Traditionally each of Cunedda's sons received a share of his lands and it was from them that many of the smaller Welsh kingdoms owed their origins. However, of these only Ceredigion grew sufficiently strong to take on the might of Demetae or Dyfed, a colony of Irish settlers in south-west Wales, eventually to form one kingdom, called Seisyllwg after its conqueror. Two other Welsh kingdoms existed in the fifth century: Powys and Gwent. Powys was in eastern Wales and formed the border between Wales and England, once the Angles migrated that far west. It was essentially the old British territory of the Cornovii, and no doubt their rulers had survived through Roman occupation to reestablish themselves. It was also from here that many British migrated south to Cornwall and Devon and from there to Brittany.

There were other British tribes in Shropshire, Herefordshire and Gloucestershire. The *Anglo-Saxon Chronicle* tells us that in 577, 'Cuthwine and Ceawlin fought against the Britons and they killed 3 kings, Coinmail and Condidan and Farinmail, in the place which is called Dyrham and took 3 cities: Gloucester and Cirencester and Bath'.

The other British kingdom of significance was Dumnonia, which originally covered Cornwall, Devon, Dorset and Somerset, but which under pressure from the Saxons was driven back into the peninsula until only Cornwall or Kernow would survive as a kingdom right up until the ninth century. (Cornwall has two carved stones commemorating two of its kings: Tristan or Drust – the legendary Tristram – who flourished in the mid sixth century and the much later king Doniert of the ninth.)

THE SAXONS, ANGLES AND JUTES

Saxons, Jutes and Angles began to settle in Britain from the middle of the fifth century, first in Kent, but Saxons and Angles were raiding and settling all along the eastern coast of Britain. They had to fight to gain their territory, and the resident British migrated westwards or were killed. There is a tragic account left by an unknown 'Chronicler of London' of this period:

The Saxons stretched out envious hands from their seaboard settlements, and presently the whole of this rich country where yet lived so many great and wealthy families, was exposed to all the miseries of war. The towns were destroyed, the farms ruined, the cattle driven away . . . nothing was brought to the port for export; the roads were closed; the river was closed. They lived now by the shore and in the recesses of the forest, who once lived in great villas, lay on silken pillows and drank the wine of Gaul and Spain.

Then we of the city saw plainly that our end was come . . . those who were left, a scanty band, gathered in the Basilica, and it was resolved that we should leave the place since we could no longer live in it. I, with my wife and children, and others who agreed to accompany me, took what we could of food and of weapons, leaving behind us the houses where our lives had been so soft and happy, and went out by the western gate, and taking refuge where we could in the forest, we began our escape . . . Every year our people are driven westward more and more . . . My sons have fallen in battle; my daughters have lost their husbands; my grand-

children are taught to look for nothing but continual war. And of
Augusta [London] have I learned nothing for many years. Where-
fore am I sure that it remains desolate and deserted to this day.

While the Celts held their kingdoms in the west, Sussex was
invaded by Aelle, where he virtually wiped out the resident British
to establish his kingdom. Cerdic led the next wave, heading a
warband from the Gewisse (who came from the Marches, and the
southern borders between Wales and Mercia) in an incursion into
what is now Wiltshire, Somerset and Gloucestershire. Cerdic was
almost certainly British and his soldiers were British and Saxon
mercenaries. They managed to establish a hold on land that
whilst predominantly British at that time was increasingly being
passed on to Saxon overlords. He managed to drive back the
British into Wales and Dumnonia, and from his battles the
kingdom of the West Saxons began to emerge. These early Saxons
spread right across parts of southern Britain in various marauding bands that gradually melded together under stronger leaders.

As the Saxons endeavoured to control the south, the Angles
were moving into eastern and middle England. And in the north,
where the Angles had made an alliance with the Picts, they fared a
little better. According to Bede, they 'extended the conflagration
from the eastern to the western shores without opposition and
established a stranglehold over nearly all the doomed island.
Public and private buildings were razed, priests were slain . . . A
few wretched survivors captured in the hills were butchered
wholesale' while others surrendered or fled abroad, eking out
'a wretched and fearful existence among the mountains, forests
and crags'.

So, after a period of a hundred years from 450 to 550 when
the Celtic kingdoms had remained dominant in Britain, fighting
among each other as much as against the Saxon and
Angle settlers, the balance began to shift. The Saxons had come
to stay.

By the close of the sixth century Kent was a rich and prosperous
place, having strong links with the Merovingian kings of France.

In fact the Jutish origins of the kingdom had given way to a major Frankish element which moulded Kent's culture. Kent was in fact the first important kingdom in England and because of its position of power and authority it was able to influence the other kingdoms. Bede recognized certain Saxon rulers as *bretwalda*, the equivalent of a high king. The third of these, Athelbert (who ruled from 580–616), was an established king for 36 years of a settled kingdom, who exerted his influence over his countrymen in matters of culture, religion, education and trade. His kingdom extended into Surrey and parts of Sussex, and also held authority over Essex.

Athelbert was the first Saxon king to convert, albeit cautiously, to Christianity. Augustine had been sent to proselytize from Rome and Athelbert welcomed his mission cautiously, meeting him under an oak tree, venerated by the Saxons, which he believed would cancel out any magic practised by the Christians. Athelbert recognized Augustine's sincerity but declared that he could not abandon the religion of his fathers. Nevertheless he allowed Augustine and his colleagues to establish a house at Canterbury and within a short period many hundreds of Athelbert's subjects had converted. Athelbert was baptized some four years later and thereafter became fervent in his support. It was a sign of his authority that he was able to arrange a meeting between Augustine and the Celtic church in the west of England, as part of Augustine's plan to bring it under Roman control.

Athelbert, with Augustine's help, also established a set of detailed law codes, bringing in a system of monetary fines (rather than payment in kind, such as livestock), allowing people to pay in instalments, and establishing the level of fine to fit the severity of the crime. The king was reckoned as overlord, so that if any crime were committed within his kingdom, the perpetrator had to recompense the king as well as the victim. His laws also gave considerable protection to women and allowed a wife to leave her husband if there was good cause. These laws not only restored a form of governance and administration to Britain, but with the emphasis on monetary compensation, also reinstated a financial system. During Athelbert's reign the first Saxon coins in England were minted at Canterbury.

The East Anglian kingdom emerged towards the end of the sixth century and its ruler Redwald was the next *bretwalde* after Athelbert and professed Christianity (though he was somewhat duplicitous in this respect). The East Anglian kingdom kept close to the former kingdom of the Iceni and would remain ferociously independent for the next 200 years.

In the north lay the kingdom of Northumbria. Northumbria at its greatest extent would include all the Scottish lowlands up to the Clyde. There was always a close relationship with the Britons of Strathclyde, the Scots of Dál Riata and the Picts whose kingdoms lay to its north. It is with Athelfrith that the real history of this kingdom begins. He had succeeded as ruler of Bernicia in 593 after his father was killed in battle against Owain of Rheged. Afterwards the young Athelfrith pursued and killed Owain, and later he earned the *soubriquets* of Athelfrith the Ferocious, as well as Athelfrith the Artful, fitting names for a powerful warrior. In 603 a confederate Scottish/Irish army moved against the English in Lothian. Losses were great on both sides but Athelfrith claimed victory and for the time being the north was his, with Bernicia extending far into the territory of the old Votadini. Then he turned his attention south, invading Deira, south of the Tees and killing their king, Athelric. He also tried to kill Athelric's brother Edwin, but the young prince escaped into exile. To legitimize his claim to Deira Athelfrith took Athelric's sister as his second wife (his first wife, Bebba, had been a Pictish princess.) By now, he controlled the whole of eastern Britain from Lothian to north of the Humber and may have exercised some authority over Lindsey, south of the Humber. In 613 he decided to hunt down Edwin who had sought sanctuary with the kings of Gwynedd and Powys, and Athelfrith advanced towards Chester, wiping out a party of monks who had come to parley with him. He then defeated the Welsh under Selyf ap Cynan at Chester. Athelfrith was finally killed in battle near Doncaster, and Edwin lived on to see his kingdom restored to him.

After settling in his kingdom Edwin (ruled 616–33) turned his attention to conquering the north. First in about 619 he expelled Ceredig from his British kingdom of Elmet; next he conquered Rheged, which gave him the gateway to the isles of Man and Anglesey and brought him into contact with his former friend Cadwallon of Gwynedd. Edwin's army drove the Welsh back to the tip of Anglesey and Cadwallon was forced to flee to Ireland. Edwin married a Christian, Athelburh. Edwin finally became the strongest ruler of Britain and eventually converted to Christianity himself. He sanctioned the conversion of the Northumbrians and successfully campaigned with the pope for the bishopric he had established at York to become an archbishopric. However, Edwin's past was to haunt him. Around 630 Cadwallon returned to power in Gwynedd and entered into an alliance with Penda, the new ruler of Mercia in a series of attacks on Northumbrian land. Eventually the two great armies met at Hatfield Chase, north of Doncaster. Edwin's army was scattered, he was killed and Cadwallon marched on through Northumbria devastating the land. Northumbria was split asunder with Bernicia being returned to the family of Athelfrith. Edwin subsequently came to be regarded as a martyr and was canonized. In fact he was a ruthless, cunning and vengeful king who manipulated people and events to his own advantage.

Penda was probably the greatest warrior of his age, the epitome of the warlord, who lived and died a pagan, dedicated to his Nordic religion. He dominated Britain from 633 to 655.

Edwin's son-in-law Oswy (ruled 642–70), who had been brought up in exile with the monks on Iona and had finally inherited the kingdoms of Bernicia and Deira, would kill Penda, after a battle in which Penda had taken his son hostage. Oswy would ultimately be responsible for the Synod of Whitby in 664, whereby the Roman church found favour over the Celtic christian church.

Penda's successors Wulfhere (ruled 658–75) and Athelred (ruled 675–705) created a major Mercian kingdom that ruled all central England and stretched as far south as Sussex, Surrey and into Kent and even the Isle of Wight, while Wessex and Kent struggled to hold on to their power in the south.

An interesting 'relative' of Penda's by marriage was Seaxburh, who became the only reigning queen of the West Saxons (672–3). She was the widow of Cenwealh, whose first wife had been Penda's sister. Twelve years after her rule, the West Saxons would have an important leader, Caedwalla, at first a roving chieftain without a kingdom, who with his band of mercenaries raided the border territories of Wessex and Mercia. He succeeded in gaining territory in the south for the West Saxons (mostly by killing off any kings who stood in his way). Thanks to his efforts Wessex became the third power in the land after Northumbria and Mercia, and he was succeeded by Ine (ruled 688–726), the first true king of the West Saxons, as distinct from a warleader. He not only established Wessex as a kingdom but introduced a code of laws and a strong administrative system to govern the land.

Northumbrian power was only broken following the death in battle of Egfrith in 685. He had believed himself invincible, having already once subjugated the southern Picts and Strathclyde, and he marched into the heart of Pictland again, to teach them another lesson, only to have his army slaughtered. Thereafter Northumbria was ruled by weaker kings, who, like the Celts, reduced their power by continual infighting. The only remaining Northumbrian king worth noting is Aldfrith (685–704), their last great king, who was a scholar and art lover. It was under his rule that many of the beautiful illuminated books of the Northumbrian monasteries (such as the Lindisfarne Gospels) were produced. Some have even attributed the poem *Beowulf*, the great Anglo-Saxon poem, to him or one of his fellows at court.

Mercian power continued under a few more kings, notably the proud and cruel Offa who ruled from 757 to 796. He was without doubt the most powerful king in Britain of his day, and his authority was acknowledged by all the other rulers of England, and to a large extent in Wales, though less so in Scotland. He is remembered for Offa's Dyke, the monumental 150-mile earthwork stretching from the estuary of the Dee to Tidenham on the Severn, built during his rule to protect his frontiers against the Welsh.

His authority was recognized by the great Charlemagne, who entered into an agreement that his son Charles would marry Offa's daughter, but when Offa made this dependent on Offa's son Egfrith marrying one of Charlemagne's daughters, the Frankish king was so enraged he broke off trading relations with England. Only after some intense negotiations were these restored and the planned marriage never materialized. While Offa had become the most influential of the Saxon rulers, he was not regarded as an equal on the stage of Europe, and the kingdom he created would soon falter under his successors.

THE FIRST KINGS
OF THE ENGLISH (802–1066)

A hot-headed young man at Offa's court was Egbert, in exile from his father's kingdom in Kent. Egbert was soon banished from Mercia, as he was seen as a problem to the West Saxon kingdom by Offa's son-in-law Beorhtric, but after Beorhtric's death, he returned to become ruler of Wessex in 802. During the first part of his reign he consolidated his position in Wessex against rival claimants, and having done that was able to underline his authority by subjugating the British of Dumnonia and absorbing Devon (though not Cornwall) into Wessex. Then from 823 onwards Egbert began to look to the other kingdoms. With the help of his son Athelwolf he regained Sussex, Surrey, Kent and Essex, and helped the East Anglians defeat and kill the Mercian kings Beornwulf and Ludeca. When he marched on Northumbria he was recognized as overlord without a fight. Although the kingdoms of Mercia and Northumbria remained in existence for another sixty years or more, Wessex was now the dominant kingdom. Egbert, who died in 838, is usually regarded as the last *bretwalda* and 'the first king of England'. The first title is certainly correct; the second is debatable. The same might be said about his successors, Athelwolf, Althelred and Alfred the Great.

Starting in Egbert's day the Vikings had begun to raid and plunder the British coast, and by the 850s they were settled along the eastern Irish coast at Dublin and Waterford under Olaf the White and the Dane Ivarr the Boneless. From here, in the short space of twenty years, they conquered the Hebrides and the Isle of Man, Deira (establishing their kingdom of Jorvik), East Anglia, and the Orkneys (and soon after Caithness and Sutherland). Throughout the 870s they encroached further into England, but it would be Alfred's defeat of the Danes at Edington that would save Wessex.

ALFRED THE GREAT
Wessex 23 April 871–26 October 899.
Born: Wantage (?) c847; Died: Winchester (?) 26 October 899,
aged 52(?) Buried: Winchester.
Married: 868, Ealhswith (d.902) of Mercia – 5 children

Alfred, a grandson of Egbert, and fourth son of Athelwolf, was born in about 847. He is certainly the best known of the West Saxon kings, though much of what we think we know about him may be myth. It is likely that as a child he accompanied his father on a pilgrimage to Rome and spent some time at the court of Charles the Bald, king of the Franks. Alfred became fascinated with the Frankish world, the court of the descendants of Charlemagne, and modelled his own court upon it, and his great passion for scholarship was stimulated by it. Alfred, as youngest son, was probably being groomed for the church, as his father was intensely religious, and it was only through the death of his elder brothers that he became king.

He first rises to preeminence in the mid 860s, when with his elder brother Athelred, he battled successfully against the Danes. But in 871 Athelred died of wounds, and though he had two infant sons, it was Alfred who was declared successor. Alfred had already proved his battle prowess, particularly at Ashdown in 870, but there was no time to celebrate his succession. Within a month he was pitched into battle with the Danes at Wilton, a day which Alfred thought he had won but the wiliness of the Danes, with their false retreat, caught the English off guard. Battle followed battle that first year, the outcomes swinging both ways, until, at the year's end, Alfred bought peace with the Danes. The Danes settled north of the Thames, where peace was also bought with the Mercians, and for a period Alfred could consolidate his army. During this time too he began to develop a navy in order to meet the Danes on their own terms.

Although the Danes suffered defeat in battle at Wareham and in a naval campaign off the south coast at Swanage, in the winter of 878 they caught the English by surprise at Chippenham, taking over the royal court, and forcing the English to flee into the surrounding marshes at Athelney in Somerset. It is to this period that belong the legends of Alfred burning the cakes and disguising himself as a harper to spy in the enemy camp. Faced with additional Danish reinforcements including a Danish fleet established in the British Channel which endeavoured to blockade Alfred, his forces in Devon, nonetheless, defeated the fleet and then, with his local knowledge, Alfred was able to outwit the Danes and lead his army out of Athelney to Selwood. There he strengthened his forces, marched on the Danes and defeated them at the battle of Ethandune (Edington). The Danes submitted and, more significantly, their leader agreed to be baptized a Christian. Peace was declared with the treaty of Wedmore.

Over the next eight peaceful years, Alfred came to be regarded by the English as their overlord, but he was never king of all England, as the Danes still held the greater part of the north and east. He created a series of 25 fortified boroughs around his kingdom, such as Oxford and Hastings, and extensively refortified London. He created seats of learning across southern England, and introduced his code of law. This was administered by local reeves (or sheriffs) and judges, and Alfred reviewed their activities in his own series of visits. This forced the local administrators to learn to read in order to ensure that the books were properly kept. Alfred also decreed that all the sons of freemen should learn to read and write, first in English and, for those destined for high office, in Latin.

Apart from a brief skirmish with the Danes in 885, peace held until 893 when another war with the Danes of East Anglia erupted and lasted until 897. The Danes caused havoc across Mercia and into Wales, but were unable to penetrate the fortifications of Wessex. Alfred reorganized the navy into a major fleet, for which he is remembered as the father of the English navy. His strength eventually drained Danish vitality and their army faded away. Although they would return again and again, Alfred had established a kingdom which, for the next few decades, was invincible.

Alfred married Ealhswith, the daughter of a Mercian nobleman and, through her mother, descended from the Mercian royal line, so that Alfred's sons could claim the royal blood of both Wessex and Mercia. Of his four children, his daughter Elfreda married Baldwin, Count of Flanders, and their great-great-great-great-grand-daughter Matilda became the wife of William the Conqueror.

Alfred's son Edward (King of the West Saxons 899–924) and grandson Athelstan (King of the English 924–39) were equally great warriors and administrators. Edward drove the Danes out of York and East Anglia, though the Norse moved into the vacuum that was left. Athelstan is, arguably, remembered as the most powerful of all West Saxon kings. He may have been illegitimate, born of a liaison between Edward and a shepherd's daughter, and was raised by Edward's sister at her court in Gloucester. Athelstan thus grew up with a loyalty towards the Mercians that his forebears had never had. He also came to an understanding with Sitric, the Norse king of York, who married his sister Eadgyth. On Sitric's death, Athelstan prevented Sitric's brother, Gothfrith from claiming the throne of York and entered York himself, the first Saxon king to do so. Later, in an effort to stop Welsh hostilities in Mercia (for they had joined forces with the Norse to carry them out), he also laid down a boundary between Wales and England, along the River Wye, and exacted a harsh tribute from the Welsh princes. It is not clear whether they ever met his demands, but Hywel Dda (possibly the greatest of Welsh rulers) recognized Athelstan's authority and became fascinated with the Saxon court, so much so that he proved his fealty by accompanying Athelstan on a punitive expedition against Constantine II of Scotland, thus ending a seven-year-old alliance Athelstan had made with the Scots. In a battle near Nottingham, Athelstan met the combined forces of Constantine and Olaf Gothfrithson of Dublin in one of the most decisive of all Saxon victories. Athelstan's reign was remembered by later annalists as a Golden Age.

It was not until the reign of Eadred (King of the English 946–55) that the Norse were finally defeated and Northumbria formally became part of England (though the earls of Bernicia retained considerable autonomy). Eadred became the first king of all the English in 954, though it was his son Edgar who was the first to be formally crowned king of the English.

EDGAR THE PEACABLE
King of the English, 1 October 959 – 8 July 975 (he was appointed king of Mercia and Northumbria from 957).
Crowned: Bath Abbey, 11 May 973.
Born: *c943.* **Died:** *Winchester, 8 July 975, aged 32.* **Buried:** *Glastonbury Abbey.*
Married: *(1) c960 Athelfleda, daughter Ormaer, ealdorman of Hertford: either divorced c961 or died c961 or c964; 1 son; (2) Elfrida (c945 – c1002), daughter Ordgar, ealdorman of Devon, and widow of Athelwald, ealdorman of East Anglia: 2 children. Also had one illegitimate child.*

The Saxon name Eadgar means 'rich in spears', which was undoubtedly a recognition of his inheritance of military power. When Edgar's uncle Eadred died in 955, his brother Edwy became king in Wessex whilst Edgar was appointed to the kingship of Mercia and Northumbria. He was only twelve at the time and did not assume full authority until he was about fifteen, by which time he was welcomed, as Edwy was a weak and unpopular king. Edgar had been raised in East Anglia, in the household of Athelstan, the ealdorman of the old territory of the Danelaw which covered all of East Anglia and Danish Mercia. As such Edgar was already a popular prince amongst the middle-English and Danes and was readily accepted as king, whereas Edwy was seen as a weak and troublesome youth. By November 957 the Mercians and Northumbrians had renounced their allegiance to Edwy. Both kings were advised (or controlled) by a strong council which had led to conflict with Edwy who had expelled bishop Dunstan. When Edgar came of age he recalled Dunstan and was enthusiastic about his ideas for reforming the English church. When Edwy died in October 959, Edgar also became king of Wessex and as the archbishopric of Canterbury was vacant with the recent death of Oda, Dunstan was appointed to that see. With the support of the king, Dunstan introduced a major programme of monastic reform, not all of which was happily accepted at the time, but which brought Saxon England in line with developments on the continent. All secular clergy were ejected, and the church officials were granted considerable independence from the crown. The most extreme of these was the creation of the soke of Peterborough, where the abbot of St Peters had almost total independence. Many of the monasteries that had been destroyed during the Danish invasions were restored. It was only a period of peace that could allow such rebuilding and change. Edgar, for all that he was not a soldier or strategist to match his father or grandfather, was able to work alongside strong and well organized ealdormen in governing the kingdom and in ensuring its safety. All the time England seemed in capable hands, the Norse and Danes bided their time.

In 973 Edgar gave a demonstration of authority. Although he would have had a formal coronation when he became king of Wessex, Dunstan believed there was a need for a major ceremony similar to those of the King of the Franks and the German Emperor. The ceremony was delayed for some years because Dunstan was unhappy with Edgar's dissolute existence. For all he supported church reform Edgar was not a particularly religious man. There were rumours about his private life. He had married a childhood friend, Athelfleda, early on, but it seems that around the year 961 either she died in childbirth or the two became separated, because of Edgar's amorous adventures with Wulfryth. Stories circulated later that Edgar had seduced a nun. But although Wulfryth later became a nun, the real story seems to be that he fell in love with a lady who bore him a child, and she either chose to enter (or was banished to) a nunnery and they probably never married. Edgar then became romantically entangled with Elfrida, who was already married, and again the scandalmongers hinted that the two might have planned the murder of her husband, Edgar's one-time foster-brother Athelwald in 964, in order to marry. Elfrida later came to epitomise the image of the wicked stepmother in her relationship with Edgar's youngest child, Edward (The Martyr). All these shenanigans caused Dunstan to counsel Edgar to change his ways. Perhaps as he passed from youth into adulthood he became less reckless, and in 973 Dunstan agreed to a major ceremony at Bath.

Following the coronation Edgar put on a display of force. His army marched from Bath to Chester along the Welsh border, showing his authority over the Welsh, while his fleet sailed through the Irish Sea, also demonstrating his subjugation of the Norse who still held power in that area at Dublin and on Man. At Chester a further ceremony took place. Edgar was rowed along the river Dee, accompanied by at least eight other kings who recognized him as their overlord. So his coronation had a double significance. For the first time a Saxon king was crowned as king of all the English, a title used by previous monarchs but never as part of their coronation. Edgar was thus the first genuine king of England. At the same time Elfrida was also crowned, the first queen of the English. This ceremony has remained essentially the same in content ever since.

Edgar's reign would be the last reign of peace and harmony in Saxon times. Thereafter the Saxon world would begin to disintegrate and within less than a century be almost wiped away.

Three years after Edgar's son Edward The Martyr was crowned in 975, he was murdered at Corfe Castle in Dorset on a visit to his stepmother Elfrida and his half-brother Athelred, who then succeeded him. The attack had clearly been premeditated and before long Elfrida was implicated in the crime as the wicked stepmother.

It is not likely that many missed Edward who suffered from fits of uncontrollable rage, but within a decade people were saying miracles were occurring alongside his bones at Wareham, and Althelred declared him a saint and martyr.

ATHELRED (II) *THE UNREADY*
King of the English, 18 March 978–December 1013, 3 February 1014–23 April 1016. Crowned: Kingston-upon-Thames, 4 April 978.
Born: *c968.* **Died:** *London, 23 April 1016, aged 48.* **Buried:** *Old St Paul's Cathedral, London.*
Married: *(1) c985, Elgiva (c963–1002), dau. Thored, ealdorman of Northumbria: 13 children; (2) 5 April 1002, Emma (c985–1052), dau. Richard, duke of Normandy: 3 children.*

Athelred is remembered colloquially and half-jokingly today as the Unready, although the nickname was really a clever pun on his name, *athel* 'noble' and *ræd* 'counsel', meaning 'noble counsel'. Throughout his reign Athelred was ill-advised and if he made his own decision, he was as likely to change his mind, hence the nickname, *ræd-less*, or lacking counsel. He was a better administrator than history has given credit, but he was a hopeless king and leader.

He was probably under ten years old when he came to the throne, and Elfrida and the Mercian ealdorman Alfhere dominated the government of England. Alfhere had been the main opponent to Edward and led the anti-monastic movement which flared up following the death of Edgar. Alfhere believed that the monasteries were becoming too rich and powerful too quickly and that they could control the shires. Alfhere was implicated in the murder of Edward. Interestingly it was he who translated Edward's body from its hasty burial at Wareham to Shaftesbury, where it was buried amongst great ceremony and talk of miracles. Alfhere remained the most powerful ealdorman until his death in 983. He succeeded in shaping Athelred's policy of reducing the power of the monasteries, although Athelred later overturned this. Alfhere also had to face the impact of the first Danish raids for thirty years.

After Alfhere's death Athelred endeavoured to exert his own authority and even his mother's considerable power waned, though Elfrida lived till 1002. There was a period in the late 980s when Athelred sought to reduce the power of the church, but he subsequently reverted to his father's interests and promoted the construction of new monasteries under the new order. He also endeavoured to update the laws of the country and reorganize local government. This culminated in the Wantage Code of 997 which, compared to past law codes, showed an unprecedented willingness to accept local customs, especially those amongst the Danes of eastern England. Many of the odd and curious anomalies that we have in our customs and codes of conduct in this country were enshrined under this Code. Had Athelred's reign been measured by his willingness and ability to reform and organize, he would have been remembered kindly, but his mettle was tested when the Danish raids returned and England was pushed to the limit.

The raids began in a comparatively small way as early as 980 and continued through to 982. Most of the raids were in the south west, but Southampton was severely damaged and London was attacked and burned in 982. Raids ceased for the next few years and perhaps Athelred was lulled into a false sense of security, for in 987 they began again, once more in the south-west and then, in 991, a major battle at Maldon in Essex, in which the Danes outwitted the East Saxons who were killed to a man. The first payment of *danegeld*, or what amounted to protection money, arose following this battle. In 994, after the Danes had invaded London, Athelred paid 16,000 pounds in *danegeld*, but this time on the basis that the Danish leader Olaf would accept Christianity and never again raid Britain. Olaf kept his promise. But his command was superseded by others who had made no such agreement, and so the raids continued. Each year the *danegeld* increased until the riches of England were savagely reduced. In addition the monasteries were plundered and destroyed and with armies being kept mobilised for most of the year men were unable to harvest. The country grew poorer, the men weaker, and spirits lower. Athelred had never been tested as a battle commander and he had no idea what to do. He also had to face desertion from amongst his own ealdormen, whose actions in fleeing the command of battle further weakened their men's morale. Athelred seemed powerless to punish them. Instead he shifted from one mad scheme to another, none of which worked and all of which reduced the country's morale further. At one point in 1009, he demanded that a whole new fleet be constructed, but he was unable to find sufficient able commanders and had no battle plans to meet the Danes in the waters they controlled. The fleet spent more time anchored off-shore than in battle, and once it moved into battle it was destroyed. Athelred did nothing to save it but left it to its fate. The venture was a disaster and drained the country's resources further. In 1002 Athelred married Emma, daughter of Richard, duke of Normandy. The marriage was almost certainly to create an alliance whereby Richard stopped the Danes using Normandy as a base for raiding southern England. Richard no doubt played his part, but the plan was another of Athelred's ineffective tactics.

Probably his worst decision was the St Brice's Day massacre on 13 November 1002. He ordered the killing of every Dane who lived in England except the Anglo-Danes of the Danelaw. It is unlikely that the edict was carried out to the letter, but there was fearful slaughter across southern England which left a bitter stain on Athelred's character. Even if the resident Danes had supported him previously, they now turned against him. The massacre brought back to English shores the Danish commander Swein who had accompanied Olaf on earlier missions. Legend has it that Swein's sister and her husband had been killed in the massacre and Swein returned to exact revenge. Swein's campaign lasted from 1003 to 1007 when Athelred agreed a peace treaty with him and paid over an immense *danegeld* of 30,000 pounds. But new commanders brought more slaughter and the whole of England became a battlefield.

By 1013 Swein held power over England and in 1016, his son Cnut or Canute succeeded to the English throne.

CANUTE, CNUT or KNUT
England 30 November 1016–12 November 1035. Crowned:
London (Old St Paul's) 6 January 1017. Canute was also
king of Denmark from 1018 and of Norway from 1028.
Born: *Denmark, c995.* **Died:** *Shaftesbury, Dorset, 12 November*
1035, aged about 40. **Buried:** *Winchester Cathedral.*
Married: *(1) c1014, Elfgiva (c996–c1044), daughter of Alfhelm,*
ealdorman of Northampton; 2 children; (2) 2 July 1017, Emma,
widow of Athelred II: 3 children.

Canute was the first Dane to be crowned as king of England. His subsequent rulership of Denmark and Norway made him the most powerful king of northern Europe. Canute had accompanied his father, Swein, on his conquest of England in 1013, when he was left in control of the Danish fleet in the north. Once his father had been elected king of England, Canute saw fit to entrench his position in the north and it was probably early in 1014 that he claimed marriage to Elfgiva, the daughter of Alfhelm, who had been ealdorman of Northumbria until his murder in 1006. Swein died early in 1014 and although the Danes elected Canute as their new king, the *witan* chose the return of Athelred whose forces drove Canute from the north. Canute was also concerned about establishing himself on the throne of Denmark, but by the time he had returned to his homeland his elder brother Harald was already ensconced as king. Canute returned to England late in 1015 and the next twelve months saw a wasting conflict between the Danes and the Saxons under Edmund Ironside. Neither side was the complete victor and in October 1016 Edmund and Canute divided England between them, with Canute taking Mercia and Northumbria. The following month Edmund died. Canute was elected king of all England and was crowned early the following year.

From a coin

The records of Canute's early reign are limited and often prejudiced against him, as are most annals of a conqueror by the conquered. He comes across as a tyrannical king who systematically murdered or exiled most of the leading Saxon nobles, including those who had crossed to his side. However, he did not eradicate the Saxon nobility as this would serve him little purpose. England was by now a well established kingdom, whereas Denmark had only recently been united and Canute was young and untested in kingship, especially in a foreign land. He needed the support and help of those who understood England and the English. Initially he divided the land into four, granting territory to three of his earls by way of military commands, and keeping

Wessex for himself. However, from 1018 he appointed Godwin as earl of Wessex and it was under Canute that Godwin became the most powerful earl in England. Canute also realized he needed to be on good terms with the church and went to great lengths to establish relationships with Wulfstan, the archbishop of York, and Lyfing, archbishop of Canterbury. It was with Wulfstan that Canute later issued his law codes, based heavily on those already promulgated by the Saxon kings. Canute was able to adapt these codes for use in Denmark. Finally Canute married Athelred's widow, Emma, in order to strengthen his right to the throne. By all accounts he was still married to Elfgiva, which has caused some commentators to presume she was his mistress. She was certainly more than that, some treating her as his 'handfast' or common-law wife according to Scandinavian custom, whilst Emma was his formal wife and queen. By this arrangement it meant that the children of Emma were heirs to the English throne, whilst the children of Elfgiva had right of succession to the throne of Denmark. In 1018 Canute returned to Denmark where, after the death of his brother, he was accepted as king. He did not return to England until 1020, but even then required regular trips to Denmark to sustain the throne, particularly during the period 1022–3. In 1020 Canute held a major council at Cirencester. There seems to have been some unrest during his absence, and Canute dealt with this by banishing Athelweard, the ealdorman of the western provinces (the former Dumnonia). The reason for his exile is unrecorded, but we can imagine he had been plotting against Canute, perhaps to restore one of Athelred's sons to the throne, the likeliest one being Edwy. Some records suggest that Edwy had been murdered by order of Canute in 1017, but William of Malmesbury records that he survived and lived in the south-west of England, perhaps under the protection of Athelweard. It may be that Edwy was murdered after Athelweard's expulsion. The next year we find Canute at odds with Thorkell the Tall, another Danish earl who had sold his services to Athelred in 1013, but who had accepted Canute's overlordship and been made earl of East Anglia. Thorkell must have challenged

Canute's authority, perhaps in his treatment of the Saxons. Thorkell, for all his early devastation of England, had married a Saxon and seems to have established a friendship. He possibly had more scruples than Canute and they disagreed over Canute's policy of government. Thorkell was temporarily banished but the two became reconciled in 1023.

Canute's reign has all the hallmarks of a powerful king who was initially uncertain in his authority. The harsh measures at the start of his reign arose through his feeling of insecurity, though he was in fact more stable in England than in Denmark. The English had suffered nearly thirty years of privations under Danish raids, and all they wanted was a restoration of peace and prosperity. The degree of support that he had in England gave him the strong base from which to consolidate his rule of Denmark and, from 1028, to conquer Norway. From 1030 he installed his eldest son, Swein (then about sixteen), as king of Norway, with his mother Elfgiva, as regent. By the mid-1020s Canute had mellowed from his earlier tyrannical rule (which was probably exaggerated in any case by the chroniclers) to one of piety. He made considerable gifts to the church in the hope of buying salvation for his soul. The famous (much later) story of Canute sitting in his throne on the beach and commanding the tide to turn may have an element of truth. Although the legend suggests that Canute wanted to demonstrate his authority over the waves – and by implication his power over the northern seas – the fact is that Canute was giving a demonstration of piety by proving that he did not have power over them. The event is traditionally sited at Bosham on the English south coast, but an earlier record, by Geoffrey Gaimar, does not refer to Canute's throne and places the episode in the Thames estuary. In 1027 Canute visited Rome and again in 1031.

Nevertheless, despite his piety, Canute sought to impose his authority not just over England but Scotland and Wales. He visited Scotland in 1031, probably not with an army of conquest, but in order to form a peace alliance with Malcolm II who had taken advantage of unrest in England during Athelred's reign to impose his authority over Bernicia and parts of North-umbria. The agreement reached between Canute and Malcolm saw Bernicia restored to England and the English-Scottish border established more or less as it is today. The *Anglo-Saxon Chronicle* records that three kings submitted to Canute in the north. In addition to Malcolm these were Mœlbœth almost certainly Macbeth, and probably Margad Ragnallson, the Norse king of Dublin who had authority over Man and the Isles. Thorfinn the Mighty, earl of Orkney, was already subject to Canute as his Norse overlord. Canute's authority over Wales was more tenuous. There is some suggestion that Rhydderch Ap Iestyn recognized Canute's authority, but that may have been an administrative convenience, judging from Rhydderch's love of power, and it is unlikely that Canute exerted any power in Wales.

The records and later folklore suggest that Canute came to love England, possibly more than his homeland. He was a monarch who had conquered and established the most powerful of all Scandinavian empires, and was recognized as one of the most important rulers of his day. He died remarkably young, aged about forty. There is evidence that he knew he was dying and had a terminal illness that lasted for many months. Yet his death must have come suddenly as Harthacanute, who should have been his successor, was in Denmark and unable to stake his claim on England. Canute was therefore succeeded by his younger (and possibility illegitimate) son Harold (I).

Canute's son Harold Harefoot (ruled 1037–40) and his elder half-brother Harthacanute (ruled 1035–7 and 1040–2) were weaklings. Like many young sons of powerful kings, Harold was spoiled and ineffectual. After his death, Harthacanute had his body exhumed from Westminster Abbey, beheaded and flung into the marshes, for it was only because he had been preoccupied with troubles in Denmark, that his younger brother had become regent and accepted as king. Harthacanute proved to be a harsh and intolerant king. He raised an excessive tax to support his fleet at four times the rate of his father's. This led to rebellion in

Worcester in 1041 which he suppressed with vicious rage, almost destroying the town. It is to this period that the legend of Lady Godiva, or Godgifu, belongs. She was the wife of Leofric, earl of Mercia, who was forced to impose the tax across his domain. The people of Coventry could not afford it and Godiva therefore rode naked through the town to persuade Leofric to reduce the tax. Although this is wholly folklore it does demonstrate the strength of opposition among the Saxon nobility to Harthacanute's taxes. Harthacanute died while drinking at a wedding party. Apparently he had a fit, but the possibility of poison cannot be ignored. He was an unpopular and much hated king and with his death (he had no heir), the kingdom passed back to the Saxons in 1042, but it would not be for long.

EDWARD THE CONFESSOR
King of England, 8 June 1042–4 January 1066.
Crowned: Winchester 3 April 1043.
Born: c1004, Islip, Oxfordshire; *Died:* Westminster, 4 January 1066, aged 61. *Buried:* Westminster Abbey.
Married: 23 January 1045 at Winchester Cathedral, Edith (c1020–75) daughter of Earl Godwin of Wessex: no children.

Edward was the only surviving son of Athelred the Unready and his second wife, Emma, the daughter of Duke Richard of Normandy. (The Vikings had not only conquered England but as early as 911, had settled in northern France where their duchy became known as Normandy, after the Northmen. These Normans became more civilized than their Norse or Danish counterparts, heavily influenced by the French courts, but they were still of Norse stock, and retained that vicious fighting streak that never admitted defeat.)

Edward was half-Norman and had spent most of his youth (since the age of nine) in exile in Normandy. He thus grew up favouring Norman customs and, never having expected to become king, was also a rather idle and dissolute man. Upon his accession he realized he had a kingdom divided between Saxons, Danes and Norse with powerful earls of all factions. It is to Edward's credit that he succeeded in governing despite these differences. Critics of Edward accuse him of being a vacillating and indecisive king, like his father, but this may have been a façade for a cunning tactician, because Edward succeeded in ruling for over twenty-three years amidst much popular support. The fact that he was prepared to make strong decisions is evident from the start of his reign, when he confiscated his mother's property because she retained control over much of the Treasury. Emma was the most powerful and probably the richest woman in England, being the widow of two previous kings (Athelred and Canute), but her support for Edward had been limited. In fact she seemed to have almost disowned her marriage to Athelred and had become a strong supporter of the Danish court. Although Edward dispossessed her she was not sent into exile but remained in England. Charges were brought against her of involvement in the death of her sons by her first marriage and in supporting the Danish king Magnus. She seems to have bought her way out of this, although the more colourful records state that a trial by ordeal was arranged. Emma purportedly walked over nine red-hot ploughshares unscathed and at this show of innocence Edward restored all her lands and property and begged her forgiveness. She lived on at Winchester where she died on 6 March 1052, aged about sixty-six.

The power base in England at this time was with Godwin, earl of Wessex, and his many sons. It was Godwin's position that secured Edward his kingship, as the English Danes had previously recognized Canute's nephew Swein as successor. Godwin had married first Canute's half-sister and after her death, Gytha, Canute's cousin. Godwin regarded himself as a kingmaker (he had succeeded in raising Harold Harefoot to the throne and expected his son Harold (II) to become king in turn). To cement this royal connection further Godwin secured the marriage of Edward to Edith, his eldest child by Gytha, in 1045. The marriage was apparently never consummated, and popular tradition has

From the Bayeux Tapestry

ascribed this to Edward's piety or effetism. Edward was to all intents married to the church. His single most lasting achievement was the construction of Westminster Abbey, which he financed personally and which was consecrated within a week of his death. Edward was not especially learned himself, but he loved to surround himself with knowledge and culture and encouraged scholarship throughout the country. With England benefitting from the first period of lasting peace for over seventy years, Edward's reign was the last glow of a Saxon golden age.

Edward had no reason to like Godwin, for all that he knew he needed his support. Godwin had been implicated in the murder of Edward's brother Alfred, who had been imprisoned and blinded in 1036/7 at the order of Harold Harefoot. Furthermore Godwin had twice changed sides, having come to power under Canute and supported Harthacanute before switching to Harold Harefoot, only to back Edward after Harold's death instead of Swein, his obvious successor. Finally, the two had politically opposed ideals. Edward was primarily a Norman. He filled his court with Normans and appointed them to the most senior posts, whilst Godwin believed these posts should be given to the Saxon and Danish nobility. It was a conflict over Edward's favouritism to the Normans that led to an argument between Edward and Godwin in 1051. Edward, now feeling secure, banished Godwin and his sons, and despatched Edith to a convent. It was not a popular move as the Godwins were held in high regard by the English. It may have been partly to ameliorate this that Edward abolished the *danegeld* in 1051, the oppressive tax that Athelred had levied to pay the Danish pirates.

During this power vacuum, William of Normandy visited Edward. William's father was Edward's cousin, and William knew that Edward had no formal heir and would not want the kingdom inherited by Godwin's sons. Although there is no record of any agreement at this time, it was later claimed that Edward nominated William as his successor. However the following year Godwin and his sons invaded England. Edward was prepared to fight but the *witan* did not want a civil war. With bad grace, Edward pardoned Godwin and restored him and his sons to their earldoms. This made them more powerful than before. Godwin also secured his son Harold as senior amongst Edward's advisers, so much so that by 1053 Edward had more or less passed all administration over to Harold, leaving himself able to devote his energies to church matters and to hunting. Surprisingly during this period Edward supported the claim of Malcolm (III) to the kingship of Scotland and gave his authority to an invasion of Scotland by Siward, earl of Northumbria, to depose Macbeth and place Malcolm on the throne. The initial onslaught was only partially successful but Malcolm eventually succeeded to the Scottish throne in 1058 and his friendship to the Saxons would prove valuable to Saxon exiles in future years.

In the meantime Harold Godwinson grew from strength to strength, and was increasingly looking like a successor to Edward, which Edward did not want. Even though he may have promised the succession to William, the anti-Norman feeling in England made this too dangerous a course to promote. Edward was thus relieved when he learned in 1054 that his nephew, known as Edward the Exile, was alive and well in Hungary. An embassy was despatched to recall him to England. As the son of Edmund Ironside he was the natural successor. His return was delayed but Edward finally arrived in England in August 1057.

Within a few weeks he was dead. Edward's succession plans were thwarted, although he now raised Edward the Exile's four-year old son, Edgar, as his heir (atheling). Edward was forced to acknowledge that should he die before Edgar came of age, Harold would be regent. As a result the final years of Edward's reign were ones of increasing uncertainty. Edward still favoured William of Normandy as his successor, whilst the English increasingly favoured Harold, at least as war-leader if Edward died before the young atheling came of age. There was another claimant, Harald Haadraada of Norway, who already ruled Orkney and the Western Isles, and believed England was his by right. In 1065, Godwin's son Tostig was deprived of his earldom in Northumbria following his inept and tyrannical rule, and was banished to Flanders. He soon threw in his lot with Harald Haadraada, so that by the end of 1065, when it was clear that Edward was dying, the English throne was under considerable threat and needed strong leadership. Thus, when Edward died in that first week of January 1066, it was Harold Godwinson who became king.

HAROLD II
King of the English 5 January – 14 October 1066.
Crowned: 6 January 1066 at Westminster Abbey.
Born: c1022 Died in battle: 14 October 1066, aged 44.
Buried: Battle, Sussex; remains later removed to Waltham Abbey, Essex.
Married: (1) c1045 Edith Swanneshals (Swan-neck): 6 children; (2) Edith (Eadgyth) (b. c1042), daughter of Alfgar, earl of Mercia, and widow of Gruffydd ap Llywelyn of Wales: 1 child.

Harold is romantically portrayed as 'the last of the Saxons' in the novel of that title by Lord Lytton. In some ways his heroic death at the battle of Hastings was a last ditch stand defending the old order against tyrannical oppression. On the other hand Harold was not a lily-white champion of virtue, he was a violent man with a vicious temper. He was, after all, Godwin's eldest son, and earl of Wessex. After his death, he had become the senior earl, and increasingly taken over the administration and government of England, while Edward had involved himself more in church affairs. By 1064 Harold was designated 'Duke of the English', tantamount to heir apparent. Harold had almost certainly instigated the mysterious death of Edward the Exile, the real heir to the throne.

He maintained a vicious campaign against the Welsh prince Gruffydd ap Llywellyn, whom he forced into submission first in 1057 and again in 1063, the latter campaign resulting in Gruffydd's death. Harold later married Gruffydd's widow, Edith, daughter of the earl of Mercia, though he already had a wife, married according to the Danish law, also called Edith (known as Swan-neck), whom he truly loved and who bore him six children.

Sometime in 1065 Harold was at sea in the English channel when his ship was blown off course and he was driven on to the coast of Normandy. This has always been a curious episode, never fully explained. Purportedly, Harold agreed that Duke William would be Edward's successor and paid homage to William. Knowing Harold's character this was unlikely, and could easily have been invented by William later, when no-one could disprove it. Whatever the circumstance, by the end of 1065 William, who had previously been made heir by Edward the Confessor, though again somewhat secretly, firmly believed he would be the next king of England. In November 1065 Tostig, Harold's brother and earl of Northumbria, having been ejected from his earldom was forced to flee the country and during that winter he planned his invasion of England.

On the night of 4/5 January, 1066, King Edward died and Harold was proclaimed and crowned king. William of Normandy regarded this as treachery and he too prepared to invade. The first to attempt it was Tostig with a fleet from Normandy. In May 1066 he harried the south coast of England round to Lindsey in the east, where he was defeated and fled to Scotland. He appealed to his cousin Swein in Denmark who was prepared to offer him an earldom, but not support for an invasion, so

From the Bayeux Tapestry

Tostig made his way to the court of Harald Haadraada, the king of Norway, and the most fearsome Viking of them all. Harald was initially unsure, knowing how strong England's defences were, but Tostig convinced him and through the summer the Norwegians prepared their fleet while William of Normandy prepared his. King Harold used the period to strengthen England's coastal defences. In September Harald Haadraada sailed with 200 warships, stopping first in Orkney where he gathered more supplies and men. He sailed with the earls Paul and Erlend down the coast to the mouth of the Tyne where Tostig waited with a further force of men from Scotland and Man. This massive force continued down the coast of Northumbria, pillaging and destroying as it went. It was met at Fulford on 20 September by an English army under earls Morcar and Edwin which was defeated. York agreed to surrender and the invaders withdrew to Stamford Bridge to await negotiators. There, on 25 September, they were surprised by King Harold's army which had undertaken a forced march north. The battle that followed was a total victory for Harold. Both the Norwegian king and Tostig were killed. But Harold had no time to relish his success. Two days later the wind that had stopped William sailing changed and his invasion began.

Harold was forced to march south again at full speed, and the two armies met at Senlac Hill, north of Hastings on 14 October. With hindsight Harold should have waited. To engage two major invasion forces at either end of the kingdom within one month required superhuman ability. The astonishing thing is that Harold almost won. The Normans' technical sophistication was of limited use against the Saxon shield-wall with which they protected the position. A retreat by the Breton forces encouraged a pursuit that exposed the English to a cavalry counter-attack, but the battle was decided by hard, attritional fighting. As dusk came on the lofted arrows were eroding the ranks of the Saxon axemen. Harold was not killed by an arrow in his eye, but he and his brothers died defending each other to the last.

Had Harold been the victor, it is a fascinating exercise in alternative reality to consider what might have become of England. Two such great victories would have made Harold secure and, seemingly invincible. He was not young, but there is no reason why he could not have reigned another twenty years or so. In that time, unless he changed his ways, the real Harold would have been revealed – the sly and devious son of Godwin. The Saxons might have continued to rule for another century. But such was not to be. All but one of Harold's sons lived into the 1080s and beyond, though we lose track of them before their deaths. Although the English initially rallied around the young atheling, Edgar, they soon capitulated to Duke William who ever after was known as William the Conqueror.

THE HOUSE
OF NORMANDY (1066–1154)

By the eleventh century the kingdoms that made up the British Isles were still agrarian. Over the centuries the Anglo-Saxons had settled in villages and had begun to clear the vast woodlands, but there were still great forests and marshes and millions of acres of moorland. Thousands upon thousands of acres of land remained unpopulated and uncultivated, and much of Britain's vast mineral resources were as yet untapped. By the time the Normans invaded England, the population had reached about one and a quarter million, with the majority living in East Anglia, while to the north there were less than four people per square mile. Because of constant warring, it was a land in decline. The arrival of the Normans would change all that. They would strengthen Britain's defences with their stone castles (many still standing to this day). They would fortify governmental institutions, the laws of the land and their direct implementation – through sheriffs and special commissioners – in turn the monarchy would itself be strengthened. For they also brought with them their feudal ways, dispossessing the English of their lands and keeping them for the crown. The Norman barons became tenants in chief of the old Anglo-Saxon manors, and in return for this favour were obliged to raise knights for the king's service in lieu of rent. The barons in their turn sublet their manors and land with equal obligations, each manor having its landless knights; the poor of the land became no more than serfs. The Normans brought in laws to protect the forests, and the royal hunting rights to all the game that lived therein. Any man (or dog) found breaking this law could be 'hambled' – that is, have his hamstring pulled and be crippled for life.

The first Norman monarchs were not sophisticated or cultured people.

WILLIAM I *THE CONQUEROR, also called THE BASTARD*
King of England, late November/early December 1066–9 September 1087. Crowned: Westminster Abbey, 25 December 1066.
Titles: *king of England, duke of Normandy and count of Maine.*
Born: *Falaise, Normandy, autumn 1028.* **Died**: *St Gervais, Rouen, 9 September 1087, aged 59.* **Buried**: *Abbey of St Stephen, Caen.*
Married: *c1053 (at Eu), Matilda (c1031–83), dau. Baldwin V of Flanders, 10 children.*

William the Conqueror, or William the Bastard as he was known in his day (though out of his hearing), was the illegitimate son of Robert I, duke of Normandy. William was also descended from Ragnald, the ancestor of the earls of Orkney. The connections between the Norman and Saxon royal families extended back to Athelred The Unready who had married Emma the sister of William's grandfather, Richard II of Normandy. William was the son of Edward the Confessor's first cousin. Researchers have been unable to find any evidence of Edward's promising the throne to William, at least amongst English documents, and its only provenance is amongst the Norman chronicles. William was later able to exact support for the claim from Harold Godwinson, earl of Wessex, who was at William's court in 1065, and the Bayeux Tapestry shows Harold offering fealty to William. So when Edward died in 1066 and Harold was crowned as king, William regarded him as a usurper.

William had already demonstrated his strength as a commander and soldier. His life was one of almost constant warfare as he carved out for himself a position as one of the most powerful and, when necessary, ruthless rulers of his day. He had succeeded to the duchy of Normandy in 1035 when just seven or eight years old. His father had died while on a pilgrimage when only 27. His mother, Herleva or Arletta, was Robert's mistress. She was the daughter of a local tanner and, legend says, Robert spied upon her while she washed clothes at the river. During William's minority there was much rivalry at the Norman court as the aristocracy struggled for power. Three of William's guardians were assassinated and the young duke knew he needed to assert his authority as soon as he was able. That opportunity came in 1047 when his cousin, Guy of Brionne, rebelled and claimed the duchy. Guy had considerable support and William needed the help of Henri I of France to win the day after a tightly fought battle. This gave William his authority but it also imprinted upon him a streak of ruthlessness which caused him to retaliate viciously against anyone who challenged him.

William's authority increased when he married Matilda, the daughter of Baldwin V, count of Flanders, a powerful ruler whose acceptance of William as a suitable son-in-law showed that William had risen above the trials of his youth. William may also have seen in Matilda a further link with his claim on the throne of England as she was a direct descendant of Alfred the Great. The pope apparently opposed this marriage for some years on the grounds of an earlier betrothal by Matilda, but it finally received his blessing in 1059.

During the decade of the 1050s William continued to consolidate his power, even to the point of incurring the enmity of his former ally, Henri I of France. William succeeded in rebuffing all attempts to invade Normandy and by 1062 had himself invaded Maine, on almost the same pretext as he would invade England four years later – that Herbert, count of Maine, had promised William the county if he died without heir. William became count of Maine in 1063. William's other conquests meant that he had support from the surrounding powers of Anjou and Brittany, whilst the new king of France, Philippe I, was under the protection of William's father-in-law, Baldwin. This meant that when William prepared to invade England in September 1066 he was able to draw not only upon his own resources within Normandy, but upon those of his allies.

From the Bayeux Tapestry

Nevertheless, this did not make William's conquest of England a certainty. He was up against one of the most aggressive armies of Europe under the command of Harold Godwinson. Harold's misfortune was that he had to face two invasions within one month. Already weakened by defeating the army of Harold Hardraada of Norway at Stamford Bridge on 25 September, his army faced a quick march back to fight William who had landed at Pevensey on 28 September. William took advantage of Harold's absence to develop his defences near Hastings and by pillaging the local farmsteads and hamlets. By so doing William succeeded in drawing Harold towards him, whereas Harold's opportunity for success lay in drawing William away from his fleet and its supplies. The two armies met at Senlac Hill (now Battle), near Hastings, on 14 October 1066. Had Harold's army not been weakened he may well have won, but they were overpowered by William's cavalry. The Saxon army submitted after the death of Harold and his brothers. That day, however, the *witan* proclaimed Edgar the Atheling as their new king but he was only a boy of thirteen or fourteen, and unable to muster any forces to retaliate against William.

For the next two months William's army moved strategically around the Kentish coast taking a circular route to London and seeking the submission of the English en route. They burned Dover, and laid waste to much of Surrey. The citizens of London prevented William crossing the Thames, so he sacked Southwark and moved west, crossing the Thames at Wallingford. Edgar submitted at Berkhamstead and the Normans then approached London from the north. Lud Gate was opened to the invader by a collaborator and, in the Battle of Ludgate Hill, countless Londoners were slain. William was crowned in Westminster Abbey on 25 December 1066, the ceremony conducted by Ealdred, archbishop of York. Cries of support from the Normans present were interpreted as an English rebellion and the guards promptly attacked the Saxons and set fire to nearby houses. William himself had to quell the panic. His reign began with terror and would remain a reign of terror for twenty years.

Although William was to style himself king of England not all of England had accepted him as king. His dominion was primarily in the south, covering all the old kingdoms of Wessex, Kent, Sussex and Essex, and stretching some way into Mercia. The powerful earls of Mercia and Northumbria, the brothers Edwin and Morcar, believed that William's design was only to conquer Wessex and accepted him as king within that domain, pleased that he had overthrown the Godwin family. They even hoped they would be accepted as kings in their territories. This short-sightedness sealed the fate of England, for had the brothers united their armies with those elsewhere in England and faced William before he became established, he might still have been defeated, but the old rivalries between Saxon families became their downfall and isolated rebellions were soon put down with the viciousness with which William became renowned.

William remained in England for three months after his coronation, during which time he appointed a wide range of Norman officials, and despatched the army to plunder the churches in order to pay his army. When he returned to Normandy in late February 1067 he took with him the most likely candidates to lead any rebellion in England, Edgar the Atheling, Stigand, the archbishop of Canterbury, and the earls Edwin and Morcar. During his absence in Normandy, where William displayed the spoils of his conquest and made most of his fame, his half-brother Bishop Odo endeavoured to impose Norman rule in England, but with minimal success. An attempted invasion by Eustace, count of Boulogne, who was Edward the Confessor's brother-in-law, was soon repelled, but the general unrest in England, especially in the north and west, continued to grow. William returned in December 1067 and began his systematic conquest of England in earnest. He turned his attention first to the west, at Exeter, where Harold's mother had taken refuge. The town submitted after a siege of eighteen days. William was comparatively lenient to the townsfolk, though he exacted payment. He also ordered the building of a castle and established a Norman nobleman, Baldwin of Brionne, as the local custodian. This became William's approach over the next few years. As he advanced upon his conquests he would build a castle from which a Norman duke or earl would maintain the peace in that territory. Initially the castles were hasty constructions of wood upon a motte-and-bailey site. It was only later that he and his successors began the construction of massive stone castles at key sites. These castles became the image of Norman power created not to defend England but to dominate it. In total 78 castles were constructed by William's order, the most famous being the Tower of London. By March 1068

William felt sufficiently secure in the south to bring his wife, Matilda, over to England where she was crowned queen. She remained in England for a year, accompanying William on his tour of conquest. Their last son, the future Henry I was born at Selby in September 1068. She returned to Normandy in 1069 and remained there until her death in 1083.

It was during 1068 that William faced his first major opposition. Earls Morcar and Edwin rebelled, and Edgar the Atheling took refuge with Malcolm III of Scotland – Malcolm married Edgar's sister Margaret the following year. The Saxons sought the support of the Welsh though clearly were not acting with any coherent plan for William was soon able to quash the rebellion by advancing on Warwick. William continued north, establishing castles at Nottingham and York. His original plans to govern northern England through the Saxon aristocracy now changed, as he believed Edwin and Morcar had forfeited their rights. From then on William redistributed the lands of the Saxons amongst the Norman and French aristocracy. The native English were not simply conquered, they were dispossessed. William was hated and despised by the English, but any attempt to display this feeling was countered by ruthless retaliation.

When William returned briefly to Normandy in early 1069, faced with a revolt in Maine, the English attacked the Normans at Durham, killing many of them. They moved on to besiege the castle at York, but by then William had returned and he not only defeated the English but sacked the city.

The English resistance was far from over. Edgar the Atheling's followers joined forces with King Swein of Denmark. Swein had as much claim to the English throne as William, if not more. He was the nephew of Canute and maintained, like William, that Edward had named him as his successor. The English had learned to co-exist with the Danes. There had been Danish kings ruling parts of England for two centuries before Canute. The armies of Swein and Edgar, along with other northern rebels, recaptured York in September 1069. Again William marched on the north, this time destroying everything in his path. This harrying of the north was the most extreme example of despoiling and genocide that England has ever seen, and for which William was never forgiven by the English. He may have conquered them, but he never ruled them.

William succeeded in buying off the Danish force and in late 1070 they retreated, after briefly returning for a second attempt. Pockets of resistance remained throughout the north, the west and especially in the Fenland of East Anglia, where the Saxon thane Hereward the Wake, perhaps the best known of the Saxon rebels, maintained the most ordered resistance to William. Hereward was joined by Earl Morcar whose brother, Edwin, had been treacherously murdered by his own men. William brought all his forces to bear upon the Isle of Ely where Hereward made the last major Saxon stand against Norman might. William's power proved irresistible. Hereward escaped, but Morcar was captured and imprisoned, and other rebels were tortured and mutilated before their release.

The last to resist William was Edgar the Atheling who had fled back to the court of King Malcolm. In the summer of 1072 William marched into Scotland to demand that Malcolm cease aiding Edgar's insurrection. Malcolm agreed and, with the Peace of Abernethy, recognized William as his overlord. He also expelled Edgar from his court. Edgar, however, did not submit to William until 1074. By the end of 1072 William believed that his conquest of England was complete. Already he had replaced many of the Saxon officials with Normans, and these included the officials of the church. Probably his most significant appointment was that of Lanfranc as archbishop of Canterbury. The Norman aristocracy was installed in lands across the length and breadth of England and their dominion established a feudal system in which all Saxons were increasingly treated as peasants.

Although William made annual visits to London, Gloucester and Winchester, he had no central headquarters so during his visits to Britain he and his court would move from one stronghold to the next. A contemporary has described this weary circuit: 'Sometimes the king declares he will leave early then slumbers till noon, while horses droop under their harness, chariots stand ready, messengers fall asleep and everyone grumbles . . . But when the king changes his mind about a destination – what chaos. Probably only one house can be found there. Then we, after wandering miles through an unknown forest, often in the dark, may find by chance some filthy hovel. Indeed, courtiers often fight for lodgings unfit for dogs.'

Although William had despoiled the land in order to subjugate the English, he had never intended to plunder it. Indeed, once he had established his authority he was keen for England to prosper so that he could benefit from the revenues. William returned to Normandy in 1072 and remained there for much of the next twelve years, needing to maintain his duchy against the opposition of the French and his former allies who were now fearful of his power. The administration of England was left in the hands of Richard Fitzgilbert and William de Warenne, two of William's most powerful barons.

William did not return to England for any significant period until 1085, when he brought over a massive army to defend the island against a planned invasion under Canute IV of Denmark. Canute, however, was murdered before the invasion began. William's restless army caused considerable hardship to the Saxons during this period. In addition William had to raise the land taxes in order to pay his sizeable army and this caused real difficulties. The problems that William had in knowing who owned what land and what its value was, so that he could levy the taxes, led to him ordering a major survey of England. The record of this survey, carried out with remarkable accuracy and speed during 1086, became known as the *Domesday Book*, and though its purpose was for William to ensure he had control over his taxes in England, the result is a rare and indispensable historical document. William, however, made little use of the document himself. He returned to Normandy at the end of 1086 where he became preoccupied with a local rebellion. In July 1087 William besieged the town of Mantes. As his horse jumped over a ditch, the pommel of his saddle ripped into his stomach. The wound became poisoned leading to peritonitis. William was carried back to Rouen in considerable pain. There he lingered on for five weeks, and died in September. His body was returned to Caen for burial but apparently the tomb was not big enough for the king was a tall man, at least five foot ten inches. As the attendants forced his body into the tomb, the already decaying and swollen corpse burst open, letting out an intense smell of putrefaction that caused most to flee the site. Only a hardy few completed the burial.

William had changed England irrevocably. His total domination had, within less than a generation, almost eradicated the Saxon aristocracy and imposed a feudal society run by a small handful of Normans. The language difficulties added further to the alienation, but perhaps the most significant difference was in the lifestyle. Although the Normans were descended from the Vikings, they no longer looked to the north as their ancestral home, unlike the Saxons whose inheritance was from northern Europe. The Normans had taken on the more sophisticated lifestyle of the French, which brought with it the power, grandeur and aloofness of an upper-class existence. William used England as his playground, establishing the New Forest in Hampshire for his hunting. He had no liking for the English or, for that matter, for England, seeing it only as a rich source of revenue. Although his harsh rule brought peace to England, where man was apparently able to travel without fear of crime, this was only because the English lived in much greater fear of revenge and retribution from their Norman overlords. It created a rift between the nobility and the common man which remained in Britain for centuries.

William was devoted to his wife Matilda, and was much saddened at her death. They had ten children. The eldest, Robert, succeeded William as duke of Normandy and count of Maine even though he had been in open rebellion against his father in his latter years. The second son, Richard, died in his twenties in 1081 while hunting in the New Forest. Two other sons, William and Henry, would succeed William as kings of England. Of his six daughters, Adela would become mother of the future king Stephen.

WILLIAM II *RUFUS*
King of England, 9 September 1087–2 August 1100;
Crowned: Westminster, 26 September 1087.
Born: *Normandy, c1057.* **Died**: *New Forest, 2 August 1100,*
aged about 43. **Buried**: *Winchester Cathedral.*

William the Conqueror's third and favourite son, William, was bequeathed the kingdom of England although many believed he might also inherit the duchy of Normandy. Normandy, however, went to his eldest brother Robert. The two were always openly hostile to one another, and had been so during their father's lifetime, with William remaining loyal to his father. Much of William's reign was spent in rivalry with Robert. The consequences were divisive: barons who held lands in both Normandy and England found it impossible to know whom to support without fear of losing their lands on one side or the other. It looked initially as if Robert's star might prevail, as barons rose in support of him in an insurrection in 1088 led by his uncle Odo. However Robert failed to capitalize on this support and William was quick to quash the rebellion, devastating Odo's estates in Kent. The rivalry between William and Robert was eventually solved to some degree in 1091, after a brief attempt at a coup by their younger brother Henry, which united William and Robert. William now showed his negotiating skills by reaching an agreement between all three brothers to their mutual benefit, and William even brought Robert to England to join him in an expedition against Malcolm III of Scotland. The position, however, was not fully resolved until 1096 when Robert decided to join the First Crusade. He pledged Normandy to William in exchange for money to raise his army. William was never officially duke of Normandy, serving instead as his brother's regent, but he was more successful than Robert and won back lands in France that Robert had lost.

In fact William was a king for whom much seemed to go right. One might almost think that God smiled on him, though such a belief would have horrified the clergy who regarded William with total disdain. Because the chronicles of the time were written by monks, the opinion has passed down in history of William as a vicious and avaricious man who was 'hated by almost all his people and abhorrent to God'. It is difficult to get an objective picture of a man who had strong and powerful enemies amongst his own barons as well as within his own family. Some have claimed that he was homosexual, his court being described as like that of the Roman emperor Caligula, with men dressed effeminately, if dressed at all. It is true that he never married, though there were later unsubstantiated rumours that he had an illegitimate son. He was portrayed as having a fiery temper, his face often flushed red, hence his nickname Rufus. The red face may be more an indication of his drinking and eating habits. He was stout, and despite being a man of action may well have had heart problems.

Despite all this William was a good soldier, who took a liking to England and endeavoured to rule justly. He attempted to conquer lands in Wales, and initially made considerable advances against the Welsh prince Gruffydd ap Cynan Gwynedd but was eventually repulsed in 1094. A second onslaught in 1098 regained ground, and several of the Welsh princes recognized William as their overlord. During this period William established a line of castles along the Welsh marches.

William also continued an uneasy relationship with the Scottish king, Malcolm III. William had spurned the Saxon prince Edgar the Atheling, who returned to Scotland and, in 1090, encouraged Malcolm to invade England again, primarily with the purpose of regaining Scottish lands in Lothian and Northumbria, and defending Cumbria. William soon rebuffed Malcolm and succeeded in renewing the Peace of Abernethy. In fact Malcolm was friendly towards William and eventually despatched Edgar as a nuisance. William did not necessarily return that friendship for, in 1092, he seized the lands around Carlisle, establishing a castle there, and when visited by Malcolm for a parley, refused to see him. As the infuriated Malcolm returned to Scotland he was attacked and killed by the Normans in Northumbria. Malcolm's brother Donald Bane claimed the throne in a period of violent upheaval against the Normans. William Rufus, however supported first Duncan II and Edgar, the sons of Malcolm III, in overthrowing Donald. Edgar, whose reign was more stable, acknowledged the help and support of the Normans and realized that thereafter he was subservient to them. William thus stamped his authority on an expanding Norman base with tentacles creeping into Wales and Scotland.

Where William really roused the wrath of the clergy was in his dealings with them. He did not seem respectful of the church, unlike his father. Although he was held in check initially by Archbishop Lanfranc, when Lanfranc died in 1089, William did not bother to appoint a successor and, instead, took advantage of the revenues himself. In the eyes of the church, William was stealing from God. They urged William to appoint Lanfranc's student and friend, Anselm, as archbishop but William refrained. It was not until William was taken ill in 1092 and believed he was dying that he gave in. As Anselm was in England at that time, William offered him the archbishopric. Anselm at first refused but, under pressure from the clergy, he accepted. This was only the start of the problems between him and William. At this time there was a schism in the papacy. Urban II was the pope installed in Rome and he was supported by Anselm, but there was a rival anti-pope in Ravenna, Clement III. William remained uncommitted. In 1095 he called a council to judge the matter. William finally agreed to support Urban, but only because he extracted acceptance from Urban that papal legates could not enter England without royal agreement. It was more an agreement of convenience than of loyalty. William in fact interpreted it as his freedom from the church. Although Anselm supported Urban, he refused to accept the way in which William had approached the issue, maintaining that church matters could not be judged in a secular court. William appealed to Urban, seeking for the pope to depose Anselm. A papal legate was despatched to England but

From Historia Anglorum

no decision was made. In the end the relationship between Anselm and William became so impossible that Anselm went into self-imposed exile in 1097.

It was little wonder that the clergy so despised William, and they had good grounds, but they may have blackened his character a little too much. There have even been recent allegations that William was a devil-worshipper and practised the black arts, but there is no real evidence for this. What it boils down to is that William was a perfectly able and capable king who was successful in most of his campaigns, but whose temperament and affectations annoyed both the church and many of his barons.

This background consequently led to much speculation about William's death. He was hunting one summer's evening in the New Forest when he was killed by an arrow apparently shot at a fleeing deer. It was immediately claimed as an accident, the offending party being Walter Tirel. Tirel always proclaimed his innocence, stating that he was nowhere near the king when the arrow was fired, but Tirel was rapidly transported back to France. The conspiracist theory is that William was murdered, perhaps by order of one of the barons who supported his brother Robert. Duncan Grinnell-Milne, in his compelling piece of detective work *The Killing of William Rufus* (1968), was convinced that William's death was part of a master plan by his brother Henry to gain the throne. Certainly there were many relieved at the death of the king, and the verdict of accidental death was satisfactory to all (except Tirel who felt he was falsely accused), so no one investigated it further. William's body was hurriedly conveyed in a farm cart to Winchester Cathedral where it was peremptorily buried in the early hours of the next morning. Though there were official mourners, everyone seemed in much greater haste to return to Westminster. There is a strong feeling in reading about William's death and Henry's succession that William was a nuisance who was now out of the way and everyone could get back to the real purpose of government.

In retrospect William's reign is a minor episode in England's history, though had he lived he might have caused more problems in his relationship with the church. It remains a fact, though, that he was not only able to sustain his kingdom in England but that he reached workable relations with the kings and princes of Scotland and Wales as well as his brother in Normandy, which demonstrates an able administrator and king for all that he was opinionated, arrogant and ill tempered. England would have many rulers who were far worse than William.

HENRY (I) BEAUCLERC
King of England 3 August 1100–1 December 1135.
Crowned: Westminster, 6 August 1100.
Titles: King of England, Duke of Normandy (from 1106) and Lord of Domfront (from 1092).
Born: Selby, Yorkshire, September 1068. Died: St Denis-le-Fermont, near Rouen, 1 December 1135, aged 67. Buried: Reading Abbey.
Married: (1) 11 November 1100, Matilda (formerly Edith), dau. of Malcolm III of Scotland; 4 children; (2) 29 January 1121, Adeliza, dau. of Geoffrey VII, Count of Louvain; no children. Henry had at least 25 illegitimate children by eight or more other women.

William and Robert had agreed that if either of them died childless, then the survivor would succeed. This effectively disinherited their youngest brother Henry who had long begrudged the fact that he had not been able to inherit his mother's estates in England bequeathed to him upon her death in 1083. Instead his father William the Conqueror believed that, as the youngest son, Henry would be destined for the church. He received a good education, hence his nickname *Beauclerc*, meaning 'fine scholar', since he was the first Norman king (and there had not been that many Saxon ones) who could read and write.

Henry was not satisfied with his lot and it was rumoured he masterminded the death of William II, making it look as though he was killed as the result of a hunting accident. If this is true then its timing was critical. In 1096 Robert of Normandy had joined the Crusade to the Holy Land and had pledged the duchy to William. By the summer of 1100 news reached England that Robert was returning, along with a new bride. Immediately upon William's death a hastily convened council elected Henry as his successor: this, despite the support that many barons had for Robert, who was on a crest of popularity following his victories in the Holy Land, even though his past record showed him as a weak ruler of Normandy. By the first week of September, when Robert had returned to Normandy, Henry had been elected and crowned. One of his first acts was to recall Anselm from exile to the archbishopric of Canterbury, and with Anselm's support Henry's position was inviolable. He further cemented it by a political marriage to Edith, the daughter of Malcolm III of Scotland and the niece of Edgar the Atheling, thus establishing alliances with the elder Saxon aristocracy and with the Scots.

From a coin

Robert raised a considerable army and invaded England in June 1101, cleverly misleading Henry whose army waited at Arundel while Robert landed at Portsmouth. It is possible that had Robert pressed home his advantage he could have defeated Henry's army. He might easily have captured Winchester, where the Treasury was held, but his army passed by that town. It stopped short of invading London, though this too was within his grasp. Instead the two armies met at Alton where Robert asked for negotiations. Clearly Robert lacked the opportunism that marked the success of his father and younger brother. Even worse, he was prepared to trust Henry. The result was that Henry agreed to pay Robert 3,000 marks annually and recognize him as the legal claimant to the throne in exchange for Henry remaining king while he lived. In the eyes of Henry and the barons possession was nine-tenths of the law, and Robert was the loser. A few years later, in 1106, Henry took control of the matter, invading Normandy and capturing his brother at Tinchebrai. Robert was brought to England and imprisoned for the rest of his life – another twenty-eight years – he was certainly over 80 when he died in 1134.

Whilst Henry was endeavouring to regain Normandy he had troubles at home with the church. Although he had recalled Anselm as archbishop of Canterbury, the relations between the two rapidly deteriorated. Anselm had fallen out with William Rufus because the latter had refused to acknowledge the authority of Rome and Anselm's rights in the reorganization of the church. Anselm reminded Henry of the papal authority in appointing clergy, since the pope had decreed as far back as 1059 that lay investiture was unlawful in the eyes of the Church. Henry would have none of this, and with other matters more pressing refused to consider it. By 1103 Anselm found his position untenable and he again went into exile. The pope threatened to excommunicate Henry and, fearful of how this would undermine his authority as king, Henry recalled Anselm and sought to negotiate a compromise. The result was that in 1106 Henry accepted clerical authority in investiture on the understanding that the clergy still recognized secular authority over the lands owned by the church. In this way Henry kept his revenues (which Anselm had maintained belonged to the church and thus to Rome) and it meant he could still agree who had possession of the property. Nevertheless when Anselm died in 1109 Henry succeeded in keeping the see of Canterbury vacant for five years.

Once Henry had secured the dukedom of Normandy he had his hands full in keeping it. Since England was now relatively safe, he found he had to spend more time in Normandy. His queen Matilda officially served as regent during these absences, but increasingly the administration came under the capable control of Roger, bishop of Salisbury. Since Henry drew heavily upon the English revenues to finance his army in Normandy as well as his extensive building projects across England, Roger developed a system for controlling the exchequer. In effect he established the basis for what would evolve into the civil service.

Although Henry would enter into battle if necessary, he sought to pave the way by treaty or diplomacy first, and in this he was admirably skilled. One such act was the marriage in January 1114 of his eldest daughter Adelaide (who adopted the name Matilda upon her marriage) to Heinrich V, Emperor of Germany, and she was crowned Empress on the same day. She was eleven years old; the Emperor was 32. Henry held Normandy against all opposition. His ultimate victory was the defeat of Louis VI of France in 1119. When peace was agreed with the pope's blessing, Henry was accepted unchallenged as duke of Normandy. Henry cemented this advance by marrying his eldest son William to Alice (who also changed her name to Matilda), the daughter of Fulk V, count of Anjou and Maine. William was only fifteen, Alice less than twelve. In 1120, as Henry's eldest son William came of age, he was made duke of Normandy, and stood in succession to the throne of England, even though Henry's eldest brother Robert and his son William were both still alive.

In the summer of 1120 Henry could be proud of his achievements. Through his own marriage and those of his children he had alliances with the strongest neighbouring royal families of Europe; others he had dominated by conquest or treaty. He had reached a satisfactory arrangement with the papacy and all looked well for the future. And then everything fell about him. In November 1120 his two eldest legitimate sons William and Richard drowned when the White Ship foundered off Barfleur while sailing from Normandy to England. He was left without a male heir, although his eldest illegitimate son, Robert Fitzroy, earl of Gloucester, now turned an eye to the throne. Henry's first wife, Matilda had died in May 1118, an event over which Henry did not seem especially concerned. He arranged a quick marriage of convenience to Adeliza, daughter of Geoffrey VII, count of Louvain. That marriage was childless, although Henry had several more illegitimate children (ultimately he would have twenty-five).

In 1125 Henry's daughter, Matilda, became a widow when the Emperor Heinrich died. She was twenty-three but had no children. In 1126, fearing he would have no further children, Henry made the barons swear an oath of fealty to Matilda as the heir-presumptive to the throne. The barons agreed, though the idea of being ruled by a queen was anathema to them. The position was further aggravated when, in May 1127, Henry arranged a second marriage for Matilda, this time with Geoffrey of Anjou, who was then only fourteen. The Normans had little affection for the Angevins and did not like to consider that Geoffrey might become their King. They began to turn their allegiance to Henry's nephew, William, the son of Duke Robert, who was known as William Clito. At this time, April 1127, he was supported by the French king, who had just made him count of Flanders. In January 1128 he married Giovanna, the daughter of the count of Burgundy. William was gradually rising in power and his right to the English throne was becoming increasingly recognized by the Norman aristocracy. However, in July 1128 he was wounded in a skirmish near St Omer and died five days later.

The barons now realised that there was little alternative to Matilda becoming their queen, but they showed increasing opposition. Geoffrey, who became count of Anjou in 1129, recognized this and though he never seems to have considered himself having any claim to the throne of England, he did consider the duchy of Normandy and asked Henry if he would give him custody of the castles along the French coast. Henry refused. Relations between Henry and Geoffrey deteriorated rapidly. They had not been helped by Matilda deciding she could not abide Geoffrey and deserting him to return to England. Henry, still with an eye on Matilda producing a grandson, sought to reconcile the two with some degree of success. Nevertheless, by 1135 Henry and Geoffrey were openly at war. Henry sailed to Normandy but soon after his arrival he became ill, apparently after eating some lampreys. Six days later he died from ptomaine poisoning. Despite having declared Matilda his heir, neither she nor the barons took up that position, and the throne was claimed by Henry's nephew, Stephen.

Henry was a highly capable king. Although he was frequently involved in warfare, either direct or diplomatic, most of this was over his lands in Normandy. For all of his long reign, after the first year, he maintained peace throughout England, though it was a peace at the cost of exacting taxes needed to maintain his army. This led to him establishing the crown exchequer, the basis of the future Treasury. With his many campaigns and international affairs, Henry had little time for anything other than pleasures of the flesh, although he did establish a royal menagerie at his manor at Woodstock, near Oxford, which is regarded as the first English zoo. It is ironic that, despite having fathered at least twenty-nine children, he was only able to leave one legitimate heir to the throne, and she was not considered seriously by Henry's barons until it became convenient to do so. For all Henry's schemes and plans during his thirty-five-year reign, the longest of any king of England since Athelred II, it all came to nought. Perhaps he schemed too much, for his efforts in his final years to find a successor meant that he found one too many, and within four years of his death, England was plunged into civil war.

STEPHEN
King of England, 22 December 1135–7 April 1141 (deposed); restored 1 November 1141–25 October 1154.
Crowned: Westminster Abbey, 26 December 1135; and again Canterbury Cathedral, 25 December 1141.
Titles: king of England, count of Mortain (before 1115) and count of Boulogne (from c1125).
Born: Blois, France, c1097. *Died*: Dover, 25 October 1154, aged 57. *Buried*: Faversham Abbey, Kent.
Married: c1125, Matilda (c1103–1152), dau. of Eustace III, count of Boulogne, 5 children. Stephen had at least five illegitimate children.

Stephen's mother, Adela, was William the Conqueror's daughter, and had inherited much of her father's strength and power, dominating her husband Stephen, count of Blois, whom she despatched to the Crusades where he was killed in 1102. She had at least ten children of whom Stephen was one of the youngest. He soon became a favourite of his uncle Henry who showered him with gifts of lands in England and Normandy, making him one of the richest men in his kingdom. His younger brother Henry likewise gained lands and titles, and was consecrated bishop of Winchester in October 1129, still an influential post at that time. This meant that both Stephen and Henry had more influence than their elder brother Theobald (whom Henry disliked), who had succeeded to the county of Blois on his father's death and had a greater right of succession to the English throne than Stephen.

In 1125, Stephen married Matilda, the niece of Henry I's first wife Matilda and granddaughter of Malcolm III of Scotland. She was also fifth in descent from Edmund Ironside. Stephen had thus married into the royal blood of Wessex. In 1126 Henry I had forced his barons to swear fealty to his daughter, the Empress Matilda, as successor in the absence of another direct male heir.

MATILDA uncrowned queen of England, known as 'Lady of the English'.
Ruled 7 April–1 November 1141. Empress of Germany, 7 January 1114–23 May 1125.
Born: *Winchester (or possibly London), August (?) 1102.* **Died**: *Abbey of Notre Dame, Rouen, 10 September 1167, aged 65.*
Buried: *Bec Abbey, Normandy; later removed to Rouen Cathedral.*
Married: *(1) 7 January 1114, at Mainz, Germany, Heinrich V (1081–1125), emperor of Germany: no children; (2) 22 May 1128, at Le Mans Cathedral, Anjou, Geoffrey, count of Anjou (1113–1151): 3 sons.*

Christened Adelaide at birth, she had adopted the name Matilda on her marriage in 1114 to the German emperor, Henry V. Since she was only twelve at this time it was clearly a political marriage and the young girl does not seem to have been especially happy. Raised in the strict atmosphere of the German court, Matilda acquired a haughty, almost arrogant nature, to some extent inherited from her father. She was used to having her own way and found it difficult to make friends. When her husband died in 1125, she had returned to England to be acknowledged as heir to her father.

Stephen had been a party to this, but, as we saw, it was not popular amongst the Normans who did not like the idea of being ruled by a woman, especially one who was now married a second time to the young count of Anjou. The Angevins were longtime enemies of the Normans in northern France, and if Matilda became queen her husband, Geoffrey, would almost certainly become king, and the Normans had even less desire to be ruled by an Angevin.

On his uncle's death in December 1135, Stephen hastened to

London from his estates in Boulogne. Although initially denied access through Dover by Matilda's half-brother, Robert of Gloucester, Stephen's resoluteness brought him to Canterbury where he gained the support of William, the archbishop. Moving on to London he gained the immediate support of the city by granting it the status of a commune, with rights of collective self-government. Stephen was crowned within three weeks of his uncle's death. This took most barons by surprise. Some were mustering their support behind Theobald. However, rather than have a divided kingdom they soon switched their allegiance to Stephen and swore fealty to him both as king of England and duke of Normandy. Stephen was helped by his brother Henry who allowed Stephen access to the royal treasury at Winchester, so that Stephen was able to bribe many of his less ardent supporters. Theobald did not pursue his claim, but Matilda was outraged. She protested, even to the pope, but Innocent II supported Stephen on the basis that certain barons and clerics maintained they had heard Henry state on his deathbed that he wished Stephen to be his successor.

For the moment Stephen was secure. In fact initially Stephen was a popular king. He had an affable nature but a firm hand and rapidly commanded respect. He was fair in his judgements and seemed to have the common touch so that he was supported by the vast majority of the English. There were, however, disputes. David I, the king of Scotland (see p. 117), invaded Northumberland and claimed the territory in the name of his niece, Matilda. In fact David's intentions were more to reclaim what he believed were his own territories by right of succession, and he used Matilda's cause as an excuse. Stephen's skirmishes against David were all successful, culminating in the Battle of the Standard in August 1138. Stephen had less success in the Welsh Marches, the stronghold of Robert of Gloucester, and it was here that Stephen's weakness lay. Although Robert had given token allegiance to Stephen it is evident that the two remained distrustful of each other. Even though Robert accompanied Stephen in 1137 in his expedition against Geoffrey of Anjou, Matilda's husband, who had been making regular incursions into Normandy, he did not act outright against Geoffrey and, by all accounts, began to support Geoffrey in his actions. In May 1138 Robert, who was then in Normandy, issued a declaration whereby he renounced his homage to Stephen. Stephen promptly forfeited Robert's lands and the only way Robert could regain them was by invading. Matilda now had an army to support her own claim to the English throne. Such were the roots of the first English civil war.

Once the rift was declared, Norman loyalties wavered and Robert was able to gain further support. It was during this period that Stephen's once sound judgement began to waver, but his determination caused him to make some ill-founded decisions that seriously weakened his position. First, in December 1138, he alienated his brother, Henry, by not supporting his claim to be archbishop of Canterbury, which went to the manipulative Theobald of Bec. Second, in June 1139, he arrested Roger, bishop of Salisbury and his nephews Alexander, bishop of Lincoln, and Nigel, bishop of Ely. These three, together with two of Roger's sons, had a tight control over much of the administration of England. It had come to Stephen's attention that all of them, under the leadership of Roger, were fortifying their castles in support of Robert of Gloucester. Stephen moved against them, arresting them on the grounds of threatening the peace. Henry of Winchester immediately denounced Stephen as infringing church authority, but Stephen's actions were subsequently upheld by the pope. In taking control of these bishops' castles Stephen had made a major military advance, but he had also made many enemies amongst their supporters. Third, after the Battle of the Standard, Stephen gave the castle at Carlisle to the Scots. This enraged Ranulf, earl of Chester, since Carlisle and Cumbria had been part of the lands of his father, which had been forfeited following his father's insurrection against Henry I. Ranulf still regarded them as part of his heritage, and to have them given to the old enemy, the Scots, was more than he could bear. From then on Ranulf became an enemy of the king and though he allied himself to Robert of Gloucester's camp, it was more for his own personal revenge than for any support of Matilda.

In September 1139 Robert and Matilda made their move. Although Stephen had the ports barred, they arrived on the south coast and found refuge at Arundel which was under the control of Henry I's second wife, Adeliza, who had recently married William d'Albini, earl of Arundel. Stephen promptly marched on Arundel, but Robert had already left through minor and well-hidden by-ways to Bristol. Stephen pursued him without success, and it seems Robert may have been aided en route by Stephen's brother Henry. Certainly Bishop Henry successfully negotiated with Stephen to release Matilda under oath and he escorted her to Robert in Bristol. From the vantage point of history this seems a remarkably naïve action, though it emphasises Stephen's chivalric nature. Evidently Stephen believed there was little support for Matilda, and his main concern was Robert. Nevertheless, with Matilda by his side, Robert was able to draw upon her right of succession and held the equivalent of a separate court in the lands faithful to him, which were mostly the old heartland of Wessex in Wiltshire, Gloucestershire and Somerset. Soon William Fitz-richard, who held lands in Cornwall, sided with Matilda. This brought another of Henry's illegitimate sons, Reginald, earl of Cornwall and the full brother of Robert of Gloucester into the fray. Nevertheless, if Stephen had managed to contain the war within the south-west, he might have finished it quickly, and certainly his impressive energy gave him the upper hand during 1140. However his position was undermined when opposition broke out in East Anglia, focused on the support for the im-prisoned Bishop Nigel of Ely. Trouble soon spread to Lincoln. Stephen had granted the Castle of Lincoln to William d'Albini, the husband of the dowager queen Adeliza. Ranulf of Chester believed he had a right to Lincoln and, although Stephen was prepared to accept this, and even granted the castle to Ranulf's half-brother William, Ranulf seemed less than satisfied. By Christmas 1140 the two brothers had seized Lincoln in their own name. The townsfolk rebelled and sent for Stephen's aid.

Stephen laid siege to the town, although Ranulf had already escaped to gain the support of Robert of Gloucester. In this he was successful and Robert advanced with a large army upon Lincoln. Stephen was advised to retreat but he stubbornly refused. Victory here could well end the civil war. Moreover Stephen had promised help to the people of Lincoln and he was not about to let them down. Despite his smaller force, Stephen led his men into battle on 2 February 1141. It was the only major battle of the civil war and could have been decisive. Stephen fought bravely but he was outnumbered and his force was defeated.

Stephen was captured and imprisoned at Bristol. Although some remained loyal to Stephen they rapidly suffered as a consequence, and before long most turned their allegiance to Matilda, in the belief that Stephen would remain permanently imprisoned. Matilda and her forces gradually assumed control.

Within a month the 'Empress' Matilda had secured the support of Henry, bishop of Winchester, which allowed her access to the royal coffers. She arrived at London a few weeks later and in April was declared 'Lady of the English'. She still preferred to be known as 'Empress', but occasionally styled herself queen. Although preparations were in hand for her coronation, that never happened. Matilda rapidly made herself unpopular. First she raised a tax on all the nobility, and then she proposed to revoke the status of commune which had been granted to London by Stephen. This allowed London to collect its own taxes for its own benefits. Matilda wanted access to these taxes. Her support in London rapidly dwindled, and when Stephen's queen, also called Matilda, was able to bring her own forces from Kent, with William of Ypres, the 'Empress' was driven out of London in June. She settled in Oxford, although she spent some weeks in the complicated siege within a siege at Winchester. It was during this and the following affrays in the surrounding countryside that Robert of Gloucester was captured and Matilda only narrowly escaped. Matilda needed Robert as head of her forces and as a consequence she had to trade for his release with the release of Stephen from captivity in Bristol.

Stephen was restored to the throne in November and enjoyed a second coronation on Christmas Day. The war was not won, but Stephen became more tenacious. England was divided, but Stephen retained the upper hand. In May 1142 Robert took a hazardous journey to Normandy to gain support from Matilda's husband, Geoffrey, but he was too busy trying to gain control of Normandy and refused assistance. Whilst Robert was absent Stephen pressed home his advantage and by December had Matilda under siege at Oxford Castle.

She was able to escape by rope from an open window and then, cloaked in white as camouflage against the snow, she crossed the frozen river and made her way to Abingdon.

It is worth noting that resident at Oxford at this time was Geoffrey of Monmouth who, just a few years earlier, had completed his *History of the Kings of Britain*. The book was dedicated to Robert of Gloucester.

The civil war would drag on for a further five years. Although Stephen continued to hold the advantage he could never rule in total confidence. A strong reminder of this came when the Empress's forces scored a notable victory over Stephen at Wilton. Stephen became less assured of his authority and frequently arrested people at a moment's notice on suspicion. Among these was the treacherous Geoffrey de Mandeville, constable of the Tower of London, who had been made earl of Essex. His support swung with the prevailing breeze and after his arrest his forces raised a rebellion in 1143, which Stephen was able to quash. For a while Robert and the 'Empress' believed they might still have a chance, especially after Geoffrey of Anjou gained control of Normandy in January 1144, but to no avail. In 1145 Robert of Gloucester's son, Philip, transferred his allegiance to Stephen. Gradually Stephen wore down opposition, but in this process England was slowly being destroyed.

In October 1147 Robert of Gloucester died, and a few months later, in the spring of 1148, Matilda returned to Normandy and never returned to England. Although she ruled as uncrowned queen for less than a year, Matilda was the first queen of all England. Had she not been so arrogant and fiery tempered, she might have been remembered more for her successes than her failures.

Her cause was taken up by her son Henry (later Henry II). Skirmishes continued throughout 1149, but nothing of any substance. The English civil war did not so much end as fizzle out. Stephen, though, was a shadow of his former self. The civil war had broken him. The strong, resolute, affable man of 1136, was now an ill, haunted, uncertain individual. His continued policies at home were thwarted by Theobald, archbishop of Canterbury, who refused Stephen's involvement in church affairs. Theobald found himself briefly exiled from England, but Stephen soon realized this worked against him. Stephen wanted to secure the succession for his son, Eustace, count of Boulogne, but he needed the approval of the archbishop to have him crowned. This Theobald refused to do. Although Stephen declared his son king of England in 1152, this was not acknowledged by the church. Stephen, now much saddened by the death of his wife in May 1152, became a broken man. In 1153 Henry of Anjou brought a force to England to establish his right to the throne. The engagements were all indecisive, not helped by Stephen's apparent lack of strength. Suddenly, in August 1153, Eustace died. Stephen's ambitions collapsed. He signed the Treaty of Wallingford with Henry in November 1153, acknowledging Henry as his heir and successor.

Stephen had less than a year to live. He spent most of these days in Kent, which had remained loyal to him, though he was in great pain from bleeding piles. He died of appendicitis at Dover in October 1154 and was buried alongside his wife and son at Faversham Abbey, which he had founded in 1147. Had Stephen's right to accession been unopposed there is no doubt that he would have ruled as a strong and popular king, but the civil war ruined the ambition and reputation of an otherwise capable, intelligent and brave king.

THE KINGDOMS OF
WALES AND OF SCOTLAND

WALES (500–1240)

The whole history of Wales from the sixth to the thirteenth century was one of constant fighting between brothers, cousins, uncles, nephews and any other relative who got in the way. And when they were not fighting each other within their kingdom, they were fighting their neighbours. In these conditions it was rare for a strong king to unite more than one kingdom and even rarer for that to remain united under his successors.

Wales was not really a country of discrete kingdoms; rather it was one where internal boundaries changed with every passing king, making up a cauldron of smaller kingdoms. Occasionally one of these would bubble to the surface and remain dominant before simmering down and awaiting the next eruption.

The major struggles for power were between Gwynedd in the north and Deheubarth in the south, with Powys and Gwent occasionally getting in the way (see map on p. 465). After Cadwallon of Gwynedd had been defeated in 634, Wales would not see another great ruler until Rhodri The Great in 844. He was what Wales had needed at the time, for the land was under threat from the Vikings. Rhodri ruled Gwynedd for thirty-four years. He was the first Welsh king to receive the epithet 'Great'.

Rhodri succeeded to the kingdom of Gwynedd on the death of his father in 844, and to the kingdom of Powys in 855 on the abdication of his uncle, Cyngen ap Cadell. Through his marriage to Angharad, the daughter of Meurig of Seisyllwg, Rhodri also came to rule that territory when Angharad's brother Gwgon drowned in 871. By the end of his reign Rhodri ruled the greater part of Wales, the most united under a single monarch since the days of Maelgwyn.

If there was any time when Wales needed a strong king, it was then. Rhodri's kingdom was under attack from the Danes to the west and the Saxons to the east. In 853 Burgred of Mercia combined forces with Athelwolf of Wessex in a major assault against the Welsh. Though they overran Powys, they were unable to defeat Rhodri and withdrew. In 855 the first Viking attack occurred on the coast of Anglesey. Rhodri marshalled his defences and, in the following year, he met a Danish fleet in battle and slew their leader, Gorm. The victory was celebrated not only in Wales, but across England and in Francia, which was also subject to Danish attacks. The Danes continued to harry the coasts of England and Ireland, and later returned to Dyfed in southern Wales, but left Anglesey alone for twenty years. This indicates that Rhodri had established significant defences to discourage any invasion. Rhodri again faced an onslaught from the Mercians in 865, when Burgred invaded as far as Anglesey but had to withdraw because of the Viking threat to his own kingdom.

For Rhodri to sustain his defences on both east and west borders shows a high degree of strategic skills and an ability to command considerable support and loyalty. There is no doubt that Rhodri gave back to the Welsh a belief in themselves and a chance to show their strength. If this had been achieved earlier and sustained by Cadwallon, the native British might well have regained much of the island, but they were never able to sustain it beyond the reign of one ruler.

With Rhodri there came a ruler who changed the culture and thinking of his people, a change which outlasted him and formed the basis for the establishment of modern Wales.

Unfortunately for Rhodri his abilities let him down after a powerful reign of over thirty years. In 877 the Danes renewed their raids on Anglesey, this time with a stronger power base in Dublin and the Western Isles. They succeeded in breaking through Rhodri's defences and he fled for safety into Ireland. He returned to Gwynedd in the following year to face an onslaught from Ceolwulf II of Mercia, himself a vassal king of the Danes, and Rhodri died in battle.

After his death his son Anarawd ruled with equal power, as did his successor Idwal. But it was nearly thirty years after Rhodri's death, before the next great leader would emerge. This was Hywel the Good.

HYWEL *DDA (The GOOD)* AP CADELL Ruled Dyfed 905–50; Seisyllwg, 920–50 – the two kingdoms combined as Deheubarth after 920; also ruled Gwynedd and Powys, 942–50

He was arguably the greatest of the Welsh rulers, and certainly the only one to be called 'Good'. By the time of his death he was king of all of Wales except Morgannwg. His date of birth is not recorded, but it was probably around 880/2. He was given Dyfed by his father Cadell ap Rhodri who had conquered it in 905, deposing the last king Rhodri ap Hyfaidd. Although Hywel ruled this as sub-king to Cadell, it was an early sign of Hywel's abilities that Cadell should entrust his new kingdom to his younger son. Hywel consolidated his rule in Dyfed by marrying Elen, the daughter of Llywarch ap Hyfaidd. When Cadell died in 909, Hywel's brother Clydog inherited Seisyllwg, but to all intents Hywel ruled Dyfed and Seisyllwg jointly with Cadell. Upon Cadell's death in 920, Hywel combined the two kingdoms to which he gave the new name of Deheubarth.

Hywel was a regular visitor to the court of the kings of England. In 918 and 927, these were meetings called by the Saxon kings to reaffirm their suzerainty and seek fealty from the other rulers of Britain. In 934, Hywel had to prove that fealty by accompanying Athelstan in his punitive expedition against Constantine II of Scotland. On none of these occasions would Hywel have relished this subordination, but he was sensible enough to know that he had neither the need nor the strength of arms to defeat the English and that he could benefit by working with them. This affiliation brought respect from the English kings and a recognition of Hywel's authority. At other times he seems to have attended the English courts as a friend, often to witness charters, and took the opportunity to study how the administration and jurisdiction operated. Though it may go too far to say he was an Anglophile, he did christen one of his children with an English name, Edwin, and the English ability to organize clearly appealed to him. He had the good sense to understand what worked well and could respect the English way of life. This was further amplified after his pilgrimage to Rome in 928. It had a marked effect upon him, not simply in the religious sense, but in recognizing the benefits that could come to a well organized kingdom, which he witnessed in France and Rome.

Hywel benefited from his association with the English. In 942 his cousin, Idwal ap Anarawd of Gwynedd, was killed in battle against the Saxons. His sons were expelled from the kingdom and the dominion of the land passed to Hywel. He was now ruler of most of Wales, with the exception of the south-east. He took this opportunity to organize and consolidate the many tribal laws of the land. Soon after 942, probably around 945, he called a great conference at Ty Gwyn ('the White House') in Dyfed (near the modern town of Whitland), with representatives from every parish. The conference met for six weeks during which time we must imagine that all of the laws were codified and differences debated. It is unlikely that within that six weeks all differences were resolved, but it provided the basis for developing a series of three law books, which represented the respective laws of Gwynedd, Deheubarth and Morgannwg. These law books established such authority that it was later said none of the laws could be amended without gathering together a similar assembly. By codifying these laws, which was apparently done under the masterful direction of a lawyer called Blegywryd, Hywel did more towards unifying the Welsh as a nation than any other ruler had sought to achieve by conquest and domination. Even when after Hywel's death his kingdom was again partitioned amongst his successors, his laws lived on, and remained the cornerstone of Welsh administration. So paramount was Hywel in his role as king and lawgiver that he was also the first and only Welsh prince to issue his own coinage. Since it was issued from the mint at Chester, Hywel must have consulted with the English over its production.

When Hywel died in 950, probably in his late sixties, he left behind a legacy that would long be remembered as a golden age in Welsh history.

As a result of the influence of Rhodri and Hywel two strong kingdoms emerged – Gwynedd in the north and Deheubarth in the south. In the south-east Gwent and Glywysing joined together to form the kingdom of Morgannwg, which remained independent, while in the east along the Marches the kingdom of Powys re-emerged under a series of powerful kings. These kingdoms retained a high degree of independence, whilst acknowledging the supremacy of the Saxons.

It would not be until the eleventh century that a ruler was to be regarded as sovereign of all Wales. This was Gruffydd ap Llywelyn.

GRUFFYDD AP LLYWELYN Gwynedd and Powys, 1039–63; Deheubarth, 1044–47 and 1055–63; from 1055 also regarded as sovereign of all Wales.
Born: date unknown but probably around 1000. *Died*: 5 August 1063.
Married: c1057, Eadgyth (i.e. Edith) (c1042–after 1070), dau. Alfgar, Earl of Mercia; 3 children.

Like the see-saw between the descendants of Augustus to be emperor of Rome, so the pendulum swung between the varied and many descendants of Rhodri Mawr for the kingship of Gwynedd. The descendants of Idwal ap Anarawd were fairly weak and usually destroyed each other by internecine battles. The other line, descended from Idwal's brother Elisedd, was stronger but had less opportunity to gain the throne. When they took it they were often dominant, as in the case of Gruffydd's father Llywelyn ap Seisyll, but the most decisive of them all was Gruffydd himself. This may seem strange for a man who, in his youth, had displayed little ambition but, matured by the instruction of his father, Gruffydd turned into a virtual war machine. He seized power in Gwynedd when Iago ab Idwal ab Meurig was murdered, and was generally welcomed by the populace who had enjoyed the reign of his father. Gruffydd first turned his ferocity against the Mercians who constantly harried the borders of Wales and in 1039 won a decisive victory at the battle of Rhyd-y-Groes, near Welshpool, where he slew Edwin, the brother of Earl Leofric of Mercia. The victory was so decisive that for a period the Saxons stopped all hostilities across the border. This allowed Gruffydd to turn his attention to South Wales with a sustained onslaught on Hywel ab Edwin of Deheubarth. The battles were intense with heavy losses on both sides and much despoiling of the land, especially around Ceredigion. After two resounding defeats, Hywel recruited an army of Vikings from Ireland and there was a climactic battle at the estuary of the river Towy in 1044, where Hywel was slain. Gruffydd's victory was brief, though, for within a few months he was challenged by Gruffydd ab Rhydderch, another of the princely descendants of Rhodri Mawr. For two years the battles continued, and when warfare did not succeed treachery was brought into play, and in 1047 over a hundred of Gruffydd ab Llywelyn's soldiers were slaughtered through deceit on the part of Gruffydd ap Rhydderch's brothers. In revenge Gruffydd laid waste to parts of Dyfed and Seisyllwg. He also went into an alliance with Swein, the new earl of Mercia, in order to have Saxon support for his claim on Deheubarth, but even this did not succeed and, for a while, Gruffydd ceased his campaigning in the south.

He turned his attention again to the eastern Marches, and sought to gain further land beyond Offa's Dyke. He entered into an alliance with Alfgar, the son of Earl Leofric of Mercia, taking advantage of rivalry between Leofric's family and that of Earl Godwin of Wessex whose son, Swein, Gruffydd's former ally, had been forced into exile in Byzantium. At about this time Gruffydd married Alfgar's daughter, Eadgyth (who would later become the wife of Harold II), who was aged about fifteen. A series of raids began in 1052 and between them Gruffydd and Alfgar gained much territory along the Marches. Saxon border patrols were overwhelmed even as far south as Westbury in Gloucestershire. In 1055 the town of Hereford was sacked and burnt.

Gruffydd was now at the height of his powers, for in 1055 he at last had his victory over Gruffydd ab Rhydderch, whom he slew in battle, and thereafter claimed the kingdom of Deheubarth. In 1056 the bishop of Hereford, Leofgar, led an army against Gruffydd but he was soundly defeated. By this time Gruffydd claimed sovereignty over all of Wales, although it was a tenuous claim that he could hold only by show of force, and not as a ruler in the normal sense. Nevertheless the English respected this authority and, in 1057, they at last sought a treaty with Gruffydd. After lengthy negotiations, led by Harold Godwinson and Earl Leofric, an agreement was reached, and Gruffydd swore his fealty to King Edward the Confessor.

One might think Gruffydd would settle down and enjoy his power and attempt to administer the rule of law across Wales, but he continued to work in alliance with Earl Alfgar, helping him to regain his lands after he was temporarily dispossessed in 1058. However, after Alfgar died in 1062, Gruffydd became vulnerable. In his old age Gruffydd let down his guard and, late in 1062, Harold Godwinson mounted a surprise attack on Gruffydd's court at Rhuddlan, destroying Gruffydd's fleet. Gruffydd escaped, but he was now a refugee. Harold, with his brother Tostig, mounted a combined attack on Wales in 1063, forcing the Welsh army into submission. Not only did Harold exact tribute and hostages but he demanded that the Welsh abandon Gruffydd. Gruffydd's own men turned on him and he was slain by Cynan ap Iago in August 1063, his head sent to Harold as a sign of the victory. Thereafter his kingdom was sub-divided by Edward and allocated to various princes. Maredudd ab Owain ab Edwin inherited Deheubarth, whilst Bleddyn ap Cynfyn and his brother Rhiwallon shared Gwynedd and Powys.

The longest reigning of all Welsh rulers was Gruffydd ap Cynan whose rule lasted some 56 years and spanned the reigns of the Norman monarchs William I and II, Henry I, Matilda and Stephen. A descendant of Rhodri Mawr, he was born in about 1055 in Ireland where his father was in exile. His mother Ragnhildr was a granddaughter of Sitric II, king of Dublin. Gruffydd was therefore of mixed Celtic and Norse blood. Early on in his career he had been captured by the Normans and held in Chester castle for some ten or twelve years but, under Henry I's rule, he made a deal with the Normans whereby he and his sons were able to retain their land in return for accepting Norman authority. He and Henry I seemed like-minded and each was prepared to tolerate the other. Gruffydd ceased to show hostility to the Normans and instead spent his time rebuilding the old glory of Gwynedd. He had a particular passion for music and stories of old, and has earned a reputation as a patron of the bardic tradition, laying down the basis for the modern *eisteddfod*. His court poet was the legendary Meilyr Brydydd.

He was clearly a survivor, for some nineteen years of his life had either been spent in exile or in prison, but his strength, willpower and ultimately his tenacity brought him the respect of the Normans. During the height of his reign, from 1100 to around 1120, Gruffydd rebuilt the pride and culture of the northern Welsh. He passed this legacy on to his son, Owain Gwynedd.

**OWAIN *GWYNEDD* AP GRUFFYDD Gwynedd,
1137–70.**
Born: Angelesey, c1100. Died: 28 November 1170, aged 70.
Buried: Bangor Cathedral.
*Married: (1) Gwladys, dau. Llywarch ap Trahern; 2 sons; (2)
Christina, dau. Gronw ap Owain; 2 sons. Owain had at least 6
illegitimate children by two or three other women.*

Owain ap Gruffydd originally earned the surname Gwynedd to
distinguish him from another prince with the same name who
became known as Owain Cyfeiliog, but the name was even more
apt, as Owain built upon the achievements of his father, Gruffydd
ap Cynan, to establish Gwynedd as a power in the land, one
which aroused respect, and not a little concern, in the English
king Henry II. By the end of his reign, Owain was being called
Owain the Great.

At the start, though, it seemed as if Gruffydd's achievements
might be split by the inevitable enmity arising among the sons
of strong monarchs, as his lands were partitioned between his
various heirs. But in fact the sons acted with one accord,
realising that between them they had the strength to dominate
Wales. This had started to happen even before Gruffydd's
death. Owain and his elder brother Cadwallon (who died in
1132) had systematically extended the borders of Gwynedd to
incorporate the territories of Meirionydd, Rhos, Rufoniog and
Dyffryn Clwyd, thereby establishing their power throughout
northern and north-west Wales. On the death of Henry I in
1135 there was a general uprising amongst the Welsh princes
to regain their territory from the Normans, taking advantage
of the political uncertainty in England which resulted in the
civil war between Stephen and Matilda. None was more
powerful or better placed to gain from this anarchy than
Owain. In 1136, the Norman lord Richard de Clare (whose
father had been given the lands of Ceredigion in 1110) was
ambushed and killed by Welsh renegades. Soon after there was

a significant battle at Crug Mawr, in northern Ceredigion, where the Welsh slaughtered a large Anglo-Norman army. Owain and another brother, Cadwaladr, used these opportunities to invade Ceredigion, taking the northern territories, and extending their hold the following year. Their attempts to break into Dyfed in 1138 failed, but Cadwaladr sought to consolidate his hold upon Ceredigion, which he maintained until 1143. Then Cadwaladr's involvement in the murder of Anarawd ap Gruffydd led to his expulsion from Wales and his exile in Ireland for a year until he was temporarily restored by his brother in 1144.

Meanwhile Owain was gradually extending his control over the territories of northern Wales, taking over one district at a time so that by 1149 almost all of the old kingdom of Powys was under his control, and the boundaries of Gwynedd once again extended from Anglesey to the estuary of the Dee. Although Owain continued to plan for further territorial expansion, the next few years saw a period of strengthening his existing domain, and it was as much his qualities as a politician as an expansionist which made him one of Wales's greatest rulers.

From a picture in the National Library of Wales

His only setback occurred in 1157. By then Henry II had come to the throne and restored political strength in England. Pope Adrian IV had granted Henry authority over the whole of Britain in 1155, and with this as his passport, Henry despatched his forces into Wales. Although Owain lost some ground, Henry did not force the king into submission. Nevertheless Owain was sensible enough to know that he needed to negotiate with Henry. Henry agreed to cease any further incursions into Gwynedd, provided Owain accepted Henry as his overlord. Henry had also taken under his wing, Owain's brother, Cadwaladr, who had been exiled in England, and had become an ally of the Norman earls of Chester and Shrewsbury. Henry required that Owain accept Cadwaladr as his partner in government in Gwynedd, which Owain did becoming, at last, reconciled to his renegade brother. Owain accepted all these terms freely. His great strength was in recognizing the benefits that came from being allied to Henry II and his great Angevin empire. It meant that the Welsh prince was regarded as a significant feudal monarch rather than as a tribal chieftain, and it was through Owain that the sovereignty of Gwynedd was recognized. Owain was regarded as the premier ruler in Wales, and was officially styled 'Prince of the Welsh' (subject to Henry as overlord), though he was still called king of Wales by his subjects. Henry publicized this at a ceremony in July 1163 at Woodstock, where all the Welsh rulers and the Scottish king assembled to pay homage to Henry. Amongst their numbers was Rhys ap Gruffydd who was still hostile to Henry, and it required Owain's authority and skills as a negotiator to convince Rhys that he should submit to Henry.

Although he maintained his fealty to Henry for the rest of his life, this did not stop Owain ensuring that the rights and status of the Welsh were acknowledged by the Normans. The ceremony of 1163 unsettled many of the Welsh princes, seeing it as domination by the Normans, and in 1164 a series of uprisings broke out all over Wales. Henry decided that a show of force was necessary and brought together a mighty army from France, Scotland and Ireland, but he mismanaged the whole operation. Owain united the Welsh armies and stood fast at Corwen, on the river Dee, awaiting the Norman onslaught. It did not happen: undone by the weather, the terrain, and the sheer size of his force, Henry retreated, taking only a few hostages. The Welsh drove home their advantage, with Owain and Cadwaladr regaining the territory they had lost ten years earlier and re-establishing the borders of Gwynedd.

Owain had a somewhat ambivalent relationship with the church. Whilst he was strongly religious he had no wish to be dictated to – a trait he shared with Henry II! He incurred the displeasure of the church when, as his second wife, he took his cousin Christina. Such a close marriage was not regarded as lawful in the eyes of the church, but Owain did not falter, and indeed his deep love for his second wife became legendary. Owain saw the authority of the see of Canterbury over the Welsh church as just as much a sign of domination as his submission to the Norman king, and whilst he saw the advantages in the latter, he did not so willingly concede the necessity for the former. He refused to accept the authority of Canterbury in appointing his local bishops, especially at Bangor, where he did not replace the bishop for thirteen years.

At the time of his death in 1170 Owain was thus master of all of North Wales, the premier prince of Wales, and was held in high regard throughout Europe. If his sons had had similar qualities, they might have avoided the civil war that broke out between them upon Owain's death and, once again, sundered the kingdom. It was left to his grandson, Llywelyn The Great (see p. 95), to restore the kingdom to its final days of glory. In the meantime in the equally powerful kingdom of Deheubarth, Rhys ap Gruffydd was also very active. His significance would be very long-term, for centuries later Henry VII, the first of the Tudor dynasty would claim descent through him from the Celtic princes of Wales.

RHYS ᴀᴘ GRUFFYDD – *THE LORD RHYS*
Deheubarth, 1155–97.
Born: *c1132 in Ireland.* **Died:** *28 April 1197, aged about 65.*
Buried: *St David's Cathedral.*
Married: *(date unknown), Gwenllian, dau. Madog ap Maredudd of Powys; 9 children, plus at least 9 illegitimate.*

In the eighteen years following the death of his father Gruffydd ap Rhys, Rhys and his brothers progressively reclaimed and rebuilt much of the old kingdom of Deheubarth, recovering lands from the Normans and from the rival kingdom of Gwynedd. Rhys had been only four when his father died, but by the age of thirteen he was involved with his brothers in various engagements so that he was already battle hardened when the early death of his brother Maredudd catapulted Rhys into power in 1155.

He came to power at the same time as Henry II of England, who felt he needed to repair the damage caused in both England and Wales during the last twenty years. As we have seen he soon tested Welsh resistance by a campaign into North Wales in 1157 that saw the submission of Owain Gwynedd. Rhys held out for a year with a display of bravado, but when Henry put it to the test in 1158, Rhys was forced to submit. His parley with Henry was costly. Rhys was forced to hand back all of the captured castles to the Norman families and was left in control of only Cantref Mawr and a few outlying territories. Deheubarth was again split asunder as if the last twenty years had been for nothing. Perhaps even more ignominious was that Rhys agreed to drop the title of king, demonstrating his total submission to Henry's authority. Ever after he was always known as *Yr Arglwydd Rhys* – 'The Lord Rhys'. Such a decision was not easily accepted. Rhys's nephew, Einion ap Anarawd, rebelled and slew the garrison at Castell Hywel. Henry returned with a show of force and Rhys had to capitulate. However, soon after Henry returned to France, Rhys attacked several castles in Dyfed, most notably Carmarthen, which resulted in a major Norman force being despatched by

Henry's illegitimate son, Reginald, earl of Cornwall. The scale of the opposition drove Rhys back into his stronghold of Cantref Mawr from which the combined forces of five Norman earls, plus the assistance of the rulers of Gwynedd, were unable to displace him. A truce was finally called and, for the next three years, Rhys remained quiet.

Then, in 1162, Rhys began again on a series of raids, taking the castle at Llandovery. When Henry returned to England in early 1163 his first mission was to penetrate into South Wales. Henry caught up with Rhys in Ceredigion. Quite how or why Rhys submitted is not clear, but there was no struggle, and Henry took Rhys away as prisoner. It is a demonstration of Henry's belief in his own strength and authority that, after a few months, he released Rhys after he had paid homage to Henry at Woodstock in July, along with Malcolm IV of Scotland and Owain Gwynedd. Rhys remained obdurate. While he had been prisoner, his nephew Einion had been murdered. The murderer was being sheltered by Roger de Clare, earl of Hertford. Once back in Wales, Rhys immediately led an army in Ceredigion destroying any Norman stronghold he found as he progressed. This was the last straw for Henry. He planned to raise a major army and subdue Wales once and for all. The threat of this at last brought

From a picture in the National Library of Wales

the various factions in Wales together into a major uprising. At the same time Henry had his own domestic problems over Thomas Becket, and his campaign of 1165 failed dramatically. Rhys seized this as an opportunity to regain all of his lost lands and within a year had rebuilt much of Deheubarth. He never was able to regain much of the land in Dyfed or along the southern coast, but most of Ceredigion and northern Ystrad Tywi was under his direct rule, and many surrounding territories were ruled by client kings.

For a period the Norman lords despaired, many of them turning their attention to Ireland to expand their power. This further annoyed Henry whose next expedition to Wales in 1170 was not to subjugate the Welsh but to bring his Norman lords back to heel. It seems that during the 1160s both sides had learned their lessons. In 1171 and 1172 Henry and Rhys held a series of meetings out of which Rhys emerged as Henry's recognized 'justiciar' in Deheubarth, a role which demonstrated that Rhys acted with the authority of Henry and had power over the administration of the law, and that meant power over the lesser rulers in South Wales. Rhys actually styled himself 'Prince of South Wales'. It was a turning point in Welsh affairs. From then on, for the second half of his reign, Rhys put aside his rebellious past and assumed the rôle of a governor, negotiator, peace-maker and king's man. He even sent a force to support Henry during the revolt of his sons in 1173. Rhys saw the benefits of Norman England and even began to imitate the Norman way of life and administration. But he did not neglect Welsh culture. He rebuilt the castle at Cardigan and, upon its completion in 1176, inaugurated there the first official *eisteddfod*. He also founded or rebuilt a number of abbeys, of which Strata Florida was the most striking example.

Unfortunately most of Rhys's achievements were built on shifting sands. They relied primarily on his own strength and stamina and on the relationship that he developed with Henry II. After Henry's death in 1189, Rhys found it difficult to receive any co-operation from Richard's government, and the protection he was allowed from the ambitions of the marcher lords also evaporated. Tensions again began to mount, intensified by unrest between Rhys's own sons. The result was that Rhys once again had to take to arms to defend himself. The main Anglo-Norman opponent was William de Breos, lord of Radnor and Builth. Initially Rhys showed his strength, but by 1194 the in-fighting within the family began to take its toll. The main trouble-maker was one of Rhys's younger sons, Maelgwyn, who was imprisoned and later handed over to Breos by his own brother Gruffydd. When Rhys secured Maelgwyn's release, it only led to more in-fighting between Maelgwyn and Gruffydd. Rhys was caught in the middle and in 1194 found himself captured and imprisoned by Maelgwyn. He was soon released, but found that other sons, Rhys Gryg and Maredudd, had captured Deheubarth's royal stronghold at Dinefwr. Rhys was incensed. Showing something of his old strength and verve he regained his castles and, in 1196, led a major campaign against the Normans. During the last few years William de Breos had succeeded in regaining some of his old territories, but in a remarkable campaign Rhys stormed and captured many of de Breos's castles and razed Norman towns to the ground. Rhys went out in a blaze of glory. He died the following spring. He was the last great ruler of southern Wales, and certainly one of Wales's greatest rulers. From out of almost nothing he rebuilt Deheubarth, and held it against overwhelming odds for over forty years. Unfortunately, as was ever the case with a strong king who ruled for so long, the rivalry between his sons soon pulled the kingdom apart.

If there is one Welsh prince everyone knows (or think they know) it is Llywelyn the Great, although some of his exploits often get confused in the public consciousness with those of his grandson, known as Llywelyn The Last. Llywelyn rightly deserved the epithet *the Great*, the most of all the Welsh rulers, almost solely for his leadership and statesmanlike abilities. Certainly he had no finesse or cultural qualities, but he was the man that Wales needed to pull it out of the Dark Ages and make it a united country. He was an ideal successor to Gruffydd ap Cynan and Owain Gwynedd his grandfather.

LLYWELYN *FAWR* (*THE GREAT*) AP IORWETH
Gwynedd (east Gwynedd from 1195) 1200–40;
incorporating Powys from 1208; overlord of Deheubarth
from 1216; regarded as prince of Wales from 1210.
Born: *Dolwyddelan, Nantconwy, c1173.* **Died:** *11 April 1240,*
aged about 66. **Buried:** *Aberconwy Abbey.*
Married: *1205, Joan, illeg. dau. King John of England; 5*
children. Llywelyn had at least one illegitimate child.

His rise to power was meteoric. His father, Iorweth Drwyndwn, had died soon after Llywelyn's birth and he was raised with his mother's relatives in Powys. By his late teens he had joined forces with his cousins, Gruffydd and Maredudd ab Cynan in their opposition to their uncles Rhodri ab Owain and Dafydd ab Owain. Llywelyn soon got the upper hand over his cousins, so that when Dafydd was deposed from East Gwynedd in 1195 Llywelyn claimed the territory as his own. Although technically he initially shared it with his uncle, Dafydd was soon squeezed out of the land, imprisoned in 1197, and then banished altogether in 1198. In 1200, his cousin Gruffydd, who had ostensibly become the ruler in West Gwynedd, died, and Llywelyn promptly annexed that territory. In 1201 and 1202 he deprived Maredudd of his lands in Llyn and Meirionydd respectively, so that by 1202 he had reunited all of Gwynedd.

Llywellyn learned from his predecessors that it was important to stay on cordial terms with the king of England. Soon after John came to power, he and Llywelyn entered into a detailed agreement. This enforced John's overlordship of Wales, and stated the terms by which Llywelyn and his own lords must render fealty; but it also recognized the authority of Welsh law and stated on what basis cases might be tried. This agreement, the oldest to survive between an English and a Welsh monarch, while definitely constituting an imposition of English overlordship, nevertheless recognized the relevance and need of Welsh law and government and thus gave Llywelyn a power in his own land that was unequalled by any previous English-Welsh relationship. Llywelyn sought to cement this accord further by marrying Joan, an illegitimate daughter of John's, in 1205. He also accompanied John on his punitive expedition against the Scots in 1209.

In the meantime Llywelyn took what opportunities presented themselves to expand his authority in Wales. His closest rival was Gwenwynwyn, the prince of Powys, who also had expansionist desires, but who overstepped the mark in 1208, literally, by several ill-disposed attacks on the marcher lands. King John reacted swiftly and deprived Gwenwynwyn of all of his lands. Llywelyn promptly annexed southern Powys and used this as a means to march into and lay claim to southern Ceredigion. He then claimed overlord-ship of the other lesser lordships in southern Wales and, by 1210, was declaring himself as prince of all Wales.

This insubordination angered John who sent two expeditions into Wales in 1211. The first suffered from poor organization but the second was highly successful, penetrating far into the strong-hold of Gwynedd. East Gwynedd was placed again under Nor-man control, and John cleverly engineered the isolation of Llywelyn by ensuring the support of the other princes. Exacting tributes were demanded and severe retribution taken on the hostages John took, including Llywelyn's illegitimate eldest son. For a few months Llywelyn was vulnerable. There was even a rival movement which sought to bring his cousin, Owain ap Dafydd, to the throne, but at the moment of crisis Llywelyn found unanimous support amongst his countrymen. In 1212 Llywelyn regrouped his forces and prepared to face the might of John's army, which he had convened with a view to total conquest of Wales.

It could have been the biggest invasion force since the Norman conquest of England but, at the last moment, John changed his plans. Domestic problems amongst his barons, which culminated in John's signing of the *Magna Carta*, meant that he turned his attention from Wales. This was not a retreat, but the Welsh regarded it as a victory. Llewelyn had not been afraid to face the might of the English, and the English had backed down. Thereafter Llywelyn felt able to recommence his onslaught against the Norman-controlled territories, regaining East Gwynedd and lands in the Marches, as well as commanding fealty from the remaining Welsh princes in Powys and Deheubarth. By 1216 Llywelyn was prince of all Wales in fact as well as title, as confirmed by the Treaty of Worcester in 1218.

Border skirmishes continued for several more years, mostly with the new regent of England, William Marshal, one of the marcher lords and the new earl of Pembroke, until his death in 1219. From 1216 to 1234 lands and castles frequently changed hands, but it was as much a period of testing as of outright hostility. The two parties came to understand each other and, with the Pact of Middle in 1234, an agreement was reached by both sides which assured a modicum of peace.

Llywelyn was determined that all he had achieved would not be broken asunder after his death so, as early as 1208 he ensured that his newly born legitimate son, Dafydd, was recognized as his heir. He also determined to revoke the Welsh law of partible succession, which had been the ruin of previous attempts to unite Wales. Llywelyn sought to introduce the rule of primogeniture so that his eldest legitimate son inherited. Although this caused a family rift between Llywelyn's eldest illegitimate son, Gruffydd, and his nominated successor, Dafydd, Llywelyn succeeded in gaining total acceptance. But Daffydd was to die at the age of thirty-seven without an heir, and it was his brother Gruffydd's son Llywelyn (the last) who succeeded him.

SCOTLAND (850–1165)

In Scotland and Wales the Celtic rule of partible succession meant that kings divided their land amongst their sons, so that the work of any king to establish a stronger and larger kingdom was immediately undone when it was subdivided amongst his successors, few of whom were of the same ability as their father. This rule had weakened the Welsh kingdoms more than the Scottish ones. The Scots of Dál Riata had been growing in power, but then fell foul of an interdynastic struggle between the main ruling family, the Cenél Gabhrán, and the Cenél Loarn, both descended from the father of the founding ruler Fergus. At the start of the eighth century this infighting weakened the Scots and allowed the king of the Picts, Angus, who was the victor of their own interdynastic struggle, to take control.

It was in the mid ninth century that the kingdoms of the Picts and the Scots united to become what we now know as Scotland. The separate kingdom of Strathclyde merged with the kingdom of the Scots in around 890. At this stage the kingdom of Scotland was centred in southern Scotland and held little authority over the Highlands which were still dominated by the Picts and the Cenél Loarn who later emerged as a separate kingdom of Moray. Further north the Vikings settled in Orkney and their authority spilled over into Caithness. The ruler responsible for the union was Kenneth MacAlpin.

> ### KENNETH MACALPIN *Scots, 840–58; and Picts, 847–58.*

Kenneth's origins are obscure and his fame rests more on the subsequent development of his dynasty than any significant actions during his own reign. Although he must have come from some branch of the ruling Cenél Gabhrán faction, his exact antecedents have never been satisfactorily identified, though a twelfth-century genealogy makes him the great-grandson of Aed Find, who ruled Dál Riata from 750–78. This is, of course, possible, but it is surprising that someone who shot to power so quickly had not otherwise already featured in the activities prevalent during the previous decade where a high ranking and ambitious prince is bound to have made his mark. The story that he succeeded his father as a sub-king of Galloway is again possible, but unlikely. What seems more likely is that Kenneth was a prince of the Cenél Gabhrán but was not necessarily resident in Dál Riata for all of his early life. He may have lived part of the time in Ireland, or elsewhere amongst the Western Highlands. It has been suggested that his father married not only a Pictish princess (Kenneth's mother) but a Norse princess, and that Kenneth thus already had strong connections with the Vikings. The Irish annals record that in 836, Gothfrith macFergus, a Gaelo-Norse half-breed, who had established himself as king of Oriel in northern Ireland and who apparently also had dominion over some of the Hebrides, visited Kenneth in Argyll in order to discuss the Viking attacks on western Scotland. Could Kenneth have negotiated some form of treaty with the Vikings which worked to their mutual benefit? In 839 the Vikings advanced through Dál Riatan territory into the heart of the land of the Picts and, in the ensuing battle at Forteviot, killed many of the Scots' and Picts' nobility. In the chaos that followed Kenneth claimed the kingship of Dál Riata. Kenneth held power by his own strength and cunning. There must have been others who believed they had a greater right to the throne or who, for whatever reasons, distrusted Kenneth, and his first few years must have been bloodthirsty, as he rid himself of his enemies and secured his right to the throne. None of this is recorded, because Kenneth subsequently became such a revered ruler that his past and origins were whitewashed to an extent, but some of his character comes through in the tale about how he deceived the Picts. Apparently he invited the Pictish nobility, then ruled by Drust Mac Ferat, to a feast. Kenneth had already dug pits around the benches and weakened the bolts holding the benches together, so that once the Picts had become drunk it was easy to release the bolts, cast the Picts into the hidden trenches and slaughter them. Whatever the real events, tradition records that Kenneth conquered the Picts by deceit and slaughter. By 847 he had united the old kingdoms, establishing them as a single entity. To do this he must have considerably subdued any remaining Pictish nobility for never again did they lay claim to their throne. Kenneth called his combined kingdom Alba, or Albany, and by the time of his grandson Donald II, thirty years later, it was already being called Scotland. Kenneth not only established his capital at Forteviot, the previous capital of the Picts, but he also established Dunkeld as the spiritual capital of Alba by removing there some of the relics of St Columba from Iona.

Kenneth's reign was violent but successful. Having taken over control of the Picts he still warred against the Angles to the south and the British of Strathclyde, and he retained an uneasy peace with the Vikings. He relied heavily on his own strength of character, though he also cemented his authority with neighbours and allies by inter-dynastic marriages through his daughters. One married Olaf, the King of Dublin; another married Aed Findliath, who became High King of Ireland in 862, whilst a third married Rhun, prince of Strathclyde. Kenneth's violent life evidently took its toll for he died of an illness, in February 858. His age is uncertain but he was probably in his late forties. He was succeeded by his brother Donald, who lasted but five years, after which came his son Constantine I, whose reign was dominated by battles or connivances with the Vikings who had settled in Ireland. With Olaf, king of the Norse Vikings in Dublin, who had married one of his sisters, Constantine conspired, along with another Viking leader, Ivarr The Boneless, to attack Dumbarton, and thus the British kingdom of Strathclyde fell.

Not long after, in 889 Strathclyde and Cumbria were merged with the kingdom of the Scots. They retained a degree of autonomy and it later became the practice that the heir to the Scottish throne was made king or prince of Strathclyde.

Constantine II, grandson of Kenneth macAlpin, was one of the longest ruling monarchs of Scotland.

CONSTANTINE II *Scotland 900–43*

Constantine, a grandson of the first Constantine, was probably little more than two years old when his father Ead died, and only in his early twenties when he succeeded his cousin Donald II, the first ruler to be termed 'King of Scotland'.

The length of Constantine's reign and his strength of character allowed him to establish Scotland as a unified kingdom. His first concerns were against the Norse who, in 902, had been driven out of their kingdom in Dublin. Their ruler in exile, Ragnall, clearly intended to establish a new kingdom in the area of Strathclyde and Cumbria, and the years 903 and 904 were ones of regular skirmishes between the Scots and the Norse. In 903 the Norse raided as far east as Dunkeld, but at this stage the Norse army seems to have withdrawn, though must always have remained a threat, for in 910 Ragnall succeeded in invading York and establishing himself as ruler. It was against this background that Constantine perceived a need to strengthen his defences around Strathclyde and Cumbria, and he established the sub-kingdom of Strathclyde in 908, with his brother Donald as its ruler. The Norse threat continued, however. Ragnall, now established in York, sought to expand his kingdom into neighbouring Bernicia and, on the death of Eadulf in 913, Ragnall expelled his successor Ealdred who fled to Constantine's court. Constantine fought two major battles against the Norse, in 914 and 918, both at Corbridge. Although the Scots suffered defeat on both occasions, it was not without heavy losses to the Norse. Ragnall was anxious not to lose his links with Dublin, which kingdom he had regained in 917, so in 918 the Norse and Scots entered into a peace treaty. Constantine then allied himself with the Norse against the Saxons of Wessex, resulting in the famous pact with Edward The Elder in 920. It is very unlikely that on this occasion Constantine regarded Edward as his overlord, despite the record of the *Anglo-Saxon Chronicle*. It is more likely that each side acknowledged the other's authority and status. This pact was subsequently renewed with Athelstan at Eamont Bridge near Penrith in July 927, a meeting which followed Athelstan's defeat of Gothfrith of Dublin, who had invaded Northumbria to claim the throne of York. Athelstan gained Constantine's agreement not to support Gothfrith, but Constantine reneged on this in 934 when he supported Gothfrith's son, Olaf, the new king of

Dublin, in his claim on the throne of York. The most flagrant sign of Constantine's support was when he gave one of his daughters to Olaf in marriage. This incensed Athelstan, who invaded Scotland as far north as Edinburgh and inflicted losses upon Constantine. He apparently also took one of Constantine's sons (probably Cellach) as hostage. Constantine's support for Olaf, however, remained steadfast and, in 937, Olaf invaded Northumbria. The armies met the Saxons at Brunanburh, where Olaf and Constantine were dealt a crushing defeat by Athelstan, regarded as one of the greatest Saxon victories. Cellach died in the battle. However, when Athelstan died two years later, Olaf ventured again to claim York and this time succeeded. Olaf's alliance with Constantine increased the latter's power.

In 943, when he must have been about sixty-five, Constantine abdicated. He was clearly still able and active, but he must also have recognized that it was time for new blood. In 943 Edmund of Wessex had resolved his problems with the Norse kings of York, which weakened Constantine's command of northern Britain. He retired to the monastery at St Andrews. During his reign Constantine had had a mixed relationship with the church. He had allied himself with the pagan Norse, had tolerated the reversion to pagan practices in Galloway and Kyle, and had delayed long in the baptism of his son Indulf. Yet as early as 906 he had agreed, with Bishop Cellach of St Andrews, to uphold the authority of the Scottish church, and he had also been a friend of St Catroe, escorting him on his mission through Scotland during the 940s. It is possible that his meeting with Catroe provided a good excuse to abdicate.

There is a long-held belief that Constantine came out of retirement in 948 to join Malcolm who had succeeded him in an invasion of England. Since he would have been at least seventy years old by then, it seems very unlikely, though it is possible that Constantine encouraged Malcolm in the enterprise. Constantine died in 952 at the monastery of St Andrews, and was almost certainly buried there.

Squabbles over succession continued for the next fifty years or so, and Kenneth II came to the throne in 971 during a period of interdynastic rivalry between the rulers of Moray, Strathclyde and Scotland. Kenneth, along with other Celtic princes, promised Edgar fealty to the English at the convention at Chester in 973, and Edgar confirmed Kenneth's right to the lands of Lothian. It was a crucial meeting in the development of defining the state of Scotland.

Kenneth was keen to preserve Scotland as a united kingdom, and endeavoured to ride the succession of dynastic rivalry by agreeing with the Scottish magnates that the succession should become patrilinear, passing from father to son, rather than alternating between dynasties. This seems to have been only partly accepted, for it would take at least a generation before the dispossessed princes passed away and the process became accepted as the norm. For six years the rivalry continued between Kenneth and Olaf, his distant cousin before Olaf was slain in 977. Then the rivalry over succession passed on to the next generation with Olaf's nephew Constantine (subsequently Constantine III – The Bald), and Kenneth's great nephew Giric (subsequently Giric II) eventually conspiring against Kenneth to cause his downfall and murder. He died in rather mysterious circumstances at Finella's Castle near Fettercairn in 995. Nevertheless it was Kenneth's son Malcolm who subsequently regained and retained the Scottish throne.

MALCOLM II MAC KENNETH
Sub-king of Cumbria and Strathclyde, 990–5, 997–1005; king of Scotland, 1005–34.
Born: *c954.* **Died:** *25 November 1034, aged 80, at Glamis Castle.* **Buried:** *Iona.*
Married: *c980 (date and spouse's name unknown): 2 or 3 daughters.*

In 990 Kenneth II had sought to establish his son Malcolm as his heir by proclaiming him king of Strathclyde and Cumbria. Since

Malcolm Mac Donald was still king of Strathclyde (unless records that suggest he died in 990 are correct) the kingdom was clearly divided, and Malcolm mac Kenneth probably ruled Cumbria. When Kenneth II was killed in 995, Malcolm was also deposed from Strathclyde, by the rival faction of Constantine III, but upon his death in 997, Malcolm regained Strathclyde. This was an unhealthy situation, as the new king of the Scots, Kenneth III, was evidently seeking to establish right of succession for his own son Giric II, who was made either co-ruler or a sub-king, possibly also in Strathclyde. The two rulers tolerated each other for eight years then, in 1005, Malcolm defeated and slew Kenneth and Giric at the battle of Monzievaird. Malcolm was not only a strong and ambitious ruler, he was a strategist and an opportunist. His long reign allowed him to expand and consolidate his kingdom, though some of his actions, not least the slaying of Kenneth and Giric, sowed seeds of discontent that would have repercussions later. Malcolm first endeavoured to establish his rulership over Bernicia, extending his lands beyond the Tweed. He was severely defeated by Uhtred of Northumbria in the siege of Durham in 1006 and it was twelve years before Malcolm again tested the lands to the south. He did, however, ensure an ally in the kingdom of Strathclyde. This kingdom was traditionally ruled by the heir to the throne. Malcolm had only daughters and his grandson, Duncan, was too young to rule, so Malcolm appointed Owen as ruler of Strathclyde. Owen was almost certainly older than Malcolm, and as the youngest son of Donald of Strathclyde had probably never entertained aspirations to kingship, so this elevation made him a strong friend and ally to Malcolm and helped strengthen the lands to the south.

In the meantime Malcolm sought to make an alliance with the Norse earls of Orkney and, in 1008, he married his daughter to Sigurd II. The main reason was to have the Norsemen as allies against the men of Moray, who for the last fifty years had worked against the main Scottish royal line, and Malcolm granted Sigurd lands as far south as Moray. Malcolm seemed to be seeking Sigurd's recognition of Malcolm as his overlord, even though the earls of Orkney were subjects of the kings of Norway. In Malcolm's eyes, though, this gave him authority over Moray, Caithness and Sutherland. The arrangement soon worked in Malcolm's favour for, in 1014, Sigurd was killed at the battle of Clontarf in Ireland and while his sons by an earlier marriage squabbled over the succession, Malcolm proclaimed his young grandson, Thorfinn, as earl of Caithness, even though he was only five. The young boy seemed to be much loved by the nobility of Orkney and by the king of Norway, so that he soon obtained claims on parts of Orkney until he became sole earl in 1030. With this support in the north Malcolm believed he had stifled the problems in Moray (even if only temporarily).

In 1018, following the annexation of Lothian two years earlier, Malcolm turned his attention to Bernicia and, with Owen of Strathclyde's help, he defeated Earl Eadulf at Carham on Tweed. Immediately afterward Malcolm bestowed much bounty on the church at Durham and claimed overlordship of southern Bernicia. In that same year he installed his grandson, Duncan, as king of Strathclyde. Malcolm was now in his early sixties, and the first king to rule the territory of Scotland as we know it today. He might have sought to rest upon his achievements. However, he needed to be ever vigilant. The rulers of Moray continued to fight for control and began a series of raids and skirmishes from the north; one of these, in 1027, resulted in the burning of Dunkeld. At the same time, Canute had established himself in England and was intent upon ensuring he had no opposition from the north. In 1031 records suggest that Canute 'invaded' Scotland, although there is some doubt as to whether he led an army, or simply made a royal visit. The latter seems more likely because, had Canute succeeded in marching north with an army and defeating Malcolm, he would almost certainly have continued with a campaign to conquer Scotland, of which he was capable. In all likelihood Canute's main aim was to secure a friendly alliance with Malcolm who, now in his mid-seventies, could in any case offer little resistance. However, either now, or soon after, Canute did reclaim Bernicia and Cumbria, with the result that the borders of Scotland as we know them today were finally established.

In his old age Malcolm did what he could to secure the throne for Duncan. In 1032 he endeavoured to slaughter the family of Kenneth III's grand-daughter Gruoch by surprising them in their fortress at Atholl and burning it to the ground. Gillecomgain was killed but Gruoch, his wife, and their son Lulach escaped. A few months later he arranged the murder of Kenneth III's great-grandson Malcolm, who was still only an infant. The next year Malcolm died, probably in his eightieth year. Later historians claimed he was murdered as part of the continuing inter-dynastic struggle, and this is just possible, though unlikely. He was the last male heir of Kenneth MacAlpine. Malcolm had lived long enough for his grandson Duncan to inherit the throne, although his future was far from certain.

DUNCAN (I) *THE GRACIOUS Strathclyde, 1018–34; Scotland, 25 November 1034–15 August 1040.*
Born: c1001. Died (killed in battle) Pitgaveny, 15 August 1040, aged 39. Buried: Iona.
Married: c1030, Sybilla, sister (some records say dau.) of Siward, earl of Northumbria: 3 sons and possibly one daughter.

Duncan was the son of Bethoc, Malcolm II's daughter, and Crinan, earl of Atholl and abbot of Dunkeld. Although Malcolm had done everything to eliminate all other rival claimants amongst the immediate descendants of Kenneth MacAlpine, he had not quashed the rival Loarn dynasty which ruled Moray. They offered little, if any, allegiance to the kings of Scotland, and certainly had little respect for Duncan. He might have inherited his grandfather's ambition, but he was not his equal as a strategist or commander. Duncan was fortunate in that soon after he inherited the throne, England was in turmoil following the death of Canute and an argument over the succession, whilst to the north Thorfinn, earl of Orkney, was also facing an internal challenge. Had Duncan struck at those moments, he might have succeeded in expanding his kingdom along the lines that Malcolm had planned. However, Duncan left it for some years, and instead found himself facing an attack by Eadulf of Bernicia in 1038, in revenge for the conquest of Durham by Malcolm twenty years earlier. Eadulf was driven back only by the help of Duncan's brother, Maldred, the regent of Strathclyde. In 1040 Duncan was ready to fight back although he chose to do it on both fronts and, by this time, Thorfinn of Orkney had regained his authority. Early in 1040 Duncan marched on Durham whilst his nephew, Moddan, led an army north to Caithness. Moddan found himself outnumbered and rapidly retreated whilst Duncan's assault on Durham was nothing short of incompetent and his army suffered heavy losses. Duncan now decided, rather late, to concentrate his forces on one front, and set out to encounter Thorfinn. He was out-manoeuvred on every front, narrowly escaping with his life in a sea battle, whilst Moddan was killed at Thurso. Duncan retreated into Moray, where any sensible commander would realize he was in unsafe territory. Although the men of Moray had for years battled against the Norsemen, they had no wish to support Duncan. The earl of Moray, Macbeth, allied himself with Thorfinn and overwelmed Duncan's army at Pitgaveny on 15 August 1040. Duncan was killed in the battle. His death was not mourned. The historical Duncan is nothing like the victim portrayed in Shakespeare's *Macbeth*. He was seen as a ruthless and incapable king. His son, Malcolm (III) was still only an infant and was not considered eligible to inherit the throne. It took the Scottish council only a short while to accept Macbeth as king.

MACBETH *Moray, 1032–57; Scotland, 15 August 1040– 15 August 1057.*
Born: *c1005.* **Died** *(killed in battle): Lumphanen, 15 August 1057, aged 52.* **Buried:** *Iona.*
Married: *c1033, Gruoch, widow of Gillecomgain, mórmaer of Moray: no children.*

The Macbeth of history was rather different from the tragic character portrayed by Shakespeare. He was the son of Findlaech, the earl of Moray of the line of Loarn, a collateral branch of the rulers of Dál Riata who now ruled much of what was soon to become Scotland. His mother, Donada, was the daughter of Malcolm II. Not much is known about his youth. His father was murdered when Macbeth was fifteen or so, and the earldom was taken by Macbeth's cousins Malcolm and subsequently Gillecomgain. It was after the latter's murder in 1032 that Macbeth, now twenty-seven, inherited the title. Whilst his predecessors had been hostile to Malcolm II and had actively sought to usurp the throne, Macbeth was less belligerent. Malcolm's cousin and successor, Duncan, however, was a far less competent king, and Duncan was killed by Macbeth's forces at Pitgaveny. Later accounts that Macbeth murdered Duncan are total fabrication.

Macbeth ruled strongly and wisely for the next fourteen years without any major mishap. Because of his close relationship with his half-brother Thorfinn, there was no conflict with the Norse of Orkney. If anything, Thorfinn knew he could rely on Macbeth's support when Thorfinn went on a punitive raid as far south as Man and North Wales in 1042. The only challenge to his rule came from his uncle Crinan, the father of Duncan and the earl of Atholl. Crinan probably sought to place his second son, Maldred, on the throne and in 1045 Crinan, then aged about seventy, staged a rebellion. The two factions met at Dunkeld where Crinan and Maldred were killed. For the next nine years there seems to have been no instability in Macbeth's reign. He was apparently a generous and pious ruler. He is described as a tall man with a ruddy complexion and fair hair. In 1050, he undertook a pilgrimage to Rome where it is recorded that he scattered gifts and money 'like seed'. This indicates that he must have had a sufficiently secure kingdom at that time, and by all accounts he was much loved by his subjects.

In 1054, however, Macbeth's world crumbled. By then Duncan's son Malcolm was twenty-three and regarded himself as the true heir to the throne of Scotland. He was supported in his efforts to regain the throne by Edward The Confessor, who placed Siward of Northumbria in charge of the invasion. Siward's forces advanced far into Scotland. Perhaps Macbeth sought to play the same tactics as Brude Mac Bili had against Egfrith of Northumbria nearly four centuries earlier. But Siward had also learned not to venture too far into enemy territory without backup and he brought his fleet into the Firth of Tay. The two armies, both of considerable size, met at Dunsinnan on 27 July 1054. This is the battle commemorated in Shakespeare's play where Macbeth had been assured by the witches that he was safe until Birnam Wood came against him. Since the battle took place on an open field (and not with Macbeth hiding in his castle as portrayed by Shakespeare), it is unlikely that Siward's troops camouflaged themselves with greenery, though one cannot discount that such tactics may have been used in part of the battle. What is more likely is that Malcolm's troops, who were essentially the men of Atholl, wore sprigs of rowan in their caps as emblems, or carried branches of rowan as cudgels. It has also been suggested that the battle site was not Dunsinnan, just north of Scone, but a few miles further east at Dundee. It is worth reflecting upon the forces involved in the battle. Although it was essentially a Northumbrian (i.e. English) army versus a Scots, Siward's forces represented the Scottish heir Malcolm. The battle was, therefore, an internal Scottish conflict. Yet most of Siward's army was made up of Scandinavian troops, whilst Macbeth's army included many Norman soldiers. Normans had settled in England during the reign of Edward the Confessor, who had been raised in Normandy and had strong Norman sympathies. However his conflict with Earl Godwin had led him to expel many Normans from England in 1051 and some had taken refuge in Scotland. Although it is not stated that Thorfinn of Orkney assisted Macbeth, it is likely that Macbeth's army included levies from across northern Scotland and thus included soldiers from Caithness and Sutherland who would have been Norse. Thus the battle that decided Macbeth's fate was essentially fought between Scandinavian factions, primarily the old enemies of Danes versus Norse. Although Macbeth was overwhelmingly defeated he was not deposed, and there were sufficient casualties amongst Siward's forces for his army to retire. Malcolm laid claim to the southern kingdom of Strathclyde and used this as his base for further incursions into Scotland. There followed three years of civil war. Malcolm's strength grew and Macbeth was driven back further into his Moray base. However, during one such retreat Macbeth found himself cut off from his main army, and he was ambushed by Malcolm's forces at Lumphanan, west of Aberdeen. Tradition states that he made his last stand in the stone circle known as the Peel Ring where he and his bodyguard were butchered. Support for Macbeth remained strong for it was not Malcolm who was chosen to succeed him but his stepson Lulach.

Macbeth's reputation as a strong, wise and generous king has been overtaken by the image portrayed by Shakespeare. Shakespeare did not invent this, however. He drew his facts from the historical records available to him which had already been distorted mostly by Hector Boece, whose *History of Scotland*, published in 1527, contained many inventions, including the characters of Banquo, the three witches, and the image we have of Lady Macbeth. The real Macbeth was revered and given a royal burial on Iona. Apart from the brief reign of Lulach (1057–8), Macbeth was the last Gaelic ruler of the Scots. With the subsequent succession of Malcolm III, Scotland shifted toward a more Anglo-Norman outlook.

MALCOLM III *CANMORE* (*BIGHEAD*)
Sub-king of Cumbria and Strathclyde, 1045–58; king of Scotland, 17 March 1058–13 November 1093. Crowned: Scone Abbey, 25 April 1058.
Born: *c1031.* **Died:** *nr Alnwick, 13 November 1093, aged 62.*
Buried: *Dunfermline Abbey (later removed to the Escorial, Madrid).*
Married: *(1) c1060, Ingibiorg (d. c1069), widow of Thorfinn, Earl of Orkney: 3 children; (2) c1069, Margaret (d. c1093), dau. Edward Atheling, son of Edmund II of England: at least 8 children.*

Many lists of Scottish kings begin with Malcolm III, even though he was the fifty-eighth in line since Fergus established the kingdom of Dál Riata in Argyll, and the twenty-second since Kenneth MacAlpin had united the Scots and the Picts. The main reason for Malcolm's apparent status is that under his rule Scotland shifted dramatically away from its Gaelic past and moved towards the Anglo-Norman world of southern Britain. Malcolm had been raised in the Anglo-Norman court of Edward The Confessor. When his father, Duncan had been killed in battle against Macbeth in 1040, Malcolm, then a young boy of eight or nine, along with his brother was hurriedly smuggled out of Scotland in fear of their lives. After the deaths of Macbeth and his stepson, Lulach, Malcolm was crowned as king of Scotland. His support was not total, with many, especially the Highlanders, preferring their old ways and customs and not seeking to follow Malcolm. Nevertheless they accepted him as overlord because of his sheer physical power and menace. He was a swaggering bully who rapidly earned the nickname of *Canmore*, or Bighead.

Malcolm began his reign by establishing alliances. Amongst his father's former enemies was Thorfinn, the earl of Orkney. It is not clear when Thorfinn died, but it is evident that he had not helped Macbeth in his fight for the monarchy, not because he did not support Macbeth (they were half brothers and allies) but because he was probably already very ill. He may have died as early as 1057 and was almost certainly dead by 1060, when Malcolm married Thorfinn's widow, Ingibiorg, and established an alliance with her sons Paul and Erlend who became the new earls of Orkney. Ingibiorg bore Malcolm three children before she died, probably around 1069. Malcolm's alliance with Orkney brought him into closer contact with Harald Haadraada, the king of Norway, and overlord of Orkney and the Western Isles. Malcolm was thus seen as an ally of Norway when, in 1066, Tostig, the brother of Harold Godwinson of Wessex, gained Haadraada's support for an invasion of England. The invasion force landed first at Orkney and sailed down the eastern coast of Scotland to the Humber estuary. Malcolm's motives are uncertain in this campaign. He was clearly a Saxon sympathizer, but evidently not a supporter of Harold Godwinson, whom he may have seen as a usurper in the south. His support for Tostig, who was nothing short of a rebellious thug, does not seem a wise choice and Malcolm would have gained little from a Norse victory beyond the possible annexation of Northumbria. He was more likely to have become a vassal of the Norwegian king. However, as we saw earlier, Harald and Tostig were killed at Stamford Bridge, and a few weeks later Harold Godwinson was killed at Senlac Hill by William duke of Normandy. At Christmas 1066 William was crowned king of England. Although Malcolm knew the Norman world – Edward the Confessor had been pro-Norman and there were many Normans at his court where Malcolm grew up as well as Norman soldiers in Malcolm's army – he was unsure what an alliance with the Normans would achieve. His initial sympathies were with the Saxons. Edgar Atheling, the Saxon heir, joined in the unsuccessful rebellion against William in 1068, and subsequently fled to Malcolm's court to seek refuge. He was accompanied by his sister Margaret whom Malcolm married the following year. This further consolidated the Scottish-Saxon alliance, but alienated Malcolm all the more from his Highland subjects, and made an enemy of William the Conqueror. It should be remembered, however, that in 1069 William's hold on England was far from secure and many believed that he

would eventually be overthrown. Edgar was almost certainly convinced he would some day regain the throne of England, and Malcolm's move was part of his framework of alliances with neighbouring powers. Malcolm supported Edgar's unsuccessful attempt to regain England in 1069 along with Swein of Denmark. The next two to three years saw Malcolm supporting a series of raids throughout northern England, coming as far south as Cleveland. William was enraged, and in 1072 he invaded Scotland and sought the submission of Malcolm at Abernathy. The terms of the treaty meant that Malcolm could no longer harbour any of William's enemies, and Edgar Atheling again became an exile. William also forced Malcolm to recognize him as his overlord, and took his son Duncan as hostage. Later English kings would regard the Treaty of Abernathy as the date of their conquest of Scotland, though it is unlikely it was viewed as that at the time. Certainly it did not stop Malcolm raiding England in 1079, though this proved equally fruitless. William sent his son Robert to negotiate with Malcolm. This achieved little, though Robert decided to add to the fortifications of the north and built the New Castle at the estuary of the Tyne. William regarded Malcolm as an irritant at this time and certainly did not view him as a ruler of equal status. Malcolm, on the other hand, living up to his nickname, believed he was just as powerful.

Under the influence of his wife Margaret, to whom he was devoted, Malcolm changed steadily from the coarse ruffian of his youth to a mature individual who had strong respect for his wife's religious and cultural beliefs and interests. Margaret had been well educated in Hungary and England and was an ardent Christian. It was under her direction that the abbey at Dunfermline was begun in 1072, to equal the one Edward the Confessor had completed at Westminster just seven years earlier. Margaret also restored the monastery on Iona, and did much to bring the Celtic church in line with the Roman. Records suggest that from 1072 the archbishopric of York was given authority over the church of Scotland. Malcolm, who was not especially religious himself, seemed content to allow

Margaret to undertake these reforms, surprisingly ignorant of their long-term effect. It is probably another example of his belief in his authority as absolute, but it is also a reminder that Malcolm truly loved Margaret and that their marriage was strong and happy.

Malcolm had evidently not forsaken his designs upon England. After the death of William I in 1087, his son Duncan was released and Malcolm again began planning an expansion of his territories. He was soon joined by Edgar Atheling, who recognized the opportunity, and in 1090 Malcolm invaded Northumbria. He was defeated by William Rufus and the terms of the Treaty of Abernathy were re-invoked. William continued to defend the north and in 1092 invaded Cumbria and built a fort at Carlisle. Malcolm and his son Edward came to meet William but were rebuffed. As they were returning north they were ambushed by Robert Mowbray, earl of Northumberland, near Alnwick and both Malcolm and Edward were killed. When Margaret, who was already extremely ill, heard the news four days later she pined away. It is an irony that Malcolm had replaced the old rule of tanistry by that of primogeniture, only to have his eldest son and heir die with him. The Scottish magnates had no idea what to do in such circumstances and civil unrest broke out. Five of his nine sons would eventually succeed him as king, though his immediate successor was his brother Donald.

Malcolm had been temporarily buried near Tynemouth. Shortly afterwards he and his wife were buried at the new Dunfermline Abbey. Following a papal inquiry in 1250 into the life and possible miracles of Margaret, she was canonized. During the Reformation their bodies were reburied at a specially built tomb in the Escorial, Madrid. In 1673 Margaret was named as one of the patron saints of Scotland.

Malcolm's reign was a clear transition from the Gaelic tradition to the acceptance of new values and beliefs. Although he was not supported in this by many of his countrymen he established a momentum that could not be stopped.

DONALD III *BANE* (*THE WHITE*) *sometimes called*
DONALBAIN *Scotland 13 November 1093–May 1094*
(deposed); restored 12 November 1094–October 1097.
Born: *c1033.* **Died:** *Rescobie, 1099, aged 66.* **Buried:** *Dunkeld
Abbey, later removed to Iona.*
Married: *(name and date unknown): 1 daughter.*

As Malcolm's younger brother Donald, for most of his life,
probably had no designs on the Scottish throne. He was almost
certainly made mórmaer (earl) of Gowrie around the year 1060
but there is no record that he played any part in Malcolm's
affairs. It is possible that the two brothers were estranged and that
Donald did not support Malcolm's and Margaret's reforms. He
lived in exile in Ireland and the Western Isles and thereby
endeared himself to the pro-Gaelic party in Scotland. After
Malcolm's and his heir Edward's death, Donald was raised to
the throne during the days of confusion over the succession.
Donald was sixty, and although his hair had probably turned
white (hence his nickname) he was evidently strong and hale of
body. Donald and his supporters promptly expelled the Norman
and Saxon refugees in Scotland. As a consequence Malcolm's
eldest son, Duncan, who had hitherto also shown no interest in
the kingship, but who had lived as a hostage at the courts of
William I and II of England for many years, came into the picture.
He was supported by William Rufus and his army defeated
Donald and drove him out of Scotland. Duncan held the throne
for only seven months (May–November 1094) before being
defeated by Donald at the battle of Monthecin in November
1094, after which Donald was restored to the throne. However,
Donald now divided the kingdom between himself and his
nephew Edmund, with Donald's rule amongst the heart of his
supporters in the Highlands north of the Forth/Clyde valley. This
arrangement survived for less than three years (November 1094–
October 1097) as another of Malcolm's sons, Edgar (October
1097–January 1107), received greater support from William II

and deposed Donald and Edmund in October 1097. Donald was blinded and imprisoned at Rescobie in Forfarshire, where he died some eighteen months later. He was buried at Dunkeld Abbey but later his remains were removed to Iona by his adherents. He was the last Scottish king to be buried there, and thus marks the end of the old tradition of Gaelic kings.

Soon after Edgar's accession Magnus III of Norway led a major expedition to his territories in northern Britain. He deposed the earls of Orkney, Paul and Erlend, who were Edgar's step-brothers, and set off on a wave of conquest around the Scottish coast. Edgar gave Magnus sovereignty over the Hebrides. These islands were heavily populated by Norse or Gallo-Norse and seemed far removed from Edgar's world. Part of this arrangement, however, meant that the holy island of Iona came under Norwegian rule. Although Edgar was sensible enough not to encourage a wave of Norman settlement in Scotland, he increased his ties with England. He was already beholden to William Rufus for gaining the throne, and was present at the coronation of Henry I in 1100. Three months later, Edgar's sister Edith married Henry, so links were tightened between the English and Scottish monarchy. Edgar lived mostly in Edinburgh and it does not appear that he ventured far beyond. He played the part of a Norman vassal to the letter and it is of little surprise that by this time the Norman kings of England began to regard Scotland, certainly the border territory, as their domain.

Edgar, who died childless in his mid-thirties, was in turn succeeded by his younger step-brother, a son of Margaret, Alexander I (The Fierce) (1107–24).

When Alexander had succeeded to the throne it was intended that he share the kingdom with his brother David.

Alexander chose not to, and David threatened to invade the kingdom, but was never able to raise a sufficiently large army. It was not until 1113 that Alexander granted David territory in Strathclyde and the Borders. Upon his accession, Alexander married Sybilla, the fifteen year old illegitimate daughter of Henry I. During the first phase of his reign Alexander was clearly

Henry's vassal: he even accompanied Henry in his campaign into Wales against Gruffydd ap Cynan in 1114. However, by the second half of his reign, Alexander had shifted back toward the heart of old Scotland, or Alba, and had taken up residence at Scone. It may be now that he earned his nickname of 'the Fierce', apparently after the ferocious way he quelled an uprising by the men of Moray. It may have been through such an indomitable strength of character that Alexander began to win over the Highland Scots, despite considerable opposition. Alexander began a programme of castle construction, including the one at Stirling. His court became one of splendour – there is mention of Arab stallions and Turkish men-at-arms. Alexander also continued his mother's reforms in anglicizing the Scottish church, and was the first to introduce coinage into Scotland. His reforms saw the introduction of the first sheriffs in Scotland as controller's of the king's peace. Thus, by the end of Alexander's reign, there had been a measurable shift toward uniting the older Scottish culture with the new Anglo-Norman world. Alexander had achieved this through his own strength and willpower, leaving a steady base for his brother David. Alexander died at Stirling Castle and was buried in Dunfermline Abbey.

DAVID (I) THE SAINT Scotland, 23(?) April 1124–24 May 1153.

Titles: king of Scotland, earl of Huntingdon and Northampton (from 1113) and prince of Cumbria (1113–1124).

Born: c1084. **Died:** Carlisle, 24 May 1153, aged about 69.

Buried: Dunfermline Abbey.

Married: 1113, Matilda (c1072–c1130), dau. Waltheof, earl of Northumberland, and widow of Simon de St Liz, earl of Northampton and Huntingdon: 4 children.

David was about forty when he came to the throne, mature in his character, his outlook and his ability to govern. He had spent much of his youth, since the year 1093, at the court of his brother-

From a 12th-century chapter

in-law, Henry I of England. Since his infancy he had been raised by Margaret with a respect for learning and the church, and it seems he had a tremendous respect for fair play. In 1113, when David married Matilda, and inherited vast lands in Northumberland, Northampton and Huntingdon, Alexander allowed David to become sub-king of the Lowlands. Since David also became earl of Huntingdon he was both a Norman baron and a Scottish king, which was immensely important in understanding the power that David was able to wield and the respect he had to be accorded by his peers.

When David became king in 1124 he continued the reforms started by his mother and brothers, but it was under David that it all came into shape. Chief of these reforms was the feudalization of lowland Scotland. Tracts of land were given to Anglo-Norman barons in exchange for their loyalty and service. Amongst them were Robert de Brus, the ancestor of Robert Bruce, who was given the lordship of Annandale, and Walter Fitzalan, who became High Steward of Scotland and thus the ancestor of the Stewart dynasty. This process was described by the disgruntled Highlanders as 'invasion by invitation', and led to at least two revolts during David's reign and eventually the declaration of independence by Somerled of Argyll after David's death. Nevertheless, David's gradual reform brought a cohesiveness to Scotland that it had previously never enjoyed, particularly in the strength of the church and the world of learning. He founded the bishoprics of Aberdeen, Brechin, Caithness, Dunblane and Ross as well as the monasteries at Holyrood, Melrose, Kinloss, Newbattle and Dundrennan. He also forged strong links with Rome. Even during his life he had come to be regarded as a saintly king by his people and the epithet Saint David remained after his death, even though he was never formally canonized. It was David who really forged Scotland as a prosperous kingdom, introducing a strong coinage, and developing towns like Berwick, Edinburgh, Jedburgh, Stirling and Perth as major trading centres from which the king drew revenues. David also redrew the Scottish administrative map, creating the counties which remained until the reorganization of 1975. Justice was dispensed by a system of justiciars. In all these things David created the modern Scotland.

In military matters he was less strong and only partly success-ful. In 1127 he agreed, along with other English barons, to recognize Henry I's daughter, Matilda, as the next ruler of England. He used this as an excuse in 1135, on the death of Henry and the succession of Stephen, to invade northern England, laying claim to Northumberland and Cumberland initially in the name of Matilda. The next three years saw considerable bloodshed in Northumberland where David's soldiers committed awful atrocities. Eventually David was defeated by the northern barons under Thurstan, archbishop of York, at Cowton Moor, near Northallerton, on 22 August 1138 at the Battle of the Standard. David continued to press his claims in the north and Stephen, unable to fight his war on two fronts, eventually reached an agreement whereby David was granted the earldom of North-umberland provided he swore fealty to Stephen. The earldom was bestowed upon David's son, Henry, who was the king designate.

David switched sides again to support Matilda when she gained the upper hand in February 1141 and he ventured as far south as London for her coronation. However, he was expelled from London in September by Stephen's troops and only narrowly escaped back to Durham without being captured. Thereafter he remained on the sidelines, a nominal supporter of the Empress, but not engaging in further conflict. In 1149 he gained a promise from Matilda's son Henry II that, should he become king, he would grant David the lands of Northumberland and Cumbria. When David died at Carlisle in May 1153 he almost certainly regarded himself as lord of all the lands from Caithness in the north to Cumbria and Northumberland in the south. Though these southern lands were never formally part of the kingdom of Scotland, David doubtless believed they would be.

Neither of David's own sons came to the throne. His firstborn, Malcolm, had been murdered in infancy, probably about 1114. Henry, who was groomed as the next king, died in 1152, aged thirty-eight. Henry's young son, Malcolm, was promptly declared the king designate, though he was only twelve.

MALCOLM IV *THE MAIDEN*
King of Scotland, 24 May 1153–9 December 1165.
Crowned: Scone Abbey, June (?) 1153.
Born: *20 March 1141.* **Died:** *Jedburgh Castle, 9 December 1165, aged 24.* **Buried:** *Dunfermline Abbey.*

It seems that for all his youth, Malcolm inherited much of the wisdom and sense of fair play of his grandfather and was not over-influenced by other external factors. He kept his head in moments of crisis and ensured he received sound advice before making decisions. Nevertheless the mere fact of his age made him less able to deal with Henry II of England. Although Henry had promised Malcolm's grandfather that he would bequeath Scotland the territories of Northumberland and Cumbria when he became king (which he did in 1154), he soon reneged upon this. In 1157 Henry met Malcolm at Chester and deprived him of these northern territories in exchange for the earldom of Huntingdon, which had been his grandfather's but had been lost in 1141. In 1159 both Malcolm and his brother William were forced to accompany Henry on a mission to Aquitaine where Henry needed to punish the count of Toulouse. The Scots perceived Malcolm operating as the vassal of Henry, although Malcolm was only delivering his feudal obligations for the honour of Huntingdon. Nevertheless this led to a series of rebellions in Scotland amongst the Highlanders who resented not only the continued anglicization of Scotland but the blatant subordination of Scotland to the English king. The first rebellion was in 1160 by Fergus of Galloway. Malcolm promptly put down this rebellion with the support of his Anglo-Norman barons, though it took two more expeditions before Fergus was eventually quashed. A further show of force in 1164 by Somerled of the Isles was equally effectively dealt with. Malcolm, for all his youth, proved himself stronger than many suspected.

Nevertheless Malcolm did not project the image of a powerful monarch. Slim, fair-haired and a declared celibate – for which he earned his nickname of 'the Maiden' – Malcolm was devoted to the church, to which he made many endowments. He never married, although it was rumoured he fathered an illegitimate child who died in infancy. Malcolm died after a short illness at the age of twenty-four, and was succeeded by his brother William.

WILLIAM *THE LYON*
King of Scotland, 9 December 1165–4 December 1214.
Crowned: Scone Abbey, 24 December 1165.
Titles: *king of Scotland; earl of Northumberland (1152–1157).*
Born: *c1143.* **Died**: *Stirling, 4 December 1214, aged 71.*
Buried: *Arbroath Abbey.*
Married: *5 September 1186 at Woodstock Palace, Oxford, Ermengarde (d. 1234), dau. Richard of Beaumont-le-Maine: 4 children. William also had at least 9 illegitimate children.*

William was twenty-two when he succeeded his brother. He had been the earl of Northumberland since the death of his father, in 1152, but the earldom was lost in 1157 as part of Malcolm's dealings with Henry II. William's ambition to regain North-umberland became an obsession during his reign and strongly dictated the subsequent events – after an initial eight years of uneasy peace, it led him to join in the revolt of Henry II's sons in 1173. William had little command over his army and was captured in 1174 and taken in chains to Falaise in Normandy. There he was forced to pay homage to Henry, acknowledging him as his overlord. He thereby became the vassal of Henry, the terms of the treaty confirming that the Scottish barons also owed their allegiance to Henry. With the Treaty of Falaise Scotland theore-tically passed into English hands. The Scots of Galloway imme-diately rebelled, led by Gilbert, the son of Fergus of Galloway. William, who had now returned to Scotland, was able to crush the rebellion with Norman support. He thereafter fortified Gallo-way with a series of burghs and castles, including those at Ayr and Dumfries, and thereafter Galloway was loyal to him.

William now endeavoured to make northern Scotland subser-vient to him. Although he was always nominally their king, the Highlanders had remained independent. In 1179, William ad-vanced into the Highlands, establishing castles at Redcastle and Dunskeath. He was soon confronted by the opposition of Donald MacWilliam, who rebelled in 1181. This Donald was a legitimate claimant to the Scottish throne. On his father's side he was the grandson of Duncan II whilst, through his mother, he was a great-grandson of Lulach. Donald believed himself the king of the Highlands, and allied himself with Harald II of Orkney in opposition to William. Donald's forces gained the upper hand for much of the next five years, taking control of Ross. It was more by chance than design that Roland of Galloway cornered Donald at Mangarnia Moor, near Inverness, on 31 July 1187 and killed him in battle. William founded burghs at Elgin and Inver-ness to further contain the north, but it was not until 1197 that Harald of Orkney gave William the opportunity to invade

Caithness and regain the northern territories. Thorfinn, Harald's son, was taken hostage. Harald's stubborness meant he refused to yield to William, and a further invasion of Caithness in 1202 caused William to react strongly. He blinded and castrated Thorfinn (from which wounds he died) and brought a mighty army into Caithness, against which Harald was unable to raise anything its equal. Thereafter Harald submitted to William, recognizing him as his overlord in Caithness.

By this period William was in a strong position. In 1189 the new English king, Richard, desperate to finance his crusade, sold all rights in Scotland back to William for 10,000 marks (or about £6,700). This was known as the Quit-claim of Canterbury. It meant that by 1202 William was undisputed king and overlord of all mainland Scotland. One other turn of fortune for William had meant that in 1192 the Pope decreed that the Scottish church was answerable directly to him, and not subordinate to Canterbury or York, which further elevated William's status. William succeeded in maintaining a tense though cordial relationship with Richard's successor John for all the latter remained the senior king. William held tightly to his control of Scotland, without being able to expand it into England. For some reason William chose not to marry until he was forty-three, and it was nearly twelve years before his first son, the future Alexander II, was born. William's brother David had also married late, and these many years without a clear heir had only added to the unease in the north and encouraged claimants to the throne. One final rebellion in Scotland, in 1211, by Godfrey, the son of Donald MacWilliam, was easily quelled, and Godfrey was executed in 1213.

William's reign, one of the longest in Scotland by an adult king, was ultimately successful, for all its darker periods. Although he never extended his kingdom, he regained all that he lost and was a stronger king by the end of his reign. His soubriquet of 'the Lyon' was added later. He was never known by that during his lifetime, and it is not believed to relate to his character, even though he was tenacious and strong in dealing with his subjects. It probably came from the symbol of the lion he used on his seal.

THE HOUSE OF ANJOU
(part 1: 1154–1272)

Although the Normans would dominate Wales and Scotland by the late thirteenth century, they still regarded their heartland as Normandy and France rather than England. England was a rich country, the revenues from which allowed the kings to finance their campaigns in France and, in the case of Richard I, the Crusades. Henry II established a large Angevin Empire where he held territories in fief to the French king across most of northern and western France. The centre of this Empire was Anjou; it also included the territories of Brittany, Aquitaine and Normandy. Henry even made moves into Ireland. Following the Treaty of Windsor, signed on 6 October 1175, Rory O'Connor, the last hereditary High King, recognized Henry as his overlord in most of eastern Ireland (primarily Meath, Leinster, Munster, Waterford and Ulster). O'Connor remained king of Connaught on payment of a tribute to Henry, and other tributory kings remained. Henry made his son John 'Lord of Ireland' in 1177.

John, the suitably nicknamed Lackland, who started with nothing, nearly ended with nothing since he died in the middle of a civil war in England in 1216, with the heir to the French throne having been brought over as king. John had already lost much of France and the recovery of the French lands would remain a passion of all successive kings down to Henry VIII.

Great changes would take place under the Angevins in England. The powers of the church and the clergy would be limited, while those of the barons would increase and finally place constraints on royal power.

The first universities of Oxford and Cambridge would be founded in 1164 and 1209, while this period is best remembered for its Crusades, and for the rise of chivalry. Meanwhile the population of the British Isles had risen to two and a half million by the beginning of the thirteenth century.

Henry, Empress Matilda's eldest son had briefly claimed the kingdom of England in 1141 during the extended civil war. His father Geoffrey, count of Anjou, became duke of Normandy in 1144. Geoffrey was frequently known as *Plantagenet* because of the sprig of broom (*planta genista*) he would wear in his cap, and this soubriquet subsequently became the surname of his descendants and the title of the royal house of England. Its official name, though, was the house of Anjou and it would dominate England for over 330 years.

HENRY II, *FITZEMPRESS or CURTMANTLE*
King of England 25 October 1154–6 July 1189. Crowned: Westminster, 19 December 1154.
Titles: king of England, duke of Normandy (from 1151), duke of Aquitaine (from 1152), count of Anjou, Touraine and Maine (from 1151).
Born: Le Mans, Maine, 5 March 1133. Died: Chinon Castle, Anjou, 6 July 1189, aged 56. Buried: Fontevrault Abbey, France.
Married: 18 May 1152, at Bordeaux Cathedral, Gascony, Eleanor (c1122–1204), dau. of William X, duke of Aquitaine, and divorcée of Louis VII, king of France: 8 children. Henry had at least 12 illegitimate children by five or more other women.

Henry had first attempted to continue his mother's war against Stephen after she had returned to Normandy in 1148, but Henry was a young squire of fifteen without sufficient resources to maintain such an effort. The next five years would see a significant change in him. When his father died in 1151 he inherited the duchy of Normandy as well as becoming count of Maine and Anjou. Eight months later he married Eleanor of Aquitaine, who was at least ten years his senior, the former wife of Louis VII of France whom Louis had divorced, ostensibly on grounds of consanguinity, but really because she had provided no male heir. This marriage infuriated Louis VII, especially when he had recognize the claim of Henry as duke of Aquitaine. Although Henry paid homage to Louis for his lands in France, he now effectively controlled more territory than the King himself. Louis sent forces against Henry as a show of power but Henry was able to contain them. In fact he felt sufficiently in control to accompany a small force to England in January 1153 in an effort to depose Stephen. In this he was unsuccessful, but Stephen was no longer disposed to fight, and most of the hostilities were between Henry and Stephen's son Eustace. In August 1153 Eustace died and this paved the way for Henry's succession which was sealed under the Treaty of Wallingford that November. By its terms Stephen continued to rule for as long as he lived but Henry was his undisputed successor. When Stephen died in October 1154, Henry succeeded to a considerable territory, subsequently called the Angevin Empire, though not known as that in Henry's day. At its peak it stretched from the Scottish border to the Pyrenees, and would include overlordship of Ireland.

From a coin

Giraldus Cambrensis wrote of him: He 'had a reddish complexion, his eyes were grey, bloodshot and flashed in anger. He had a fiery countenance, his voice was tremulous and his neck bent a little forward . . . he had an enormous paunch, rather by fault of nature than from gross feeding [for] in all things he was moderate, even parsimonious'.

The energy with which Henry set about establishing his authority over his territories was awesome. This was helped by the papal bull issued in 1155 by the new Pope Adrian IV (the only English pope – Nicholas Breakspeare), which decreed that Henry had authority over the whole of Britain, including Scotland, Wales and Ireland. In the space of two years (1155–7) Henry had destroyed many of the castles established by barons during the civil war, and which he referred to as 'dens of thieves'; he had negotiated terms with Malcolm IV of Scotland, whereby Cumbria and Northumberland returned to English rule; and he had invaded Wales and brought the Welsh princes to heel. This last enterprise nearly cost him his life, however, when he was ambushed by the heir of Gwynedd, Cynan ab Owain. Henry's strength of character, his papal authority, and the immense resources upon which he could draw made him an impossible man to challenge, and by 1158 he had restored an order to England and its subservient kingdoms which it had not known to such a degree for many lifetimes. Wales would continue to be a thorn in his side for much of his reign, but he never considered it as much of a problem compared to other priorities. Subsequent campaigns of 1167 and 1177 served to remind successive Welsh rulers of his authority.

From 1158 to 1163 Henry was back in France. In July 1158 his brother Geoffrey had died. Geoffrey had in 1150 been made count of Nantes, one half of the duchy of Brittany, and on Geoffrey's death Henry sought to gain control. He was foiled by the speed with which the exiled duke, Conan IV, reclaimed his lands. Conan had been confirmed as earl of Richmond by Henry in 1156, and Conan was forced to acknowledge Henry's overlordship in Brittany. In 1166 Henry arranged a marriage between his son Geoffrey and Conan's daughter Constance, and thereafter Conan handed over the administration of Brittany to Henry to direct on behalf of the children. Henry's main thrust during 1159 and 1160 was against Toulouse, which he regarded as part of his wife's territory in Aquitaine. The French king, Louis VII, came to the defence of his brother-in-law, the count of Toulouse, and Henry had to withdraw rather than fight his French overlord. Toulouse and Aquitaine remained in dispute between Henry and Louis for the rest of their reigns.

The most notorious aspect of Henry's reign was his relationship with Thomas à Becket. Becket was a personal friend of Henry's. Born in London, the son of a wealthy merchant, he was well educated and had trained as a knight before his father's misfortunes obliged him to become a clerk, entering the household of Theobald, the archbishop of Canterbury, in 1142. He became an expert at canonical jurisprudence, and was appointed archdeacon of Canterbury in 1154 and chancellor of England in 1155. He fought alongside Henry in Toulouse and became wealthy. His election as the next archbishop of Canterbury in May 1162 came as a surprise to many, and was not universally accepted amongst other churchmen because of Becket's background and worldliness. It was probably this that caused Becket to change so radically in character in order to prove his devotion to the church. Henry, who thought he had an ally within the church who would help him in ecclesiatical disputes which had so plagued past kings, found that he had an unpredictable opponent. Henry's short temper did not allow this to last for long and matters came to a head over the issue of clergy who broke the law. Henry maintained at a council held in October 1163 that these 'criminous clerks' should be unfrocked and tried in a lay court. Becket maintained that they would be tried by ecclesiastical courts. Henry appealed to the new pope (Alexander III), who requested that Becket be more conciliatory. Henry now presented Becket with a series of terms, known as the Constitutions of Clarendon, where in January 1164 the council was held. Becket argued tenaciously but eventually submitted. Henry believed that he had succeeded but, soon after Becket repented his change of heart and began lobbying the bishops. Henry was furious. He summoned Becket on various charges, including a debt of 44,000 marks (about £30,000) as owing since his days as chancellor. Becket was found guilty and his estates forfeited. He fled to France where he spent two years at the Cistercian abbey of Pontigny in Burgundy before the pope gave due attention to his cause. Becket pleaded personally before him in Rome, and Alexander restored him to the see of Canterbury. But Becket could still not return to England. He remained in France where he wrote letters of exhortation to the bishops, threatening excommunication unless they heeded his words.

In the meantime Henry had more pressing matters in hand. The pope's support and the Clarendon verdict had allowed Henry to start breaking down the old feudal system in England, making local baronial courts subordinate to a strong central court. He reestablished the jury system and introduced a new code of laws.

By a series of dynastic marriages Henry was establishing himself as one of the most powerful men in Europe. Already in 1160 he had arranged a marriage between his eldest surviving son Henry (aged two), and Margaret (aged two), daughter of Louis VII of France. Louis had not expected a confirmed marriage for many years after the betrothal agreement. But Henry had offered his support to the new pope, Alexander III, in 1160, whose succession was disputed, and in repayment, Alexander carried out the marriage. With her marriage Margaret brought a dowry of several castles in France. Then, in February 1168 Henry's eldest daughter Matilda was married to Heinrich the Lion, Duke of Saxony and Bavaria, while his youngest daughters were betrothed to the kings of Castile and Sicily.

Henry's dispute with Becket returned to haunt him in 1170. In that year Henry determined to have his eldest son Henry formally crowned as king of England. Louis VII constantly objected to Henry's schemes and objected to the coronation of June 1170 firstly on the grounds that his daughter had not been crowned queen at the same time but also that it was unlawful. The coronation should have been conducted by Thomas Becket, the authorised representative of the pope. Becket was still in exile in France at that time so the archbishop of York conducted the ceremony.

This coronation effectively elevated Henry himself into an imperial role. Becket condemned this when he returned to England later that year. Becket was welcomed by the general populace as a hero: their champion against baronial oppression. Henry could not understand why Becket was always so quarrelsome. It was during one such moment of frustration that Henry uttered his notorious words: 'Is there none will rid me of this turbulent priest?' Four knights, hearing these words and determined to prove themselves, immediately left Henry's court in Normandy, arriving at Canterbury on 29 December 1170 where they slew Becket within the cathedral. Although the murder shocked Christendom, it had not been at Henry's direct bidding. The knights each did their penance. Henry donned sackcloth, and apologized to the pope, but he soon weathered the storm. Everyone realized that Becket was best out of the way, though he was rapidly canonized in 1173.

Henry's attention turned to Ireland. He already believed he had ostensible authority over the country but plans for an earlier invasion in 1155 had been shelved. However in 1170 Richard Fitzgilbert, the earl of Pembroke, known as Richard Strongbow, invaded Ireland at the request of the dispossessed king of Leinster, Diarmaid MacMurchada. Diarmaid had earlier appealed to Henry who had offered him his support, but gave him no direct help. Strongbow's forces however soon captured Waterford and Dublin. Strongbow married Diarmaid's daughter. Henry II became suspicious of Strongbow's intentions and brought his own army into Ireland in 1171. Henry's forces were too powerful for the Irish. They nicknamed them the *gaill glassa*, or 'grey foreigners', from their armour which had not been seen before in Ireland. Henry soon established authority over eastern Ireland, especially the kingdoms of Leinster and Meath, whose rulers acknowledged his overlordship in the Treaty of Windsor in October 1175. Hugh de Lacy was made the first lord of Meath and remained as Henry's viceroy in Ireland, though his later aspirations to the kingship led to his assassination. Henry's youngest son, John, was styled king of Ireland from 1177, though this was no more than an honorific as the hereditary kings of Ireland still ruled. John later adopted the more appropriate title lord of Ireland.

John's title was part of a settlement in a dispute between Henry and his children that rocked his final years. The 'Young King' Henry was not satisfied with his authority in name only and wanted more. Although he was crowned a second time along with his wife by the new Archbishop of Canterbury, in August 1172, when he was created not only king of England but duke of Normandy and count of Anjou, he was still dissatisfied. There is the tale that at the banquet the father waited upon his own son, remarking that 'No other king in Christendom has such a butler', to which the son retorted, 'It is only fitting that the son of a count should wait on the son of a king.' This new status stirred Richard and Geoffrey into rebellion in 1173, which brought with it opportunists from elsewhere in the realm, including William The Lyon (see p. 121) of Scotland. William had long had designs on Northumberland and Cumbria which he believed were his inheritance. He invaded northern England in 1173 but was captured and taken prisoner to Henry in Normandy and forced to pay homage. The sons were supported by their mother Eleanor of Aquitaine, from whom Henry had drifted apart by the late 1160s. The problem intensified after 1180 when Louis VII was succeeded by Philippe II, a far less scrupulous monarch who was keen to shatter the Angevin Empire and agreed to help Henry's sons against their father. Henry's world which he had so painstakingly created was now in danger of collapsing.

The young Henry was an ungrateful child and, encouraged by his mother, Eleanor of Aquitaine, he rose up in revolt against his father when the old king attempted to transfer three of Henry's key castles to John. The 'Young King' sought his mother's help with the result that Eleanor was imprisoned. This led to the other sons coming into the fray, and the next decade saw an embittered rivalry between Henry and his sons. The 'Young King' did not survive to inherit the throne, as he died of a fever at Martel Castle in Turenne on 11 June 1183, aged twenty-eight.

Henry's third son, Geoffrey, was killed in an accident at a tournament in Paris in August 1186. Although this might have simplified the battle between Henry and his sons, it focused the attention on the rivalry between Richard, the eldest surviving heir and Eleanor's favourite, and John, the youngest and Henry's favourite. Henry had spent most of these latter years in France, visiting England only for official duties. It was in France that he faced the army of Richard and King Philippe, with whom was also his favourite son John. This broke Henry's spirit. He was already ill and prematurely aged. He no longer had the energy to fight and agreed terms with Philippe at Colombières on 4 July 1189. Two days later he died from a massive haemorrhage, cursing his sons to the last. He was only 56 years of age. His widow, Eleanor, would live for a further fifteen years, dying at the remarkable age of 82, the oldest of any English queen consort until the twentieth century. She still continued to exert an influence over her scheming children, of whom Richard now inherited the throne of England.

RICHARD (I) *LIONHEART*
King of England, 6 July 1189–6 April 1199. Crowned:
Westminster Abbey, 2 September 1189.
Titles: *king of England, duke of Normandy and duke of Aquitaine (from 1172).*
Born: *Beaumont Palace, Oxford, 8 September 1157.* **Died**: *Chalus, Aquitaine, 6 April 1199, aged 41.* **Buried**: *Fontevrault Abbey, Anjou.*
Married: *12 May 1191, at Limassol, Cyprus, Berengaria (c1163–after 1230), dau. of Sancho VI, king of Navarre: no children. Richard had one or possibly two illegitimate children.*

Probably no other historical king of England has so much legend attached to him and so much reputation which is ill founded. We know Richard as the Lionhearted, or *Coeur-de-Lion*, the brave and intrepid champion of Christendom against the infidel, and he is one of our national heroes. And yet the truth is so very different.

Richard had little interest in England and certainly not in the administrative demands of government. In his youth he had not expected to become king, as his elder brother Henry (The Young King) was heir to the throne. In 1172 he was invested with the duchy of Aquitaine, the inheritance of his mother, Eleanor. Like all the sons of Henry II, Richard seemed a less than grateful child. He was devoted to his mother and, when she had been imprisoned, Richard had joined in the rebellion of his brothers against their father seeking to gain more authority. Henry was still able to rebuff them at this time, but the relationship between father and sons soured over the years, with Richard's brother John being the favourite. Richard had one passion in life. He loved to fight. The thrill of battle never left him. In his youth he had trained as a knight and was a champion of the tourney. His courage and strength soon became the wonder of Aquitaine where he spent several years in battle against the rebellious barons. His military skill was evident when he took the hitherto impregnable castle of Taillebourg in 1179. Richard was 'tall in stature, of handsome appearance, his hair between red and reddish yellow, straight-limbed, rather long in the arms, the better for drawing the sword or more effective for attack; nonetheless his legs were long, and his entire person was well proportioned,' wrote a contemporary. He seems to have attracted as much attention from men as from women and there is almost certainly some truth in the belief that Richard had homosexual inclinations.

After the death of his elder brother Henry in 1183 Richard became his father's heir. Henry hoped that Richard would pass Aquitaine on to John, but Richard had no such intention. Henry's efforts to gain land back from his sons for John only led to warfare between Richard and his father. In 1189 Richard had joined forces with Philippe II of France and beat his father into submission. When Henry died a few days later, Richard travelled promptly to England to be crowned, pausing briefly in Normandy to be acknowledged Duke.

Richard's coronation was marred by the persecution of the Jews that broke out in London and later in other cities, especially York. Two years earlier Saladin's forces had captured Jerusalem, and the cry went up across Europe to regain the heart of Christendom from the infidel. Henry II had originally been asked to lead the Crusade, and Richard had been anxious to take part, but with them both fighting each other nothing had happened. With Henry's death, Richard's one ambition now was to lead an army against the Saracens. His stay in Britain was brief, sufficient to raise finances and resources for the Crusade. This included the infamous Quit-claim of Canterbury whereby Richard sold all rights in Scotland back to William The Lyon for 10,000 marks. He returned to France in December 1189 and would not set foot in England again for four years, and then only for two months. Although king of England for ten years he spent only six months in his kingdom. He left the administration of England in the hands of William Long-champ, a loyal and capable chancellor whose short temper and arrogance caused considerable friction with other barons and for a period forced him to retreat to Normandy.

From Historia Anglorum

Richard combined forces with Philippe II of France and set off for the Holy Land in July 1190. The vast army encountered transportation difficulties when their fleet was delayed and they decided to winter in Sicily. Richard's sister Joanna was the recently widowed queen of Sicily and Richard was less than satisfied with her treatment by the new king Tancred. A skirmish broke out between the crusaders and the inhabitants of Messina which resulted in Richard capturing the town. This enabled him to negotiate favourable terms with Tancred, which not only brought the release of Joanna, but much needed funds for the Crusade. It was not a happy winter in Sicily, however. Richard and Philippe quarrelled over Richard's planned marriage with Philippe's sister Alys. They had been betrothed for over twenty years, but during that time Alys had almost certainly become the mistress of Richard's father Henry. She was not exactly a shining example of virtue and Richard, who had little interest in the fair sex, declined to marry her. In the midst of this quarrel, Eleanor of Aquitaine arrived in Sicily with a new bride for her son, Berengaria of Navarre. Incensed, Philippe sailed on ahead to the Holy Land. Richard followed in April 1191, but en route the ship carrying his young bride and his sister was nearly captured by Isaac Comnenus, a Byzantine rebel who had usurped power on Cyprus. In the resultant battle Richard conquered Cyprus, which he subsequently sold to Guy de Lusignan, the exiled king of Jerusalem. While in Cyprus, Richard married Berengaria. There were to be no children of this marriage. Although Richard may have been homosexual (and he certainly had a fascination for Berengaria's brother Sancho) he had at least one illegitimate child, Philip, who became lord of Cognac, probably the offspring of a lady at court in Aquitaine, a child of Richard's youth.

Richard reached the Holy Land in June 1191 and his forces helped conclude the siege of Acre, which had been deadlocked for almost two years, and where the besiegers were themselves besieged by Saladin's army. Richard however fell out with Duke Leopold of Austria, whom he insulted. Both Leopold and King Philippe of France soon returned home. Richard killed the prisoners taken at Acre and marched down the coast to Jaffa, winning a victory at Arsuf en route. However his forces were unable to penetrate inland to Jerusalem and, in September 1192, Richard was forced to conclude a three-year treaty with Saladin. Although Richard's Crusade failed in its prime objective, his exploits were amplified in their telling so that his English and French subjects elevated him to the status of a super-hero. In fact he was an extremely arrogant, petulant king, with a vicious temper and a total lack of moral scruples.

Richard returned to Europe in October 1192 but his ship was wrecked in the Adriatic and he was forced to travel across land. When he entered the territories of his enemy Leopold of Austria he apparently disguised himself as a woodsman, but he betrayed himself because of his fine gloves and was handed over to the Emperor Heinrich VI, who demanded a ransom of 150,000 marks. Richard was held captive for fifteen months while negotiations ensued and the ransom was raised. The negotiations were conducted by Richard's new justiciar, Hubert Walter, who had accompanied him to Palestine and who had arrived safely home. Hubert not only succeeded in raising the ransom but also quashed the attempted revolt by John to gain the throne. John's ineptitude nevertheless lost him lands in northern France. It is to this period that the romantic legend belongs of Richard's minstrel Blondel travelling from one castle to another in Austria and singing Richard's favourite song until he heard Richard sing back in response from the castle of Dürrenstein. Like most legends it probably has a core of truth.

Richard was eventually released and returned to England in March 1194. Despite John's treachery, Richard forgave him, merely admonishing him for acting like a child. He devoted the remaining years of his life to regaining his lost territories in France. He left for France in May 1194 and never returned to England. He seemed little concerned about the problems that his absence had caused elsewhere in Britain, particularly in Wales where warfare had broken out between the various rulers, and also in the Irish Sea where Ragnald of Man ruled as a pirate. Henry II had held these upstarts in check, but Richard showed no such interest.

Although Richard made peace with Philippe II on more than one occasion, war always broke out again. Nevertheless Richard reconquered all of his former territories and, in building new fortifications, left them stronger than before. He received an arrow wound during a skirmish at the castle of Chalus in the Limousin, and he died from the infection a few days later in April 1199. Richard spent his entire life as a warrior. He was an excellent soldier, fearless, brave and a great tactician, but he was useless at anything else. He left no heir, and had also spent a considerable fortune on his exploits. The English, in their usual way of preferring the legend to the facts, have long cherished the memory of a man who, in fact, had no interest in England other than as a source of revenue, and who was a ruthless fighting machine who made enemies of most of the royalty of Europe.

Berengaria survived Richard by over thirty years. She settled in Le Mans where she helped finance the construction of the Abbey of L'Epau where she was later buried. It is often stated that Berengaria was the only queen of England never to set foot in the country. She never did so during Richard's reign, but she made occasional visits after his death until she settled down as a nun at L'Epau.

JOHN LACKLAND
King of England: 6 April 1199–18 October 1216. Crowned: Westminster Abbey, 27 May 1199.

Titles: king of England, lord of Ireland (from 1177), count of Mortain (from 1189) and duke of Normandy (1199–1203).

Born: Beaumont Palace, Oxford, 24 December 1167. **Died**: Newark Castle, 18 October 1216, aged 48. **Buried**: Worcester Cathedral.

Married: (1) 29 August 1189, at Marlborough Castle, Isabella (c1175–1217), dau. of William, earl of Gloucester; divorced 1199: no children; (2) 24 August 1200, at Bordeaux Cathedral, Isabella (c1187–1246), dau. of Aymer Taillefer, count of Angoulême: 5 children. John also had at least twelve illegitimate children.

John was the youngest and favourite son of Henry II and Eleanor of Aquitaine. His mother was forty-five when he was born and she had already given birth to nine children. As the youngest child John had no immediate inheritance, Henry's patrimony having already been divided amongst his other children. John thus earned the nickname *Lackland*.

After Henry II's conquest of eastern Ireland in 1175, John was invested with the honorary title of king (later lord) of Ireland, though it carried no authority or land. In 1185 John was despatched to Ireland to conclude the conquest, but instead he alienated the native kings by ridiculing their dress and appearance, and angered his soldiers by spending their pay.

John was clearly a spoiled child, but he did not waste his childhood. He had received a good education and took a special interest in law and administration. He was the youngest male child by some eight years and there is little doubt that his elder brothers continued to treat him as a child. He did not get on with them particularly well and followed his own solitary pursuits. He became extremely petulant, but also shrewd, finding ways of achieving his own ends. His brothers, and others who knew him closely, found they could not trust him. When Richard left for the Crusades in 1190, he granted John sufficient territory in France in the hope it would keep him out of mischief, and ordered him not to set foot in England. But John's passion for power ruled his head and the moment Richard left, John determined to overthrow William Longchamp, whom Richard had left in charge. Richard heard of John's activities and sent Walter of Coutances to assist Longchamp. John was forced to retire to his estates but then paid homage to Philippe II of France, who had returned (ahead of Richard) from the Crusade in 1191. When Richard eventually returned to England in March 1194, John lost many of his lands in Normandy but Richard soon forgave him. Nevertheless with Richard close at hand, winning back his lands in France, John was not able to make more trouble. In fact he assisted Richard in his wars and Richard appointed him his heir.

When Richard died in 1199 John was accepted as king in

England, but not by the Angevin territories in France, who preferred his nephew Arthur of Brittany. Arthur, and his sister Eleanor, were the children of John's elder brother Geoffrey, and had stronger claims, on the principle of primogeniture, to the throne than John did. John's subsequent actions did not help the situation. Little over a year after his coronation he divorced his wife and married Isabella of Angoulême. Their marriage was tempestuous – both highly sexed and strong-willed, they were well matched – but the marriage was also the cause of John's downfall. She was already betrothed to Hugh de Lusignan, who complained to Philippe of France. He summoned John to answer the case but John refused, enabling Philippe to confiscate all John's lands in France. In the ensuing conflict, which broke out in the spring of 1202, John defended his lands admirably, including a mercy dash to save his besieged mother. Unfortunately John made a singular error of judgement in capturing and imprisoning Arthur and his sister. Arthur was never heard of again, but by Easter 1203 there were strong rumours that his mutilated body had been seen in the river Seine. Blame attached itself to John, with many believing he had killed Arthur in a fit of rage. Arthur's fate unsettled the barons in Brittany, Normandy and Anjou, and their distrust of John increased. John found it difficult to defend his lands. He escaped to England in December 1203, leaving his Norman subjects to their fate. He succeeded in negotiating a truce for two years thus enabling him to hold on to most of Poitou, but by 1206 he was forced to surrender all his territories north of the Loire.

John needed resources to re-establish an army to regain his French lands and though this was the main focus of his energies for the next few years he did not neglect the administration of England. It is unfortunate that John is remembered as a harsh king because to his subjects he was exceedingly fair, ensuring that the law was properly administered. In fact he was probably too fair, since he often angered his barons with his judgements against them in favour of their tenants. He further alienated the barons by levying severe taxes and strengthening the forest laws to increase his income. The most hated tax was 'scutage'. This was levied on

From the Charter Roll of Waterford

those barons who declined military service, which became increasingly common amongst those who had no lands in France and thus had no desire to fight abroad. Moreover many were less and less inclined to want to fight for John, and scutage became seen as an onerous punishment for their disloyalty. John did not seem to worry about annoying his barons. He had a good sense of humour and delighted in anything that ridiculed or deflated pomposity. This angered his barons even more, though John's common subjects found it a redeeming feature.

John's delight at challenging authority went a step too far, however, with the pope. In 1207 John rejected the new archbishop of Canterbury, Stephen Langton, and refused to accept the pope's injunction that Langton be re-installed. As a result in 1208 England was placed under an interdict that stopped all church services, and then John was excommunicated. This did not worry John because he used the opportunity to confiscate church revenues which provided much needed funds for his military endeavours. Between 1208 and 1211 John undertook several successful campaigns throughout Britain, which bought him time with his restless nobles. Campaigns in Scotland, Ireland and Wales during these years brought the rebellious lords and vassals to order and demonstrated that John did possess military skills. In fact John's defeat of Llywelyn The Great (see p. 95) in 1211 was perhaps his single most effective victory. He was able to exact severe tribute from these vassals to add to his growing treasury. John planned a further campaign in 1212 but by then other priorities took over. A rumoured murder plot, a threatened rebellion by his barons, a planned invasion by Philippe of France, and the threat of deposition by the pope made John reconsider his position. This was where he demonstrated his cunning. His negotiations with Pope Innocent III lifted the interdict on the basis that John would hold his lands as a fiefdom of the papacy. Innocent thereafter supported John in his actions against his barons, and even against Philippe.

John now had the finances and the papal support he needed. He had to capitalize on this by regaining his lands in France. His campaign, which began in July 1213, was initially successful. He routed the French fleet and won a number of battles. However, the following year, whilst campaigning in Poitou, John's allies were defeated at Bouvines in Flanders, which weakened John's position. He was forced to agree a peace treaty with France. In the eyes of the barons this was seen as a defeat. Their patience snapped. They rebelled openly and civil war broke out in May 1215. The hostilities were brief as John was betrayed. Within a month London fell. John met the rebels at Runnymede on 15 June 1215, where he was forced to sign a charter, agreeing to restore many of the rights that the church and barons believed they had lost, not just during John's reign but that of Henry II. This later became known as the Great Charter or *Magna Carta*. It was not so very earth-shattering at the time, but it rapidly became the symbol of the success of the barons over their oppressive king. John soon denounced the charter as having been signed under duress and was supported in his actions by the pope.

Civil war again broke out and this time the rebel barons

declared Louis, the son of Philippe of France, as their king. Louis was able to land at Sandwich in May 1216 and advance on London unopposed. John was forced to retreat. Although he retained much of the West Country, the rest of England was opposed to him. Campaigning in the Fens, he crossed the Wash and headed towards Lincoln, but misjudged the tides. His treasures and crown jewels were lost, and it must have seemed as if his kingdom was lost with them. He soon caught a fever, not helped by his over-eating, which led to dysentery. He died a few days later aged only forty-eight. There was some suggestion that he might have been poisoned. He was succeeded by his nine-year-old son Henry III. Queen Isabella retired to her estates in France where she married the son of her original lover, Hugh de Lusignan, and lived a further thirty years.

History has judged John rather more harshly than he deserves. He was a man who believed the world owed him something and created enemies by refusing to take authority seriously. But there were many who remained intensely loyal to him, otherwise there could not have been a civil war, and he certainly cared for England and the English more than his brothers or his father. It would be from him, and not from his brothers, that two of England's greatest kings, Edward I and Edward III, were to descend.

HENRY III
King of England: 18 October 1216–16 November 1272.
Crowned: Gloucester, 28 October 1216, and again at Westminster, 17 May 1220.
Titles: king of England, duke of Normandy (until 1259) and Aquitaine.
Born: Winchester Castle, 1 October 1207; Died: Westminster, 16 November 1272, aged 65. Buried: Westminster Abbey.
Married: 14 January 1236, at Canterbury Cathedral, Eleanor (c1223–1291), dau. of Raymond Berenger, count of Provence: 9 children.

Henry inherited the English throne at a difficult time. He was only nine years old. England was riven by civil war, with London and the south-east controlled by Louis, the son of the French king. It did not take long for the appointed regent, William Marshal, and the justiciar, Hubert de Burgh, however, to defeat the rebel barons and to bribe Louis into departing. Young Henry had been crowned in a makeshift ceremony at Gloucester Cathedral, where the royal family had fled. Because John had lost the crown jewels in the Wash during his Lincoln campaign, Henry was crowned with his mother's own bracelet or torque. Henry was fortunate in having William Marshal as his regent. William was probably the most respected man in England. He was a brave and valiant knight, the epitome of chivalry, and had loyally served Henry II, Richard and John. He vowed to carry the young king head-high on his shoulders rather than submit to French domination. By the time Marshal died in 1219, he had restored law and order to the kingdom. Young Henry was crowned again, this time with new regalia, at Westminster Abbey in May 1220. He was still only twelve, and would not assume authority for another seven years. With the passing of Marshal, Henry became the pawn of two men whose self-aggrandisement and poor advice would cause Henry's long reign to be regarded as weak and ineffectual. These men were Hubert de Burgh and Peter des Roches. De Burgh, who became regent after 1219, was an extremely able and talented soldier, and had served under both Richard and John. He continued the struggle against the barons and foiled the plot to capture Henry in 1223. However, de Burgh's actions in France were less successful, with Aquitaine being lost in 1224, though Gascony, the southern part of Aquitaine, was regained the following year.

Henry assumed direct rule in 1227, although Hubert de Burgh remained the chief justiciar until 1232. By then he and Henry had fallen out because Henry needed money to continue his campaigns to recover his territories in France. The royal treasury was almost empty. Henry accused the justiciar of using the money for his own endeavours and de Burgh was imprisoned. The main

architect of de Burgh's fall was his rival, Peter des Roches, bishop
of Winchester who, along with Stephen Segrave, now become the
equivalent of prime ministers in England. Des Roches was from
Poitou, which was no longer in English hands, thus the barons
became unsettled when des Roches filled most of the offices of his
state with his fellow Poitevins. England was coming under foreign
rule. Edmund Rich, archbishop of Canterbury, along with William Marshal's son, Richard (who had been declared a traitor
because of his opposition to des Roches's government) led a
delegation of barons to entreat Henry to expel the Poitevins.
Henry capitulated in 1234. He not only expelled the Poitevins,
but dismissed Roches and Segrave and took full government, into
his own hands. Henry had come to realize that he ignored the
authority and power of his barons at his peril. Even though Henry
had reaffirmed the terms of the Magna Carta, he did not particularly abide by them. He was essentially thoughtless in his views
of the barons, and rather than follow their counsel he began to fill
his court with others, mostly from France. This process was
accelerated after Henry's marriage to Eleanor, the daughter of
Raymond Berenger, count of Provence, in January 1236 and the
marriage of Eleanor's sister, Margaret, to Louis IX, the king of
France. Although this further angered the English barons it had a
remarkable effect upon English culture. France was at this time at
the height of literary and architectural art. French literature,
especially the chansons and romans de gestes, spilled over into
England, and the many chivalric romances, including those which
built the stories of king Arthur and his knights, came into their
final form during Henry's reign. It also saw a massive increase
in the building and restoration of churches, castles and other
religious houses in the Gothic art form. Many of our great historic
castles date in their existing form from this period. This includes
Westminster Abbey which was sumptuously restored and
improved for the coronation of Eleanor of Provence in 1236.

The seeds of discontent that grew between Henry and his
barons were now firmly sown and regularly watered. Not only
did Henry fail to recognize the rights and privileges of the barons,

From a contemporary document

turning instead to his own court favourites for their counsel and advice and showering them with honours, but he continued to place onerous tax obligations upon his barons, including the infamous scutage. The barons might have tolerated the latter had the money gone towards successful military campaigns, but this did not happen. Although Henry was not a good soldier, having lost most of his lands in France, he was a good negotiator. He established a strong alliance with Scotland in 1237 under the Treaty of York, which more or less established the existing boundary between England and Scotland; whilst the Treaty of Woodstock in 1247 established a similar arrangement with the Welsh princes. The reduction in border skirmishes meant that the marcher lords and northern barons could turn their attentions again to matters of state, and they did not like what they saw. In 1250 Henry took the Cross, determined to undertake a Crusade. This may have been a diversionary tactic to raise the spirit of his nobles. It did not work, however, because Henry never did embark upon his Crusade. Instead, influenced by the pope, he used the money raised for the Crusade to support the pope in his battle against Manfred, the usurping king of Sicily. In return the pope nominated Henry's young son, Edmund (known as Crouchback because of his deformity), as the king of Sicily, in

1254. The enterprise was, however, doomed and the pope eventually deprived Edmund of the title and bestowed it upon Charles of Anjou, Henry's brother-in-law, in 1266. In the meantime Henry had concluded the Treaty of Paris in 1259 with Louis IX of France, whereby he renounced his rights in Normandy, Maine and Anjou, but retained Gascony as a fiefdom subject to Louis.

As with his father, Henry was perceived by the barons as an inept king who taxed them to the hilt, ignored their counsel, and wasted resources on unsuccessful foreign campaigns. The Sicilian campaign was the final straw. Opposition to Henry was voiced first by the Marshal of England, Roger Bigod, earl of Norfolk, at the Council of Westminster in 1258, which was followed rapidly by what became called the Mad Parliament at Oxford. There Henry was forced to acknowledge a new charter known as the Provisions of Oxford, where he grudgingly agreed that the barons were allowed to select one half of the King's council, instead of the King having absolute discretion. Amongst these barons was Simon de Montfort, Henry's brother-in-law, with whom Henry's relationship had soured over the years. Simon was almost as high-handed and authoritarian as Henry, having caused an uprising in Gascony during his governorship. In 1260, when Henry returned from concluding the Treaty of Paris, he denounced de Montfort and overturned the Provisions of Oxford, obtaining papal support for his actions. The events of fifty years earlier repeated themselves and England slid into the abyss of civil war. Arbitration over the application of the provisions was made by Louis of France, who found in favour of the king in 1264.

In April, hostilities broke out. The baronial army was supported by the Welsh princes under Llywelyn ap Gruffydd. As we saw, Henry's supporters were initially successful, capturing Simon de Montfort's son (also called Simon) at Northampton in April 1264, but the elder de Montfort fought back and, in the Battle of Lewes on 14 May, defeated and captured Henry. The king was forced to call a parliament at which he acknowledged the barons' demands. During the course of the next year the barons, under de Montfort, succeeded in gaining the king's assent to most of their proposals. However, in July 1265, Henry's eldest son, Edward (later Edward I), escaped from custody and raised an army against de Montfort. At the ensuing battle of Evesham on 4 August 1265, de Montfort and his supporters were savagely defeated and Henry returned to power.

Henry now overturned all the acts forced upon him by the barons in the previous year and decreed grievous punishments against the barons and others who had sided with the revolution. Having exacted his revenge he became more conciliatory, granting certain privileges to the barons under the Treaty of Marlborough in 1267, and also recognizing Llywelyn as prince of Wales under the Treaty of Montgomery that same year. Henry retained his executive role and it would not be true to say that he granted the first parliament as we know it today. Nevertheless, the concessions of his final years went some way towards establishing a council of peers.

Now aged sixty, Henry began to suffer from approaching senility. He left much of the government to his son Edward and devoted his time to pursuing the arts, including completing the rebuilding of Westminster Abbey, which remains the greatest legacy of his day. He was apparently griefstricken at the death of his brother Richard in April 1272, and dementia overcame him. He died seven months later.

Henry had been king for a remarkable fifty-six years, the longest reign of any English monarch up to that time, although ten of those years were in his minority. Despite that length of reign, Henry III is rather a forgotten king. People are more likely to recognize the name Simon de Montfort and know of his rebellion than to know anything about Henry III. This serves to demonstrate the weakness of Henry's character and his inability to govern strongly, but he was not all bad. He believed in his absolute right to rule, and was unsympathetic to his barons, but he was pious, loving (a devoted family man) and preferred to seek peace wherever possible rather than wage war. Although that may have damned him in the eyes of his barons, it encour-

Uniting the Kingdoms

KINGDOMS STILL DIVIDED

WALES (1246–84)

In Wales, as we have seen the greatest of the Welsh rulers Llywelyn the Great, acknowledged ruler of Wales from 1216, had endeavoured to secure the succession for his descendants, but everything crumbled after his death in 1240. Llywelyn ap Gruffydd would seek to hold the kingdom together but would meet his death fighting in 1282. With the Statute of Wales, issued by Edward I on 19 March 1284, Wales would pass under the government of England, and the direct rule of its king, who would, for ever afterwards, appoint his own son as the new prince of Wales.

Llywelyn was the last native ruler of Wales. The sudden death of his uncle, Dafydd ap Llywelyn, just as events had turned in his favour had enabled Henry III to sweep through Wales, meeting no organized resistance and, one by one, the minor princes had submitted to him. The Treaty of Woodstock on 30 April 1247 concluded the affair and saw Llywelyn and his elder brother **Owain, the senior princes of Gwynedd, also submit to Henry.**

LLYWELYN (II) AP GRUFFYDD (*LLYWELYN THE LAST*)

Gwynedd (west Gwynedd from 25 February 1246, effectively 30 April 1247) June 1255–11 December 1282; styled Prince of Wales from 1258.

Born: *date unknown, but probably c1225.* **Died:** *11 December 1282, aged about 57.* **Buried:** *Cwm Hir Abbey.*

Married: *13 October 1278 at Worcester, Eleanor, dau. Simon de Montfort; 1 daughter.*

The Treaty had been severe. Henry invoked many clauses from previous agreements and reclaimed vast areas of Wales directly for the crown, including some territory that had been lost since the reign of Owain Gwynedd, a century earlier. These lands were incorporated as part of England in perpetuity. Moreover, whilst Henry still respected Welsh law, the Treaty had brought with it certain obligations which required the recognition of English law. Any lasting vestige of Welsh autonomy had been quashed. Owain and Llywelyn were allowed to administer Gwynedd, which now consisted of Anglesey and the few *cantrefi* on the adjacent mainland, as vassals to Henry.

However, Llywelyn had more political acumen than Henry gave him credit. Over the next eight years he entered into a series of secret alliances with neighbouring princes ensuring their support. In June 1255 he met his brothers Owain and Dafydd in battle at Bryn Derwin. They were defeated and imprisoned and Llywelyn became sole ruler of Gwynedd. The following year Llywelyn called in his support and his new alliance conquered East Gwynedd, ejecting its English lords. Over the next two years, Llywelyn swept through Wales reclaiming all the territory lost to Henry. Although Henry attempted a punitive expedition in August 1257, it failed dismally and Henry, already in serious trouble at home with his barons, was forced to reach an agreement with Llywelyn in 1258 which granted him authority over the conquered lands. At that point Llywelyn declared himself

'Prince of Wales', and the native princes transferred their fealty from Henry to him. Under the Peace of Montgomery, agreed with Henry III in 1267, Llywelyn was recognized as the sovereign of Wales. Wales (which at this time still excluded some of the territories in the south) for the first and only time had become a single sovereign state. In the decade leading up to 1267, Llywelyn had allied himself to Simon de Montfort, and this resulted in considerable gains as Llywelyn took control of much land in the Welsh Marches. Llywelyn also contracted to marry de Montfort's daughter, Eleanor, in 1265.

After de Montfort's death, as Llywelyn endeavoured to consolidate his principality into a more unified whole, it became increasingly apparent that his territories were held together more by fear and the strength of his own personality than by any inherent loyalties. His actions to sustain law and order became increasingly severe, and respect for the prince visibly evaporated. Also the lack of an heir fuelled factionalism. In 1274 a plot against his life by his brother Dafydd and Gruffydd ap Gwenwynwyn of southern Powys was uncovered; the two conspirators fleeing to England. Llywelyn promptly overran Gruffydd's lands. That year saw a new king on the throne of England, Edward I, who openly supported the two princes. Edward did not initially plan to enter into conflict with Llywelyn – the two in fact had a high degree of respect for each other. However, Llywelyn's failure to attend Edward's coronation in 1274 or pay homage to Edward, despite several demands, angered Edward irretrievably. Moreover, Llywelyn's high-handedness towards the church in wanting a share of revenues caused as much dissension among church officials, as other actions did among his lords and subjects. The last straw came when Llywelyn refused to pay homage in 1276, despite Edward travelling to Chester. In reaction Edward stopped Llywelyn's bride-to-be, Eleanor de Montfort, travelling to Wales and detained her at Windsor. Llywelyn's hot-headedness and pride made it impossible for him to climb down and the two were set on a collision course. In November 1276 Llywelyn was declared a rebel and hostilities began. Edward

From a picture in the National of Wales

knew he could soon turn the dissension amongst the Welsh to his advantage. His first test of the Welsh borders in 1276 saw resistance crumble immediately in northern Powys where its prince, Llywelyn ap Gruffydd ap Madog promptly changed his allegiance to Edward. Edward's progress through Wales was systematic and clinical. Within a year Llywelyn was forced to submit and, under the Treaty of Aberconwy, he was relegated to ruling only the heartland of Gwynedd, west of the Conway. Although he retained the title 'Prince of Wales', it was meaningless. He was also forced to share that kingdom again with his brother Owain, who was resettled in the cantref of Llyn in 1278.

Although humiliated, Llywelyn maintained his dignity. He treated Edward with the utmost respect and endeavoured to maintain amicable relations, while also seeking to regain his hold on Wales. Over the next four years he began to re-cement relationships with the various princes across Wales. In some cases he was successful; in others woefully unsuccessful. Territorial disputes, especially with Gruffydd ap Gwenwynwyn, who had been restored by Edward in southern Powys, began to fray Llywelyn's temper. Throughout this period Wales was in uneasy humour, uncertain over the degree to which they should support Llywelyn or respect Edward. In the end it was the inevitable unrestrained irresponsibility of Llywelyn's brother Dafydd that sealed the fate of Wales. Dafydd, in league with Llywelyn ap

Gruffydd ap Madog of Powys, ravaged the borders around Oswestry in March 1282. Whether or not Llywelyn was himself aware of the revolt, he was soon caught up in it and had no other choice but to become its leader. Edward was outraged and, though he had to react swiftly, he planned his strategy with cool deliberation, marshalling forces that would be powerful enough to resolve the matter once and for all. It was a much harder struggle than in 1277, but Edward was relentless. Victory would almost certainly have been his, even if Llywelyn himself had not been killed in December 1282. He was killed, not in a pitched battle, but in a scuffle by an opportunist who did not realise at the time who he was. The war continued for four more months under the command of Dafydd, but in April 1283 he surrendered at Castell y Bere and was imprisoned. In October he was executed for treason. With the Statute of Wales, issued on 19 March 1284, Wales passed under the government of England. All the local princes were dispossessed, and the political face of Wales was changed for ever, the old kingdoms replaced by new counties and a provincial administration run by a governor-general.

Llywelyn's daughter, Gwenllian, was sent to a nunnery where she remained till she died in 1337. Dafydd's daughters were likewise consigned to nunneries while his two sons were imprisoned for the rest of their lives: Llywelyn died in 1288; Owain, some time after 1305. Alone of all the royal family, Rhodri ap Gruffydd, who had sold his inheritance to Llywelyn as early as 1272, lived on as a lord of the manor in Surrey and in Cheshire, dying in 1315. His grandson, Owain ap Thomas ap Rhodri, who lived much of his life in France, held pretensions to invade Wales and reclaim the principality. He received a modicum of support at the time, and there were even rumours of an invasion between 1369 and 1372, but his plans came to nothing and he was assassinated in 1378. The only successful attempt to regain the principality would come under Owain Glyn Dwr in 1400, during the reign of Henry IV.

SCOTLAND (1214–1371)

Although William the Lyon had successfully wrested back Scotland from the English, succeeding monarchs – Alexander II, Alexander III, Margaret, Maid of Norway and John Balliol – had over the years once more become tied into a state of fealty to the English crown. Had Alexander III, who had been a strong monarch, not met such an untimely death by riding over a cliff at the age of forty-four, things might have worked out differently, but after his demise, his strong realm was plunged into a period of darkness that would lead to war.

Scotland at this time was still a land divided. The authority of the Scottish kings effectively covered the lowlands and the Borders plus much of the eastern seaboard. Orkney, Shetland and the Western Isles, as far south as the Isle of Man, were still answerable to the king of Norway, whilst the Highlands on the mainland, where the people were Gaelic speaking, regarded themselves as independent even if recognizing the authority of the crown. The Isle of Man had always had a degree of independence especially since it became the base of the formidable Godred Crovan in 1079. A few generations later Somerled established his own Kingdom of the Isles in 1156. Both of these rulers and their successors acknowledged the sovereignty of Norway, not Scotland. Their lands remained separate kingdoms until they were officially ceded to Scotland under the Treaty of Perth of 2 July 1266. This followed the defeat of the Norse at the Battle of Largs three years earlier and the subsequent subjugation of the islands and mainland territories by Alexander III. Alexander later invested the title of Lord of the Isles in the head of the Macdonald family and over the next two centuries these lords would operate as if they were kings in their own right, frequently opposing the Scottish monarch. Orkney remained under Norse sovereignty until 20 May 1469.

In the meantime the kingdom of Scotland itself came under threat with the death, on 26 September 1290, of Margaret, known as the Maid of Norway, the infant queen of Scotland. There was no immediate successor to the throne though there were no shortage of claimants. The Scottish lords agreed that Edward I of England would arbitrate upon the final shortlist of thirteen claimants. There followed an interregnum of over two years whilst the English king and his judges decided. In the meantime Edward took advantage of the situation by claiming the Isle of Man for England in 1290 and apart from efforts by Scotland to reclaim it in 1293 and again in 1313, it remained an English territory thereafter.

On 17 November 1292 Edward I would nominate John Balliol as Scottish king, a justifiable decision but one also convenient to Edward as Balliol had strong English sympathies. Balliol subsequently cast off the English yoke but following his defeat at Dunbar he would be forced to abdicate in July 1296. Edward set about bringing Scotland under English control and his first act was to remove the Stone of Destiny from Scone and bring it to Westminster. In effect he had taken the heart out of Scotland. Distracted by problems with France, Edward was unable to hammer home his advantage straightaway with the consequence that there was time for rebellion to ferment in Scotland, first under William Wallace and then under Robert Bruce. Edward I would die without seeing Scotland absorbed into England even though he had proceeded as far as preparing a new constitution. His son, Edward II, was a much weaker ruler and after his defeat at Bannockburn in June 1314, Scotland was lost to the English. It was not, however, till the Treaty of Northampton on 4 May 1328 that the English formally recognized the sovereign independence of Scotland.

Robert Bruce applied to the Pope for recognition of Scotland as a sovereign state with the authority to anoint its monarchs. The Scottish kings had no such right previously and this had always made them secondary to the English kings in the eyes of the Church. Pope John XXII granted this right to Robert on 13 June 1329, though unfortunately for Robert he had died six days earlier and did not know of his success. Nevertheless the combination of the

Treaty of Northampton and the papal bull meant that Robert's successor, David II, was the first Scottish king to be crowned and anointed as monarch of an independent sovereign state.

ROBERT (I) *THE BRUCE*
Ruled 25 March 1306–7 June 1329. Crowned: Scone Abbey, 27 March 1306.
Titles: *king of Scotland; earl of Carrick (from 1292), lord of Annandale (from 1304).*
Born: *Turnberry Castle, 11 July 1274.* **Died**: *Cardross Castle, Dumbarton, 7 June 1329, aged 54.* **Buried**: *Dunfermline Abbey (though his heart was buried at Melrose Abbey).*
Married: *(1) c1295, Isabella, dau. Donald, earl of Mar: 1 child; (2) c1302, Elizabeth (d. 1327), dau. Robert de Burgh, earl of Ulster and Connaught: 4 children.*

The ancestor of Robert the Bruce was a Norman knight, also called Robert, who accompanied William the Conqueror on his invasion in 1066. This Robert de Bruis, who took his name from his family estates at Bruis near Cherbourg, received extensive lands in Yorkshire. His son, also called Robert, was made lord of Annandale by David I of Scotland in 1124. This Robert's grandson, another Robert, married David's great-granddaughter Isabel in 1220. Their son, Robert le Brus (1210–1295) was at one time heir to the throne and competitor for the crown of Scotland against John Balliol in 1292. His son, Robert (1243–1304) was the father of the famous Robert the Bruce, who succeeded him as lord of Annandale in 1304.

Robert would originally swear fealty to Edward I of Scotland in 1296, when he inherited the title of Earl of Carrick. His father had sought the Scottish crown from Edward, but had been refused. Robert would remain loyal to Edward until 1297, when he supported the revolt of William Wallace. After Wallace's defeat in 1298, Edward laid waste to Robert's lands. Nevertheless he made his peace with Edward and in 1299 Robert was made one of the four regents of Scotland. Robert's pride made it difficult for him to work alongside his co-regent John Comyn, the son of another competitor of 1292 and a descendant of Duncan III, but they needed to work together. In 1305 Edward executed Wallace and prepared an ordinance for the governance of Scotland. Its independence was soon to be a thing of the past. In February 1306 Bruce and Comyn met at Greyfriars church in Dumfries, endeavouring to resolve their rival claims to the throne and to plan a course of action against Edward. An argument followed in which Robert stabbed Comyn, who subsequently died. Robert knew he would be excommunicated and would thereby lose his right to the throne. Rather than flee, he acted on impulse and hurriedly gathered his supporters together and within six weeks had crowned himself king of Scotland. His support was far from complete. There were many who regarded him as a young hothead, but there were enough to rally round him as a symbol of Scottish kingship. Robert had been present at the execution of William Wallace and knew what would happen if he failed. He was therefore determined to succeed, regardless of the odds.

At first luck went against him. He was defeated by the earl of Pembroke who captured Perth and drove Bruce west into Atholl. Bruce was defeated again soon after by Comyn's uncle, Macdougal of Loarn, who forced Bruce further west, until he was driven out of Scotland and sought refuge on the Isle of Rathlin off the Irish coast. It is at this time that the memorable legend arose of Bruce hiding in a cave and, being inspired by a spider defiantly re-weaving its web against the weather, to resolve 'if at first you don't succeed, try, try again.'

Robert rallied. Early in 1307 he surprised the English at Carrick, who had garrisoned his own castle of Turnberry, and later that year defeated Pembroke at Loudon Hill. Edward I marched against Bruce but died before reaching Scotland. The campaign would be prematurely abandoned by his son, Edward II, and Bruce went from strength to strength. Over the next six years the English garrisons were driven out of Scotland. By 1314 only two castles remained in English hands: Berwick and Stirling. The governor of Stirling promised to hand over the castle unless the English sent reinforcements by 24 June. This galvanized Edward II into belated action. His forces arrived and engaged the Scottish at Bannockburn on 24 June 1314. This was one of the Scot's greatest victories. Edward's force of over 20,000 men were totally defeated by Robert's army of half its number.

Although skirmishes continued for the next decade, Robert's victory allowed a degree of respite in the hostilities. Robert even had time to support his brother, Edward, who had been made high king of Ireland in May 1316, but who was killed at the Battle of Dundall in October 1318. Edward Bruce was, for a time, recognized as Robert's heir. One might imagine the possibilities had Scotland's king also been high king of Ireland. After Edward's death the succession passed to Robert's infant grandson, the child of his daughter Marjorie and Walter, the steward of Scotland. Although this child later ruled as Robert II, Robert the Bruce eventually sired his own heir, David II.

Robert still needed to make his peace with the pope, who had excommunicated him. By 1320 the Scots had compiled what became known as the Declaration of Arbroath, which not only established the sovereignty of Scotland but defined Robert's right to the throne. It has been described as 'the most remarkable statement of nationalism in medieval Europe'. It took Pope John XXII eight years to reach a decision. He eventually lifted his excommunication in 1328 and recognized Robert's right to the kingship. The same year saw the Treaty of Northampton between Robert and Edward III of England, which also recognized the independence of Scotland.

In the intervening years when not fighting, Robert had done his best to bring law and order back to a country rent by civil unrest. He instigated a major rebuilding programme and sought to re-establish trade. Scotland at last began to be restored. In early 1329 Robert prepared to set off for the Holy Land, but he died of leprosy before leaving Scotland. Although he was buried at Dunfermline, his heart was carried on the Crusade to atone for his sins and was eventually returned to Scotland and interred at Melrose Abbey. The young hothead and turncoat had become the saviour of Scotland and was long after remembered as 'Good King Robert'.

DAVID II

Ruled 7 June 1329–August 1332 (deposed); restored 16 December 1332–March 1333 (deposed); restored 1336–22 February 1371. Crowned: Scone Abbey, 24 November 1331. **Born***: Dunfermline Palace, 5 March 1324.* **Died***: Edinburgh Castle, 22 February 1371, aged 46.* **Buried***: Holyrood Abbey.* **Married***: (1) 17 July 1328, at Berwick, Joanna (1321–62), dau Edward II of England: no children; (2) 13 (?) February 1364, at Inchmahome Priory, Aberfoyle, Margaret (d.1375), dau. Sir Malcolm Drummond; divorced 20 March 1370: no children.*

David was Robert (I), the Bruce's only son, and was only five when his father died. He had already been married to Joanna, the sister of Edward III of England, since July 1328. He was four, she was seven. Although they remained married for thirty-four years, they had no children and it was, apparently, a loveless marriage. This was symbolic of David's early life where, for much of the time, he was a puppet controlled by other forces. This made him a rather dissolute youth who took some while to live up to the expectations others had of him. Of particular significance, though, was David's coronation. Although he was only seven, and probably not that aware of the import, he was the first king of Scotland to be anointed with the symbol of papal approval, and to be crowned jointly with his wife. Nevertheless, it did him little good. Nine months later his forces were defeated by those of Edward Balliol (son of John) who, supported by Edward III, had sought to regain what he believed was his rightful inheritance. Although Edward was crowned in September 1332, he was deposed three months later and David was restored. The overthrow of Balliol allowed

Edward III to act. He invaded Scotland, defeating all opposition at Halidon Hill on 19 July 1333. At this stage David was taken for safety to the court of Philippe VI of France. Although he was restored to the throne in 1336, he remained in exile in France until it was felt safe for his return to Scotland in 1341, when he was seventeen.

An uneasy peace ensued for the next five years. By then the French were at war with the English and asked the Scots for assistance. David invaded England but was defeated by the forces of Archbishop William de la Zouche at Neville's Cross, near Durham, on 17 October 1346. David fought valiantly but was captured and held prisoner in England for the next eleven years. His nephew, Robert, remained steward of Scotland during this period when, to all intents and purposes, Scotland was subservient to England. Nevertheless, Edward's war with France meant his attention was elsewhere and the governance of Scotland continued unhindered. David was eventually released in 1357 under the terms of the Treaty of Berwick, whereby David had to pay Edward the staggering sum of 100,000 merks (about £67,000) in ten equal instalments. This was never fully paid, but David paid occasional instalments as and when it was necessary to stave off the ambitious Edward. David even proposed that Edward's second son, Lionel, should succeed him as king of Scotland, should David die childless. The Scottish Parliament rejected this proposal, and the death of Lionel in 1368 brought an end to the idea, but it was another factor in David's attempts to hold Edward at bay. Nevertheless whenever David sought to impose a tax to raise the instalments for the ransom he was met with outright rebellion, particularly from John, the lord of the Isles. It required considerable negotiation, mostly by Robert the Steward, to restore an alliance. David did his best to re-establish the financial and civil strength of Scotland, despite the depredations of the Black Death which had severely reduced the population of Scotland and England whilst David was in captivity. Although David was never held in such esteem as his father, his final years showed that he was not totally the weak or inadequate king as he was later remembered. He just had the misfortune at living at the same time as Edward III, one of Europe's strongest monarchs. Robert died childless in 1371 and he was succeeded by his nephew, Robert, the first king of the Stewart dynasty.

THE HOUSE OF ANJOU
(part II: 1272–1399)

The Angevins' rule for a further 120 years in many ways marked a grim period for the ordinary man. Not only were there the invasions into Wales and Scotland to quell uprisings, and the Hundred Years' War with France, but the climate of the fourteenth century turned to one of constant rain, which in turn fostered pandemics of the plague which raged across Europe in 1348–9 and again in 1361, 1375 and 1390. There were two types of plague: the pneumonic plague, which spread by droplet infection like the common cold, and the Black Death carried by flea-infested rats. Within the space of a few years, the kingdoms of Britain had lost a third of their population: some one and a half million people succumbed. Now there were fewer people left to pay taxes, fewer revenues for the royal coffers, despite the sovereign's extravagant lifestyle, though wages for those skilled craftsmen who had survived rose. In 1381 the poorer classes revolted: in town and countryside, in separate outbreaks virtually all over the country. The immediate reason was the poll tax, brought about by the heavy costs of war. This was imposed no less than three times within the space of a few years, and rose from four pence to one shilling a head. But discontent had also been festering for a long time about the obligations which the peasants owed to the lords of the manors.

For the nobility and those at court, however, it was a time of increasing wealth and cultural splendour. The wool trade began to expand rapidly in the mid fourteenth century, bringing enormous prosperity. Although nobility was largely by descent, wealth became a yardstick for social class, whereby, for example, only those with annual incomes exceeding £40 could apply to become a knight. And in 1460 an Act of Parliament was passed laying down rules for the type of dress and quality of cloth that could be used by each social class.

The notion of chivalry with its elegance and strict codes of courtly behaviour had spread throughout Europe, and the first works of literature in vernacular English were being written by William Langland and Geoffrey Chaucer (whose wife's sister was first John of Gaunt's mistress, then his wife). With Wyclif's translation of the Bible into English, the use of English rather than French or Latin was soon to mean that literacy was no longer only the prerogative of the court and the clergy.

EDWARD (I) *LONGSHANKS*
Ruled 16 November 1272–7 July 1307. Crowned:
Westminster Abbey, 19 August 1274.
Titles*: king of England, Wales (from 1284), Man (from 1290),*
Scotland (from 1296), lord of Ireland, duke of Gascony (from
1254), earl of Chester (from 1254).
Born*: Palace of Westminster, 17 June 1239. **Died***: Burgh-on-Sands,
*near Carlisle, 7 July 1307, aged 68. **Buried***: Westminster Abbey.
Married*: (1) October 1254, at Las Huelgas, Castile, Eleanor*
(1241–90), dau. of Ferdinand III, king of Castile: 16 children; (2) 10
September 1299, at Canterbury Cathedral, Margaret (c1279–1318)
dau. of Philippe III, king of France: 3 children. Edward is reputed to
have had one illegitimate child, although the claim is suspect.

Edward I is certainly the greatest of the Plantagenet kings of England and one of the most important of all English kings. The soubriquets applied to him give some indication of his abilities: 'the Lawgiver', 'the Hammer of the Scots', 'the Father of the Mother of Parliaments', 'the English Justinian', let alone his personal nickname of Longshanks, which was not derogatory. Edward was a tall man, healthy, strong and immensely powerful, a born soldier.

He was the eldest son of Henry III, born when his father had already reigned for over twenty years. Thanks to his father's long reign, Edward was able to ascend to the throne in the flower of his manhood. Thankfully he had also matured, for his youth, whilst spent as part of a loving family, was also tempestuous. In 1254, when only fifteen, he was married to Eleanor, the infanta of Castile, who was barely thirteen. Her name would be given to many inns and taverns, one of which, in south London became corrupted into the Elephant and Castle. It was a political marriage in order to protect the southern borders of Gascony, England's last possession in France, the governship of which had been in the hands of Simon de Montfort. Edward was invested as duke of Gascony at the time of his marriage, and acknowledged his fealty to the French king, the sainted Louis IX. However, Edward's command of Gascony does not seem to have been any less turbulent than De Montfort's. It appears Edward ruled with a strong hand and was not averse to severe retribution if any of his subjects challenged his authority.

At the same time (1254) Edward had been invested with lands in Wales and Ireland, and his first experience of warfare came in the uprisings in Wales when in 1256 the Welsh, under Llywelyn ap Gruffydd, rebelled against the English imposition of a system of county administration. Peace was rapidly concluded because Henry III was facing his own internal problems in the rebellion of the barons. Edward initially sided with Simon de Montfort in producing the Provisions of Westminster in 1259, but later supported his father in the war that broke out in 1264. It was Edward who captured the younger Simon de Montfort at Northampton, but it was also Edward's youthful rashness that led to his capture alongside his father at the battle of Lewes later that year. As we have seen, Edward succeeded in escaping his custody a year later and in August 1265 routed and killed the elder De Montfort at the battle of Evesham. Henry's retribution on the disaffected barons was severe and those who were disinherited fought back from a stronghold at Ely in 1267. It was Edward who overpowered the barons, and it was his military skill and show of strength that helped bring peace to England by 1269.

Edward was now thirty and, in 1270, set out on a long-awaited Crusade to the Holy Land. Although his escapades were not entirely glorious, there was much derring-do suitable for later retellings in adventure stories. Edward succeeded in relieving Acre from one of its many sieges by the troops of the sultan of Egypt, and won a victory at Haifa, but he was also wounded by a poisoned dagger wielded by an Assassin. Had he died English history would have been significantly different, and there would certainly have been a succession crisis with no adult heir. Edward recovered, however; this was later said to be thanks to his wife who sucked the poison from the wound. He was in Sicily on his way home when, in November 1272, he learned of his father's death. It is an indication of how confident Edward was in his English regents that he did not hurry home. Instead he travelled triumphantly through Italy as a Crusader hero and new king, and on through France to pay homage to the new French king, Philippe III. He eventually returned to England on 2 August 1274, with his coronation held seventeen days later.

The coronation was a momentous occasion, but a small cloud over it would cast a long shadow. Llywelyn ap Gruffydd, the prince of Wales, failed to attend to pay homage. Edward commanded him to attend his court on two later occasions and even travelled to Chester in 1276 to make it easier. When Llywelyn rebuffed him for a third time, Edward acted with lightning effect. He declared Llywelyn a rebel and thus anyone supporting him would be a traitor.

Edward brought his forces into Powys and opposition immediately crumbled. He was able to penetrate into Gwynedd and force Llywelyn into submission. Under the Treaty of Aberconwy in November 1277, Llywelyn retained the now hollow title of Prince of Wales, and held authority over only Gwynedd, west of the Conway, which he was forced to share with his brother. Llywelyn, though humiliated, endeavoured to remain respectful of Edward to the extent that in October 1278 Edward allowed the long promised marriage between Llywelyn, and his cousin, Eleanor, the daughter of Simon de Montfort. This arrangement had been made in 1265, when Eleanor was only thirteen. Unfortunately Eleanor died in childbirth four years later, just at the time that actions by Llywelyn's brother Dafydd caused a further rebellion in Wales and Llywelyn, possibly against his will, was forced back into the limelight. Edward, believing he had previously treated Llywelyn with surprising leniency, was furious. Although the Welsh offered more resistance than in 1278, Edward was able to call upon much greater resources than the Welsh. Victory was almost certain to be Edward's, but it was made more complete when Llywelyn was killed in a skirmish in December 1282. His renegade brother held out for a further four months but was arrested in April 1283 and executed for treason six months later.

Edward was no longer prepared to tolerate the perpetual hostility from the Welsh. On 19 March 1284 the Statute of Wales was enacted, bringing Wales under the direct government of England. Wales now held the status of a colony of the Crown, and justice was administered by three sheriffs. Edward also set up a series of new lordships, some of which were granted to the dispossessed Welsh princes, but others to Edward's own barons. In June 1284 Edward celebrated his conquest of Wales by holding an Arthurian Round Table court at Nefyn. The festivities were so well attended that the floor of the court gave way under the strain. One of the legends attached to this period is that Edward promised he would grant them a prince who had been born on their own soil, and promptly presented to them his infant son, Edward, who had been born at Caernarvon. Edward was not officially invested as prince of Wales until February 1301.

From the Cotton MS, British Library

The Welsh exploits were but one chapter of Edward's early reign, though a significant one. Much of his energy was directed toward a survey of England and a reformation of feudal jurisdictions in the country's legal system. Soon after his coronation he despatched commissioners throughout his kingdom to establish who held what authority over what land and whether there had been any abuse of power. Hitherto barons holding lands in fief from the king had often administered the king's laws within their territories, but many abused this privilege. In many cases barons claimed this had been their right since time immemorial, because they were unable to produce charters granting them such authority. Edward recognized that authority granted in the time of Henry II (his great grandfather) was early enough to qualify as time immemorial, particularly given the unstable years of Stephen and Matilda's civil war, but anything more recent had to be supported by written evidence. With this established Edward was able to put the collection of taxes and other revenues on a much firmer footing, and he was also enabled to reconstruct his authority and that of his barons in a more clearly codified set of laws. Edward needed clarity over his revenues to enable him to finance his extensive military campaigns. This time, however, he determined to appease the barons by gaining their assent to his tax collection.

The combination of tax and legislative reforms in consultation with his peers was what brought about the evolution of government by Parliament. A Great Council had met since the time of John, but it did not have the representative element of a formal Parliament. With his Statute of Westminster in 1275 Edward inaugurated reforms which led, over the next twenty years, to the establishment of a formal parliament. During this process Edward was quick to punish those who had abused their authority. In this way Edward endeared himself to the commoners of England, who saw him as their saviour. The one group to which Edward did not endear himself was the Jews. In 1278 he had passed an enactment which allowed all Jews in England to be arrested on the grounds of coin-clipping. Some 280 of them were hanged. The Jews had been one of the main alternative sources of income in England, but the Crusades had brought a reaction against them. While barons and royalty were keen to borrow their money, they had no desire to repay it and even introduced laws to stop the Jews claiming land in forfeit for non-payment. By Edward's reign the Jews were themselves becoming impoverished and the rising tide of nationalism in England increased the public antipathy to them. In 1290 Edward expelled all of the Jews from England, over 16,000 of them, on the grounds of usury. Thereafter the merchants became royal creditors, especially those from Venice and Lombardy in Italy.

Edward had long set his eyes on the conquest of Scotland. An opportunity arose in 1290 when Margaret, the infant queen of Scotland (and Edward's great-niece) died. Edward had previously agreed with Alexander III (King of Scotland 1249–1286) that the young queen would marry his son and heir Edward, which he hoped would lead to the union of England and Scotland. Margaret's death scuppered that plan, but Edward was now consulted by the Scottish magnates to adjudicate over the succession. In 1292, Edward eventually nominated John Balliol, a fair decision, but also a weaker choice than the other primary candidate, Robert le Brus, and one whom Edward could more easily dominate. Nevertheless over the next few years the Scots grew tired of

John as a spineless pawn of Edward and incited him into rebellion in 1295. This came as a result of a difficult set of circumstances which now plagued Edward. In 1294 the French king Philippe IV had taken possession of Gascony. Edward had summoned a parliament to approve the collection of taxes for his campaign against France, but there was considerable resentment, especially north of the border where the Scots were expected to pay a tax for a war against the French, whom they regarded as their ally. At that same time, in October 1294, the Welsh took advantage of the French diversion to rebel, with Madog ap Llywelyn declaring himself prince of Wales. Edward was now facing rebellion on three fronts. It is evidence of his mastery of the situation that he was able to resolve all three in quick succession. From December 1294 to March 1295 he led his armies into Wales, defeated all opposition and slaughtered the main ringleaders. Back in England Edward summoned the first Model Parliament, which consisted of representatives of all three estates: the church, the barons and the shires and towns. With the agreement of this parliament he was able to raise further revenues and enact plans for his campaigns in Scotland and France. Edward took his forces north, sacked and plundered Berwick in March 1296 and defeated John Balliol at Dunbar on 27 April. John surrendered two months later and was imprisoned in the Tower of London. Edward proudly seized the symbol of Scottish kingship, the Stone of Scone, which he brought south to Westminster, where it would remain for seven hundred years. Edward now believed he had conquered Scotland and left three magnates in authority. He needed to turn his attention to France. Parliament was less keen to raise further revenues for a French campaign, but regardless Edward sailed for France in 1297 and, through the intervention of the pope, was able to make a truce with France whereby he also regained control of Gascony. Thus in the space of two years Edward had held his possessions on two fronts and extended them on a third. The Scottish advance, however, was more chequered than Edward had anticipated. His three administrators proved unequal to their task and the tyrannical oppression of one of them,

William Ormsby, had stirred the Scots back into revolt under William Wallace. Edward now led a further army north, defeating Wallace at Falkirk on 22 July 1298.

Over the next few years Edward sought the total subjugation of the Scots. His many campaigns, which culminated in the capture and execution of Wallace in August 1305, seemed to deliver Scotland firmly into his hands. And yet, even as he was in the process of confirming a constitution for Scotland another rebellion erupted, this time under Robert the Bruce. Despite his age and increasing infirmity, Edward prepared for a further campaign. He marched north and was in sight of Scotland when he died of dysentery at Burgh-on-Sands near Carlisle in July 1307. Edward believed he had conquered the Scots and thus must have died disappointed at not seeing his vision complete. Nevertheless, unlike any ruler before him (and most since), he had the skill, strength and authority to undertake the task and failed ultimately only by his underestimation of the strength of the Scottish spirit.

Edward's first wife, Eleanor, had died in 1290 of a fever near Grantham while she was travelling north to meet Edward in Scotland. Edward had been devoted to her and was sorely grieved at her death. As her body was conveyed back to London, he established crosses at the sites where her body rested each night. There were originally twelve of these, of which the best known were at Waltham and Charing Cross. Eleanor had borne Edward sixteen children, the most from one legitimate union to any king of England. However few of these survived infancy and only four of them outlived Edward. Three of these were daughters, but the fourth was Eleanor's youngest son Edward. King Edward had remarried in 1299, this time to Margaret the sister of Philippe IV of France. It was another political marriage yet, although Edward was sixty and Margaret scarcely twenty, the match seemed to work, and Margaret bore Edward three more children.

Although Edward failed to conquer Scotland, his conquest of Wales has left its mark on Britain ever since, though possibly his most lasting legacy was the firm establishment of Parliament. He would be succeeded by his son Edward.

EDWARD II
Ruled 8 July 1307–25 January 1327 (abdicated). Crowned: Westminster Abbey, 25 February 1308.
Titles: *king of England and Scotland, lord of Ireland; prince of Wales (from 1301), duke of Aquitaine (from 1306).*
Born: *Caernarvon Castle, 25 April 1284.* **Died** *(murdered): Berkeley Castle, Gloucestershire, 21 September 1327, aged 43.*
Buried: *Gloucester Cathedral.*
Married: *25 January 1308, at Boulogne Cathedral, Isabella (c1292–1358) dau. of Philippe IV, king of France: 4 children; Edward may also have had one illegitimate child.*

Edward II's reign was amongst the most despairing in history, cast into even greater notoriety because it was locked between the reigns of those two giants – his father, Edward I, and his son, Edward III. He was regarded as a weak king, not only through his lack of military ambition, but because of his total lack of interest in matters of state. He preferred gardening and basket-weaving to soldiery and government. Had he not been so easily influenced by his court favourites, he might have served better. The problem stemmed from his lonely childhood. Although he was the fourteenth of Edward's nineteen children, few of his brethren survived infancy and he never knew them. Of his elder sisters, three were married before Edward was six, while a fourth entered a nunnery around the time he was born. Only Elizabeth was close to Edward in age and would have been his closest childhood companion. Edward was already sixteen by the time his half-brother Thomas was born. Although his father was a devoted family man, his continued absence in his wars against Wales, Scotland and France left Edward to fend for himself, and the death of his mother when he was only six left him bereft.

As so often happens with lonely children (especially child heirs) they welcome anyone who shows them friendship and do not recognize when that friendship may be false, seeking only fame or riches. His closest childhood friend was Piers Gaveston, a rather handsome but affected knight from Gascony. The two of them led extravagant lifestyles, finding enjoyment in the disruption of ceremony and the annoyance of members of court, whom Gaveston delighted in calling by rude nicknames. Their inseparability and manner of dress caused the old king to believe they may have shared a homosexual relationship and Gaveston was banished from court on several occasions, but after the king's death, young Edward called Piers back. To the horror of the court magnates, Piers was made the earl of Cornwall (a title usually reserved for the king's sons), he was married to Edward's niece, Margaret, and when Edward went to France to collect his bride, Isabella, he made Piers regent. Piers made all the arrangements for the coronation, tried to outshine all others present by his manner of dress and had the highest honour of carrying the king's crown. Gaveston disgraced himself at the celebrations by his outward display of affection for Edward, which distressed the young queen. Gaveston further incurred the wrath of the court by bungling the banqueting arrangements resulting in a poorly cooked and late meal.

The barons prevailed upon Edward to banish Gaveston, which Edward did by making him regent of Ireland in 1308, but within a year Gaveston had returned. Gaveston continued to abuse the barons with his wit and sarcasm, but probably what annoyed the barons more was that despite his foppishness, Gaveston was a good knight. He often arranged tournaments, only to defeat any knight who rode against him. One of these, the king's cousin, Thomas, earl of Lancaster, was incensed by this ignominy. Thomas was no man to upset. He was one of the most powerful in England, with vast estates and a huge private army. By nature he was vicious and haughty, caring only for himself. He led the opposition against the king and in the parliament of 1310 forced the king to agree to a committee of twenty-eight barons, known as the Lords Ordainer, who in effect governed the country. They forced Edward to agree to **Gaveston's permanent exile. Edward made him lord of Man, but**

Gaveston could not stay away and turned up at the king's Christmas celebrations, as arrogant and obnoxious as ever. A group of barons, led by Lancaster, arrested Gaveston and executed him in June 1312 on the grounds that he was an enemy of the state. The barons soon realized Gaveston's execution was a mistake as it polarized opinion in England. There were those who believed the Lords Ordainer had acted unlawfully. The leader of this opposition was Hugh le Despenser, a long-time supporter of the king and a friend of Gaveston's. He and his son (Hugh the Younger) inveigled their way into the king's favour. By 1313, Hugh the Younger had become the king's chamberlain and closest adviser.

By this time Edward determined that he had to do something about Scotland. He had accompanied his father on several of his expeditions to Scotland in the early years of the century, and had been with his father on his final march north in 1307. The old king's last words had been to command young Edward to defeat the Scots. Edward had none of the military skills or leadership of his father and, though he tentatively crossed the border into Ayrshire, he rapidly retreated to the pleasures of the court, leaving Robert the Bruce to reclaim and rebuild Scotland. Edward led another brief foray to the Scottish borders in the autumn of 1310 and, meeting no opposition, regarded his expedition as a victory. However Robert merely bided his time and, on Edward's departure, returned to conquering castles and expelling the English. By the end of 1313 the only castle remaining in English hands was Stirling, which was under siege by Robert's brother. The governor of the castle, Sir Philip de Mowbray, declared that, if English reinforcements were not sent by 24 June 1314, he would surrender the castle to the Scots. Edward felt compelled to do something for the prestige of the English. On the eve of the appointed day he arrived at Stirling with one of the largest armies ever assembled in England. Although some estimates assigned it 100,000 men, it was probably closer to 20,000, but it still outnumbered the Scots two to one. Despite their numerical disadvantage, the Scots had spent months preparing for this battle and Bruce chose the site close to the Bannock Burn with precision. The English were forced into a course of action for which the Scots were ready, and almost from the outset the English infantry were thrown into chaos as they stumbled into prepared pits, whilst the cavalry were limited because of the surrounding bogland. The defeat was one of the worst ever to befall an English king. Edward fled from the battlefield, first trying to find shelter at Stirling Castle itself, probably one of the more extreme examples of stupidity from any English king, and then escaping by way of Dunbar back to London. Edward left Robert to his own devices, and though it was still another fourteen years before Scotland's independence was formally recognized, it was effective from the battle of Bannockburn.

Edward's reputation was at its nadir. England was torn between two opposing factions. The country was governed by the Lords Ordainer under Thomas of Lancaster, whilst the king's party was increasingly controlled by Hugh le Despenser. Although no official civil war broke out, there was a total state of anarchy with opposing factions fighting their own private battles, whilst the Scots plundered the north of England with almost complete freedom. To add to the problems England was laid low by a dire famine. It was only due to the negotiations of Aymer de Valence, earl of Pembroke, one of the more honourable and pragmatic nobles, that a form of reconciliation was made between the king and Lancaster in 1318. Had Edward seen fit to change his ways, matters might have improved, but Edward's conviction of his absolute authority only increased his intransigence. He listened only to his court favourites, the two Despensers, whom he showered in riches, and rebuffed his barons. Hugh the Younger had been created lord of Glamorgan and used the opportunity of further unrest amongst the dispossessed Welsh lords to establish an extensive domain in southern Wales. This development was opposed by Roger Mortimer, the most prominent of the marcher lords, who saw the Despensers' authority challenging his own in Wales. A confrontation in 1321 between Edward and Lancaster, supported by the Welsh marcher lords, caused Edward to agree temporarily to exiling the Despensers.

This was more because Edward feared a rebellion among the Welsh being supported by a Celtic alliance with Scotland, and he needed to pacify the Welsh leaders. They hated Mortimer more than Despenser. It should not be forgotten that Edward had been invested as prince of Wales in 1301 which, at that time, was not solely an honorific title. The Welsh took it seriously, as did Edward, and in the years before he became king he administered Welsh affairs and pronounced upon petitions far more effectively than he was ever able to do as king of England. Wales was specially his own, and the Welsh recognized this. In 1322, this allowed Edward, for once, to become his own man and act with uncharacteristic resolution. He led an army against Roger Mortimer, whom he captured and imprisoned in the Tower of London in January 1322. He then led an army against Thomas of Lancaster, who was defeated at Boroughbridge, captured and beheaded at Pontefract in March 1322. Flushed with success Edward continued north and laid waste to Scotland, his army reaching as far as Edinburgh before his luck ran out. He then retreated with all haste, pursued by a Scottish army, losing his baggage and plunder en route, but escaping with his life and a degree of dignity. Edward discovered further treachery along the Scottish borders where his warden of the Marches, Andrew Hartcla, had been conspiring with the Scots to allow them inroads to Cumberland. Hartcla was executed, and Edward agreed a truce with Scotland in May 1323.

The years 1321 to 1323 were the most decisive of Edward's life and showed his abilities when he put his mind to it. But he soon relapsed. The Despensers were recalled and they continued to create significant domains for themselves, especially in Wales, where they were allied with Rhys ap Gruffydd, who became sheriff of Carmarthen and was a strong supporter of the royal cause in Wales. The Despensers now caused the enmity of Edward's queen, Isabella. It seems that after the death of Lancaster, Isabella grew distant from Edward. It is difficult to say how close they ever were, since Edward had insulted Isabella at their coronation by his show of affection for Gaveston, but she had borne the king four children.

The last, Joan, had been born in July 1321. Isabella now began openly to confront the king, spurred on almost certainly by Roger Mortimer, with whom Isabella became more closely acquainted at the Tower of London. The Despensers contrived with Edward to have Isabella deprived of her estates in 1324, but they underestimated her cunning. Relations with France were once again hostile and Isabella requested that she visit the king of France, her brother, to aid negotiations. Edward agreed. No sooner was Isabella in France than she was joined by Roger Mortimer, who lived with her openly as her lover.

When her young son Edward arrived in France to pay homage for the lands of Ponthieu and Aquitaine, of which he was made respectively count and duke in September 1325, Isabella refused to allow him to return to England, in defiance of Edward's authority. She and Roger now raised an army to depose Edward and establish her son on the throne. The French king, Charles IV, with a remarkable display of honour, would not allow Isabella to conduct these affairs in France, especially with her open adultery with Mortimer, and she was exiled to Hainault, where the count allowed her to recruit an army of mercenaries from the Low Countries. Isabella and Mortimer sailed for England, landing at Harwich on 24 September 1326. Edward showed little resistance, retreating to his stronghold in Wales. Over the next two months his supporters were captured and executed, including the Despensers, and the king was eventually taken at Pen-rhys in the Rhondda on 16 December. He was held captive at Kenilworth Castle, where he was well treated by his cousin, Henry, the new earl of Lancaster and brother of the executed Thomas. Isabella called a parliament on 20 January 1327 to seek the deposition of Edward, but the parliament had no authority without the king's presence. Edward refused until he was given the ultimatum that his son's inheritance might also be forfeit, at which point he capitulated and abdicated in favour of his son on 25 January.

Edward was now transported to Berkeley Castle in Gloucestershire, where his rescue was attempted by Rhys ap Gruffydd. Isabella and Mortimer feared that Edward might yet make a resurgence, and so Mortimer arranged for Edward's death. He did not want it to appear that violence had been committed against the king. He was hoping it might appear as a natural death, or suicide. However, attempts to starve the king did not work, and in the end Edward was held down while a red hot poker was inserted into his bowels. There were some rumours, however, that another victim was found to serve as a body whilst Edward was smuggled out of England and spent his final years as a hermit in Lombardy. The idea of the former ostentatious monarch being able to live as a hermit, regardless of his situation, beggars belief, however. He was buried at Gloucester Cathedral where a beautiful alabaster effigy was raised above the tomb by his son. Edward's death roused considerable sympathy amongst his subjects, especially the Welsh, and his memory was venerated for many years. It was not until 1330 that his death was avenged. Roger Mortimer was tried and executed, and Queen Isabella was placed in confinement at Castle Rising in Norfolk. She lived on for thirty years after her husband's death, dying on 22 August 1358 and was buried at Greyfriars Church at Newgate in London. Though a strangely matched couple, Edward and Isabella produced one of England's greatest kings, Edward III.

EDWARD III

Ruled 25 January 1327–21 June 1377. Crowned: Westminster Abbey, 1 February 1327.

Titles: king of England, duke of Aquitaine (from 1325), earl of Chester (from 1312), count of Ponthieu and Montreuil (from 1325), lord of Ireland, king of France (from 1340).

Born: Windsor Castle, 13 November 1312. **Died:** Sheen Palace, Surrey, 21 June 1377, aged 64. **Buried:** Westminster Abbey.

Married: 24 January 1328, at York Minster, Philippa (1311–69) dau. of William V, count of Hainault and Holland: 13 children. Edward also had at least three illegitimate children by his mistress Alice Perrers (c1348–1400).

Any king must have seemed an improvement after the embarrassing reign of Edward II, but England was fortunate in that his son, Edward III, was both a great king and a popular one. Although his reign was not as glorious as subsequent romancers and chroniclers liked to maintain, it was remarkable and one that England needed to restore its self-esteem and its position in Europe.

The start of Edward's reign was less momentous. He had been raised to the throne following the forced abdication of his father. He was only fourteen and was in the manipulative hands of his mother, Isabella of France, and her paramour, Roger Mortimer. They had detained Edward in France the previous year when he had gone to pay homage to the French king Charles IV for his lands in Aquitaine and Ponthieu, and it was under Isabella's standard that Edward returned to England in September 1326 to be proclaimed 'Keeper of the Realm'. Edward remained under the control of Isabella and Mortimer, though there was some saving grace in that the head of the regency council was Henry of Lancaster, a cousin of Edward's father and a more moderate man than most. The murder of Edward's father at the instigation of Mortimer shocked the nation, but the young king was in no position to do much about it at the time. Despite his youth he had led an army into northern England in the summer of 1327 to counter the attacks made by the Scots on the borders. After a month trying to track down the enemy amongst the wild country, Edward was forced to admit defeat and he returned dejected to York. Negotiations were opened with the Scots resulting in the Treaty of Northampton in May 1328 where the independence of the Scots was recognized. Edward's sister Joan was betrothed to Robert The Bruce's infant son, David (II), and they were married that July at Berwick. Edward in the meantime had married his long-time betrothed, Philippa of Hainault, who had travelled to York for the wedding in January 1328. Their marriage was happy and fruitful, far more so than England's alliance with Scotland which was always threatened by the uneasy *ménage à trois* between Scotland, England and France.

From the tomb, Wesminster Abbey

That same year Charles IV of France died without an heir. Edward believed he had a more direct claim, through his mother, as grandson of Philippe IV of France and nephew of Charles IV. The French did not recognize inheritance through the female line and overturned Edward's claim in favour of Charles's cousin, Philippe de Valois. In any case there was no way that the French would be ruled by an English king, but that did not stop Edward's ambitions. He did not press his claim for the moment, but paid homage to the new king for his lands in France, and bided his time.

In the meantime Edward took control of his own affairs. There was a rising tide of feeling against his mother, Isabella, and Mortimer, who were now living openly together. Mortimer was continuing to seek retribution against the supporters of Edward II, including the young king's uncle, Edmund, earl of Kent, who was executed in March 1330. Edward decided that enough was enough. With the support of Henry of Lancaster, Edward's men (including William de Montacute, King of Man) seized Mortimer at Nottingham Castle, apparently dragging him from Isabella's embrace. He was tried and convicted, and was hanged, drawn and quartered at the new place of execution at Tyburn in London. (He was the first of many thousands to be executed there over the next 450 years.) On 20 October Edward assumed personal responsibility. He was to receive unanimous support from his barons. They recognized in him a quality that reminded them of the great days of Edward I. Edward used the facilities of the Parliament to ensure that the barons received a fair opportunity to contribute to debates, and he often took their advice. Whilst he remained superior, in the regal sense, he did not demean the barons.

Clearly none of this would have worked had Edward not proved himself an able soldier and king. His first opportunity came against the long standing enemy, Scotland. Edward Balliol maintained his right to the throne of Scotland against the family of Bruce and Edward supported his claim. In August 1332 Edward overthrew David II. Even though David was Edward's brother-in-law, Edward continued to support Balliol, and Balliol recognized him as his overlord at Roxburgh on 23 November 1332. Consequently, when Balliol was himself overthrown a month later, Edward III responded, providing forces to support Balliol's endeavours to regain the throne. Edward's army won a crushing victory over the Scots at Halidon Hill on 19 July 1333. Here, for the first time, the strength of the English and Welsh longbowmen played their part in seriously weakening the Scots forces. Balliol was restored and a year later, in June 1334, gave to the English crown almost all of the border country between the Forth and the Tweed, which was immediately governed as part of England. The Scots however fought back. Balliol was deposed again, and although he soon regained the throne it became evident that Balliol could only rule with English support. When he was overthrown again in 1336, he gave up and David II was restored. Edward did not pursue rights to Scottish territory, because his attention shifted to France. France and Scotland had long been allies and Edward was only too aware that united the two could seriously damage England. Moreover the many Gascons living in England had a right of appeal in the courts to the French king, through Edward's fealty for his lands in Gascony. Edward recognized that these problems would be solved if his claim to the throne of France was upheld. He revived this claim in 1337 and declared his intentions to fight for it. This was the start of what became known as the Hundred Years' War.

Supported by his barons, Edward crossed to Antwerp and invaded France in 1338. Philippe VI refused to fight, and the next eighteen months saw only minor and relatively unsuccessful skirmishes. However, in 1340 Edward won a major sea battle off the port of Sluys in Holland, and this emboldened him enough to declare himself king of France. He even challenged Philippe to decide the matter in single combat, but Philippe refused. For the next three years Edward was unable to make any advance, and the cost of maintaining his army and fleet became crippling. He reached a truce with Philippe in 1343, but that truce was conveniently broken in 1345. Now Edward's luck changed. His great general, Henry, earl of Derby, regained Gascony, and Edward followed up with a major invasion force. Landing in Normandy in July 1346, he harried his way through northern France with much pillaging and destruction, which galvanized Philippe into action. The two armies met at Crécy, near the Somme, on 26 August. Again it was the power of the longbow that gave the victory to Edward. His army moved on to Calais, to which he laid siege for several months until the citizens submitted, on the verge of starvation. Edward was prepared to sack and destroy the city but his queen, Philippa, who had accompanied him on the campaign, pleaded for their lives. While the siege was continuing Edward received excellent news from England. The Scots had sought to take advantage of Edward's absence by invading northern England, but their forces were routed by the archbishop of York at Neville's Cross in October 1346. David II was captured and taken as prisoner to England. A peace treaty was concluded in France and Edward returned to England.

The next few years may be seen both as the zenith of Edward's reign but also some of the darkest days in Britain. Edward, triumphant in his victory over France, and with David of Scotland his prisoner, established a court par excellence at Windsor Castle. Edward operated his Court on the model of the Arthurian Round Table. Arthur was his hero, and many of the incidents later related by Thomas Malory in his *Morte d'Arthur* have their counterparts in Edward's tournaments and chivalric quests. The world of Edward III was the world of Arthur. Edward planned to instigate an Order of the Round Table, which was eventually called the Most Noble Order of the Garter when he established it in 1348. It was the highest order of chivalry limited always to a select group of twenty-five or so knights. It was first bestowed upon Edward's eldest son, Edward, the Black Prince, and included among its illustrious ranks his second cousin, Henry, earl of Derby (later duke of Lancaster and grandfather of the future king Henry IV), and Roger Mortimer, the grandson of his mother's lover. These honours and the opportunity to prove themselves to the king resulted in a rare camaraderie between the king and his nobles, one which helped sustain the successes of the first half of Edward's reign. Edward called to his court the greatest knights from throughout Europe who would prove their valour and strength in his tournaments. It was a period of considerable glory and prestige for England.

However this splendour was darkened by the Black Death, the name given to the virulent bubonic plague that swept through Europe, reaching its height in the north in 1348. Almost a third of the population of Britain (or almost a million people) died from it. Over 200 people a day died in London alone for over two years. Edward's thirteen-year old daughter Joan died of it in Bordeaux in September 1348, as did his infant son Thomas, but although others of the court succumbed, the plague left the royal family surprisingly unscathed. Nevertheless it devastated the English economy and reduced the manpower on which Edward could call, but this was the same throughout Europe. It was through the remarkable ability of Edward's officials that the finances and administration of England were sustained through this period.

Philippe VI of France died in August 1350 and with the succession of his son, Jean II, hostilities broke out again with England. Jean, known as the Good, refused to acknowledge Edward's overlordship but likewise refused to fight until Edward's tactics of plunder and destruction drew the French out. A series of battles, of which the most decisive was at Poitiers in September 1356 under the command of Edward's son, Edward the Black Prince, brought French government to the verge of anarchy. Jean II was taken captive to England. Unable to agree terms, Edward III invaded France in 1359, hoping at last to gain control. However, the continuance of the bubonic plague and a devastatingly severe winter weakened the English as much as the French and Edward was unable to strike the final blow. A treaty was nevertheless agreed at Brétigny in 1360. By this Edward's sovereignty was recognized over his former lands in France, primarily Aquitaine and Calais. In return Edward dropped his claim to the throne of France.

The year 1360 remains the peak of Edward's reign as the remaining sixteen years were ones of slow and sad decline. The plague returned with increasing virulence in 1361. The French king Jean was never able to raise his ransom (set at half a million pounds) and died in London in 1364. His son, Charles V, ascended the French throne and encouraged the French subjects of the English in Aquitaine to rebel. Although Edward tried to negotiate with France relations worsened. The great triumphs of the Black Prince faded as his health failed, and were replaced by the ignominious defeats of his brother John of Gaunt. The war became protracted and costly and, when the French plundered and burnt Portsmouth in 1369, English opinion began to turn away from the king. This was further aggravated when Edward drew upon church revenues in order to finance the conflict. By 1374 Edward had lost much of Aquitaine, and the French regained control over most of the English territories except Calais and a coastal strip in southern Gascony, near Bayonne.

Edward's health and spirit also failed. His wife, Philippa, died in August 1369 of an illness akin to dropsy. They had been married for forty years and by all accounts had remained very happy. Philippa had grown rather portly in her last years which added to her overall character as a friendly, homely, motherly woman whom the nation greatly loved. In her final years Edward had found himself drawn to Alice Perrers, one of his wife's chamber ladies, who became his mistress. Although she satisfied the old king's physical desires – in fact she bore him at least three children – she was also scheming and grasping and made his final years a misery. She was banished from the court in 1376. It was likely that she was the cause of the king contracting gonorrhoea. To add to the king's sadness, his eldest son, Edward the Black Prince, who had turned against his father's policies, died in June 1376. The king's final year was spent in much loneliness and sadness aware that the administration about him was crumbling. He died of a stroke at Sheen Palace in June 1377. He was succeeded by his grandson, Richard II. Although his reign is remembered for its great days of glorious knighthood and con-quest, it was this and the Black Death that drove the country into poverty and near ruin and was the basis for the collapse of the Plantagenet dynasty in the next generation. Edward III cannot be denied the epitaph of a great king, but like so many other great kings he bequeathed little to his successors.

RICHARD II
Ruled 22 June 1377–29 September 1399 (abdicated).
Crowned: Westminster Abbey, 16 July 1377.
Titles: *king of England; prince of Wales, earl of Cornwall and earl of Chester (from 1376).*
Born: *Bordeaux, Gascony, 6 January 1367.* **Died**: *Pontefract Castle, on or about 14 February 1400, aged 33.* **Buried**: *initially Kings Langley, then removed to Westminster Abbey in 1413.*
Married: *(1) January 1382, at Westminster, Anne (1366–94) dau. Charles IV, Holy Roman Emperor and king of Bohemia: no children; (2) 4 November 1396, at Calais, Isabella (1389–1409), dau. of Charles VI of France: no children.*

Richard whose father was Edward, the Black Prince, was only ten when he ascended the throne. The Black Prince had been renowned throughout Christendom for his knightly valour. He had all the prowess of the Plantaganet line, but he also inherited their violent temper. Edward also proved himself a poor administrator and, for all that he was loved by the nation, he would probably have made a poor king. Richard's mother was also something of a character. She was Joan, the granddaughter of Edward I through his second marriage. Although she was known as the Fair Maid of Kent, she was older than Edward (she was 33, he was 31) and had already contracted a bigamous marriage to William Montague, earl of Salisbury, and borne five children to her first husband, Sir Thomas Holland. She was a loving mother to Richard and his elder brother Edward, who died young, but was not the most virtuous. We have an image of the young Richard striving to live up to his responsibilities but surrounded by lecherous and grasping relatives all endeavouring to gain more than their fair share of the action. This no doubt made Richard all the more determined to assert his authority, a characteristic that would eventually cost him his life.

No formal regent was appointed on Richard's accession. Control of the government was initially assumed by Parliament, but this increasingly passed into the hands of his uncle, John of Gaunt, duke of Lancaster, who was the most powerful man in England and who also had claims on the kingship of Castile. Some contemporaries believed that Gaunt himself had pretensions to the throne but, if he did, these did not come to the fore and he remained one of the staunchest supporters of his nephew throughout his minority and into his kingship. Richard early proved his courage and strong spirit with the Peasant's Revolt of 1381. In 1377 the first poll tax had been introduced to help finance the wars with France and campaigns in Scotland, Wales and Ireland. It was unpopular but was tolerated, though the increases in the tax in 1379 and 1380 caused considerable unrest. In June 1381 one of the tax collectors was killed by Wat Tyler of Dartford in Kent because of the taxman's attack on Tyler's

From a painting in Winchester Abbey

daughter. Tyler's colleagues came to his aid in defence and a force of around 100,000 evolved around Tyler as its leader to march on the capital. The rebels killed Simon of Sudbury, archbishop of Canterbury, and Robert Hales, the treasurer. The establishment had already raised the anger of the English common folk by proceedings against the religious reformer John Wycliffe, whose challenge to authority had gained popularity among the peasants. Richard appeased the rebels, promising to grant them their wishes. Although this satisfied many of them, a core remained with whom the king agreed to parley the following day at Smithfield. Here Wat Tyler became more presumptuous and raised his hand several times to the young king. Tyler was struck down by the Lord Mayor of London, William Walworth, and killed. The remaining peasants prepared to fight, but Richard risked placing himself in front of them and subdued their wrath. He led them out of the city, and many were attacked and killed by Sir Robert Knollys. Richard emerged from this with increased prestige, not only amongst his own barons, who respected his bravery, but surprisingly amongst the English common folk who held him in regard as their champion against oppression, even though he had in effect betrayed them, especially as he never instigated the reforms he promised. This success, though, influenced Richard's later life when he came to regard himself as a champion of England and one not to be dictated to by anyone, whether his barons or his subjects.

Nevertheless Richard's relationship with his court soon became divided. Much of this came at the instigation of Richard's close friend, his chamberlain, Robert de Vere, earl of Oxford, and of his advisor and later chancellor, Michael de la Pole. Richard bestowed much bounty upon these two colleagues which incurred the enmity of the court circle, whose opposition polarised around the leadership of Richard Fitzalan, earl of Arundel. By the mid 1380s Richard II's court had become divided along exactly the same lines as that of Edward II seventy years earlier. Richard even made the same mistake as Edward by seeking to gain glory by an expedition to Scotland in 1385. This had been occasioned by a show of might by a combined army of Scots and French, the French having allied themselves with Scotland against a common enemy. Although the army had caused havoc in Northumberland, it retreated against the might of Richard's army and though Richard marched through southern Scotland, laying waste as he went, the two armies did not once meet, and Richard retreated without a victory. The Scots bided their time for three years and then made further devastating raids on Northumberland. By that time Richard was in less of a position to respond because he was fighting for his own right to govern.

Richard had caused the final rift with his enemies in 1386, when he made Robert de Vere duke of Ireland with full powers of regency, and Michael de la Pole chancellor, without consultation with Parliament. When later that year John of Gaunt, who had maintained the stability in government, sailed to Castile to defend his right to the throne, Richard's opponents took the opportunity to act against Richard. They were led by his uncle, Thomas, duke of Gloucester, with the earl of Arundel and Thomas Beauchamp, earl of Warwick. Together with Thomas Mowbray, earl of Nottingham, and Richard's cousin, Henry Bolingbroke, son of John of Gaunt, these five opponents became known as the Lords Appellant. Their private armies allowed them effectively to assume control of the country. They forced Richard to hand over his courtiers for trial. Richard did not, but retribution was still carried out. Some, like de Vere and de la Pole, escaped but had their lands forfeited, but others were rounded up and executed. For a while, although furious with the Lords Appellant, Richard complied with their wishes. Although he declared himself of age in 1389 and assumed full kingship, he carried out no vengeance upon the Lords Appellant, although he did dismiss most of the counsellors imposed upon him and replaced them with his own favourites. A relative period of calm followed over the next six years, during which time Richard successfully brought a settlement to the turbulence in Ireland in 1394 and concluded a twenty-eight year peace treaty with France in 1396. One major sadness was the death of Richard's wife, Anne of Bohemia, of the plague in June 1394. She was only twenty-eight. Richard was so grief stricken that he had the palace at Sheen, where she died, razed to the ground. They had had no children. Two years later, as part of his peace treaty with France, Richard married Isabella, the seven-year-old daughter of the French king Charles VI.

With troubles concluded abroad Richard believed he was now operating from a position of strength. In the summer of 1397 he had Gloucester, Arundel and Warwick arrested. Gloucester was despatched to Calais where he was murdered. Arundel and Warwick were tried before a parliament now firmly under Richard's control. Arundel was found guilty and executed. Warwick so prostrated himself before the king that he was reprieved but banished to the Isle of Man, under the lordship of William le Scrope. As for Mowbray and Henry Bolingbroke, both had, in fact, been comparatively loyal to Richard. Many believed that Mowbray may have personally murdered Thomas of Gloucester. However in early 1398 they were both accused of treason and challenged to a trial by combat. Richard intervened before the contest. Mowbray was exiled for life and deprived of his lands, whilst Henry was exiled for ten years.

Richard now ruled as a total despot, assuming absolute power. He dominated his court and parliament and all lived in fear of his wrath. All of the viciousness and arrogance of the Plantagenet temperament become focused in Richard. He became the embodiment of the adage that absolute power corrupts absolutely. In his youth and when controlled by his parliament Richard had demonstrated both his courage and an ability to govern wisely, but this was now all laid aside in his desire for total control. For those who remained his favourites this was no problem as he continued to bestow his favours upon them. Richard was no warrior king, for all he was an able soldier, but like Edward II, Richard became a dilettante. He is credited with inventing the handkerchief, which may say much for his lifestyle, but there is no denying that his court encouraged the development of cultural pursuits. It was during his reign that Geoffrey Chaucer wrote his *Canterbury Tales* (1387). The rise of literature also brought with it the rise of criticism, and two other poets, William Langland and John Gower, both wrote remonstrances against Richard II's reign.

When John of Gaunt died in February 1399 Richard, instead of pardoning Henry Bolingbroke and allowing him to return to his estates, extended his banishment for life and forfeited his lands. He thereby made a dangerous enemy. In May 1399 Richard left for Ireland in order to quell the unrest. On 4 July Henry Bolingbroke landed in Yorkshire with a small army. The number soon swelled as Henry marched south. Richard returned to meet him but his support rapidly dwindled. Deserted, Richard was forced to submit to Henry at Flint on 19 August 1399. He was imprisoned in the Tower of London. Henry now used the precedent established by the deposition of Edward II to seek the abdication of Richard. It was complicated by the fact that Henry was not the direct heir. Richard was childless and the next in line to the throne was Edmund Mortimer, earl of March, who was descended from Edward III's son Lionel, the elder brother of John of Gaunt. However, Edmund was only eight, and there was no benefit following the revolution in installing an eight-year-old king. Parliament thus agreed that Henry should succeed. Richard II eventually consented to abdicate on 29 September 1399, and Henry came to the throne as Henry IV.

THE HOUSES OF LANCASTER AND YORK
(1399–1485)

With the population decimated by plague, wages for work on the land grew higher and so did the price of food. Once again, rebellion and lawlessness were rife. Henry IV would be constantly hampered by lack of funds.

Under Henry IV in 1400 and 1402 Acts of Parliament were passed restricting the rights of Welshmen. Henceforth the Welsh were only allowed to hold subordinate roles.

Wales, under Owain Glyn Dwr would challenge the English monarchy and for a while maintain its independence. And Henry IV's attack on Scotland would end in his defeat. His son, Henry V, an abler and more popular king, would inherit the rebellion in Wales and finally quell it for the last time. And he would also invade France, winning the Battle of Agincourt against all odds, bringing Normandy once again under British control. But his French conquests would be gradually eroded under the rule of his successor Henry VI and by 1453, only Calais would remain an English possession.

Then, for the next thirty years England would be plunged into interdynastic strife (in a series of civil wars that would later become known as the Wars of the Roses – so named after the different coloured roses of the families' coats of arms – white for House of Lancaster, red for the House of York) as the descendants of the Plantagenet king Edward III contested for the English throne.

HENRY IV *BOLINGBROKE*
Ruled 30 September 1399–20 March 1413.
Crowned: Westminster Abbey, 13 October 1399.
Titles: king of England, earl of Derby (from 1377), earl of Northampton and Hereford (from 1384), duke of Hereford (from 1397), duke of Lancaster, earl of Leicester and earl of Lincoln (from 1399).
Born: Bolingbroke Castle, Lincolnshire, 3 April 1367 (or 1366),
Died: Westminster Abbey, 20 March 1413, aged 45. Buried: Canterbury Cathedral.
Married: (1) before 10 February 1381, at Arundel, Sussex, Mary (c1369–94), dau. of Humphrey de Bohun, earl of Hereford: 7 children; (2) 3 April 1402 (by proxy) at Eltham Palace, Kent, Joan (c1370–1437), dau. of Charles II, king of Navarre, and widow of John de Montfort, duke of Brittany: no children.

Henry was the first king of the House of Lancaster, but he was still a Plantagenet. Both he and Richard II, whose throne he usurped, were grandsons of Edward III. Henry's father was John of Gaunt, who had been the premier lord in England after the death of Edward III in 1377. Henry had been born at Bolingbroke Castle and was often called Henry Bolingbroke. His mother (whom he scarcely knew, as she died of the Black Death when he was three) was Blanche, the daughter of Henry, duke of Lancaster, and great-great-grandaughter of Henry III. Bolingbroke was initially induced by his uncle, Thomas, duke of

Gloucester, to oppose Richard's court favourites and he became one of the Lords Appellant, who effectively governed the country during the late 1380s. However he stepped down from this role a year later in 1389 and in subsequent years appeared as a supporter of the king. In 1390 Henry embarked on the first of his adventures, joining the Teutonic Knights on an expedition to Lithuania in the war over the Polish succession. Two years later Henry undertook a pilgrimage to Jerusalem, though his greater triumph was the grand journey he took through the courts of Europe on both the outward and return trips, where he was treated regally and evidently held in high esteem. At this time of his life Henry was still comparatively handsome, although he was rather short. He had inherited the Plantagenet red hair which, when he grew a beard, gave him a rather fiery appearance. In later life Henry developed a very severe form of eczema, to the extent that many believed he was suffering from leprosy, something he could have caught in his early travels. It is quite possible that the malady was stress-connected considering the difficult life Henry later led as king.

Henry was a good man for the king to have on his side, but Richard II did not seem to appreciate this. In 1398 Richard delighted in banishing Henry into exile on the grounds of past treasonable acts. The banishment was originally for ten years. In February 1399 Henry succeeded his father as Duke of Lancaster. King Richard chose to deprive Henry of his estates and extend the sentence to life. Henry invaded England in July and within six weeks Richard submitted to him. Henry succeeded in convincing Parliament of his eligibility to the throne (Edmund Mortimer, earl of March, had a prior claim, but he was only seven years old). Nevertheless it was an uneasy succession. For all that nearly everyone welcomed Henry over Richard, those who had supported Richard became concerned for their own lives and estates. Within months of his succession Henry found his life threatened in a rebellion organized by the earls of Kent, Salisbury and Huntingdon. Henry's retribution upon the earls and their supporters was swift and violent. It is likely that in its aftermath

Henry also ordered the murder of the king who was starved to death, though the guilt of this continued to haunt Henry for the rest of his life.

Within a few months Henry faced a further revolt, this time in Wales, where Owain Glyn Dwr was declared prince in September 1400. Although the initial revolt was swiftly put down by Henry, Owain was not caught and several years of guerilla warfare followed.

OWAIN GLYN DWR or GLENDOWER Prince of Wales, 1400–16.

The last Welsh national to claim the title 'Prince of Wales'. He was descended on his father's side from Madog ap Maredudd, the last ruler of a united Powys, and on his mother's side from Rhys ap Gruffydd, the Lord Rhys of Deheubarth. Later chroniclers would also find a distant link with the families of Owain Gwynedd but, even without that, after the murder of Owain ap Thomas in 1378, whose pretensions to the Welsh throne in 1372 had caused an upsurge of Welsh pride and nationalism, Owain Glyn Dwr was certainly the primary contender to the principality of Wales. Little is known of his early life. He was born around 1354 and on his father's death in 1370, inherited estates in Powys and Meirionydd. Sometime around 1383 he married Margaret, the daughter of David Hanmer, a justice of the King's Bench, and it is likely that up to this time, Owain had been receiving legal training. He also served a military apprenticeship, between 1383 and 1387, in northern England, Scotland and France. He settled down to the life of a country squire, building himself fine new houses and estates at Sycharth and Glyndyfrdwy. Although the next decade gave no indication of Owain's future intentions it is evident that he was held in high regard by the Welsh and that

From a portrait in the National Library of Wales

increasingly he became the voice for their complaints of ill-treatment by their English overlords. It seems that it was a boundary dispute with his English neighbour that suddenly caused tempers to flare. Everything came to a head on 16 September 1400 when Owain's supporters declared him prince of Wales.

After an initial show of power in late 1400, which was followed by an equally quick punitive expedition by Henry IV, Owain went into hiding for several months. During this period, although English agents were searching for him, he was able to maintain a guerilla campaign. Encouraged by Owain's acts other rebellions broke out across Wales, the most momentous being the capture of Conway Castle in April 1401. By August 1401 Owain's forces were tightening their grip over north-west Wales, and a further expedition by Henry IV only strengthened national resistance and brought support to the Welsh from Scotland and Ireland. In June 1402 Owain made a further show of force at the battle of Bryn Glas, where he overwhelmed an English levy and put fear into the marcher lords. The leader of that levy, Edmund Mortimer, was captured and won over to the Welsh cause, marrying Glyn Dwr's daughter Katherine. Owain soon began to win over other factions from England, most notably the Percy family, who held the earldom of Northumberland and, by the end of 1403, he was receiving support from the French. Owain's successes came to their peak in 1404 when he summoned a parliament at Machynlleth, on the borders of Powys and Meirionydd, and soon after he contracted a Franco-Welsh alliance. The support of the French resulted in major gains in south Wales during 1405. It was in July 1405 that Owain held his second parliament. He had also, by now, gained the support of the Welsh church through his own support in the long-running dispute over the autonomy of St David's.

By this stage, however, Owain's ambitions seem to have grown unrealistically. It seems that during 1405 his alliance with Henry Percy, earl of Northumberland, and Edmund Mortimer reached the stage where they were plotting the overthrow of Henry IV and the division of England and Wales between them. Such plans required significant forces, support and finances. These were all available in some measure but not sufficiently co-ordinated and, by the end of 1405, Owain's fortunes began to founder. Northumberland was the first to suffer defeat and he withdrew his forces. Further promised support from the French and Scots did not materialize and by late 1406 Owain was in retreat before a more organized offensive by the English king. With the death of the earl of Northumberland in 1408, Owain's English support evaporated. Gradually castle after castle was regained by the English, the last two – Aberystwyth and Harlech – falling from Owain's hands in 1409. Edmund Mortimer died in the siege of Harlech, and Owain's wife and several of his children and grandchildren were captured. Thereafter Owain and his son Maredudd remained in hiding. There were occasional skirmishes in the mountain fastness of north-west Wales, and Owain was never betrayed, but the revolt was over and Wales was subdued. It is possible that his final days were spent in a remote part of Herefordshire. It is presumed Owain died either late in 1415 or early in 1416. It was not until April 1421 that Owain's son, Maredudd, accepted a pardon. Owain's resting place is not known, allowing him to pass into legend like Arthur as a saviour who might one day return.

Support for Owain grew, not only amongst the Welsh, but amongst the English barons who had their own axes to grind. Key amongst these were the marcher lords, the Mortimers, who believed that their heir, Edmund, was the rightful king of England. This heir's uncle, also called Edmund, was won over to the Welsh cause and married Glyn Dwr's daughter. Owain also found support from Henry Percy, the son of the earl of Northumberland. Young Percy, better known as Hotspur, was a vain and intolerant individual who never believed he had received just recognition for his border successes against the Scots. Moreover his wife was Mortimer's sister. In 1403 Hotspur threw in his lot with Glyn Dwr and Mortimer. Henry reacted quickly, before Hotspur and Mortimer could combine forces, and confronted Hotspur at the battle of Shrewsbury on 21 July 1403. Hotspur was killed and his uncle, the earl of Worcester, was captured and executed. Hotspur's father, Henry, earl of Northumberland, was spared, but he continued to plot against the king. By 1405 it became evident that Mortimer and Percy were planning to overthrow Henry and share England between them. Both Thomas Mowbray, the Earl Marshal of England, and Richard Scrope, archbishop of York, became involved in the plot. The rebel army was defeated and this time Henry showed no mercy, though there was a great outcry when the archbishop was executed. Although the earl of Northumberland escaped to Scotland, he died in February 1408. Soon after Edmund Mortimer died during the siege of Harlech and the Welsh rebellion faded away.

At last by 1408 Henry felt reasonably safe. Two years earlier he had taken James I of Scotland captive when the young heir to the throne was being sent to France for safety. James remained at the court of the English king for the next seventeen years and, with him as hostage, England's relationship with Scotland remained stable. Moreover threats from France diminished as the French became riven by their own civil war. Unfortunately for Henry his physical constitution gave way and for several years, between 1406 and 1409, there were concerns for his life. In addition to the stress of keeping his throne amid widespread opposition, Henry had struggled to sustain the administration and finance of England. Henry placed considerable demands upon his treasury, and Parliament often argued against him. Henry remained moderate throughout, careful to avoid a confrontation that might cost him his throne. He relied increasingly on his council to help him run his government. However, it became evident that his illness was taking its toll and that Henry was finding it difficult to govern. By 1409 his son, Prince Henry, was made chancellor in place of the king's favoured Thomas Arundel, archbishop of Canterbury. Arundel returned in 1411 amidst a quarrel between the King and his council, in which it seems it had been proposed that Henry abdicate in favour of his son. Henry refused. Rumours abounded that Prince Henry was going to take the throne by force, but that never happened. He had little time to wait. Henry's strange wasting disease took his life in March 1413, two weeks before his forty-sixth birthday. The valiant knight of twenty years earlier had been worn out by the stress of government and ill health. Nevertheless he had established a united kingdom, and passed on the throne to his son, Henry V, who would become one of England's best known kings.

Henry had desired that he be buried at Canterbury Cathedral rather than Westminster Abbey. There is a story that while a ship bore his coffin down the Thames a storm erupted and the king's body was washed overboard. The sailors later substituted another body. When Henry's tomb at Canterbury was opened in 1832, the simplicity of the remains suggested that the story may have been true. Henry was succeeded by his son Henry.

HENRY V
Ruled 20 March 1413–31 August 1422.
Crowned: Westminster Abbey, 9 April 1413.
Titles: king of England; prince of Wales, duke of Cornwall, earl of Chester and prince of Aquitaine (from October 1399); duke of Aquitaine and duke of Lancaster (from November 1399).
Born: Monmouth Castle, 16 September 1387. Died: Bois-de-Vincennes, France, 31 August 1422, aged 34. Buried: Westminster Abbey.
Married: 2 June 1420, at Troyes Cathedral, France, Katherine (1401–37), dau. of Charles VI, king of France: 1 son (Henry VI).

Henry from his youth demonstrated his abilities as a resourceful and valiant soldier. Even though he was only fifteen, Henry fought alongside his father in the war against the Welsh rebels under Owain Glyn Dwr, and later against the English rebels, Henry 'Hotspur' Percy and Edmund Mortimer. By the time he was eighteen Henry was heavily involved in working with his father's council of administrators. The young king was so admired that, when his father grew weak from a wasting disease, there was a call for the father to abdicate in his son's favour. This did not happen, and it is not proven that the prince wanted it to happen, but it is evident that in the king's final years he and his son disagreed over several matters. Chief amongst these was England's involvement in France. Henry IV had chosen to press again England's claims to French territories, and an opportunity had arisen in 1407 when civil war broke out in France during one of Charles VI's increasing bouts of insanity, between two factions – the Burgundians and the Armagnacs. Henry IV supported the latter but Prince Henry supported the Burgundians. Their dispute was never resolved, and the king's supporters used it as an opportunity to discredit the prince. However when Henry IV died in 1413, and Prince Henry became king, these disputes were rapidly resolved. Henry was quick to forget old grievances, even to the point of granting the last Plantagenet king, Richard II, a proper state burial at Westminster.

Henry focused his intentions single-mindedly on regaining the lands in France and galvanized Parliament into total support. His initial negotiations with the French proved fruitless – not surprisingly considering Henry's wish to have the whole of the old Angevin Empire restored. When negotiations ceased, Henry invaded on 11 August 1415. He successfully besieged Harfleur and then, on 25 October, confronted the French army at Agincourt. Although the French outnumbered the English three-to-one, their rash tactics against the English and Welsh longbowmen proved disastrous. The flower of French chivalry died on that day. It is reported that the French lost some six thousand men compared to four hundred English.

Although Agincourt was a major victory, it was not decisive because France did not immediately fall to Henry. But his success had caused the French to be extremely wary of Henry, and it earned Henry tremendous support in England. He also succeeded in gaining Sigismund, the Holy Roman Emperor, as his ally and together they won the support of John, duke of Burgundy. Starting again in August 1417, Henry pursued his campaign through Normandy which fell to him in the spring of 1419. A few months later the duke of Burgundy was murdered, and Henry found that his own claim on the French throne was now supported by all Burgundians in total defiance of the Armagnac party, adherents of the Dauphin, Charles. Henry signed the Treaty of Troyes with the Burgundians in May 1420, which recognized him as the heir to the French throne. To seal the alliance Henry married Katherine, daughter of the French king. Henry brought his bride back to England in February 1421 and spent the next few months in a triumphant tour of the land. It was soured slightly by the news of the death of his brother, Thomas, duke of Clarence, at the battle of

Baugé in France in March. By June Henry was back in France, continuing his battle for the kingdom. The Dauphin's stronghold at Meaux fell to him in May 1422 after a long siege. Unfortunately Henry had become very ill during the winter, almost certainly with dysentery, and his health worsened during the summer. He died on 31 August 1422, aged only thirty-four. It was a cruel blow of fate. Less than six weeks later the French king died. Like Moses, Henry was in sight of his kingdom but was denied entry into it. Nevertheless Henry bequeathed to his infant son a kingdom greater than any since the days of Henry II.

Our image of Henry is probably drawn mostly from his portrayal by Laurence Olivier in the film version of Shakespeare's *Henry V*, but Olivier's own portrayal was based on a painting of Henry that shows a rather humourless, determined young man with a hard face, an over-large nose, thin eyebrows and a clipped monkish haircut. Although Henry's reign had been the shortest of any English king since the Norman conquest (even Richard I's was three months longer), it was one of the most successful. No other king gained such united support from his barons and no other king regained so much territory and held it. There is no way of knowing how Henry would have maintained his two kingdoms had he lived and his reign might have ended in failure, like Edward III's. But Henry was also a tireless administrator who, despite the pressure of his military campaigns, continued to respond to petitions from England and meet the needs and demands of his court. His ability to hold together his parliament despite the immense strain upon the treasury of his campaigns is further testimony to his abilities. Henry also remained fond of and on good terms with his step-mother, Joan of Navarre, even though she was accused of witchcraft in 1417 and imprisoned at Pevensey Castle. His ability to handle all of these eventualities and triumph in them all was remarkable. His early death was a tragic loss to England. His wife, Katherine, subsequently formed a romantic alliance with Owain Tudor, and most probably married in secret. By him she had four or five children, and died giving birth to the last in 1437. By her son Edmund, she was the grandmother of Henry VII.

From a painting in the National Portrait Gallery

HENRY VI
Ruled England 1 September 1422–4 March 1461 (deposed);
restored 3 October 1470–11 April 1471 (deposed again).
Crowned: Westminster Abbey, 6 November 1429, and
again at St Paul's Cathedral, 6 October 1470. Also
declared king of France, 11 October 1422. Crowned:
Cathedral of Notre Dame de Paris, 16 December 1431.
Titles: *king of England and France; duke of Cornwall (from birth).*
Born: *Windsor Castle, 6 December 1421.* **Died** *(murdered):*
Tower of London, 21 May 1471, aged 49. **Buried**: *Chertsey*
Abbey, Surrey, but removed to Windsor Castle in 1485.
Married: *22 April 1445 at Titchfield Abbey: Margaret*
(1429–82), dau. of René, duke of Anjou and king of Naples:
1 son.

Henry VI is a prime example of the wrong king at the wrong time, and that made for a very tragic reign. His father had been strong and charismatic, a king whose single-mindedness in recovering the former Norman territories in France had led to him being recognized as heir to the French throne. His son was not even nine months old when his father died. Six weeks after inheriting the English throne, young Henry was also declared king of France with the death of Charles VI, his grandfather. Had Henry V lived he would have had the strength of character to take advantage of the situation, but with only an infant king, the new empire required something special to unite it. That something special was not there. In fact the empire soon became a victim of the same tensions that had threatened both thrones for as long as there had been kings: inter-dynastic rivalries, and hatred and suspicion of court favourites.

Although Henry was officially king of France, he never had much opportunity to rule it. In France Charles VI's nineteen-year-old son was also declared king as Charles VII. He held most of the southern provinces while Henry's regent, his uncle, John, duke of Bedford, governed the northern provinces for England. The battle for France dragged on, lacking the relentless drive and power of Henry V. Bedford endeavoured to consolidate the gains the English had made so that the benefits could be ploughed back to the crown and thus reduce the drain of the war on the English treasury. However this meant that any final victory was perpetually deferred. Neither Bedford nor the rather weak-willed Charles VII had sufficient skill to conclude the battle. The key to the fighting centred around Orléans which came under siege in 1427. This was the period of Joan of Arc who galvanized the French into action. Although she was only seventeen she led an army into Orléans and raised the siege in May 1429. The spirit of victory was restored to the French and a wave of national pride engulfed the country as they regained lands from the English along the Loire Valley. Charles was crowned king of France in June 1429. This concerned Bedford who urged on the coronation of young Henry. He was crowned king of England in November

1429, but it was another two years before he was crowned as king of France in 1431. He was the only king ever to be formally crowned in both countries. However, although it had been hoped this would instil a similar nationalistic fervour in the English, it achieved nothing. The French were gaining the upper hand and the English were losing all of the lands Henry V had gained. In 1435 the Duke of Burgundy, in whose name the English had first invaded France, reached an agreement with Charles VII known as the Treaty of Arras. From then on the English cause in France was lost; Charles entered Paris in 1436. Apparently when Henry learned of Burgundy's defection he cried. Although he retained the title of king of France, it held no authority. The conflict would continue for another eighteen years until the death of England's dashing champion John Talbot, earl of Shrewsbury, at Castillon in 1453. With that defeat England's Hundred Years' War with France came to an end. The only French territory remaining in English hands was Calais.

Henry did not declare himself of age until November 1437, just before his sixteenth birthday. Until then the protector of England had been his uncle, Humphrey, duke of Gloucester. No one seemed to like Gloucester, and he was not trusted with full regency powers, which had remained with Bedford until his death in 1435. The result was constant wrangles in Parliament as Gloucester endeavoured to exercise his authority. At times even the young king interceded to calm matters, although no one took much notice of young Henry. During his upbringing he had been told to behave himself and not believe himself to have absolute authority. By the time he took the reins of government he was already a pawn of the most powerful statesmen and was too weak willed to exert any power. This was not because he did not believe he should, it was mostly because he was not interested. People are not simply born kings, they have to be them, and Henry had no will to govern. As a result he invested power and authority in the hands of those he most trusted and, as Henry was amazingly naive, these tended to be the least scrupulous of people. Amongst them was William de la Pole, earl of Suffolk, and grandson of

Michael de la Pole who had been one of Richard II's court favourites. Although de la Pole ingratiated himself into Henry's affections, and became his steward in 1435, he had good intentions since he was a peacemaker at heart. However, his solution for peace effectively meant the loss of France, and his chief opponent in this was Humphrey of Gloucester who was in favour of continuing the war of conquest. In other times, history might have been on the side of Suffolk, but in the years so soon after Henry V's great victories and with so many lives and resources expended, the English nation was not for sacrificing France. Nevertheless, because of his closeness to the king, Suffolk was able to plot his course for some years.

It was through Suffolk's negotiations that Henry married Margaret of Anjou in 1444 with terms that should have brought peace. What many did not know until later was that one of the terms in order to extend the truce was that Henry would surrender Maine, to which he agreed. There was uproar when the truth was known to the extent that Henry no longer felt safe in London. Margaret of Anjou together with the Earl of Suffolk convinced Henry that his uncle was plotting an uprising. Humphrey of Gloucester was arrested and confined at Bury St Edmunds in February 1447, where he died a week later. Many believed that he was murdered, probably on Suffolk's orders. Suffolk, realizing his unpopularity, switched from peacemaker to warmonger and invaded Brittany in 1449. This brought the conflict into Normandy which the French conquered by September 1450. Suffolk could not escape the loss of Normandy. Even before the war was concluded, Suffolk was arrested and impeached. Henry, hoping to save his life, had him banished, but his ship was intercepted at Dover and Suffolk was executed. Suffolk and his allies now became the scapegoat for all that had gone wrong both in France and with the mismanagement of English affairs. This was the main cause for the revolution led by John Cade in May 1450 which followed much the same course as the Peasants' Revolt of seventy years earlier, except that Henry VI did not show the bravery of the young Richard II. The revolt ran its course over the next two months before Cade's death. His rebellion was an opportunity to purge government, but Henry took little action. Instead he created further polarization by appointing Edmund Beaufort, the Duke of Somerset (and Henry V's first cousin), as his closest adviser. Somerset had once been a good soldier, but his role as lieutenant of France had coincided with the loss of most of the English lands, and he was regarded as the focal point for English failure. He was also the sworn enemy of Richard, duke of York (who was Henry V's second cousin). York had been effectively banished to Ireland in 1447, because of his sympathy for Humphrey of Gloucester. However in August 1450 he returned to England, supported by his army, and demanded his place on the Council.

The next few years were tense ones as the rivalry between Somerset and York grew: a rivalry that would erupt into the Wars of the Roses. Somerset had the upper hand to begin with, because of his direct link with the king, but matters changed after August 1453 when the king became afflicted by the first bouts of mental decline that would darken his later years. This was almost certainly inherited from his grandfather, the king of France, who also had bouts of imbecility. Exactly what was wrong with Henry is not certain, but he lost all memory and reason and would sit for weeks devoid of expression or awareness in a deep melancholia. The depression may have been triggered by the loss of France. It came just two months before the birth of Henry's first (and only) son, Edward. The king gave no sign of acknowledging the child and when, eighteen months later, Henry's reason returned, he had no idea where the child came from, believing it must have been born of the Holy Ghost.

Richard of York was made 'Protector of the Realm' in March 1454 and promptly had Somerset arrested and imprisoned in the Tower. However, a year later, when Henry recovered, the king had Somerset released and York dismissed. York's entreaties to the king were ignored and the inevitable conflict broke out at St Albans on 22 May 1455. The battle was brief and Somerset was killed. That should have been an end of any hostilities, because

Henry seemed prepared to be reconciled to Richard of York. When another bout of madness struck Henry in November 1455, Richard was again made protector but was again dismissed in February 1456. With Henry scarcely able to govern, his queen, Margaret, took up his cause. She despised the arrogant haughtiness of York and encouraged the new duke of Somerset, Henry Beaufort, against him. By 1458 the flames of war were being fanned across England between the Yorkists, supported by Richard Neville, earl of Salisbury, and his son, also Richard Neville, earl of Warwick, on the one side, and the Lancastrians, under the figurehead of Henry VI, but really led by Margaret of Anjou, supported by Somerset and Henry Percy, the third earl of Northumberland. With the battle of Ludlow in 1459 the Wars of the Roses began in earnest. At that battle the Yorkists were routed and Richard of York fled to Wales and then Ireland, while his supporters sought refuge in Calais. The following year the Calais element defeated the Lancastrians at Northampton, and Richard of York returned to England. He now formally placed his claim to the throne before Parliament in September 1460. The following month his right was acknowledged and he was declared the heir to the throne, in place of Henry's son Edward. Henry, his mind failing rapidly, agreed, but Margaret of Anjou was not so easily pacified. She raised a further army in the north and met the Yorkists at Wakefield on 30 December. York was killed in the battle, whilst Salisbury was captured and murdered. Margaret marched on London, defeating the earl of Warwick at St Albans early in 1461. Warwick managed to recruit another army, together with York's son, Edward, and they marched into London in triumph in March 1461. Edward declared himself king (as Edward IV). His forces marched north, following the retreating army of Henry and Margaret, and the two clashed at Towton near Tadcaster in Yorkshire. There, in the middle of a snowstorm, the Lancastrian army was defeated. Henry and Margaret fled to Scotland, where they were given refuge by the young king James III. Henry bought support from the Scots by granting them Berwick, but the military aid he was given proved useless in the abortive battle at Carlisle. Edward was soon after crowned king of England. He outsmarted every move made by Margaret of Anjou, including her alliance with France, to try and regain the crown and, after three years, Henry became an embarrassment to the Scots. He was smuggled out of Scotland and spent a year in refuge in northern England, until he was betrayed and captured by English forces in July 1465 and imprisoned in the Tower of London.

Had Henry been of the same arrogant disposition as Edward II and Richard II, both of whom had been murdered in prison, Henry might have expected his days to be numbered. But following an amazing reversal in the fortunes of Edward IV, Henry suddenly found himself removed from the Tower on 3 October 1470 and reinstated as king. The earl of Warwick had changed his allegiance to Henry and even went so far, two months later, as to marry his daughter Anne to the king's son, Edward. Henry's 'readeption', as it was known, was not to last for long. Edward IV returned with an army in April and defeated and killed Warwick. The king was again captured and imprisoned. His wife's army arrived too late to save him. She and her supporters were defeated at Tewkesbury on 4 May 1471, where the young Prince Edward was killed. Margaret was also imprisoned in the Tower and on that same night, 21 May, Henry was stabbed to death. Just who killed him was never revealed, though his body was displayed in its coffin the next day as if he had died naturally, so as to avoid any later rebellion to restore him.

Margaret of Anjou remained in prison, first at the Tower, then Windsor and finally Wallingford, before being released to return to her father's estates at Angers in 1475. Her appearance had become as wretched as Henry's, exhausted by years of trial and tribulation. Had she been the queen of a stronger king, they would have made a remarkable pair and doubtless ruled with considerable effect, but Margaret had the misfortune to be married to a king who began weak and sank into mental decline. He should have been a younger brother and left government to

John, duke of Bedford, who was much more able. Henry was more a scholar than a statesman. Although his reign led to the Wars of the Roses, he and his queen may best be remembered as the founders of King's College (1441) and Queen's College (1448) at Cambridge.

EDWARD IV
Ruled 4 March 1461–3 October 1470, deposed; restored 11 April 1471–9 April 1483. Crowned: Westminster Abbey, 28 June 1461.
Titles: king of England and France, earl of March (from birth), duke of York, earl of Ulster and earl of Cambridge (from 1460).
Born: Rouen, Normandy, 28 April 1442. Died: Palace of Westminster, 9 April 1483, aged 40. Buried: St George's Chapel, Windsor.
Married: 1 May 1464, at Grafton Regis, Northamptonshire, Elizabeth (c1437–92) dau. of Richard Wydville, 1st Earl Rivers: 10 children. Edward also had at least four illegitimate children.

Edward IV was the first king of the House of York though, like his predecessor Henry VI, he was a Plantagenet. Both were descended from Edward III, Henry through Edward's son John of Gaunt, and Edward through a younger son, Edmund, duke of York (and in the female line through Lionel, duke of Clarence). Edward IV's father was Richard, duke of York, who, in 1460, had been declared heir to the throne, though he died soon after in battle at Wakefield. Edward, who was only eighteen, was able to rally support along with his cousin Richard Neville, earl of Warwick, and successfully invaded London. He was declared king on 4 March 1461, and just over three weeks later decisively defeated the forces of Henry VI at Towton, probably the bloodiest battle fought on English soil, and this secured his claim on the throne. Henry VI and Margaret of Anjou fled to Scotland, seeking sanctuary with James III.

Edward IV was welcomed to the throne. Although he was

young he had already proved himself an able soldier. Moreover he was tall (six foot three inches) and handsome with a dashing smile, golden brown hair and winning ways – he could, for instance, always remember the names of his knights and officials and something about them, which endeared him to the court. Nevertheless all the time Henry VI lived, Edward's claim on the throne could not be regarded as secure. He needed to rule wisely and ensure the support of his noblemen. He did this by limiting the previous practice of court favourites. Instead he placed the control of Crown lands under court officials, confiscating many of the lands previously bequeathed to Lancastrian sympathizers. He set about making England profitable through foreign trade, including his own commercial ventures, to the extent that he was eventually able to make the Crown solvent, rather than buried in debt as under previous kings. He did his best to make the Crown and government administratively efficient and financially sound, though it must be admitted that one reason he reduced administrative costs was in order for more money to be spent on himself and the image of the king so that his court was as resplendent as those in France and Burgundy.

Once Edward felt firmly established as king he left the work of defeating the remaining outposts of Lancastrian resistance, which were mostly in the north, to his cousins Richard and John Neville. Edward knew how much he owed to Richard Neville for his position as king and Neville was highly rewarded. He would later earn the reputation as Warwick, the King-maker. He was made the Chamberlain of England, as well as receiving many other honours and considerable land. He became the second most powerful man in England. After the battle of Hexham in May 1464, where the last important Lancastrian resistance was crushed, John Neville was given the earldom of Northumberland, the hereditary title of the Percy family. With the Nevilles supporting him, Edward's position was secure, and therefore Edward's next act was one of the greatest folly.

Edward was a highly sexed man, and his actions were as much ruled by his lust as by his brain. Warwick, under his own initiative, had been working to secure an alliance with the French king Louis XI, who still supported Henry VI. The proposed treaty of friendship was to be sealed by the marriage between Edward IV and a French princess, Bona of Savoy. Warwick continued the negotiations throughout 1464 with a view to concluding them in October. Edward was not fully supportive of the negotiations as he favoured a treaty with England's older ally, Burgundy, which was itself at loggerheads with France. Edward's marriage was therefore a powerful bargaining tool. Yet Edward married in secret to an English lady and, to make matters worse, the marriage might even have been bigamous.

Although more rumour than fact, Edward had a reputation for taking many of the ladies of the court to his bed. All the time he was an honourable bachelor, and all the time this led to no consequences, everyone turned a blind eye. However, in May 1464, under the pretext of a hunting trip, Edward entered into a secret marriage with Elizabeth Wydville (often called Woodville), daughter of the 1st Lord Rivers, and the widow of Sir John Grey. The story went that Edward lusted after her but she would not submit without a promise of marriage. Edward agreed, probably not meaning it, but Elizabeth held him to his word. Edward was reputed often to make promises for sex with the ladies of the court, and this reputation would later be the downfall of his family. When news of his marriage leaked out – amazingly he kept it secret for four months – there was uproar. There was even a rumour that Edward had made a similar marriage compact with Lady Eleanor Butler a year or two earlier. How much of this was true has never been satisfactorily resolved, and the rumour was probably a fabrication built upon Edward's known philandering, but it was later a major weapon to be used against the legitimacy of his children by Elizabeth. What made matters worse was that Edward had married into a family of Lancastrian sympathizers: Elizabeth's father had married a second time to Jacquetta of Luxembourg, the widow of Henry V's brother John, duke of Bedford. Elizabeth's father, brother and her former husband had all fought on the side of Henry VI. Warwick was the most outraged at the marriage. It had humiliated him in the face of the French king and lost him his opportunity to gain lands and titles in France. Moreover it meant that the Wydville family now advanced in status and threatened to equal or even overthrow his stature as the second most powerful man in England.

Although Warwick continued to work with Edward and the Wydvilles over the next few years, he became increasingly exasperated at Edward's persistence in allying with Burgundy while Warwick tried to cement an alliance with France. Also when Edward thwarted Warwick's proposals of marriage contracts between his family and the king's, Warwick realized that differences between them were becoming irreconcilable. The last straw came when Edward married his sister, Margaret, to Charles, duke of Burgundy, in July 1468. Warwick withdrew his support from Edward and began to side with Edward's over-ambitious brother, George, duke of Clarence, who desired the kingship. Warwick was also supported by Louis XI, who promised Warwick lands in France if he successfully overthrew Edward. Warwick had not at this stage moved across to the Lancastrian cause, though he knew that Louis still supported Margaret of Anjou. Warwick's intention was to depose Edward and make George king in his place. In July 1469 Warwick succeeded in securing the marriage between George and and his daughter Isabella which Edward had so long opposed. Warwick now supported a series of uprisings that began in northern England. Although Edward was still a popular king amongst his subjects, his marriage had sullied his reputation and Elizabeth was never a popular queen. Warwick, on the other hand, was always a popular hero, seen by many as the nation's deliverer, and when in mid-July, Warwick issued a proclamation declaring that Edward must reform his ways or suffer deposition, Warwick received enormous support. Edward at first procrastinated, perhaps a little too sure of himself, and found himself trapped at Nottingham by a rebel army. A relief force was defeated and, although it allowed Edward's escape, Edward realized that his army was outnumbered. A battle was out of the question and, wisely, Edward dispersed his army and allowed himself to be captured by Warwick. Warwick imprisoned the king and sought to govern in his name, but was unable to find support in Parliament and, with government crumbling, he began to incur the wrath of the populace for imprisoning their sovereign. Warwick had no choice but to release Edward, who returned to London in October 1469 amidst much public acclaim. Although on the surface, Edward reconciled himself with Warwick and his brother George, Warwick knew that his authority was now limited. Grudgingly, if he was to achieve any restoration of his power, he needed to throw in his lot with Louis XI and Margaret of Anjou and defect to the Lancastrian cause. Supported by the Lancastrians, Warwick again fomented rebellion in the autumn of 1470, and their invasion fleet landed at Dartmouth in September. Edward was caught ill prepared. John Neville sent his army purportedly to support Edward but, at the last moment, declared his support for Henry VI. Edward suddenly realized that his forces were considerably outnumbered and his only recourse was to flee. He left England on 2 October seeking refuge with his brother-in-law, the Duke of Burgundy. Warwick seized the opportunity, brought Henry VI out of imprisonment in the Tower and restored him to the throne.

Had Warwick withheld his zeal, Henry's restoration might have remained permanent, but urged on by Louis XI, Warwick and Louis declared war on Burgundy. Charles, who until then had not wished to be involved, was now compelled to grant Edward a fleet and an army, and on 11 March 1471 Edward returned to England. Edward's skills as a soldier and general now became apparent. Although outnumbered three to one, Edward's army soundly defeated Warwick's at the battle of Barnet, on Easter Sunday, where both Warwick and his brother John were killed. Edward marched victoriously into London and was restored to the throne. Six weeks later Edward defeated the army of Margaret of Anjou at Tewkesbury on 4 May, where Margaret's son, Prince Edward, was killed. Edward IV was once more firmly in command of his realm. To ensure there was no further rebellion in favour of Henry VI, Edward ordered that the old king be murdered, though the public message was that he had died naturally and his body was put on display to curb any rumours.

The second half of Edward's reign lacks the glory and excitement of the first, although it was more administratively sound. It was during this period that Edward was able to carry through the reforms he had started in the previous decade, which led to better executed offices of the Crown, more effective administration of the law, and generally profitable and safe trade throughout England. The Crown became self-financing, and the loss of burdensome taxes made Edward even more popular amongst his subjects. He exerted considerable diplomacy abroad, developing strong alliances with the dukes of Brittany and Burgundy and with the king of Aragon. In July 1475 Edward determined to recapture the former English lands in France but his own invasion army was not matched by the promised reinforcements from Burgundy, and Edward had no choice but to negotiate peace with Louis. This was almost certainly the better outcome for, despite Edward's superior generalship, continued conflict in France was bound to have financial repercussions that might have soured Edward's popularity. As it was, Edward's brothers Richard (see Richard III) and George both saw the peace treaty as an ignominious defeat. George, who still believed he should be king, began to plot against his brother. This time Edward had him arrested and tried for treason. Found guilty, George was executed in February 1478. The traditional story is that George was drowned in a butt of malmsey wine.

Edward was a great patron of the arts, and a pioneer patron of printing. Although he personally preferred the illuminated manuscript, he encouraged William Caxton in his pursuits, and in November 1477 helped finance the first book printed in England, *The Dictes and Sayenges of the Phylosophers*, which had been translated by the queen's brother, Anthony, Lord Rivers. Edward also financed major building works at Windsor Castle and Eltham Palace in Kent. Ultimately, however, he fell victim to his own love of food. His continued gorging had made him fat and lazy and the once virile and strong king had become stout and inactive. His health began to fail and he became subject to an increasing number of ailments. Just which one killed him has never been satisfactorily resolved. He died just before his forty-first birthday, probably of pneumonia, though it has been conjectured that he had contracted typhoid or may even have been poisoned. Certainly some attributed his death to a surfeit of food. Had he reigned longer Edward might well have been regarded as a great king. He was without doubt a strong one, and governed intelligently, though in his private life he was unwise and naïve, and his actions ultimately proved fatal to his dynasty.

EDWARD V
Ruled 9 April–25 June 1483, deposed, never crowned.
Titles: king of England; prince of Wales, earl of Chester and duke of Cornwall (1471–83), earl of March and earl of Pembroke (from 1479).
Born: Westminster Abbey, 4 November 1470. **Died**: *Tower of London, probably 3 September 1483, aged 12.* **Buried**: *Tower of London and subsequently Westminster Abbey.*

Edward did not live long enough to enjoy any of the benefits of kingship, only its hardships. He and his brother Richard, duke of York, are immortalized in history as the ill-fated 'Princes in the Tower' whose deaths have become one of the best known historical mysteries.

The likelihood of Edward ever becoming king seemed doomed from the start. Although his father Edward IV had been a popular king, his mother, Elizabeth Wydville, was not so universally liked. Possibly had Edward been their first born, he might have been old enough to take control himself at the time of his father's sudden and unexpected death. His eldest sister, Elizabeth, was then seventeen, and at that age Edward could have assumed royal authority. But he was his father's fourth child, and was born at the lowest ebb in Edward IV's reign, when the king had fled

England and Elizabeth had sought sanctuary in Westminster Abbey. Although his father regained the throne, young Edward grew up in a family where there was considerable hostility between his father and his uncles, George, duke of Clarence, and Richard, duke of Gloucester (later Richard III). Nevertheless the child had a good education and a regal bearing and may, in due course, have made a fine king.

However upon his father's death, his uncle Richard rapidly manipulated events to establish himself as 'Lord High Protector' of England. Young Edward was holding court as prince of Wales at Ludlow and travelled to London under the protection of his mother's brother, Earl Rivers. They were met at Stony Stratford by Richard, on his way to London from York. Thereafter he escorted Edward to London and, though professing absolute loyalty, he was already planning on assuming the kingship himself. Edward and his brother were installed in the Tower of London which, at that time, was still a royal residence and not solely a prison, but the young king's freedom was totally restricted and he never left the Tower again. Plans for his coronation were delayed and in June 1483 Bishop Stillington, almost certainly at the instigation of Richard, announced his belief that Edward IV's marriage to Elizabeth Wydville had been illegal because Edward already had a pre-contract marriage arrangement with Lady Eleanor Butler. As a consequence his children by his second marriage were illegitimate. Although no evidence for this first marriage was ever produced, such was Edward IV's reputation as a womaniser that it was easily believed, and Richard was able to gain the support of Parliament in declaring the young king illegitimate and he was summarily deposed on 25 June 1483. His period as king can scarcely be honoured with the description of a reign, since he had no opportunity to exercise any authority, but he was the true heir to the throne and as such had the shortest reign of any legitimate king after the Norman Conquest.

Rumours began almost immediately of the fate of Edward and his brother Richard, Duke of York. The last they were seen was in July 1483, but there is circumstantial evidence to suggest that they lived for another four or five weeks. Over the centuries there has been considerable speculation as to what became of the Princes and who caused their deaths. Had they died naturally it would have been in Richard III's interests to make it known. Some believe the boys survived Richard's reign and that they were subsequently murdered on the orders of Henry VII. The fact that their fate remained such a secret allowed two pretenders to the throne to emerge during Henry VII's reign, Lambert Simnel and Perkin Warbeck, both of whom claimed that they were Edward's younger brother Richard. It was not until the year 1674 that the remains of two young children were found buried in the Tower of London. These were treated as the bones of Edward and Richard and were reburied in an urn in Westminster Abbey. More recent research on these bones, whilst inconclusive, was suggestive that they were the remains of the young Princes. The likely explanation of their deaths is the one given to Henry VII by Sir James Tyrrell, who declared under torture that he had smothered the two children by order of Richard III. Henry VII chose to maintain its secrecy because he had earlier shown favour to Tyrrell and it might be implied that Henry had sanctioned the death of the Princes. Nevertheless the thorough research conducted by Alison Weir in her book *The Princes in the Tower* makes it clear that the only person who could have been responsible for their deaths was Richard III.

RICHARD III *CROOKBACK*
26 June 1483–22 August 1485. Crowned: Westminster Abbey, 6 July 1483.

Titles: *king of England; duke of Gloucester (from 1461).*
Born: *Fotheringay Castle, Northamptonshire, 2 October 1452.*
Died *(in battle): Bosworth Field, Leicestershire, 22 August 1485, aged 33.* **Buried**: *Greyfriars Abbey, Leicester.*
Married: *Anne (1456–85) dau. Richard Neville, earl of Warwick, and widow of Edward, prince of Wales: 1 son. Richard had at least four illegitimate children.*

Richard III has long been regarded as one of England's most villainous kings and, though many revisionists have sought to clear his name, the evidence continues to suggest that Richard was as conniving in his personal affairs as history dictates, but not necessarily any more conniving than many of his predecessors. He was certainly not the evil monster portrayed by Shakespeare in his play *Richard III* and, though he probably had a slight deformity in his shoulder, he was not a hunch-back.

Richard was the younger brother of Edward IV. His was apparently a difficult birth, and he seems to have been a delicate child, but grew through all of this into a strong and resourceful young man, albeit short. He was only nine when his brother became king, after a childhood where he was frequently moved to safe custody as the fortunes of his father, Richard, duke of York, waxed and waned during the Wars of the Roses. Five months after his brother became king, Richard was created duke of Gloucester. Although young, he was well aware of the actions of his elder brother George, duke of Clarence, who, encouraged by Richard Neville, earl of Warwick, rebelled against Edward in 1469, but Richard remained loyal to Edward. As Warwick rapidly fell from grace, starting in 1469 and culminating in his death at the battle of Barnet in 1471, Richard benefited, being granted many of Warwick's titles and much of his land in the north. By 1471 Richard was Constable and Lord High Admiral of England, chief justice of the Welsh Marches, chief steward, chamberlain of South Wales, Great Chamberlain of England and chief steward of the Duchy of Lancaster. In 1472, though still only nineteen, Richard married Anne Neville, the daughter of the earl of Warwick, herself a descendant of Edward III and the widow of Edward, prince of Wales, the son of Henry VI. Their only child, Edward, was born early in 1476. Through this marriage Richard became entitled to half of the Warwick estates, which caused considerable acrimony with his brother, George, who felt that the reapportionment of Warwick's lands was unequal. During these years Richard strengthened his hold on the north of England governing it on Edward's behalf. He became known as 'Lord of the North', ruling it as king in all but name. His chief residence was his castle at Middleham in Yorkshire, a strong yet comfortable castle which became known as the Windsor of the North. Richard accompanied Edward on his expedition to France in 1475, and the only show of dissension between Richard and Edward was over the peace treaty, which Richard held to be dishonourable. Nevertheless, Richard remained loyal to Edward during the continued defiance of George, resulting in George's execution. Richard strengthened his hold on the north and even turned his eyes towards Scotland. He conducted several campaigns against James III resulting, in 1482, in regaining Berwick and advancing into Edinburgh. During all this period Richard was highly regarded by his peers and subjects, both as a just administrator and as a wise and strong general. To all intents Richard ruled northern England, which was recognized when he was granted palatine powers in the west March in 1483. Two months afterwards Edward IV died unexpectedly and his will named Richard as 'Lord High Protector of the Realm' during Edward V's infancy.

Thereafter matters moved swiftly. Richard knew that he needed to assert his authority before the Wydvilles – the family of Edward's widowed queen – did so. Richard hastened down from York while the Wydvilles were bringing the young heir from Ludlow. Richard met them at Stony Stratford, took the young king under his protection, escorted him to London, and placed him in the Tower. The Tower was still a royal residence in those days, but it was also a strong fortress, and once there the king was entirely under Richard's power. Predictably the Wydvilles reacted, and Richard was able to represent their actions as being treasonable. Anthony Wydville, the queen's brother, was executed without trial. Richard meted out the same fate to Lord Hastings, once his loyal supporter and a staunch opponent of the Wydvilles. However when Hastings realised that Richard was seeking to claim the throne and depose Edward, he objected and was promptly arrested and executed. Richard now broadcast the belief that Edward V was illegitimate, because Edward IV had entered into a previous marriage contract. Parliament recognized this claim on 25 June, when the young king was deposed, and Richard was proclaimed king the next day. He had secured the throne quickly and quite ruthlessly in eleven weeks. By the standards of his day, while one might not condone his actions, one can understand them. The rivalry between the Yorkists and the Lancastrians was not at an end and England needed a strong ruler with full authority. Even acting as protector, Richard could not always count on the full support of Parliament. He thus needed to be rid of the young king. His main rivals were the Wydvilles whom Richard and most Yorkist supporters opposed, so it was crucial that they did not gain power. Seen in this light Richard's quick actions were those of a shrewd, calculating tactician who knew how to control and manipulate. Morals aside he was a very clever man.

With Edward V deposed, it remains questionable why the young king and his brother had then to be killed. Richard probably recognized that the Act of Parliament that had over-thrown Edward's legitimacy could as easily be revoked and, so long as the princes were alive, they remained a threat to his overall control. It seems likely that Richard ordered their deaths in early September 1483 while he was on a state tour of the realm and outside the capital, but although rumours were rife about the fate of the princes, the real facts about their deaths did not come to light during Richard's lifetime.

Although secure on the throne, Richard had to deal with some residual rebellions. The main threat came from his once loyal supporter Henry Stafford, duke of Buckingham, who had entered an alliance with the Wydvilles and with Henry Tudor who, through his mother, was another descendant of Edward III and the last Lancastrian claimant. Buckingham's revolt was, however, ill planned and thwarted by rainstorms, and he was captured without battle and executed at Salisbury on 2 November 1483. Henry Tudor remained in Brittany but continued to ally himself with the Wydvilles and awaited his opportunity.

There is little doubt that Richard governed as a wise and

competent king. This suggests two sides to his character. But though he may have been ruthlessly ambitious and duplicitous in his desire for kingship, he enjoyed the power of governance and treated his subjects fairly. He was highly regarded as a monarch by the English and by his contemporaries in Europe. Though it might seem hypocritical, Richard railed against the poor English morals and issued proclamations to uphold moral standards. Richard was, in fact, a very pious man, a staunch supporter of the church and generally loyal to his wife. He had fathered several illegitimate children before his marriage, but the records are unclear as to whether he continued to maintain mistresses afterwards. He was distraught when his young son, Edward, who had always had a weak constitution, died in April 1484, aged only eight. Richard's wife, Anne, was too weak to bear another child. She was consumptive and died within the year, in March 1485. Later stories implied Richard had poisoned her because of his plans to marry his niece, Elizabeth of York, in order to father a new heir to the throne. This never occurred, and it is not clear how serious Richard's plans were to this effect, and it may have only been to thwart Henry Tudor's plans to marry Elizabeth.

Henry Tudor's planned invasion happened in August 1485. The two armies met at Market Bosworth, just west of Leicester. Had Richard succeeded, his authority to rule would have been unchallenged. However the battle was soon over. Richard charged straight into the thick of it, intent upon killing Henry Tudor himself, and was killed in the close-fought action. His naked body was carried on a pack-horse to Leicester for burial. According to tradition Richard's crown was found on the battlefield under a hawthorn bush.

When his brief reign is viewed in the round, Richard was undoubtedly a worthy king. He was as capable of taking the kingdom forward into a new age as his ultimate successors. History as written has chosen to focus on the vicious and ruthless side of his character rather than a balanced view. Richard was certainly not someone to have as either your friend or your enemy, but he was a better king than many who had come before

THE HOUSE OF TUDOR
(1485–1603)

It was somewhat ironic that Richard III's successor to the English throne should be of Welsh descent, for the Welsh had been condemned to subordinate roles for so long. Henry VII and Henry VIII would now revoke the prejudicial laws, giving the Welsh equal rights.

The arrival of the Tudors heralded a new age. With Henry VII came increasing peace, prosperity and enlightenment. This was the age of the great voyages of exploration – of Columbus and Cabot, Magellan, Pizarro, Hawkins, Drake and Ralegh. Mercator would complete his first map of the world. And on the high seas, England and Spain would become the great rivals for supremacy. Portugal would establish trading links with India, and by the end of Elizabeth's reign the first charter for the East India Company would be granted.

The latter part of this period became a time of religious upheaval and intolerance, as Protestantism vied with Catholicism. Luther would be condemned as a heretic, Latimer and Tyndale burnt at the stake for their beliefs. Under Henry VIII

3,000 monasteries would be destroyed, while 300 Martyrs were burnt at the stake at Queen Mary's orders.

The wool trade continued to prosper. In fact, sheep had become so prolific that Henry VII had to introduce a new law restricting the number of sheep anyone could hold, for common lands were being enclosed for pasture, and villages erased for more pasture. Henry sought to wrest the cloth trade from Flanders for the English and this too would become a new source of wealth.

HENRY VII

Ruled 22 August 1485–21 April 1509. Crowned: Westminster Abbey, 30 October 1485.

Titles: *king of England; earl of Richmond (from birth).*

Born: *Pembroke Castle, 28 January 1457.* **Died**: *Richmond Palace, 21 April 1509, aged 52.* **Buried**: *Westminster Abbey.*

Married: *18 January 1486, at Westminster Abbey: Elizabeth (1466–1503), dau. of Edward IV: 8 children. Henry allegedly had one illegitimate son, though this seems to have been disproved.*

The first of the Tudor kings of England, Henry's claim to the throne was extremely tenuous. He was descended from Edward III's son John of Gaunt, but only through his mistress Katherine Swynford. Their child, John Beaufort, was made duke of Somerset and his granddaughter, Margaret, was Henry VII's mother, giving birth when she was only thirteen. The Beauforts' claim on the English throne had once been declared illegitimate, but it was later legalized. Henry's more authentic claim was from the Welsh rulers. His father, Edmund Tudor, earl of Richmond, was eighth in line from Rhys ap Gruffydd, the Lord Rhys of Deheubarth, and through him Henry could claim descent from the Celtic princes of Wales and as far back as the pre-Saxon rulers of Britain. Rightly or wrongly Henry argued that the blood of Arthur flowed in his veins, and he even named his first-born son Arthur to emphasize that connection.

Nevertheless Henry was aware that his right to the throne by descent was not strong, there were at least a dozen others with a better claim – even assuming he knew that Edward V and Richard, Duke of York (the 'Princes in the Tower') were dead. His real claim was by right of conquest. He had defeated Richard III at Bosworth and was a popular claimant. His uncle, the notorious Jasper Tudor, a colourful adventurer had been amongst the staunchest supporters of the Lancastrians in the Wars of the Roses. The Tudor name brought with it an aura of daring and excitement. The nobility had not fully supported Richard III, but neither were they especially supportive of Richard's nephew, Edward, earl of Warwick, who was then only ten years old, but who had the strongest claim to the throne by right of descent. Henry VII grew to resent Edward's existence and found reasons to have him imprisoned and later executed for treason in 1499. Henry strengthened his claim on the throne by marrying Elizabeth of York, the eldest daughter of Edward IV, thereby uniting the houses of York and Lancaster under the new dynasty. Richard III had declared Edward IV's children illegitimate, and one of Henry's first Acts of Parliament was to legitimize them again. It only serves to emphasize, however, the questionable entitlement that Henry had to the throne. He knew this and was forever fearful of other claimants. It is no coincidence that during Henry's reign two significant pretenders came forward, Lambert Simnel and Perkin Warbeck. Henry was gracious to the first, and patient to the latter.

Henry's childhood had been one of exile and estrangement. His father had died before his birth and his young mother remarried. Henry was raised by his uncle, Jasper, until Pembroke Castle fell to the Yorkists in 1461, when Henry's custody passed to William Herbert, soon created Baron Herbert and earl of Pembroke. Henry received a good education and was raised as a prospective husband for Herbert's daughter Maud, but all this changed when Herbert was executed for treason in 1469, and soon after Henry was reunited with his uncle Jasper, who was welcomed back at court with the restoration of Henry VI in 1470. The king even

From a portrait dated 1505

recognized Henry Tudor as a likely heir. Fortunes changed again when Edward IV recovered the crown, and both Jasper and Henry fled Britain to seek refuge in Brittany. Despite attempts by Edward to find them they survived. Little is known of this period, but judging from Henry's later nature it was evident that he learned to survive by his wits and to trust no one. It was this wily but dashing soldier who defeated Richard III at Bosworth in 1485 and inherited the throne of England.

Yet Henry forever remained a nervous king. Despite his success over the various claimants to the throne, who remained troublesome throughout the first half of his reign, Henry was anxious to establish his authority amongst his peers in Europe. He received the backing of Pope Innocent VIII in 1486, who recognized his right to the throne and threatened excommunication to any who challenged that right. With the birth of his son, Arthur, in September 1486, Henry was keen to make a strong alliance with the rulers of Aragon, Ferdinand and Isabella, whose court was one of the richest in Europe. Their daughter, Katherine, had been born a few months earlier than Arthur, and negotiations over their betrothal began as early as 1489. They were eventually married in 1499.

The link with Spain became even more important following Columbus's discovery of a route to the Indies (or so was then believed) in 1492. Columbus claimed these islands in the name of

Ferdinand and Isabella. Henry took considerable interest in trade and exploration, though he had failed to help finance Columbus's expedition. He certainly did not overlook a second opportunity and in 1496 authorized and financed a voyage of discovery by the Genoese sailor Giovanni Caboto, who set sail from Bristol in 1497 and discovered Newfoundland (five hundred years after the Vikings), though he also believed these to be the lands of the Great Khan.

Henry was keen to avoid expensive wars and thus needed an alliance with England's centuries-old foe, France. Key to this was an alliance with Scotland. While pursuing one political marriage with Spain, Henry also negotiated another with Scotland. As early as 1487 plans were afoot to arrange no less than three marriages between the Scottish and English royal houses. The strength of James III's friendship with the English (see p. 274) angered many Scottish nobles and resulted in James's murder in 1488. Negotiations were not reopened until 1495, when the pretender Perkin Warbeck found favour with both James IV of Scotland (see p. 280) and the scheming German emperor, Maximilian I, who agreed to support the Scots against the English. This forced Henry to enter into discussions with Scotland with a view to encouraging Scotland to drop the Auld Alliance with France. Whilst James IV never agreed to this, a peace treaty was agreed between England and Scotland in 1502 and James IV married Henry's eldest daughter Margaret in August 1503. Henry had also negotiated an alliance with Maximilian in February 1496.

SIMNEL, LAMBERT. Pretender to the throne of England, crowned in Ireland as Edward VI of England on 24 May 1487. Simnel, who was aged only eleven or twelve, was a pawn in the dynastic struggles that had led to the Wars of the Roses and had not yet settled down at the start of the reign of Henry VII. Simnel was of humble origin, and his real name is not known — contemporary records call him John, not Lambert, and even his surname is suspect. He was purportedly the son of an Oxford joiner and had been born in 1475. He was raised and educated by a local priest, Richard Simon, and through him came under the wing of John de la Pole, earl of Lincoln, the son of Edward IV's sister, Elizabeth. Lincoln had been nominated as his heir by Richard III and he believed he could use Simnel as a means to attain the throne. Henry VII's claim to the English throne was primarily by right of conquest, not by descent. There had been considerable secrecy during the reign of Richard III over the fate of Edward IV's sons, Edward (Edward V) and Richard, duke of York – the 'Princes in the Tower'. Also, on his accession, Henry VII had imprisoned Edward, earl of Warwick, another nephew of Edward IV. Simnel was the same age as Warwick, and only slightly younger than Richard of York. When Lincoln first put forward Simnel's claim it was as Prince Richard, but this was soon changed to Edward of Warwick. For his safety Simnel was taken to Ireland in late 1486, where there were many Yorkist supporters. Although Henry VII soon discovered the truth about Simnel and declared him an impostor in February 1487, bringing the real Warwick out of the Tower to prove he was alive, the support for Simnel grew and he was crowned in Dublin Cathedral as Edward VI. With Simnel as his figurehead, Lincoln led an invasion force into England in June 1487 but it was decisively beaten at the battle of Stoke on 16 June, where Lincoln was killed. Simnel, being still a minor, was pardoned by Henry who was kind to the boy. He allowed him to work in the royal kitchens and he was eventually elevated to the role of the king's falconer. He died in 1525, aged about fifty. He fared considerably better than the subsequent pretender, Perkin Warbeck.

WARBECK, PERKIN. Pretender to the throne of England, who proclaimed himself as Richard IV in 1494. Like the earlier claimant, Lambert Simnel, Warbeck took advantage of the tenuousness of Henry VII's claim to the English throne and the uncertainty over the fates of rightful heirs. He was in truth the son of a French official, John de Werbecque, and had been born at Tournai in Picardy in 1474. He subsequently gained work as a merchant's assistant and, while in Ireland in 1491, he gained the support of the Yorkists, first claiming to be Edward, earl of Warwick, then an illegitimate son of Richard III, and finally Richard, duke of York, the younger son of Edward IV and one of the 'Princes in the Tower', whose fate was still uncertain. Warbeck may have already intrigued with Edward IV's sister, Margaret of Burgundy who, in November 1492, recognized him as her nephew and the rightful heir to the English throne. Warbeck travelled through Europe, gaining support and recognition, most importantly from Maximilian I, the new German emperor, who urged Warbeck to invade England. It was with Maximilian's encouragement that Warbeck proclaimed himself as Richard IV in October 1494 and returned to Ireland to raise an invasion force. Henry VII, however, had been quick to respond, and had succeeded in arresting most of the English nobility who supported Warbeck. For over a year Warbeck vacillated between Ireland and the Netherlands, seeking to gain support, every time finding himself bettered by Henry VII. He eventually turned to James IV of Scotland who offered to help. James even married Warbeck to his cousin, Lady Catherine Gordon, daughter of the earl of Huntly, in January 1496. Their eventual invasion of England ended up as no more than a border skirmish in September 1496. By then Warbeck had already lost the support of the Emperor Maximilian and James IV. Warbeck emerged as a whinging, self-centred individual with a high opinion of himself but little ability. Warbeck's last refuge was in Cornwall, where the Cornish had rebelled against Henry VII's taxes. Warbeck raised a local force and in September 1497 besieged Exeter, but with little success. He fled and was captured a month later and imprisoned. Henry was lenient with Warbeck, allowing him to live at court, but when Warbeck sought to escape, he was imprisoned in the Tower, close to the real earl of Warwick. As was almost certainly intended, the two managed to communicate and plotted a conspiracy. As a consequence they were both charged with treason and executed. Warbeck was hanged at Tyburn on 23 November 1499, aged twenty-five.

Henry VII's ancestry meant he was held in high regard by the Welsh, and although he did not especially show them any favour, neither did he show them any hostility. In fact as his reign progressed, so members of the Welsh nobility were appointed to senior posts and granted territory in Wales, particularly the Marches. As a result the English domination of Wales by the marcher lords ceased. For the first time in generations, there was harmony between England, Wales and Scotland, with Henry's foreign negotiations bringing greater peace with his European counterparts. This was perhaps Henry's greatest legacy. Although he was only continuing policies already initiated by Edward IV, the upsurge of trade and exploration at the start of Henry's reign, against a background of increased peace, prosperity, and also enlightenment, gives the feeling that, with the arrival of the Tudors, a new age had begun. Admittedly this was probably more evident in hindsight than at the time.

However the final years of Henry's reign were ones of personal sadness and increasing loneliness. His eldest son, Arthur, had died childless of consumption in April 1502, aged only fifteen. Henry's wife Elizabeth died ten months later following the birth of their eighth child, who also died. Henry, who had never been a trusting or a happy king, became all the more surly, and retreated further into private life. Under his instruction Sheen Palace, which had been badly damaged by fire in 1497, was rebuilt and made all the more lavish as Richmond Palace, and it was here that he retired, keeping himself more to himself. His health failed and he had increasing bouts of asthma and gout. He died at Richmond Palace in 1509, aged 52.

Although Henry's reign is seen as the start of England's glory and the birth of Modern England, with the end of the Middle Ages, in truth his main achievement was in uniting a previously divided England and bringing harmony with Wales and Scotland, which provided a solid base upon which his successors, Henry VIII and Elizabeth, could build. Personally Henry was a sad king – faithful to his wife, but cautious with his affections and perhaps never truly enjoying the success that he achieved. Henry would be succeeded by his third child and second son.

HENRY VIII
Ruled 22 April 1509–28 January 1547. Crowned:
Westminster Abbey, 24 June 1509.
Titles: *king of England and (from 1542) of Ireland; duke of York (from 1494), duke of Cornwall (from 1502), prince of Wales and earl of Chester (from 1504).*
Born: *Greenwich Palace, Kent, 28 June 1491.* **Died**: *Whitehall Palace, London, 28 January 1547, aged 55.* **Buried**: *Windsor Castle.*
Married: *(1) 11 June 1509, at Greenwich Palace, Katherine (1485–1536), dau. Ferdinand II, king of Aragon; marriage annulled 23 May 1533: 6 children;*
(2) 25 January 1533, at York Place (renamed Whitehall Palace), London, Anne (c1500–36), dau. Thomas Boleyn, earl of Wiltshire; marriage declared invalid 17 May 1536: 3 children;
(3) 30 May 1536, at Whitehall Palace, London, Jane (c1508–37), dau. Sir John Seymour; died in childbirth: 1 son;

(4) 6 January 1540, at Greenwich Palace, Anne (1515–57), dau. Johann, duke of Cleves; marriage annulled 9 July 1540: no children;

(5) 28 July 1540, at Oatlands Palace, Surrey, Katherine (c1520–42) dau. Lord Edmund Howard; executed 13 February 1542: no children;

(6) 12 July 1543, at Hampton Court Palace, Katherine (c1512–48), dau. Sir Thomas Parr: no children.

Henry also had at least two illegitimate children, and probably more.

Henry VIII is probably the best known king of England and may even be the most notorious (though there are plenty to compete for that title). Some may argue he was also the most important king of England because of the status which he brought to his kingdom along with the establishment of the Church of England. Certainly his reign saw some of the most significant developments in England since the time of Edward I.

Henry was not born to be king. As a younger son of Henry VII he had been groomed for the church, receiving a substantial classical education. However, Henry's elder brother Arthur died of consumption and Henry, still only ten, became heir apparent. Unlike his father, who was reserved and surly, Henry was a happy child who delighted in all manner of sports and entertainment. Not only did he master French and Latin, and become an excellent rider and athlete, but he was a fine dancer and musician – the music of *Greensleeves* has long been attributed to him. He also had a natural authority and self-command, and enjoyed touring England and presenting himself to his subjects, which made him a very popular prince and king. Although the nickname 'Bluff King Hal' was only accorded to him posthumously, it fitted his character well. Moreover unlike his predecessors for the past one hundred years (and arguably longer), Henry was the first to inherit a comparatively united kingdom, as an assured successor with every right of inheritance to the throne.

His father had established good relationships with the leading countries of Europe, and with no foreign wars for some years, the country's finances were strong. England was in the best shape financially, spiritually and administratively that it had been for a long time.

Henry was two months off his eighteenth birthday when his father died. He was a handsome, well proportioned youth, in love with life and the world. He happily obeyed his father's dying wish that he marry his elder brother's widow, Katherine of Aragon, in order to continue the alliance with Spain. They were married six weeks later and two weeks after that there was a double coronation in Westminster Abbey at the height of midsummer, with much feasting and merrymaking.

Henry was more interested in enjoying himself than bothering with the day to day affairs of government. He satisfied himself that his ministers could be trusted, and left the overall direction of affairs to William Warham, archbishop of Canterbury, Thomas Howard, earl of Surrey (later 2nd duke of Norfolk), who was the Lord Treasurer, Bishop Richard Foxe and, after 1514, to Thomas Wolsey. Henry rid the courts of Edmund Dudley and Sir Richard Empson, two key ministers in Henry VII's reign who were the architects of a strict tax regime and had become hated by the populace. Henry had them executed on the grounds of 'constructive treason', as they had sought to arm their men as Henry VII lay dying.

Henry preferred to involve himself in European affairs, playing the role of an international magnate not confined to an English backwater. He supported his father-in-law, Ferdinand of Aragon, against the Moors in 1511, and joined Pope Julius II, along with Venice and Spain, in the Holy League against France, which was formed that October. This increased the friction between England and Scotland (France's old ally), which was exacerbated by border skirmishes and sea raids. James IV of Scotland, who was Henry's brother-in-law, insisted that, if Henry remained part of the Holy League, the only outcome could be war between Scotland and England. Henry seemed undisturbed. In June 1513 Henry led an invasion force to Calais. James IV took advantage to invade England, something Henry had anticipated and so despatched Thomas Howard to counter. The result was the battle of Flodden on 9 September 1513, where James IV and the flower of Scottish nobility fell. Since the heir, James V (see p. 286), was only a year old, Henry's sister, Margaret, became the Scottish regent. She did not receive the support of the Scottish aristocracy, but for a period, although skirmishes continued, the battle with Scotland was won, and Henry was victorious. He was also victorious in France, leading the successful sieges of Thérouanne and Tournai, whilst his forces defeated the French at the battle of the Spurs, at Guinegate, on 16 August 1513. The name of the battle signified the speed of the French retreat. Thomas Wolsey negotiated peace terms with France, one of the terms being the marriage of Henry's sister Mary to Louis XII of France in August 1514. The marriage was short lived as Louis died only a few months later. Mary then angered Henry by running away with his close friend Charles Brandon, duke of Suffolk, and marrying in secret in February 1515. They were eventually pardoned, upon payment of an exacting fine, and they would subsequently become the grandparents of the ill-fated Lady Jane Grey.

Henry wanted to be the centre of the European stage. When the Holy Roman Emperor, Maximilian I, died in January 1519, Henry stood as a candidate to succeed him, having earlier been encouraged by Maximilian himself who regarded him as a good prospect. However, the electors selected from the controlling Hapsburg family. When Pope Leo X died in December 1521, Henry strove to have an English pope, nominating Thomas Wolsey but without success. Europe seemed a world closed to Henry and it frustrated him that a man of his abilities was denied greater influence in European affairs. It was probably this attitude that shaped his dealings with the new French king, François. In June 1520 Wolsey was able to engineer a summit meeting at Guisnes, near Calais, which became known as the Field of the Cloth of Gold because of the extravagance of the display, each

From a portrait by Holbein

party trying to outshine the other. Another peace treaty was negotiated, though it too was short lived.

This period was one of change in Europe. Most significant, as far as England was concerned, was the reforming zeal of the German scholar and preacher, Martin Luther, who began a prolonged series of attacks upon the Papacy and the Catholic church, including his book *On the Babylonish Captivity of the Church* in 1520. Henry had remained a staunch supporter of the Pope and felt compelled to respond to Luther's attacks. Together with Thomas More and John Fisher, Henry wrote *Defence of the Seven Sacraments*, which became a best-seller throughout Europe. In recognition of his support the Pope conferred on Henry in 1521 the title of *Fidei Defensor*, or Defender of the Faith, a title which has been used by all subsequent English monarchs, regardless of their faith. Within a few years it would seem a singularly inappropriate title for Henry.

He was becoming increasingly concerned about the birth of an heir. His wife, Katherine, had borne him six children, but only one of these, Mary, had survived infancy. His eldest son, Henry, born in 1511, had died after only seven weeks. Their last born child died within hours of its birth in November 1518. By 1526, when Katherine had turned forty, it was evident that Henry would not have a son. It was unthinkable that he would be succeeded by a girl. He began to believe that the fault lay with him, and that he had committed a sin against the church in marrying his brother's widow, even though the marriage had received papal blessing. It was especially galling as in June 1519 Henry's mistress, Elizabeth Blount, who was only seventeen, had borne him a baby boy, who became Henry Fitzroy, duke of Richmond. Although illegitimate, Henry began to regard this boy as his likely heir if he were unable to produce a legitimate child. Also by 1527 Henry had become infatuated with the twenty-five-year-old Anne Boleyn, whose elder sister, Mary, had been Henry's mistress for some years. Anne refused to be simply his mistress and played for higher stakes. Wolsey entered into negotiations with the pope formally to annul Henry's marriage with Katherine. The new pope, Clement VII, was traditional in his outlook and a vehement opposer of Lutheranism. At first it looked as if he might accommodate Henry, but the pope then succumbed to the power of the Holy Roman Emperor, Charles V, who was the nephew of Henry's wife. Clement refused to accept that his predecessor's dispensation for Henry's marriage could have been in error, yet whilst he did not reject Henry's request outright, he procrastinated in every way possible, setting up a commission to review the issue.

The affair dragged on for six years, during which time Clement was seen by more and more countries as a weak pope. The whole of Scandinavia broke with Rome and introduced Lutheranism, beginning in 1527. Henry's adviser, Thomas Cromwell, advised the same. His inability to resolve the matter had seen Wolsey fall from power. He was arrested for treason in November 1530, but died soon after.

Cromwell now moved matters ahead and it was under his guidance that Henry became the Head of a separate Church of England with the authority to appoint his own archbishops and bishops. Thomas Cranmer, his newly appointed archbishop of

Canterbury, pronounced on 23 May 1533 that Henry's marriage with Katherine was void. Henry had already taken this as read, as he had secretly wedded Anne Boleyn in January 1533, when she was already a month pregnant. The pope refused to accept the pronouncement, and in July 1533 he declared the divorce and remarriage void, and prepared to excommunicate Henry. The excommunication was suspended, but it was reaffirmed by Clement's successor, Paul III, who was however unable to gain the international support he desired to formalize the sentence. This merely served to force Henry further down his chosen road rather than allow for reconciliation. In fact Henry was at great pains to demonstrate that his argument was only against the pope, not the church. The significant change was that Henry was 'Head of the Church' in his dominions, or (like the pope) God's representative. Otherwise, changes were limited, and Henry emphasised this with the publication of the *Act of the Six Articles* in 1539 which re-affirmed doctrines inherited from the Church of Rome. Nevertheless there were those who could not support Henry in his role as Head of the Church, such as Sir Thomas More and Bishop John Fisher, who refused to acknowledge this and were executed in 1535.

Henry's next move was to appoint a commission to report on the state of the monasteries. Cromwell had long believed that the monasteries were too powerful and were likely to lead any pro-Roman resistance to change. Following the report Parliament legislated in 1536 for the suppression of all small monasteries on grounds that they were uneconomic and, on the strength of this, dissolved all remaining monasteries in 1539. This caused considerable anguish throughout England, but especially in the north, where there was a rebellion known as the Pilgrimage of Grace. This rebellion was not just about the monasteries. Dissatisfaction had been fermenting for some time and the Acts of Dissolution were the final spark. Peasants were rebelling against the enclosure of common lands, which limited their ability to farm because of high rents. The rebellion began in Lincolnshire in October 1536 and spread through Yorkshire under the command of Robert Aske. Henry appeared conciliatory and defused the rebellion by promises, none of which he fulfilled, and some months later he had Aske and over two hundred of the rebels executed. This punishment was a salutory lesson to all and Cromwell's commissioners met little resistance as they moved from county to county closing the monasteries. The last to fall was Waltham Abbey in Essex in March 1540. Although the Crown benefitted considerably from the closure of the monasteries, since most of the profits arising passed to Henry who was always desperate for money for his foreign exploits, the ultimate beneficiaries were the local landed gentry who, once the monastery was closed and ransacked, acquired most of the land and remaining properties. It was the greatest shift in land ownership since the Norman Conquest.

Henry's early delight over Anne Boleyn's pregnancy soon faded when she gave birth to a girl, the future Elizabeth (I). This was followed by two stillborn children. A fourth child was miscarried following a fall Henry had from a horse in January 1536 which left him unconscious and the shock brought on Anne's labour. Henry recovered, though the injury led to complications in his later years with a severely ulcerated leg. By now Henry had lost all interest in Anne – he even maintained he had been seduced by witchcraft. As a sign of this, Catholics later ascribed to Anne a shrivelled sixth finger. He readily believed charges of her infidelity and adultery and she was arrested, tried and found guilty of treason and executed on 19 May 1536. Just two days before Archbishop Cranmer declared Anne's marriage to Henry null and void, probably on the rather tenuous grounds that Henry had formerly had a relationship with her sister Mary.

During the previous two years Henry had become besotted with one of Anne's ladies-in-waiting, Jane Seymour, a not especially attractive lady but one who beguiled Henry with her coquettish ways. They were married eleven days after Anne's execution and the marriage was a happy one, albeit brief. Jane was never crowned queen because an outbreak of plague in London delayed the coronation and then Jane became pregnant.

Henry was overjoyed when Jane gave birth to a boy, the future Edward VI, but Jane was seriously weakened by the birth and died twelve days later in the midst of Henry's celebrations. Because she had given him a son and heir, Jane remained the favourite of Henry's wives and after his death he was laid beside her in St George's Chapel, Windsor.

For his next wife Henry looked to Europe. Because of the papal bull isolating him, Henry was fearful that the French, the Hapsburgs or both would invade England and depose him. As a consequence Henry sought a political marriage with Germany and, through the advice of Thomas Cromwell, settled on Anne, the sister of the duke of Cleves in Germany. Although Henry admired her portrait, he was horrified when he first met Anne in January 1540 but by then marriage arrangements had proceeded too far. Henry feared the backlash if he withdrew. Although they were wed on 6 January, the marriage was never consummated and both parties readily agreed to a divorce which went through seven months later. Henry was generous to Anne, because of her compliance, and the two remained good friends.

Unfortunately for Henry his next marriage, which was almost on the rebound, was to the beautiful teenage Katherine Howard, a cousin of Anne Boleyn's. He and Katherine were married within three weeks of the divorce and Henry delighted in his young bride, who seemed to put the spring back in his step, even though by now he was becoming grossly fat and ageing fast.

Evidently Katherine soon tired of her husband, thirty years her senior, and turned to her former lovers. She was soon betrayed, charged with treason and executed on 13 February 1542. Henry had at first refused to believe the charges and never quite recovered from her loss.

When he entered into his final marriage in the following year it was to an older lady, already twice widowed, Katherine Parr. By all accounts Henry was now after a companion rather than a lover, and in Parr he found a woman with whom he could converse on a wide range of subjects and who served as an excellent stepmother to his three surviving children, Mary, Elizabeth and Edward, who were reconciled for the first time in 1543.

During these tempestuous marriages Henry had not ignored the international scene, or indeed the state of Britain. He regarded the British Isles as his own empire, and had made a move towards consolidating it in 1536 with what has since been called the Act of Union, which officially incorporated Wales as part of England, rather than as a separate province. He was unable to enact the same legislation for Ireland, although his father had made the Irish parliament subject to the English. A rebellion led by the Fitzgeralds in Ireland in 1534 had been summarily dealt with and in 1542 Henry declared himself king rather than lord of Ireland.

Henry also kept a constant eye on the intrigues between France and Scotland and had even visited France to meet the king, though the two could never reconcile their views. Relationships with Scotland soured. Henry regarded it as an affront when James V (see p. 286) failed to keep a meeting at York in September 1541 and future meetings were postponed because of the interference of the French king. Henry grew tired of the Scots, and the last connection between them ended when his sister, Margaret, died in November 1541.

The following year saw Henry prepared to go to war with Scotland and, although no formal declaration was made, hostilities broke out in a series of scraps and skirmishes with the upper hand going to the Scots. However a Scottish force of some 10,000 was soundly defeated by 3,000 English at Solway Moss in November 1542. The Scots had appeared as such a disorganized rabble that the defeat was a double disgrace, and soon after James V pined away in despair. Henry now pursued a marriage alliance between his son Edward and James's infant daughter Mary and, under the terms of a peace treaty concluded in July 1543, Mary was to marry Edward in her tenth year. This treaty was never ratified by the Scots while the pro-French nobles did everything to undermine it. Hostilities continued between England and Scotland throughout the 1540s, with Scotland using this as an excuse to argue that the treaty was invalid. Henry had marginally better success with France, concluding a treaty with François in 1546.

Henry died on 28 January 1547, aged only 55, but a victim of his gross conduct. Despite the major reforms that he had made he was not a great initiator, relying instead on such great men as Wolsey and Cromwell whom he cast aside when no longer needed. At times he ruled like a despot, engineering everything to his own ends. Yet he could wield that power without it destroying him and it is true to say that no other English king could have undertaken such reforms and succeeded. It was through Henry, the first king to be referred to as His Majesty, that the modern English state was created.

EDWARD VI
Ruled 28 January 1547–6 July 1553. Crowned: Westminster Abbey, 20 February 1547.
Titles: *king of England and duke of Cornwall.*
Born: *Hampton Court Palace, 12 October 1537.* **Died**: *Greenwich Palace, 6 July 1553, aged 15.* **Buried**: *Westminster Abbey.*

As had happened so many times before, a strong and powerful king was followed by a weak one. Edward VI was Henry's only surviving son and was only nine when his father died (Henry Fitzroy had died in 1536). His mother, Jane Seymour, had died giving birth, and though in his youth he seemed healthy, it became evident that he had a weak constitution. He had the potential to be a wise and powerful king, for he received an extensive education, and was raised with considerable care by his step-mother Katherine Parr. His childhood seemed to pass him by. Thrust into kingship and surrounded by scholarly men, Edward tried to run before he could walk, combining precocity with much of his father's stubborness and self-centredness.

Edward's uncle, Edward Seymour, duke of Somerset, was made 'Protector of the Realm' during Edward's minority and started the reign with an invasion of Scotland to enforce the marriage treaty between Edward and Mary, Queen of Scots. Although he defeated the Scots at Pinkie in September he was unable to break the Scots' resolve and in fact drove them closer to a marriage alliance with France. Edward was surrounded by rival factions who sought to control the king's mind when he was still too young to understand fully the motives for his actions. It seems that he genuinely regretted having to agree to the execution of Thomas Seymour, who had become his step-father, on grounds of high treason in March 1549, and in 1552 he also agreed to the execution of the protector, Somerset, who had presumed on his authority and been ousted from power in October 1549. In his wake the over ambitious John Dudley, earl of Warwick (and soon to be created duke of Northumberland) came to power, operating as protector in all but name.

Edward had been raised a Protestant and at the outset of his reign Protestant reform continued at an even greater pace than before due to the unremitting zeal of the Protector Somerset. All shrines and pictures of saints were destroyed, many processions were banned and the number of official ceremonies reduced. The first English Prayer Book was issued in 1548. There was much Catholic discontent throughout England, though the only manifestation of it was a rebellion in Devon in the summer of 1549 against the *Common Prayer Book* and this was promptly dealt with by Lord Russell. At the same time, in East Anglia, there was a repeat of the problems which had given rise to the Pilgrimage of Grace in 1536, when local peasants, under the leadership of Robert Kett, a tanner, rebelled against the enclosure of common land. Kett gathered together a force of 10,000 men to blockade Norwich, but the rebels were defeated by John Dudley and Kett was hanged.

Edward founded a number of grammar schools throughout England which still bear his name, and he also established a workhouse for the poor at Bridewell and Christ's Hospital in London. It seems that the young king had a genuine concern to help the poor and needy as well as to promote education and learning. Although he was moulded into a zealous Protestant, he evidently promoted it with good intent. It was as much his concern as it was Northumberland's, that if he died young all the Protestant reform would be undone if his half-sister Mary, a staunch Catholic, came to the throne. He thus complied with Northumberland's plans in promoting Lady Jane Grey as his successor.

Edward's last year was one of much suffering. He contracted consumption and also suffered from congenital syphilis, passed on from his father. His death was a merciful blessing for him, but it would turn the country into a period of turmoil.

JANE 'THE NINE DAYS QUEEN'
Proclaimed Queen of England, 10 July 1553. Deposed 19 July 1553.
Born: Bradgate Manor, Leicestershire, October 1537. *Died (executed)*: 12 February 1554, aged 16. *Buried*: Tower of London.
Married: 21 May 1553, at Durham House, London, Guilford (1536–54) son of John Dudley, duke of Northumberland. No children.

Jane was the innocent victim of the schemes of her ambitious and recent father-in-law, John Dudley, Duke of Northumberland, to continue the Protestant faith in England after the death of Edward VI in preference to the Catholic princess Mary (I). Jane was the granddaughter of Mary, the sister of Henry VIII, and under the latter's will, Mary's children had right of succession only after the deaths of his own children and their heirs. Edward VI signed an amendment to his father's will only a few weeks before his own death which set aside his sisters' claims to the throne and nominated Jane. Just a month earlier Northumberland, who had assumed the role (if not the title) of protector of the realm during Edward's minority, had arranged the marriage of his son Guilford to Jane. Jane did not particularly like Guilford, although their subsequent adversity drew them together.

Jane was formally offered the crown in accordance with Edward VI's wishes, and declared queen, against her own better judgement, by the Council on 9 July 1553. Jane did not want to be queen of England, but when she accepted the crown, she did so recognizing it would help the Protestant reform. She was publicly proclaimed queen the following day. She was an extremely well educated and well mannered child who in other circumstances would have made an excellent queen consort. She was obdurate that her husband would not be jointly proclaimed king. The nobility were affronted by Northumberland's scheme. There was also overwhelming public support for Mary. Jane retained the title of queen for just nine days. Northumberland's army was defeated, and he was arrested and beheaded. Jane and her husband were also arrested and imprisoned in the Tower. Mary was prepared to be lenient with them, recognizing their unfortunate position, but Jane's fate was sealed when her father, Henry Grey, duke of Suffolk, became involved in Sir Thomas Wyatt's rebellion against Mary. Jane refused to recant her Protestantism and on 12 February 1554 she was executed, having been found guilty of treason.

MARY (I), 'BLOODY MARY'
Ruled England, 19 July 1553–17 November 1558. Crowned: Westminster Abbey, 1 October 1553. Also queen consort of Spain: 16 January 1556–17 November 1558.
Born: *Greenwich Palace, Kent, 18 February 1516.* **Died**: *St James's Palace, London, 17 November 1558, aged 42.* **Buried**: *Westminster Abbey.*
Married: *25 July 1554, at Winchester Cathedral, Philip (1527–98) son of Charles V, Holy Roman Emperor. No children.*

Mary was the eldest surviving daughter of Henry VIII and his first wife, Katherine of Aragon and, as such, she was despatched in 1525 to Ludlow Castle, styled Princess of Wales. When Henry's marriage to Katherine was declared void by Thomas Cranmer in

1533, Mary, who was then seventeen, was declared illegitimate. Mary, who was a well educated child and a capable linguist and musician, was devoted to her mother and hated the separation. She steadfastly refused to accept that the marriage was not legitimate and indeed regarded her father's second marriage to Anne Boleyn as bigamous and false. She had a violent and volatile relationship with her stepmother and disliked her young half-sister Elizabeth. Mary remained obdurate throughout Henry's reign, refusing to accept the Protestant Reformation.

Jane Seymour, Henry's third wife, worked hard to reconcile father and daughter, but the family were not fully reunited until Henry's last wife, Katherine Parr, who succeeded in bringing them all together, united, at last, in their support for the young Edward VI. Mary's right to the throne was recognized in Henry's will, in succession to Edward. However Edward subsequently amended his father's will to disbar Mary from the throne for fear that she would undo all of the Protestant reforms enacted during Edward's brief reign. He, as we have seen, nominated his cousin, Jane, as his successor, but although Jane was proclaimed as queen, she did not receive the support of her peers or the populace and was rapidly dethroned. Mary entered London in triumph on 3 August 1553 and was crowned two months later. Since neither Jane nor the Empress Matilda had been crowned, Mary was the first genuine queen regnant of England. It is perhaps ironic that at the same time Scotland was also ruled by a Queen Mary, who was her first cousin (see p. 291).

As feared by the reformers, Mary did begin to reverse the legislation passed during her half-brother's reign and restore as much of the old order as she believed possible. She was cautious, because she did not want to provoke religious disorder and strove, instead, to find a balance. She reinstated some of the Catholic bishops and imprisoned certain zealous reformers, but she did not dare overturn her father's enactment which would have restored the Pope's supremacy. She did, however, pass an act which invalidated her father's divorce from Katherine of Aragon, restoring Mary's legitimacy and automatically bastardizing Elizabeth.

Mary had never married; in fact she had come to regard herself as a spinster. It is true that she was not very attractive and she had inherited congenital syphilis from her father which not only gave her a weak constitution, with regular headaches and poor eyesight, but gave her a form of rhinitis which meant that her breath was always foul-smelling. This hardly endeared her to anyone and if there was to be any marriage at all it would be a political one. Her choice settled on Philip of Spain, the son of the Holy Roman Emperor, Charles V. Parliament petitioned the Queen to reconsider and to seek a husband from within England, but Mary steadfastly refused. Her choice of Philip was extremely unpopular, with many believing that Philip would use the opportunity to enforce his own control over England and that Mary would become a Spanish puppet.

A group of conspirators including Sir James Crofts and Sir Thomas Wyatt plotted against Mary but the intended *coup* was ill planned and only Wyatt's rebellion in Kent, which began on 25 January 1554, carried any force. It was, however, soon quashed, many of the ringleaders were captured, tried and executed. The Princess Elizabeth was also implicated in the *coup* and briefly confined to the Tower of London.

Mary's marriage with Philip went ahead in July 1554. In accordance with Spanish tradition, Philip was granted the title of king (although he was only the king consort). Eighteen months later Philip's father abdicated, relinquishing to him the throne of Spain. Mary likewise assumed the title of Queen of Spain. It is also worth an aside here and noting that when Mary Queen of Scots married François, the French Dauphin in April 1558, he likewise became king consort of Scotland. Although Mary fell in love with Philip, the love was not reciprocated. Philip left for Spain in August 1555, returning to England only once between March and June 1557. His treatment of Mary was callous and left her heart-broken.

In November 1554 Cardinal Reginald Pole, the papal legate (and subsequently archbishop of Canterbury) announced that England had been absolved of papal censures and was restored to the Holy See. Whilst this was welcomed by many, in its wake came the papal requirement that all heretics must be burned at the stake. It was from this moment that Mary's reign of terror began, which earned her the title of Bloody Mary. Almost certainly much of it was not of her own desire, but between February 1555 and November 1558 almost 300 victims perished cruelly in the flames. These included Thomas Cranmer, archbishop of Canterbury, and the famous example of Hugh Latimer, bishop of Worcester and Nicholas Ridley, bishop of London, who were burned outside Balliol College, Oxford. These executions were recorded and published, during Elizabeth's reign, by John Foxe in his best-selling *Acts and Monuments of these latter and perilous days* (1563), now popularly known as *Foxe's Book of Martyrs*.

Another conspiracy was hatched against Mary in December 1555, called the Dudley Conspiracy after one of its main architects, Sir Henry Dudley. The idea was to rob the finances from the Exchequer, depose Mary and Philip, and raise Elizabeth to the throne. It was also intended to secure her marriage to Edward Courtenay, a distant relative descended from Edward IV. However before the plot could be achieved news of it leaked out and by March 1556 most of the conspirators were either arrested or had fled to France. There were other plots, all of which failed, but England remained in a sorry state. The last blow to national pride came when Philip convinced Mary and the English Parliament to join Spain in its war against France. As a result of the conflict England lost Calais, its last possession in France.

Mary's husband had returned to Spain and never came back to her. Although she believed she might be pregnant, she had never conceived. Both of these facts caused a depression which added to her overall ill-health, and the loss of Calais as well as all of the Protestant persecutions caused Mary to regard her reign as a total failure. Her famous remark, 'when I am dead, you will find Philip and Calais engraved upon my heart', was not without substance. She died in the early hours of 17 November 1558, her constitution further weakened by influenza. A few weeks earlier Mary had reluctantly conceded that her half-sister, Elizabeth, would be her successor.

ELIZABETH (I)
Ruled England 17 November 1558–24 March 1603.
Crowned: Westminster Abbey, 15 January 1559.
Born: Greenwich Palace, 7 September 1533. **Died:** Richmond
Palace, 24 March 1603, aged 69. **Buried:** Westminster Abbey.

Elizabeth was the only surviving child of Henry VIII and Anne
Boleyn. She was a disappointment to her father, who had anticipated a son and heir. She scarcely knew her mother, who was
executed when Elizabeth was thirty-two months old, and the
infant Elizabeth despatched to Hatfield Palace in Hertfordshire.
She was also disowned by her sister, Mary, the start of a bitter
rivalry that festered for twenty-five years. When Anne Boleyn's
marriage to Henry was declared void, Elizabeth became illegitimate, as had Mary before her, and was thus barred from
inheriting the throne. It was only later, satisfied that he would
be succeeded by his son Edward VI, that Henry recognized Mary
and Elizabeth as potential successors if Edward's line failed.
Typically for Henry, however, he was prepared to recognize
Elizabeth as the 'heiress of a kingdom' in his negotiations with
France over the possible betrothal of Elizabeth to Charles, duke of
Angoulême, the younger son of the French king. Nothing came of
this or of any other possible childhood proposals, but it was
evident that the only real benefit Henry saw in his daughter was
as barter in any political alliance.

Elizabeth was extremely well educated and was a precocious
and intelligent child. She mercifully escaped the congenital syphilis passed by her father to his other children, and grew into a
strong and healthy child who delighted in riding, hunting, archery
and dancing and who became a proficient linguist. It was not until
1543 that Henry's last wife, Katherine Parr, brought all of the
children together in a united household and proved an excellent
stepmother. Whilst Elizabeth and Mary tolerated each other they
never became close. Elizabeth always regarded herself as a rightful heiress. Though supportive of Edward VI, she was seen as a

threat and a liability by Mary when she became queen in 1553. Elizabeth had been raised within her father's newly reformed Church of England while Mary remained defiantly Catholic. During Mary's reign there were terrible persecutions of the reformers after years of ardent Protestantism in Edward's reign. Mary even believed that Elizabeth had plotted against her in a number of conspiracies and had her sister confined first to the Tower of London and then to Woodstock, near Oxford. Thus, when Edward and Mary both died childless, it was with much relief and a belief by Elizabeth that 'this is the Lord's doing,' that she inherited the throne. Her accession was welcomed throughout the land.

Elizabeth had all the credentials for a strong queen. She inherited much from her father – her physical strength and resolution, her vicious temper, her cruelty, but also a delight in pomp, a passion for power and a general joy of life. From her mother, apart from her youthful beauty, she inherited a degree of insincerity and a tendency towards jealousy. She also had an interest in astrology, consulting the alchemist John Dee over the most propitious date for her coronation. His forecast evidently worked, for not only did Elizabeth go on to reign for nearly forty-five years, longer than any king since Edward III, and also live longer than any English monarch since Penda, but her reign was undoubtedly the most glorious England had seen and one which firmly established England as a world power.

Elizabeth's first pressing responsibility was to resolve the religious division in England. She did not want a backlash against the Protestant persecutions of Mary's reign, but neither did she want the rampant Protestantism of Edward's. She sought to strike a balance, accommodating both religions, so that although Protestantism became the national religion, she did not regard it as wrong if there were those who wished to hear the Roman mass in private. But she disliked the more extreme Calvinist tendencies in Protestantism. Those who acted wisely would be safe in Elizabeth's realm, but she would not tolerate any who sought to test her will. Nevertheless, throughout her reign there were many Catholic conspiracies seeking to overthrow Elizabeth. This became worse after 1570 when the Pope, tired of seeking Elizabeth's compliance to the authority of Rome, issued a bull deposing her. Since she took no notice of this, it only strengthened her role as 'Supreme Governor of the Church of England' and meant that anyone who continued to practise Catholicism was effectively a traitor. Much against her own wishes, religious persecution returned after 1570 and this only aggravated the Catholic cause against her. This in turn widened the rift between England and Scotland and led to the darkest shadow cast over her reign, the treatment of Mary Queen of Scots (see p. 291), her cousin and a claimant on the English throne.

The relationship between Scotland and England had been one of near constant hostility for a thousand years. Mary of Scotland was still in her teens when Elizabeth came to the throne, but as the queen consort of the king of France she exerted authority in two strong Catholic countries. Mary's mother, Mary of Guise, who was the queen regent in Scotland, was an even more ardent Catholic and it was her desire to place her daughter on the English throne. There were many Scots who feared that Scotland would become a puppet state of France, and the growing number of Protestants made Scotland a land divided. Elizabeth took advantage of this, secretly supporting the Scottish Protestants in their work against the two Maries. The Scottish rebels soon became too powerful to overlook and Mary of Guise sought aid from France. A French invasion became a probability, and advance troops landed in Scotland. Elizabeth was able to use this situation, albeit reluctantly, to enter into an alliance with Scotland in February 1560 (Treaty of Berwick), whereby England promised troops to help repel the French. Despite some rather scrappy fighting by the English, the French decided to negotiate, circumstances hastened by the death of Mary of Guise. The Treaty of Edinburgh was signed on 6 July.

Five months later François II of France died and in August 1561 the widowed Mary returned to her native Scotland, much to the horror of the English who had hoped she would stay in France. Her power there had been eclipsed by the rise of Catherine de Medici, mother of the young king Charles IX, and Catherine bore no love for the Guises. Whilst this helped Anglo-French relations, Mary's return to Scotland might have stirred up old rivalries. In August 1560 the Scottish Parliament had abolished the pope's authority and brought its Protestant church more in line with England's, but Mary remained a Catholic. To her credit, Mary was conciliatory and her charm captivated her Scottish subjects who soon welcomed her return. However, she refused to ratify the Treaty of Edinburgh, the terms of which would have denied her any possible succession to the English throne, and she actively sought to be regarded as Elizabeth's heir presumptive in the absence of any children. Plans for a meeting between Mary and Elizabeth nearly came to fruition in August 1562, but the eruption of civil war in France between the Catholic Guises and the Huguenots (Protestants) made the situation too tense. It was the closest Elizabeth and Mary ever came to meeting. Aggravatingly Elizabeth refused to name a successor, even after a near fatal bout of smallpox in October 1562, always maintaining that although she had no desire to marry, for the sake of the succession one day she would and produce an heir. Mary of Scotland, on the other hand, was actively in pursuit of a new husband and there was fear in England that if she married the heir of a strong Catholic country, she would have the power to invade England and oust Elizabeth. This was made all the more potent when negotiations opened between Scotland and Spain for the marriage between Mary and the heir to the Spanish throne, Don Carlos. These only ceased when Don Carlos was declared insane. Mary however lost her controlling hand when she fell in love with her cousin, Lord Darnley. The marriage proved unpopular and the subsequent events, including the murder of Mary's secretary, David Rizzio, the mysterious death of Darnley in February 1567 and Mary's affair with and rapid marriage to Lord Bothwell, brought about the fall from grace of Mary and her subsequent deposition.

From a portrait by Nicholas Hilliard, c1575

From July 1567 Mary was a captive, and in May 1568 she was driven out of Scotland and threw herself upon Elizabeth's mercy. Elizabeth was outwardly supportive but maintained she could not harbour Mary while the stigma of her involvement in the death of Darnley was unresolved. Mary remained in prison, first at Carlisle, and then in a series of castles in northern England. This continued for nineteen years with the inevitable consequence that Catholic factions used Mary as the figurehead for their cause. There were several conspiracies during this period culminating in the Babington Plot in the summer of 1586. Plans were well advanced for the murder of Elizabeth and there were hopes of a Spanish invasion, when Babington was betrayed. Mary was aware of Babington's schemes and as a consequence was herself tried for treason, found guilty and, with much reluctance on Elizabeth's part, executed. At this same time Elizabeth had bestowed a pension upon Mary's son, James VI, in effect recognizing him as her heir.

Just why Elizabeth did not marry is the matter of some conjecture. Her dedication to the throne and her people led her to say that she was married to the nation in much the same way as she believed her bishops were married to the church. She expressed a low opinion of any bishop who chose to marry. Her own haughtiness and belief in her absolute authority almost certainly meant she would have found it difficult to share government with anyone, for although she might remain queen, any husband, especially one of the proper status, could not have been denied his views. It was more a problem over whom to marry rather than whether to marry, and that problem was never resolved. It was not helped by the fact that Elizabeth's first love was almost certainly her favourite – Robert Dudley, earl of Leicester, the brother of Guilford Dudley, husband of Lady Jane Grey. Dudley was already married, to Amy Robsart, whose mysterious death in 1560 caused many to believe that Dudley had murdered her. Thus tainted, Dudley was no suitable candidate as Elizabeth's husband, even though he pursued his suit for the next twenty years. He remained something of a philanderer and adventurer and died in 1588. Elizabeth was much saddened by his death for although she had other court favourites, such as Sir Christopher Hatton, the captain of the bodyguard, and, most notably, Robert Devereux, earl of Essex, the flame burned strongest for Dudley and he never left her heart.

Nevertheless Elizabeth recognized that a political marriage was necessary both for producing an heir and for strengthening England's position in Europe, but she constantly prevaricated over her choice, using it for political bargaining. For a period she had to be the most eligible spinster in Europe, and various royal families made their approaches. Early in her reign there had been negotiations with Philip II of Spain, the former husband of Elizabeth's sister Mary, but these were dropped when Elizabeth confirmed her opposition to papal sovereignty in 1559. The main contender then became Charles, the archduke of Austria, and younger son of the Holy Roman Emperor Ferdinand. He was an ideal candidate and, had Elizabeth been given more support from her brilliant and long-suffering adviser, William Cecil, the marriage might have happened. But Cecil counselled against it,

Elizabeth became more involved with Dudley and negotiations collapsed in 1567 on religious grounds. By the time Elizabeth came to reconsider Charles in 1570 he was betrothed to another. Now approaching 37, Elizabeth's eligibility was failing. If she was going to marry she needed to marry soon. Negotiations opened with Henri, duke of Anjou, the younger brother of Charles IX, king of France (who had also been a suitor at one stage). Negotiations again failed on religious grounds (and possibly because of Henri's sexual practices – he was bisexual and a transvestite) and so Anjou's younger brother François, duke of Alençon, stepped into the frame. The age difference between the two was considerable, and it was not helped by the fact that the French persecution of the Huguenots aggravated the Anglo-French religious balance. Nevertheless Elizabeth apparently became enchanted with the diminutive young Duke, whom she nicknamed 'frog' when she first met him in 1579. Though negotiations were erratic Elizabeth caused a sensation in November 1581, when she announced that she would marry him. This was really a ploy on Elizabeth's part to increase her bargaining power with the French as she was not that sincere in her proposals to marry.

All came to naught in 1584 when Alençon died. He was the last serious suitor for by now Elizabeth was past the age of successfully bearing a healthy child. It is almost certain that despite her many favourites, Elizabeth remained a virgin all her life. She actually delighted in her virginity, deploying it as a strength, and became known as 'the Virgin Queen'. Walter Ralegh, another court favourite, named the territory in North America Virginia in her honour in 1584. Elizabeth refused to acknowledge that she was ageing. She wore a wig (as she had lost much of her own hair), whitened her face with a mixture of lead and arsenic to hide the scarring from the smallpox, and even rubbed urine into her face to remove wrinkles. She could not hide her blackened teeth arising from her love of sugar.

During all these years England had been fighting an unofficial conflict with Spain. Philip II of Spain was infuriated by England's blatant piracy of Spanish ships from the New World. Spain and Portugal dominated the seas, and in 1580 Philip became king of Portugal as well as Spain, thus increasing his maritime and merchant strength. In 1493 the then pope had partitioned the New World between Spain and Portugal and now the bounty of the Americas was united in Philip. Spain had exerted an almost tyrannical exploitation of the New World, forbidding other countries access to the lands. In 1562 an English seaman, John Hawkins, had found a way round this by trading directly with the Spanish in Hispaniola over slaves. The venture proved profitable and two more followed, this time with Elizabeth as a shareholder, but the third expedition fell foul of the Spanish and only just limped home in early 1569. Hawkins's fellow captain, Francis Drake, now regarded it as open season on the Spanish and from 1572 he began to plunder Spanish enterprises in Central and South America. By 1577 Drake had been introduced to Elizabeth and she unofficially encouraged his activities against Spain. In December 1577 Drake set off on what would become his voyage around the world, plundering Spanish vessels in both South America and the East Indies. It has been estimated that the total value of Drake's booty was worth about £450,000, which would be many millions at today's rates. He returned to England in September 1580 and became a national hero. He was knighted in April 1581.

Philip's relationship with England continued to sour. England's support to the Netherlands against Spain was the final straw in 1585. After the execution of Mary Queen of Scots, Philip believed he had a divine right to invade England, a major heretical aggressor, and contended that he had a claim on the English throne, because he was distantly descended from Edward III. In July 1587 Philip secured a treaty with the pope approving the conquest of England, provided that the land was restored to Catholicism. The pope allowed Philip to choose whomever he wished as England's ruler. While these negotiations were in hand Drake led a punitive expedition into Spain, capturing and destroying many Spanish vessels. The culmination of all this was one of the most famous confrontations of all time when Philip sent his apparently invincible Armada against England in July 1588. Philip's venture was doomed by the weather even more than by the superiority of English seamanship and the better design of the English ships, which allowed them to hug the water and dart through the waves. By comparison the huge and imposing Spanish galleons were a liability in strong winds. Although Elizabeth had hesitated at first about the confrontation with the Armada, the defeat of Spain's might was one of the most important victories in English history. Conflict with Spain dragged on for another fifteen years. In April 1596 the Spaniards turned up on Elizabeth's doorstep by capturing Calais. A joint Anglo-Dutch offensive was made against Spain under the command of Essex. It captured and plundered Cadiz, destroying much of the fleet, and returning home rich with booty, little of which the queen saw as most of it ended up in the hands of the looters. Philip despatched a second Armada in October 1596, but this again fell foul of the weather as did, this time, the English fleet. This was the last major battle against Spain although hostilities continued beyond Philip II's death in September 1598, and even beyond Elizabeth's.

The end of the century saw England at the height of her power. Her great sea captains and explorers – Francis Drake, Walter Ralegh, Martin Frobisher, John Hawkins – meant that she effectively 'ruled the waves'. Literature blossomed – this was the age of Francis Bacon, William Shakespeare, Christopher Marlowe, Sir Philip Sidney and Edmund Spenser, whose *Faerie Queene* (first part, 1589; second part 1596) was dedicated to Elizabeth. Scientific study did not advance quite so quickly in England as it did in the Protestant parts of Europe, but there were some great physicists and speculative thinkers who emerged in Elizabeth's time, with Sir Francis Bacon again head and shoulders above them.

The last drama to be enacted during Elizabeth's reign was the revolution in Ireland and the subsequent fate of the earl of Essex. Hugh O'Neill, earl of Tyrone, had been in rebellion against the

English for some years, and this reached a climax in August 1598 when O'Neill massacred an English force sent to relieve the fort at Blackwater. The Irish were now in open revolt and England sent in an army. The earl of Essex jumped at the opportunity to take command, hoping that this might restore his favour with the queen, who had been cold to him since Essex had quarrelled with her ministers William Cecil, now Lord Burghley, and his son Robert over the possibility that Elizabeth might negotiate for peace with Spain. This had followed an alleged assassination plot against the queen organized by Rodrigo Lopez, a Portuguese Jew supposedly in the pay of Philip of Spain, and involving Ferdinando Stanley, king of the Isle of Man. Elizabeth had some suspicions that Essex had concocted the whole story in order to get back into her favour. Many did not believe that Essex was a capable commander, but the queen supported him and gave him all the men and finances he needed. Elizabeth would have been only too happy to be rid of Ireland, except that she feared it falling to a foreign power, especially to Spain. There had been other rebellions during her reign, that of Shane O'Neill in Ulster during the 1560s, the Fitzmaurice rising of 1569–73 and the Desmond rebellion of 1579–83. These received harsh retaliation from the English, slaughtering young and old alike and keeping the island savagely repressed. Elizabeth had hopes that Essex might similarly subdue the rebels, but instead he spent the summer of 1599 moving about the island and achieving little. He negotiated terms with O'Neill, after losing more than half his force to the unhealthiness of the Irish environment, and returned home without permission. Essex expected to be regarded as a hero, but instead the queen and the Privy Council showed him nothing but contempt. Essex was censured and humiliated. Essex sought his revenge upon the Council, but was caught and tried for high treason and executed in February 1601. Although Elizabeth was saddened by Essex's death, she was delighted when his successor in Ireland, Lord Mountjoy, succeeded in defeating Tyrone in December 1601 and in reaching an agreement with Spanish opportunists who had invaded Kinsale that September. Tyrone's

SCOTLAND: THE HOUSE OF STEWART (1371–1625)

Robert the Bruce's daughter Marjorie had married Walter, the sixth High Steward of Scotland and a descendant of Walter Fitzalan who had received large estates from David I along with the hereditary title of Steward of Scotland. So Steward or Stewart had become the family name. Marjorie had died in childbirth, but the baby survived to become Robert II.

Just as in England, by Robert II's day, the influence of the Normans had turned what had been a nation of tribes into a feudal society and the powerful Celtic earls – the *mormaers* – had been brought into a feudal relationship with the king. There was strong central and local government, and a number of burghs had been founded – these were communities in which merchants and tradesmen had specific rights. As townships, many of their inhabitants were English and they were English-speaking. Gaelic speakers formed much of the rural population, for Scotland was mainly an agricultural community, and exports of wool from the ubiquitous sheep were booming.

As in England too, the Black Death struck Scotland in a series of plagues between 1349 and 1401, and Scotland lost a third of its population. As a consequence landlords were only too anxious to get tenants for their land even if it meant granting them their freedom and by the mid fourteenth century Scotland had no more serfs.

However, in certain respects, the social structure in Scotland differed from England, for by the fourteenth century it was a land of two distinct identities and cultures (and in some respects remains so today). There were – and still are – the Lowlanders and the Highlanders. In 1380, John of Fordun described them thus: the Lowlanders were 'domestic', had 'civilized habits', and were 'trusty, patient, urbane, decent in their attire', while those of the Highlands were 'savage and untamed, rude and independent, given to rapine, easy living . . . comely in person but unsightly in dress, hostile to the English . . . and exceedingly cruel'.

Pastoral farming was favoured in the Highlands because the land could quickly be cleared for a fight, and tenants looked forward to their lord's feuds, for warfare rather than farming was their true pleasure in life.

Over the next century or so, despite warring clans, plots, treason and murder, by the reign of James IV, Scotland could boast a large and colourful, immensely cultured – and expensive – court which conversed in at least six languages, for James IV was, *par excellence*, a prince of the Renaissance. An impression of the court's sheer liveliness can be gained from the poet William Dunbar's list of people serving in it: servants, officials, churchmen, courtiers, craftsmen, doctors in law and medicine, diviners, rhetoricians, philosophers, astrologers, artists and orators, men of arms and valiant knights, musicians, minstrels, horsemen, hurlers and flingers, coinmakers, carvers and carpenters, builders of boats and ships, masons, shipwrights, glaziers, goldsmiths and jewellers, pointers, painters and apothecaries. James IV and his wife Margaret Tudor would be fitting ancestors to the first king of Scotland and England.

ROBERT II

Ruled 22 February 1371–19 April 1390; crowned: Scone Abbey, 26 March 1371.

Titles: king of Scotland; earl of Atholl (1342–67), earl of Strathearn (1357?–69).

Born: Paisley, 2 March 1316. *Died*: Dundonald Castle, Ayrshire, 19 April 1390, aged 74. *Buried*: Scone Abbey.

Married: (1) 1336, with a second ceremony in 1348, Elizabeth Mure of Rowallan, Ayrshire: 10 children; (2) May 1355, Euphemia (c1330–87), dau. of Hugh, earl of Ross: 4 children. Robert had at least 8 illegitimate children.

Robert had been named the Bruce's heir if Bruce did not have a son of his own, but in the event David was born and succeeded. Although his nephew, Robert was eight years older than David, and grew into a tall, strong youth with good manners and a generous disposition. He was liked by all, and many wished that he had become king. He was twice the regent or guardian of Scotland during David's enforced absences. David, however, regarded Robert as something of a traitor. Robert had withdrawn his forces from the battle of Neville's Cross in 1346 at which David was captured. Robert governed the kingdom for the next eleven years with as much weakness as he would when he subsequently became king, although the kingdom was plagued by the Black Death.

Robert finally succeeded to the kingship in 1371 when he was nearly fifty-five and not the man he had been. He was described as red-eyed and enfeebled and was known as 'Auld Blearie'. Perhaps this was partly due to his amorous adventures – he fathered at least twenty children, possibly more. Under his aegis, the kingdom became poorer and ill-controlled with many crimes going unpunished. Lawlessness grew. There was a vicious and destructive raid by Richard II in 1385, which included the burning of Edinburgh, leading to a number of border incidents, the most notable of which was the battle of Otterburn on 5 August 1388. Here the earl of March defeated and captured Henry Percy ('Hotspur'), the son of the earl of Northumberland. From about 1384, by which time Robert was growing senile, the general administration of affairs passed to his son John, earl of Carrick, who would become Robert III.

ROBERT III
Ruled 19 April 1390–4 April 1406; crowned: Scone Abbey, 14 August 1390.
Titles: king of Scotland; earl of Carrick (from 1368).
Born: c1337. Died: Dundonald Castle, 4 April 1406, aged 68(?). Buried: Paisley Abbey.
Married: c1366, Annabella Drummond (c1350–1401), dau. Sir John Drummond of Stobhall: 7 children. Robert III also had one known illegitimate child.

Two years before his succession, John was kicked by a horse and became an invalid. Because his abilities to govern were severely limited, much of the administration was carried out by his younger brother, also called Robert. This Robert was created duke of Albany in 1398. Albany was ambitious and took over almost complete control of the kingdom from the day of his brother's accession, but in 1393 the king decided to take the administration back into his own hands, with disastrous results. Robert III was about as incapable at governing as his father. The 1390s saw bribery and corruption throughout the Scottish lowlands, with money flowing from the government's coffers into the hands of the newly created barons (the many sons of Robert II) and their vassals. Even worse the rift widened between the Lowlands and the Highlands. The clans strengthened, with clan warfare becoming rife. Donald MacDonald, lord of the Isles, ruled his lands as a separate kingdom. Robert III was unable to exercise any authority over them. They were more responsive to his younger brother, Alexander, the earl of Buchan and self-styled

'Wolf of Badenoch', who became little more than a bandit leader. He married into the family of the lord of the Isles and to some extent became their proxy king in the North.

Robert III sank further into a state of depression, stating to his wife that he should be buried in a dungheap with the epitaph 'Here lies the worst of kings and the most miserable of men.' Annabella called a special council in April 1398 at which her eldest son, David, then still only nineteen, was made 'Lieutenant of the Realm'. In his actions his primary adviser was his uncle, the ambitious Albany. David proved to be as inept as his father, being of a dissolute and licentious nature. When the English king Henry IV decided to invade Scotland in 1400, he was able to reach Edinburgh without much opposition. He lay siege to the castle but was eventually forced to retire through want of supplies. The Scots seemed powerless to respond. After Annabella died in 1401, Albany had David thrown into prison at Falkland Palace in Fife where he left him to starve to death.

Scottish fortunes did not revive. In September 1402 they made an expedition against the English to retaliate for the raid on Edinburgh, but were totally defeated by the earl of Northumberland at Homildon Hill.

David's younger brother, James, who was only seven, became heir to the throne. In 1406 the king entrusted the boy, then aged eleven, to the care of Sir David Fleming, to be smuggled out of Scotland to safety in France as he was in danger from Albany. Unfortunately everything went wrong. The sea and high tides limited shipping; Sir David was waylaid and killed; and when James was eventually hidden on a cargo ship by Henry St. Clair, it was attacked by pirates. The young boy was captured and taken to Henry IV, who promptly imprisoned him in the Tower of London. When news reached King Robert, he retired to his ancestral home at Rothesay and there pined away from grief.

ROBERT STEWART, *DUKE OF ALBANY*. **Governor of Scotland, 1406–20.**

Titles: earl of Menteith (from 1361), earl of Fife (briefly before March 1372), duke of Albany (from 1398).
Born: c1340. Died: Stirling Castle, 3 September 1420, aged 80. Buried: Dunfermline Abbey.
Married: (1) 1361, Margaret Graham, countess of Menteith (c1330–1380?): 7 children; (2) 1380, Muriella Keith (d. 1449): 5 children.

Robert was the ambitious and certainly most capable son of Robert II who sought to gain the crown of Scotland for himself and his own progeny. With the increasing senility of his father during the 1380s, Robert took on more of the country's administrative affairs, and after his brother John's accident in 1368, Robert became the senior administrator. He was not formally styled governor, even after the succession of his brother (as Robert III), for all that the power was almost wholly in his hands. The king sought to regain control of the government between 1393 and 1398 but that was a disaster. In April 1398 the king's son, David, was made 'Lieutenant of the Realm', and Robert, now duke of Albany, was his primary adviser. From April 1402 Robert was more or less in full control. After James, now heir, was captured by pirates and imprisoned in the Tower of London, and Robert III had died of grief. Robert Stewart was officially inaugurated as the governor of Scotland in 1406. Although he never held the title of king, he held the equivalent power, signing all the documents in his name and ensuring that his son, Murdoch succeeded him as governor. Nevertheless Robert realized that he was not all-powerful and could be toppled, so he sought to govern without alienating either the leading barons or the common folk. For the former, he allowed them ample use of the crown's revenues; and for the latter, he decreed that no taxes should be levied. As a result the kingdom grew poorer by the day and there was general lawlessness. Robert delegated the general administration of southern Scotland to Archibald, the earl of Douglas who had married Robert's niece Margaret, whilst northern Scotland was in the hands of Alexander, the earl of Mar and son of Robert's brother, Alexander, the notorious Wolf of Badenoch. Although Douglas was a capable soldier and administrator, Alexander Stewart was little more than a robber baron who held the Highlands under his sway. Robert did nothing to reduce his power and it would be fair to say that by the time of Robert's death, at the age of eighty, Scotland was in straitened and corrupt circumstances.

JAMES I
Ruled 4 April 1406–21 February 1437.
Crowned: Scone Abbey, 21 May 1424.
Titles: king of Scotland; duke of Rothesay and earl of Carrick (from 1404).
Born: Dunfermline Palace, 25 July 1394. **Died** *(assassinated): Perth, 21 February 1437, aged 43.* **Buried:** *Perth.*
Married: 2 February 1424, in Southwark, London, Joan Beaufort (d. 1445), dau. John, earl of Somerset, and great-granddaughter of Edward III: 8 children.

Although young James's freedom was restricted while kept in the Tower of London, he was not totally deprived of his liberty as he spent most of his time with King Henry at Windsor and on his progress about England. As a consequence James gained not only an excellent education, but considerable knowledge of court administration and governance, almost certainly better than he would have received at home. James also accompanied Henry V on military service in France, learning much about soldiery and military tactics. He also acquired literary skills. Not only is he the first Scottish king of whom evidence of his handwriting survives, he was also something of a poet. One of his poems, *The Kingis Quair*, is not only an autobiography of his years of captivity but records how he fell in love with his future wife. By the end of his captivity, he was thirty. He had outlived Henry IV and Henry V, and was living during the minority of Henry VI. The English had problems in their continuing conflict with France and saw an opportunity in restoring James to the throne as a way of stopping the Scottish support for the French. Under the Treaty of London, James was given his freedom, in return for a payment of 60,000 merks (£40,000) to cover the cost of his upkeep and education (a neat euphemism for a ransom). Before returning to Scotland James married his sweetheart, Joan Beaufort, the niece of Richard II and a granddaughter of John of Gaunt. James was eventually crowned king of Scotland in May 1424, at last king of a land he had not seen for eighteen years.

The Scotland he inherited was in a pitiful state. To a man raised in the comparatively prosperous south, the condition of Scotland must have cut him to the quick. It was controlled, though not governed, by his cousin Murdoch and his wayward sons. James had been able to keep in touch with the Douglas family, whose earl, Archibald had married James's sister Margaret in 1390 or earlier. Archibald had endeavoured to govern southern Scotland and had by 1424 disassociated himself from Murdoch. It was Douglas who helped engineer James's release. James devoted all his energies to restoring the land. His first measure was to rid Scotland of its lawless governors. Within a month of his coronation James had imprisoned his cousin's son, Walter Stewart, who controlled the fortress of Dumbarton and was thus not only influencing the trade into the western Highlands and pocketing most of the revenues for himself, but was also controlling the despatch of forces to France, which James had agreed to stop under the Treaty of London. Over the next few months James imprisoned the earl of Lennox (Murdoch's father-in-law), Murdoch himself, Murdoch's wife Elizabeth and his son Alexander. Murdoch's youngest son, James, led a revolt in the area of Lennox and sacked Dumbarton. Although he escaped to Ireland where he remained in exile, his actions sounded the death knell for the other members of his family. Lennox, Murdoch, Walter and Alexander were all executed at Stirling Castle on 24 and 25 May 1425.

James next sought to minimize the possibility of challenge from among his uncles and cousins who were descendants of his grandfather's second marriage, which was regarded as more legal than his first and thus may have represented a stronger legal challenge to James's right to the throne. James deprived the young Malise Graham of his right to the earldom of Strathearn, claiming it could not be passed on through his mother, the only daughter of Robert II's, son David, who had died in 1389. Malise was despatched to England as one of the hostages held against payment of James's ransom. James recognized the seniority of his ageing uncle Walter, the second son of Robert II's second marriage, who was earl of Atholl, and he created him earl of Strathearn in July 1427. This was tantamount to recognizing Walter's right of succession (and that of his sons Alexander and David) to the Scottish throne. It would have dire consequences later in James's reign.

James next turned his attention towards the Highlands. The MacDonald clan had assumed almost absolute power under Donald II and Alexander II, lords of the Isles. The Highlanders did not regard themselves as subjects of the Scottish king, but were a law unto themselves, not that there were any laws to control them. In 1428 James called a meeting of clan leaders at Inverness. Once there he arrested them, executing the more powerful ringleaders. In this he showed that he was not a king to be trusted. At his worst he was cruel, vicious and vindictive, and gave no inch to his enemies. Alexander of the Isles was released, but promptly led an uprising and, although he was soon re-captured and forced to do obeisance to James, the clan warfare continued for a few more years until an uneasy peace was agreed in 1435.

In addition to curbing the powers of the clans and nobles, James sought to reintroduce strong laws. He passed a considerable number during the first few years of his rule, ranging from the banning of football (football hooliganism must be older than we think!) and the introduction of licensing hours for drinking, to organized fire-fighting and the control of tax collection. He briefly introduced direct taxation in 1424, but it was so unpopular that he repealed it, though he reintroduced it in 1431. He also developed trade with his close European neighbours and, despite the Treaty of London, re-opened relationships with France by renewing the Auld Alliance. His eldest daughter, Margaret, was betrothed to the Dauphin of France in 1428, though the marriage did not happen until 1436, when she was still only eleven. Other daughters were married to dukes and counts of some consequence throughout Europe. It seemed for a while, though, that James might not leave a male heir. It was not until October 1430 that his wife was delivered of male twins, Alexander and James. Alexander soon died, but James survived.

It was inevitable that James's ruthless actions in order to regain stability and control in Scotland would make him enemies. In the summer of 1436, a disastrous attempt to regain Roxburgh, from which James was forced to retreat, lowered his prestige farther and demonstrated his lack of control over his nobles, who had sought to create trouble at home while James was away. James spent that Christmas at Perth. Legend has it that a local seer warned him that he would not return south alive. While retiring for the night on 20 February, he and his wife were attacked by a group of assassins. His wife, who tried to protect him, was wounded, and James, who fled into an underground vault, was cornered and hacked to death. Ironically James had recently bricked off one end of this vault because tennis balls ended up down there and, in so doing, he had stopped off his means of escape.

The conspirators were led by Sir Robert Graham, the uncle of

Malise Graham whom James had slighted at the start of his reign. Also involved in the plot were Walter Stewart, earl of Strathearn, whom James had once favoured, and his grandson Robert, whom Walter had hoped would be made king. The assassins were all caught, tortured and executed. Walter received his crown: a red-hot one of iron. James's widow, Joan, lived a further eight years and married a second time: to James Stewart, the famous 'Black Knight of Lorne'. The then lieutenant of Scotland, Alexander Livingstone, feared that they might abduct the child king (James II) and so had them arrested in 1439 – they were released on condition that they would not attempt to retain custody of the child.

JAMES II
Ruled 21 February 1437–3 August 1460.
Crowned: Holyrood Abbey, 25 March 1437.
Titles: king of Scotland; duke of Rothesay (from 1431).
Born: Holyrood Palace, Edinburgh, 16 October 1430. Died (in battle): Roxburgh, 3 August 1460, aged 29. Buried: Holyrood Abbey.
Married: 3 July 1449, at Holyrood Abbey, Mary (1433–63), dau. Arnold, duke of Gueldres: 7 children. James also had at least one illegitimate child.

James bore a large birthmark which caused him to be known as James of the Fiery Face. He was only six when his father was murdered. He remained in the care of his mother, Joan, until she remarried in 1439, when she was barred from having any dealings with him. The new lieutenant of Scotland and the real power in the land was a relative unknown, Sir Alexander Livingstone, governor of Stirling Castle. The queen and her infant son had first sought refuge in Edinburgh Castle, governed by Sir William Crichton, and a wrangle broke out between Livingstone and Crichton as to who should have possession of the boy. These two officials remained in rivalry for several years, exercising authority over the boy and through him over the land. Crichton, in particular, became involved in the rivalry over the succession between the king and the Douglas family. The fifth earl of Douglas, Archibald, was James II's cousin, and he married Euphemia Graham, a great-granddaughter of Robert II. His sons, William and David thus had a strong title to the Scottish throne. When Archibald died in 1439, James was faced with the young upstart William, the sixth earl, a born trouble-maker. Crichton, acting on behalf of the king, invited the two brothers, William and David, to a feast at Edinburgh Castle on 28 November 1440. At the end of the meal a black bull's head was placed on the table as a symbol of death. The two brothers were then seized and subjected to a mock trial at which James pleaded for their release. They were, however, found guilty of treason and immediately executed. The Douglases were thereafter the sworn enemies of James and of Crichton and, as the family regained their power, they supported Alexander Livingstone, engineering events from behind the scenes effectively to control the kingdom.

Throughout the 1440s, Scotland once again became a land of civil strife with rivalry between baronial factions. By 1449 when James II, now eighteen, assumed his full powers as king the Livingstone family had control over almost all the key offices and castles. Almost immediately, he arrested most of the Livingstone officials. They were imprisoned and two of them were subsequently executed. Their fall from power was as sudden and mysterious as their rise. Soon after, William Douglas, the new earl, set off to France and Italy, probably to escape the king, who may have learned of the Douglas's assistance to the Livingstones. When William returned, in 1450, his relationship with the king remained cordial if distant, but James became incensed when he found that William had entered into an alliance with the earl of Ross, who was also the lord of the Isles. Douglas was invited to dine with James on 22 February 1452, where James asked Douglas to break the alliance. Douglas refused, and James stabbed him in the neck. The attack was probably unpremeditated and the murder not planned, but its results were disastrous.

William Douglas's brother, James, the new earl, withdrew his allegiance from the king and declared his allegiance to the English king Henry VI. The Douglas family now united under a common cause against James II.

When conflict erupted it came as part of the English Wars of the Roses. James supported the Lancastrians while the Douglases supported the House of York, so that the war, which began with the battle of St Albans in May 1455, had its echo on Scottish fields. James, however, used his devious tactics in setting one noble house against another, and used his own strong support in the south to defeat the Douglases within a matter of months. James relied heavily on a new form of artillery, the cannon. These had only recently been introduced into Scotland, and James used his wife's connections in the Low Countries to acquire a monopoly on these giant guns. Castles had no protection against cannon power and soon fell to his siege train. It is likely that one of these cannon was the mighty Mons Meg, still on display at Edinburgh Castle. The power of the Douglases was destroyed once and for all. The earl survived but fled to England.

Over the next few years James aggressively revoked many of the acts and settlements agreed during his minority and removed many hereditary entitlements. Few earls were safe in their castles, as James reclaimed many of them as possessions of the crown. In effect the old feudal system was ended as many lands now became forfeit. James also updated many of the laws promulgated by his father and introduced many new ones, regulating dress and improving education. Glasgow University was established in 1451.

By the end of the 1450s James had a powerful hold over Scotland. He may not have been liked by many of his subjects, but he was respected. He could have had ahead of him a long and effective reign. But his delight in the power of the cannon which had won him his kingdom, was also his undoing. In August 1460 James was laying siege to Roxburgh Castle in support of Henry VI. His wife arrived on the scene and James was keen to fire a special salvo in her honour. As he ignited one cannon it exploded and killed him. James's heir, also called James, was only eight. It looked as if the events at the start of the last two reigns were to be repeated.

JAMES III
Ruled 3 August 1460–11 June 1488.
Crowned: Kelso Abbey, 10 August 1460.
Titles: king of Scotland; duke of Rothesay (from birth).
Born: St Andrew's Castle, Fife, May 1452. **Died** *(murdered): Milltown, 11 June 1488, aged 36.* **Buried:** *Cambuskenneth Abbey.*
Married: 10 July 1469, at Holyrood Abbey, Margaret (1456–86), dau. Christian I of Denmark and Norway: 3 sons.

Once again Scotland found itself under the control of a council of regents. This was initially headed by young James's mother, Mary of Gueldres, a remarkably able woman, though she found herself opposed by James Kennedy, bishop of St Andrews.

Scotland supported the Lancastrian cause in the English Wars of the Roses and it was to Scotland that the Lancastrian king, Henry VI, fled after his defeat at Towton at the end of March 1461. The Scots gave him refuge and, in return, Henry restored Berwick to Scottish hands. (It had been in English hands since 1296, and its recovery was a further boost to the regency following the recapture of Roxburgh the previous year.) An attempt to aid Henry with military support was less successful as Scottish forces were defeated at Carlisle in June.

A few weeks later Edward IV was crowned king of England. He soon entered into a treaty with the earl of Douglas and John II, lord of the Isles, which was sealed in February 1462. This gained Edward the support of those rebels against the Scottish throne. Mary, the queen mother, realized that if Scotland entered into its own treaty with Edward, the agreement with Douglas and John would be worthless. She was strongly opposed in this by Kennedy and the two parties – known as the 'Young Lords' headed by

Mary and the 'Old Lords' headed by Kennedy – almost rent the country apart. Mary did enter into negotiations with Edward, but was unable to bring these to a satisfactory conclusion before illness resulted in her early death on 1 December 1463, aged thirty.

Meanwhile the Scots had been actively supporting Margaret of Anjou, Henry VI's wife, who had brought an army from France and was endeavouring to regain castles in northern England. However, when Edward agreed a truce with France in the autumn of 1463, the Lancastrian cause seemed hopelessly lost. Kennedy was forced to realize that the queen mother was right. Within days of her death, negotiations began between Kennedy and Edward IV that resulted in a truce. Henry VI was smuggled out of Scotland in March 1464 but, after two ignominious defeats, he was captured and imprisoned in the Tower of London. Soon after this John of the Isles realized that his power had been annulled and although he technically resumed his allegiance to James III, he continued to rule as if independent of the crown.

Kennedy died in July 1465. Had he or the queen mother lived longer Scotland would have been spared the rise to power of the Boyd family, under the guiding control of Sir Alexander Boyd, governor of Edinburgh Castle. He entered into an alliance with Gilbert Kennedy, brother of the late Bishop Kennedy, and with Robert, Lord Fleming. Between them they were able to gain sufficient support from other members of the nobility to sustain their audacious plans. In July 1466, while the young king was hearing his accounts at Linlithgow Castle, Boyd and Fleming lured James out on to a hunt and kidnapped him, hiding him away at Edinburgh Castle. When Parliament was held that October, James, who was still only fourteen, stated that his abduction had been made by royal agreement. Boyd was appointed the King's guardian and keeper of the royal fortresses. His elder brother, Robert, was already earl of Kilmarnock and now became the lord chamberlain. Robert's son, Thomas, married the king's elder sister, Mary, in April 1467 and was created earl of Arran. The consequent grants of land made him the senior lord of the country. For a little under three years the Boyds dominated the control of Scotland. Unlike the Livingstones, in the previous reign, the Boyds did not go for absolute power, preferring to drain the revenues for their own profit, and enjoy the use of their authority. Their fall would be as sudden as their rise.

The same Parliament that had acknowledged their authority had discussed the matter of the debt owed by Scotland to Norway for the annual rent due on the Hebrides which had been accumulating for over forty years. It was now becoming an embarrassment, and default could result in the restoration of the Hebrides to Norway. It had already been suggested some years earlier that Scotland would benefit from a marriage with the crown of Norway and negotiations began in 1468. It was Thomas Boyd who led these negotiations and, although the end result was of considerable benefit to Scotland, it did not help the Boyds. With the marriage of James III to Margaret of Norway in July 1469 the debt owing on the Western Isles was written off. King Christian agreed to pay 60,000 florins (£20,000) as a dowry. However, 50,000 of these were offset against Norway pledging its rights in Orkney to Scotland. When payment came to be made, Christian could not raise the 10,000 florins and instead further pledged his rights in the Shetlands to Scotland. By 1470, therefore, Scotland found itself in ownership of the Northern Isles, which had been in Norwegian hands for almost 600 years, and in full ownership of the Hebrides. The last Norse earl of Orkney had died eighty years earlier and the earldom had been held by the St Clair family. William resigned his earldom to the Crown in 1471, and was compensated with lands in Fife. St Clair's daughter, Katherine, married James III's brother Alexander in 1475. The kingdom of Scotland was now at its full extent.

With his marriage, James III assumed full regal authority and his supporters acted immediately. The Boyds were found guilty of treason and sentenced to death. Lord Boyd fled to England, where he remained in refuge but died within a year at Alnwick Castle. Thomas Boyd was warned by his wife Mary. He had been returning from Denmark but was able to set sail again. He was stripped of his title and remained in exile until his death in 1473. Alexander was less fortunate. He was arrested and executed in November 1469.

The reign of James III is a something of a paradox. The tradition passed down to us is of a dilettante who abandoned his nobles and the government of his people for his fascination for the arts and sciences. He is also portrayed as a weakling king who hid himself away in his castle and refrained from defending his country from the designs of the English. He was accused of being an anglophile, which was true, though this was not necessarily as heinous as implied. James was rather shrewder than he might at first seem. At the start of his reign he benefitted from a remarkable period of peace and prosperity which Scotland had not enjoyed for many years. The increased size and wealth of his realm, the relative calm with England and the reconciliation with John of the Isles, who was eventually brought to book in 1476, allowed James to explore other areas of interest. The fact that he tended to ignore the aristocracy in favour of artists and artisans should have been no bad thing. He encouraged learning: poetry, music, painting, astronomy, architecture and engineering all seem to have prospered during his reign. It should come as little surprise that he placed more trust in the middle class artisans than in the nobility who, hitherto, had given him little comfort. A case in point relates to the bishopric of St Andrews. In August 1472, due to the negotiations of the bishop, Patrick Graham, St Andrews was granted archiepiscopal status by the pope. This was a tremendous honour for Scotland, as this released it from the control of the archbishopric of York which had long claimed supremacy over Scotland. However Graham, who was a nephew of the former Bishop James Kennedy and was distantly related to James III, saw this as an opportunity to increase his authority over the king and certainly over all the clergy of Scotland. Opposition immediately arose against Graham, who was perceived as a megalomaniac. James III placed his court physician and astrologer, William Scheves, as head of this opposition faction. Scheves succeeded in making himself archbishop in 1478. Graham was deposed by papal bull on the grounds of heresy and simony and died insane soon after. The clergy seem prepared to accept Scheves, for all that he was not of noble birth, but Scheves turned out to be something of an adventurer and later turned against James III.

James's relations with England continued to remain cordial and, with the birth of his son (the future James IV) in 1473, he entered into arrangements with Edward IV that once the prince reached his majority he would marry one of Edward's daughters. This was exceedingly beneficial for Scotland, though it was not necessarily perceived as such by all those north of the border. By the close of the 1470s James was being held in disdain by many of his subjects because of his anglophilia and because of his apparent abrogation of his kingly duties in favour of the arts. The nobility came to believe that these artisans, particularly the mason Robert Cochrane, were effectively running the government. James was even believed to have cultivated an interest in alchemy and the black arts. The Scottish aristocracy turned their allegiance to James's younger brothers, Alexander, duke of Albany, regarded as one of the greatest knights in Europe and the father of chivalry, and John, earl of Mar, another gifted knight and statesmen. It seems that these two brothers had all the knightly and kingly virtues in which James failed. Discovering the ambition of his brothers in the summer of 1479, James stripped them of their titles. Both were imprisoned at Craigmillar Castle in Edinburgh, where John died soon after, many believe murdered. Alexander escaped and sought refuge in France.

Although James was temporarily rid of his ambitious brother, he was still surrounded by many disaffected barons who were increasingly dissatisfied at James's reluctance to confront Edward IV of England. Edward was openly plotting war against France, Scotland's old ally, and doing his best to ally himself with James's old enemies, including John of the Isles and James, earl of Douglas. Hostilities broke out on the English border in the spring of 1480. Attempts at reconciliation proved fruitless and by the close of 1481 Scotland and England were at war. Alexander, the king's brother, chose to side with Edward IV against James and, from June 1482 was openly styling himself as Alexander IV, king of Scotland. James was eventually forced to lead an army into England. However he took with him his court favourites, which angered the earls. While encamped at Lauder the earls, led by Archibald, earl of Angus, parleyed with the king and besought him to surrender his favourites and to cease circulation of the debased coinage which James had issued. James refused and, in anger, the earls seized the king's favourites, including Cochrane, and the king's musician, William Roger, and hanged them at the bridge into the town. James himself was arrested and imprisoned at Edinburgh Castle. Alexander marched on Scotland and concluded peace with England. Part of the price was that England regained Berwick in August 1482, which had been in Scottish hands for only twenty-one years. Thereafter Berwick would remain English.

Alexander chose not to usurp the throne, even though he could almost certainly have counted on the support of the Scottish aristocracy and of the English king. Instead he released James from prison in October 1482. The two, for a while, were reconciled, but by early 1483 they were back in conflict. The death of Edward IV in April 1483 robbed Alexander of his English support and two months later James was able to drive Alexander out of Scotland. He eventually sought refuge in France, where he was killed in an accident at a tournament in 1485.

James's reign should have taken a turn for the better over the next few years. However, he was sadly affected by the death of his wife in July 1486 and thereafter increased his seclusion in his royal homes. Nevertheless he pursued, with singular dedication, the desire to formalize a marriage between his son and the royal house of England, even to the extent of suggesting a marriage between himself and Edward IV's widow. James pursued this throughout the short reign of Richard III and into the early years of Henry VII. This apparent passion for England further angered the Scottish earls, who were already disaffected by James's continued mismanagement of financial affairs.

Eventually, in the spring of 1488, the earls, led by Angus, Argyll and Gray, broke into open rebellion. James sought refuge in the north where he raised an army of supporters. The two factions met at Sauchieburn, near Bannockburn, on 11 June 1488. James's army was defeated and the king fled the battlefield. There are several stories of his fate, the most colorful of which is that he fell from his horse and was helped to safety by a local woman drawing water from a well. He told her his identity and she went in search of a priest but, when she revealed James's whereabouts, a local opportunist found the king and killed him. More likely is that soldiers, pursuing James from the battlefield found his horse and soon discovered him in refuge, apparently at a local mill, where he was slain. It is not known who killed the king.

James III was in all probability a misunderstood king who severely miscalculated the power of his nobles. He was not as foolish as some made out since he succeeded in maintaining periods of considerable peace and prosperity in Scotland, despite the activities of his brothers and their supporters and the tactics of the English crown. Had he been less strong-willed and more conciliatory, he might have made a fine monarch. He was succeeded by his son, another James.

JAMES IV

Ruled 11 June 1488–9 September 1513. Crowned: Scone Abbey, 26 June 1488.

Titles: king of Scotland; duke of Rothesay, earl of Carrick and lord of Cunningham (from birth).

Born: 17 March 1473. *Died* (in battle): Flodden Field, 9 September 1513, aged 40. *Buried:* possibly Sheen Abbey, Surrey, though his exact resting place is not known.

Married: 8 August 1503, at Holyrood Abbey, Margaret (1489–1541), dau. Henry VII of England (the marriage had earlier been performed by proxy on 25 January 1502): 6 children. James had at least seven illegitimate children, and it is claimed he was secretly married to Margaret Drummond, by whom he had one child and who was poisoned in 1502.

The reign of James IV saw Scotland (and Europe) emerge from the Middle Ages and enter a new age. This transition meant that although the young James (who was fifteen when his father was killed) took after his father in his patronage of the arts and sciences, it had become more acceptable and James was not pilloried because of it. It also helped that James was a strong king who did not ignore his nobles and, for the most part, earned their respect and support. His abilities as a politician and negotiator were appreciated and, despite the relative insignificance of his kingdom on the European stage, he could hold his own and maintain an influential voice. It was this which, by his own misfortune, would lead to his tragic death.

James was quick to bring his country back to order after the strife of the last year of his father's reign. In his first parliament, led by the earl of Argyll, they annulled all grants and enactments made by James III earlier that year and issued summons of treason against all those who still opposed the new king. Only three of these were dealt with summarily. The earl of Buchan was fully pardoned, whilst the lords of Bothwell and Montgrenane were stripped of their estates, but did not forfeit their lives. All others were pardoned and the heirs of those who had died at the battle of Sauchieburn were allowed to inherit their estates. Furthermore the absolution of the pope himself, Innocent VIII, was sought for all of those who had risen against James III on the basis of his interest in alchemy and the black arts. Within less than a year James had gained peace with most of his nobles, though matters were soured by the rebellion of Robert, Lord Lyle, the Justice General, and John Stewart, a distant cousin of the king, who had been created earl of Lennox. These two seemed dissatisfied with the share of the spoils, and they found unexpected support from Lord Forbes of Aberdeen. The insurrection broke out in April 1489 when the lords garrisoned their castles against the king. The sieges lasted throughout the summer but by October the castles had been taken and the lords' lands declared forfeit. With a remarkable act of clemency James later forgave the lords and restored their titles.

That same year saw a naval victory by Scotland against English ships which had been harrying the Firth of Forth. James's naval commander, Sir Andrew Wood, not only captured these ships, but defeated a punitive expedition sent by Henry VII against James later that summer. This victory did much to raise the spirits of the Scottish populace.

James used Wood in his activities amongst the Hebrides to help root out the rebellious supporters of Angus of the Isles. Angus was murdered in 1490, but his cousin, Alexander, was no less troublesome in the Isles. Eventually James took action against the aged MacDonald lord, John II, in May 1493. His lands were declared forfeit and he was summoned to appear before James IV and declare his submission. John complied and the title of Lord of the Isles ceased. Although hostilities remained amongst the Isles, James had dealt the final blow to the great adversary of his forebears. With such time as he was able James spent much of the 1490s visiting and taking measures throughout the Isles to restore order and loyalty. His actions were persistent and persuasive and he moved forward by occasional victories. For instance the flagrant opposition of Sir John of Islay, who stormed Dunaverty Castle in April 1494 and hanged James's new governor before the king's very eyes, was followed with swift retribution upon Sir John and his accomplices. The uprising of Alexander of Lochalsh in 1496 was similarly swiftly dealt with by James's supporters, and Alexander was slain. There were still further rebellions, the main one being lead by Torquil Macleod, the lord of Lewis, who now regarded himself as the primary hereditary ruler of the Isles. He had taken under his wing Donald Dubh, grandson of John of the Isles, who had escaped from prison in 1501 and by 1503 was prepared to lead his assault on the Scots king. It took three summers before Donald was captured, in 1505, but by then the measures that James took in order to subdue the Isles and guarantee the support of the chieftains were having effect. Firstly, James had agreed to grant land by charter to the chieftains provided they gave him their fealty. Secondly, following Donald's rebellion, James established two sheriffs over the Isles to administer justice, while the government of the Isles was given to the Earl of Huntly in the north and the earl of Argyll in the south.

From a portrait in the National Gallery of Scotland

Throughout his reign James endeavoured to maintain peace with England, though in this he was fraught with dilemma. Since 1492 James had been aware of the endeavours of Perkin Warbeck, the pretender to the English throne who had begun his campaign in 1490. He rapidly gained the support of many princes of Europe, including James IV whom he first visited in 1495. James believed Warbeck's claims and, as a sign of his support, he not only wrote to the king of the Romans, Maximilian, offering his support if Maximilian should take action against Henry VII, but he married Warbeck to his cousin, Lady Catherine Gordon, in January 1496. In September 1496 James and Warbeck invaded Northumberland but the skirmishes proved fruitless and the two parties retreated after a little over two weeks. Warbeck became incensed at the way James had conducted the forces and Warbeck now fell out of favour. Although James continued to honour him as his guest for many more months, at the risk of war with England, Warbeck was eventually despatched from Scotland to France in July 1497. These hostilities, however, had led to a series of border skirmishes which remained until peace was eventually restored between England and Scotland in September 1497 through the medium of the Spanish ambassador Pedro de Ayala. Somewhat languidly James and Henry sought to strengthen this peace, reviving the aims of James's father in seeking a marriage between the royal families of Scotland and England. James was in his late twenties and his failure to marry and produce an heir was the cause of some consternation in Scotland. There were rumours that James had secretly married one of his mistresses, Margaret, the daughter of Lord Drummond, and that this would complicate arrangements with the English. Margaret Drummond was poisoned, along with her two sisters, early in 1502. After three years of negotiation a marriage treaty was signed in January 1502 between James IV and Henry VII's twelve-year-old daughter Margaret Tudor. The same day a formal peace treaty in perpetuity was signed between the two nations. This treaty also had papal blessing, so that, if it were broken the transgressor would face excommunication. That this perpetuity was to last only eleven years was one of the unfortunate twists of fate. The official marriage between James and Margaret took place at Holyrood in August 1503. Through this union the crowns of Scotland and England would eventually be united under James IV's great-grandson 100 years later.

Political endeavours aside, James continued to pursue his interests in the arts and sciences and encourage learning. Of great significance in this respect was his statute of 1496, which purports to be the first compulsory education act, making it incumbent upon all barons and gentlemen to send their sons to school from the age of eight, to remain there until they had mastered Latin. James had a fascination himself for all forms of study, especially medicine and dentistry. He apparently experimented in pulling the teeth of his own barber. The King's College at Aberdeen was founded in 1495, teaching among other subjects, medicine and in 1506 the Royal College of Surgeons was established in Edinburgh. Among the most colourful of James's doctors was John Damian, an alchemist, who was appointed abbot of Tongland in 1504. This eccentric experimented with flying and made his own wings, with which he plunged to his death from Stirling Castle in 1513. James was also concerned about the morals of the nation. Among his many statutes was a ban on the playing of football in 1491, though he evidently enjoyed the game himself for there is a record that he purchased footballs for his own pleasure in 1497! To enforce his regulations James often accompanied the court justiciars, but from 1504 he established a permanent court in Edinburgh (or wherever the king held his court) which met daily and became the supreme court of justice in Scotland until superseded by the Court of Session in 1532.

James also encouraged the arts. The priest William Dunbar became Scotland's first equivalent of the poet laureate, receiving a pension from James in 1500 and thereafter penning poems for official occasions, notably *The Thistle and the Rose* to commemorate James's wedding in 1503. In 1507 the bookseller Andrew Myllar, financed by the king's clerk Walter Chapman, brought the first printing press into Scotland.

Although James now had a formal treaty with England, he also had a long-standing treaty with his old allies, France. This caused him another major dilemma when his brother-in-law Henry VIII prepared to do battle against France. Whom should James support? The war had come about because of the machinations of the pope, Julius II. Although James had supported the need for a holy war against the Turks, he was taken aback when he found that in 1511 Julius declared Louis XII of France a schismatic because he had dared to question the pope's actions. Julius formed a Holy League of Spain, Austria and England against France. James could not support this, finding that he too questioned the pope's decision. The Auld Alliance between France and Scotland held good, but it meant that England and Scotland were again on opposing sides. Henry did not especially want war with Scotland, but James maintained that so long as Henry continued aggression against France there could be no peace between them. As part of his preparations, James strengthened his fleet and constructed the mighty battleship the *Great Michael*. At 240 feet long and with space for 300 sailors, over 100 gunners and 1,000 soldiers, it was the largest ship yet built. Despite many efforts to ensure peace, border skirmishes and sea battles grew between the two nations until they could no longer avoid full hostilities. When Henry invaded France in June 1513, James declared war on England. The first major and decisive battle was at Flodden Field, just south of the border near Coldstream. Here, despite fighting valiantly, James was killed. With him died thirteen earls, fourteen lords, his twenty year-old son Alexander, whom he had made archbishop of St Andrews, and many hundreds of knights and soldiers. The English commander, the earl of Surrey, had also suffered considerable losses, and he did not follow up his victory by an incursion into Scotland. For the moment the battle was won.

There is an interesting aftermath. The historical account states that James's body was found on the battlefield by the English and was conveyed to Berwick and then to London, where it was kept at Richmond Palace for some time before being interred at Sheen Abbey. However rumours began to arise that James had not died at Flodden and that the body was that of a lookalike, or one so disfigured in the fighting to make identity uncertain. There was one rumour that James had survived the battle but was murdered soon after by Lord Home. Others maintained that James had gone on a pilgrimage to the Holy Land, from where he never returned. All of this is fanciful but was sufficient to provide James's widow, Margaret, who remarried in 1514, with an excuse to obtain a divorce from her second husband on the grounds that James had still been alive when the second marriage took place. The exact whereabouts of James's remains is still a mystery. He was succeeded by his seventeen-month-old son James.

JAMES V
Ruled 9 September 1513–14 December 1542.
Crowned: Stirling Castle, 21 September 1513.
Titles: *king of Scotland; duke of Rothesay (from birth).*
Born: *Linlithgow Palace, 10 April 1512.* **Died**: *Falkland Palace, 14 December 1542, aged 30.* **Buried**: *Holyrood Abbey.*
Married: *(1) 1 January 1537, at Notre Dame, Paris, Madeleine (1520–37), dau. Franois I of France; (2) 12 June 1538, at St Andrews Cathedral, Fife, Mary (1515–60), dau. Claude I, Duke of Guise-Lorraine: 3 children. James also had at least nine illegitimate children.*

A special crown and sceptre was made for the infant's coronation twelve days after his fathers death. James V's whole reign, half of which was in his minority, was filled with attempts at diplomacy between France and the papacy, most of which were successful, but which ultimately proved a disaster for the king.

Immediately upon his succession, his mother, Margaret Tudor, set herself up as regent but, since she was English and the sister of the aggressor Henry VIII, she scarcely commanded much support. The Scottish council preferred John, duke of Albany, the son of James III's brother Alexander, who was next in line to the throne. John had been born and raised in France – in fact he could not speak Scottish. The French king was not confident the Scots would continue to support him and did not sanction the return of Albany so for some months there was an uneasy stalemate. In April 1514 James IV's posthumous son, Alexander was born. He became the new heir to the throne, which helped ease some of the tension between the factions which supported Stewart and Albany succession. Then in August 1514, Margaret Tudor married the untrustworthy Archibald Douglas, earl of Angus. Thus, under the terms of James IV's will, she was excluded from her guardianship of the young king and this increased the demand for a new regent. Since in that same month, France and England entered into a peace treaty, Louis approved the return of Albany to Scotland on the promise that he maintain peace between Scotland and England.

Although there were suspicions that Albany had his own designs upon the Scottish throne he never gave evidence of this and in fact showed remarkable skill in handling a difficult situation. The only rebellion against him came from Alexander, Lord Home, who was already regarded as having played a dubious role at Flodden. He was promptly arrested and executed in 1516. Albany succeeded in administering justice and upholding the rule of law with admirable credit, though not without cost. Records show that he and his retinue drained the Scottish coffers and left the nation virtually bankrupt. Nevertheless, he was eventually accepted by the remaining Scottish factions once it was evident that Albany agreed that the French-Scottish alliance against England should be renewed. The new French king, François, was less supportive and when Albany returned to France to enter into negotiations in 1517 he found himself detained there for four years. During his absence the Council of Regents that he had established soon broke down. This led to the notorious Cleansing of the Causeway in April 1520: a street fight between the Douglases (under the earl of Angus) and the Hamiltons (under the earl of Arran) which resulted in the Hamiltons being driven out of the capital.

In 1521 Henry VIII entered into an alliance with the emperor Charles V which reopened hostilities with France. The Anglo-French treaty was thus broken and François sought to renew his alliance with Scotland. Albany returned to Edinburgh with a treaty to be ratified by the Scots council. The Scots however had no desire to be merely the pawns of the French and it was a further two years of negotiations before the Scots agreed to support the French. Albany returned to Scotland in 1523 with men and finances, to find not only an antipathy to French soldiers in Scotland, but an increasing fear of attacking England. Past severe defeats began to make the Scots think twice about a renewed alliance with France. Albany returned to France in 1524 and never returned. He died there in 1536. The Douglases sought to take over control. The earl of Angus declared himself the new governor and keeper of the king. He effectively imprisoned the fourteen-year-old James at Edinburgh Castle in 1526, while he and his family took over the official posts. This action was not supported by Angus's wife, Margaret Tudor, who succeeded in divorcing Angus in 1527. She eventually managed to make contact with her son who escaped from Edinburgh Castle in 1528 and was given refuge at Stirling Castle. Angus's lands were declared forfeit and he fled to England.

Now, at sixteen, James entered into his majority. The years of his youth had forced him into a position from which he could not retreat. He pursued his hostility to Angus with vitriolic vigour, though further conflict broke out before the Douglases were eventually banished from Scotland in November 1528. James's opposition to Angus, who had been the focus of the pro-English faction in Scotland, meant that any hope of reconciliation with England was limited. However James found that Henry had too much else to consider than to open hostilities with Scotland and a five-year peace treaty was concluded with England at Berwick in December 1528. This allowed James some respite to restore order to his fractured realm. He took action against the chieftains of the borders who were openly defying alliance to either Scottish or English monarchs. His punitive raids on the borders in 1529 and 1530 were decisive, especially the second, when he hanged nearly fifty rebels of the Armstrong clan of Liddesdale without trial. Although this restored peace to the Borders it brought further enmity from the Border folk towards James, whom they felt they could no longer trust.

James next turned his attention to the Western Isles. Although the chiefs of the Isles had shown their allegiance to James's father, old rivalries had broken out during Albany's governorship and this erupted into full fury in 1528 when the Macleans took up arms against the Campbells for revenge for the murder of Lord Maclean by John Campbell, the brother of the earl of Argyll. Despite his youth James was able to use his authority and powers of diplomacy in negotiation with the Macleans by which he won the support of the chieftains of the Isles. James arrested and imprisoned Archibald Campbell, earl of Argyll, in 1531. These actions in the Highlands and Borders, while restoring peace, had also alienated James from many key nobles. When he needed their support in later years it was not forthcoming.

James re-opened negotiations with France and also with the pope. Clement VII's own relationship with Henry VIII had deteriorated beyond redemption and the pope was fearful that James might follow in his uncle's footsteps. Although James had no intention of doing this he nevertheless milked the situation for what it was worth, which resulted in his receiving an extensive annuity from the pope. This enabled James to replenish his bankrupt coffers and to re-establish a rule of law in Scotland by founding the Courts of Justice in 1532. Relations with England were tense, but as France was keeping peace with England and did not want to have to support Scotland in a war with Henry, the French were able to facilitate a new Anglo-Scottish peace treaty which was more lasting. James also sought to marry into the French royal house. He had long expected a betrothal to a daughter of the king of France, and when another planned marriage was rejected, James married Madeleine, the French king's sixteen-year-old daughter on 1 January 1537. The one objection to the marriage had been the young girl's weak constitution and the worst fears were proved right. Soon after she was brought to Scotland that summer she died, after a marriage of only seven months. James was distraught, but he soon entered into a new marriage alliance with Mary of Guise-Lorraine, whose first marriage to Louis de Longueville had also ended in 1537 with the duke's death. This girl was a more robust twenty-three year old and had borne her first husband two sons.

James was to prove an unsuccessful father. His firstborn son, James, died after eleven months in April 1541. Three days later his second born son, Robert, died aged only eight days. That following November, James's mother, Margaret, died, and with her passing went the last family link between James and his uncle Henry. At the same time James's relationship with his nobles was worsening. He remained an extremely popular king amongst the general public, and he was welcomed on a tour of Scotland during the summer of 1541 when the nation shared in his and his wife's grief.

By 1542 the relationship between England and France had worsened. A projected meeting between James and Henry VIII was stopped by François and the inevitable conflict became a reality. No formal declaration of war was made, but a series of border conflicts led to an incursion of Henry's men under the duke of Norfolk into Scottish territory in the summer of 1542. James's army followed Norfolk but refused to cross the border, again arguing that they were not going to do France's dirty work. James succeeded in raising another army but as it came to face the

English army at Solway Moss in November 1542, James found his earls would not support him and the army broke into disarray. The English victory was easy. Scarcely anyone was killed, and James's army was routed.

It seems that after this defeat James lost the will to live. With no heir to the throne, no support from his nobles and no ability to fight the English, he took to his bed in early December. Even the news of the birth of a daughter, the future Mary, Queen of Scots, did nothing to raise his spirits and he died of depression a week later, aged only thirty. His defiant opposition to Henry VIII's Protestantism had established the course of conflict between his heiress, Mary, and the English crown that would prove both a disaster and ultimate success for the Scottish crown.

MARY queen of Scotland and France
Queen of Scots, 14 December 1542–24 July 1567 (abdicated); Crowned: Stirling Castle, 9 September 1543. Queen consort of France, 10 July 1559–5 December 1560. Born: Linlithgow Palace, 8 December 1542. Died (executed): Fotheringhay Castle, 8 February 1587, aged 44. Buried: Peterborough Cathedral, later removed to Westminster Abbey in 1612.
Married: (1) 24 April 1558, at Notre Dame, Paris, François (1544–60), son of Henri II of France: no children; (2) 29 July 1565, at Holyrood Palace, Henry, lord Darnley (1545–67), son of Matthew Stewart 4th earl of Lennox: one son; (3) 15 May 1567, at Holyrood Palace, James, earl of Bothwell (1535–78): stillborn twins.

Mary was only one week old when her father died. Since Mary's elder brothers had both died in infancy, there must have been some concern that Mary might not survive. Although her mother, Mary of Guise, remained the child's protector, she was not made regent. That role fell to the heir presumptive, James Hamilton, second earl of Arran and great-grandson of James II. Unlike past governors, however, Hamilton was not his own man and was easily influenced. The next five years saw Hamilton battered between the various pro-English and pro-French factions that dominated Scottish politics. The prize was in gaining a marriage treaty with the young princess. Hamilton entertained the hope that she would become the bride of his own son, James. Henry VIII conspired to make her the wife of his son Prince Edward, the future Edward VI, by the Treaty of Greenwich, which was never ratified. When the Scots, under Cardinal Beaton, archbishop of St Andrews, ended this arrangement, English forces harried the Scottish borders in 1544 and 1545, which served only to strengthen the Scottish opposition to the English. Beaton was a fervid papist and ordered the burning of several heretics, notably George Wishart in 1546. It was probably as a result of this that Beaton was murdered in May 1546, though whether for his sympathy with England or Protestantism was not entirely clear. It was at this same time that John Knox was forced into exile following his own persecutions as a 'heretic'. He found refuge on the Continent but returned to Scotland in 1559 as its most fervent Protestant.

When Henry VIII died on 28 January 1547 the French began to exert a stronger influence in Scotland, particularly after the defeat of the Scots by the English Protector, the duke of Somerset, at Pinkie in September 1547. The Scots convinced Hamilton that the best place for Mary's safety was in France and she set sail in July 1548. Mary grew up in the glittering French court and was carefully educated as a French woman. For the next decade the Scots found themselves the pawn of French affairs, becoming embroiled in the war between France and Spain and consequently with England. Any chance of reconciliation with England, whose new queen Mary Tudor had reverted to Catholicism, was thwarted by the French hostilities. Scotland was powerless to conduct its own affairs, even after their twelve-year-old queen, Mary, had decreed in 1554 that she wished to choose her own Governor. James Hamilton was replaced by Mary of Guise, the queen mother, who acted as much the agent for France as for Scotland.

It was against this background that Mary was married to the French Dauphin, François, on 24 April 1558. She was fifteen; he was fourteen. Only a year later, Henri II of France died in a tournament. Mary became queen consort of France and her husband, king François II. To many Scotland had now lost its sovereignty to the kingdom of France.

Considerable opposition to France grew in Scotland and although there was no outright rebellion it did allow the growth of Scottish reformists who supported English Protestantism. When the English queen Mary died in 1558, and it became evident that her successor, Elizabeth, would follow her father's opposition to the pope and reintroduce the Church of England, the Scottish Protestants turned to England for support in driving out the French. Elizabeth, still not sure of her position, did not initially provide open support, but did not stop the action of her countrymen in their designs. A little earlier the French had recaptured Calais, the only English possession remaining in France, and set about the persecution of the English Protestants in France. Mary of Guise, the queen regent, carried out the same actions in Scotland. The Scottish Protestants and their supporters, who were now becoming openly hostile to the French, sought to depose the queen regent and instal their own Regent. They first sought to follow James Stewart, Mary's illegitimate half-brother, but by December 1559 James Hamilton (sometimes called the earl of Arran), son of the heir presumptive, escaped from captivity and this allowed his father, now known as the duke of Châtelherault, to return to Scotland and resume control. Civil war plagued Scotland over the next six months. Elizabeth of England eventually sent troops to support the Scots against the French. There were no decisive victories, however, and peace was only restored with the death of the queen mother in June 1560. Thereafter the Treaty of Edinburgh called for the peaceful retreat from Scotland of English and French troops. A parliament was called that September in the names of Mary and François II of France.

From a contemporary portrait

Although an uneasy peace returned to Scotland, there were many loyalists who believed that Mary would remain in France and possibly abdicate her position as queen of Scotland. If she did, then the crown would fall to the Hamiltons, the younger of whom was currently pursuing the hand of Elizabeth of England. All this changed, however, in December 1560, when the young French king died. Mary became the dowager Queen of France with her own estates and income, but was without support in France, as the new king, Charles IX, was under the power of his mother, Catherine de Medici. Mary determined to return to Scotland. The younger James Hamilton had already contacted Mary, reminding her of their childhood friendship. If they should marry, the Scottish lines of succession would come together and James would become the rightful king. Mary, however, rejected his suit. When she returned to Scotland in August 1561 she sailed to meet her half-brother, Lord James Stewart, at Leith rather than the Hamiltons at Dumbarton. Thereafter the younger Arran's mind began to fail and within a year he was incarcerated as insane.

Mary did not rush into marriage. Instead she worked with her councillors and church representatives to establish a moderate rule in Scotland acceptable by all. In this she achieved remarkable results. Her grace and good humour made her appeal to the general populace, and her desire to be seen about her kingdom increased her popularity. Mary, although at heart a Catholic, allowed religious freedom. She succeeded in walking this middle road by her sheer strength of character. Her supporters talked openly of her as the successor to the English throne and whilst they tried to unite Mary and Elizabeth in common views, Elizabeth's increasing antagonism towards Mary failed to bring about what could have been a strong union. The need for Mary to marry had caused some consternation amongst official circles but, in 1564, Mary fell in love with Henry Stewart, Lord Darnley, her second cousin and next in line to the Scottish throne. Although it seemed a natural match, it was unpopular amongst Mary's nobility. The marriage, which took place in July 1565, was enacted according to the Catholic rites and this ruffled the feathers of the reformers. Moreover, the rise to power of Darnley removed Châtelherault and James Stewart (now earl of Moray) from any likelihood of succession. Although these two nobles rebelled they were soon defeated by Mary who led her own troops into battle. The nobles, however, believed that Mary was neglecting their interests which were supplanted by her own court favourites, especially the court secretary and musician David Rizzio.

Darnley also believed Mary was having an affair with Rizzio and, in March 1566, he and his fellow lords murdered Rizzio in front of Mary. It is possible that the conspirators also intended to murder Mary, but she escaped, along with Darnley, with whom she became briefly reconciled.

However, Mary's position was now endangered. The birth of her son (the future James VI) and his baptism by Catholic rites, further alienated the Protestants. Her reconciliation with Darnley was brief, and she began a new liaison with James Hepburn, earl of Bothwell. Bothwell was disliked and distrusted by the other leading nobles, including Mary's own half-brother. Again she was blinded by passion. The two of them conspired to remove Darnley from the scene. This did not necessarily mean his murder, although a divorce might have meant the succession of Mary's young son becoming void. In fact Mary sought to reconcile herself again with Darnley when, on 10 February 1567, he was murdered under somewhat mysterious circumstances at his lodgings in the Provost's House near Holyrood. A tremendous explosion nearly destroyed the house, suggesting the conspirators had sought to murder both Darnley and Mary, except that Mary was not there and Darnley was found smothered in the grounds. The full facts behind Darnley's murder were not satisfactorily resolved despite several convictions and the unseemly haste by which Bothwell divorced his wife, was acquitted of any part in Darnley's death, and then married Mary on 15 May, only added to the suspicion. Mary had now turned her back on the Catholic faith for she was married by Protestant rites. However, Mary's actions had discredited her in the eyes of many of her lords and her people. A confederacy of lords united with the outward purpose of rescuing Mary from the traitor Bothwell, but with the real objective of replacing Mary with their own choice, her young son, James. Although Mary and Bothwell fled they were soon captured. Mary was despatched to the castle of Lochleven where, on 24 July 1567 she agreed to abdicate. Bothwell was stripped of all his titles and lands. He fled to Orkney and then to Norway where he remained in exile, dying in Denmark in 1578. While at Lochleven Mary miscarried twins.

In May 1568 Mary escaped from Lochleven and rapidly raised a considerable army but it was defeated by the supporters of the young king James at Langside on 13 May and Mary fled into England. She threw herself under the protection of Queen Elizabeth, but this resulted in Mary's imprisonment at Carlisle on suspicion of involvement in Darnley's murder. A commission which looked into Mary's affairs reached no clear conclusion. This did not wholly clear her name and Elizabeth, who had avoided speaking with Mary, consigned the Scottish queen to further imprisonment, for her own safety, in a series of castles – Bolton, Tutbury, Wingfield. Mary still had supporters, both in Scotland and England and there were many papists who yearned for the restoration of Mary and the overthrow of Elizabeth. While at Wingfield in 1569 she became romantically entangled with Thomas Howard, the Duke of Norfolk, who had investigated the Darnley enquiry on Elizabeth's behalf. Norfolk hatched a scheme with the Florentine financier, Roberto di Ridolfi, to free Mary, overthrow Elizabeth and restore Catholicism. The plan failed. Ridolfi escaped. Norfolk was imprisoned and executed. Mary was now doomed to finish her life imprisoned in a further series of castles and fortified houses: Chatsworth, Sheffield, Chartley and finally Fotheringhay. Throughout this period she managed to involve herself in various intrigues and plots against the English crown, becoming more and more dangerous. Amongst these was the plot of Antony Babington in 1586, who was encouraged by a Catholic priest, John Ballard, to head a conspiracy against Elizabeth. They were betrayed by double agents including Gilbert Gifford and Anthony Tyrrell. Letters from Mary to Babington were found. Ballard and Babington were executed. Mary was tried and convicted of treason. Elizabeth delayed signing her death warrant for three months, but Mary was finally beheaded at Fotheringhay Castle on 8 February 1587. There were many who wondered why her son, James VI, now of age and in full sovereignty of Scotland, had taken no action to save her. But James, who had never really known his mother, was plotting his own future and was in no mood to complicate matters. Mary went to the executioner's block bravely and with honour – a victim perhaps of her own pride and recklessness, but ultimately a pawn in the power vortex of love, religion and politics.

JAMES VI, also **JAMES I** of England.
Ruled 24 July 1567–27 March 1625. Crowned king of Scotland: Stirling Castle, 29 July 1567.
Full name and titles: James Charles, king of Scotland and (from 1603) England; duke of Rothesay (from birth), duke of Albany, earl of Ross and baron Ardmannoch (from 1567).

> **Born:** *Edinburgh Castle, 19 June 1566.* **Died:** *Theobalds Park, Hertfordshire, 27 March 1625, aged 58.* **Buried:** *Westminster Abbey.*
> **Married:** *23 November 1589, at Oslo, Norway, Anne (1574– 1619), dau. Frederick II of Denmark and Norway: 9 children.*

We tend to think of James VI more as James I king of England, overlooking the fact that he had been king of Scotland already for thirty-six years, twenty-three of those since he had taken the reins of government. He was the first king to rule the whole of Britain (only the Isle of Man retained a separate kingship but was subject to the Crown).

James, the only son of Mary Queen of Scots and Henry Stewart, Lord Darnley, was, through both his parents, the great-grandson of Margaret Tudor, sister to Henry VIII of England, and he was thus heir to the English throne should Elizabeth, the queen of England, have no children. He was just thirteen months old when his mother was forced to abdicate and, as with other Stewart kings of Scotland, his reign began under a regency amid intense rivalry. His mother was still alive and her supporters, the papists, led by John Hamilton, archbishop of St Andrews, were still powerful amongst the Scots. Also, accusations were still flying over the murder of his father, Lord Darnley. Both his mother and his uncle, the earl of Moray, were implicated. Although both were eventually cleared of the charges, Moray (who almost certainly was a party to it) succeeded in casting the blame on to William Maitland of Lethington, who had been Mary's secretary of state. Maitland was thrown into prison but was never tried and, though released, later died of poison.

Moray became regent. He was the head of the pro-Reformation faction that opposed Mary. Although he had his enemies, Moray was a strong and able governor. Had he been conceived on the right side of the sheets he would have been a good king. He succeeded in subduing rebels in the Borders as no previous monarch had, and it was primarily through his guidance that

Protestantism spread throughout Scotland and took too strong a hold to fail. Nevertheless his enemies eventually got the better of him, and in January 1570 Moray was murdered by James Hamilton of Bothwellhaugh, nephew of Archbishop Hamilton. Although the younger Hamilton was not brought to book, his uncle was. Elizabeth of England knew that Hamilton was the power behind a series of border incidents. She took advantage of the divisions between the Scottish nobility to encourage Matthew Stewart, earl of Lennox and James's grandfather, to attack and devastate Hamilton's lands. Lennox was promoted to the regency. Although he was becoming old and weak, he was still a passionate supporter of the king and in the ensuing months he captured Archbishop Hamilton who was tried, found guilty of complicity in the murders of Darnley and Stewart, and hanged. Over the ensuing months Lennox pressed home his advantage. His Protestant faction eventually won the day, though Lennox himself was shot and killed in a skirmish in Stirling in September 1571.

The next regent was John Erskine, earl of Mar, who governed for just over a year, but the real power behind the throne, and the next regent, was James Douglas, earl of Morton. Morton had his enemies but he established a firm and stable government. He was the strongest champion of the Protestant cause, to the extent of passing legislation that enabled justiciars to levy fines for non-conformity to the new faith. Although he was briefly ousted from the regency by the earls of Argyll and Atholl in 1578, he regained control for a further two years. The young king did not like Morton, who was cold and ruthless. James had been starved of parental affection throughout his childhood, and this allowed him to warm to the ebullient and avuncular Esmé Stuart, a cousin of his father's, who had been raised in France but who was also an heir to the throne. He came as an agent to Scotland in 1579 in the hope of converting the country back to Catholicism. Through his urbanity he soon won the affection of the young king and succeeded in overthrowing Morton who was charged with involvement in the murder of Darnley. Morton was arrested and executed in 1581. Stuart's true colours however now emerged and the threat of a popish plot caused the more extreme Protestant faction to react. William Ruthven seized James in August 1582 and refused to release him until James agreed to the banishment of Esmé Stuart. Once this was accomplished James was freed in June 1583. The episode, known as the Ruthven Raid, demonstrated what a powerful force Protestantism had become by the late sixteenth century, and how much the king was perceived as the figurehead in determining the direction of the church.

James's relationship with Esmé has caused some to regard James as homosexual, or at least bi-sexual. It is quite likely as, starved of affection in his youth, James showered love and affection on anyone who showed him a personal interest. James had not been the most attractive of children. He was short and walked with a rolling gait that was suggestive of rickets. He had somewhat bulbous eyes and apparently had trouble swallowing so that he frequently drooled. This affliction also affected his speech which was, at times, slurred. How much of this picture of James was the product of his enemies is less easy to interpret, because much of it is recorded by later English chroniclers, some of whom found it difficult to understand James's broad Scottish accent. Other more dangerous rumours were spread about James. The most extreme was that he was a changeling child, swapped because Mary's had been stillborn. Some noticed a remarkable resemblance with John Erskine, earl of Mar. The remains of a newborn baby were found at Edinburgh Castle during renovations in the nineteenth century, but nothing was proved. The same rumours would be spread about James II of England's only surviving son, the Old Pretender (see p. 338).

Although James had exercised some authority in government since 1578, by 1583, at the age of seventeen, he decided he would no longer be the pawn of factions within his aristocracy. All those who attempted to control him, such as James Stewart, the new earl of Arran (and cousin of the previous earl, James Hamilton, former suitor of Mary, Queen of Scots), found their power

From a portrait by Paul van Somer, 1620

rapidly curtailed. By 1586 James had established a government of moderates who moved along with his own wishes towards a firm relationship with England and a strong control over Protestant affairs. This did not stop James being an eternally nervous king, in regular fear of assassination, a consequence of his upbringing rather than of his current state. It also made him cautious in his foreign affairs. By 1586 he had reached an informal agreement with Elizabeth of England whereby he became her successor, and James would do nothing to endanger that. For that reason he remained silent while his mother was tried and executed in February 1587, and remained neutral during England's war with Spain and the invasion of the Spanish Armada in July 1588.

The death of Mary, Queen of Scots, reduced the power of the Catholic faction who now had no figurehead. Most of the Catholics were in the north of Scotland where Protestantism had barely reached. The Highlanders professed Catholicism, but many still held true to the old Celtic church, whilst others often practised pagan worship. (Claims of witchcraft amongst the Highlanders were rife in the 1590s. James compiled a volume railing against witchcraft and satanism called *Dæmonologie*

[1597] and in 1603 introduced an act with the aim of abolishing its practice, though with little effect.) It was these northern Scots who still held dialogue with the Spanish and were a threat to Scottish uniformity – not that that was new in Scottish history. The Highlands and the Lowlands had seldom been one kingdom, for all they might have purported to be one country. Nevertheless, James could not have the north siding with Spain and creating a Catholic kingdom north of the Clyde. In 1589 he quashed one potential rebellion when he discovered that the earls of Huntly and Errol had been in communication with Spain over a invasion. James treated the earls lightly. But in 1592 James became aware of similar plans again involving Huntly and Errol, this time in league with the earls of Angus and Bothwell. James bided his time, working matters to his own advantage until in 1594 he was able to surprise the earls and banish them from the kingdom.

At the same time he was increasingly nervous of the power of the Protestants, especially once Presbyterianism was introduced by Act of Parliament in 1592. These reformists regarded themselves as beholden only to God, not to the King. The King was as much a vassal of God as were they, and God's spokesman on Earth was the General Assembly. This meant that James VI effectively had no authority over the church, a matter of which Andrew Melville, the instigator of Presbyterianism, was prone to remind the king. James VI now worked one faction against another. In 1596 he recalled the northern earls and stated that these and other northern magnates should have their own equal representation on the General Assembly. Hitherto the Assembly had been composed almost entirely of earls from the south under the domination of Melville. Moreover, although Melville believed James could not abolish the General Assembly, James had statutory control over the holding of any assembly. He could thus control when the Assembly could meet and who was on it. In one quite masterful stroke he weakened the power of the Presbyterians and ensured the northern earls were no longer isolated. He was soon to remind Melville and his colleagues of his own belief in the authority of kingship. In 1599 he produced his book,

Basilikon Doron, which espoused the divine right of kings. It was a direct challenge to Melville's Presbyterianism. Fifty years later it would lead to the death of James's son Charles.

After 1596 James was in complete control of his kingdom. Occasional skirmishes erupted, but nothing that seriously endangered his authority. The worst example was the Gowrie Conspiracy in August 1600 when it was alleged Alexander Ruthven, the brother of the earl of Gowrie, lured James to his house in Perth on some pretext only then to attack James. In the resultant fracas, Ruthven and the earl were killed. There has been some speculation over whether James fabricated this story to explain the death of Gowrie to whom James owed considerable sums of money, but the weight of opinion has settled in favour of James. Gowrie's primary opposition to James had been over his passion to unite England and Scotland, for which purpose James had planned to raise an army to ensure his succession.

James had used the authority of kingship to unite a kingdom more completely than any previous Scottish king. He still did not crack the inveterate obstinacy of the Highlanders who paid him mock allegiance but otherwise played by their own rules, but he had little interest in them anyway. By now Elizabeth of England was in her sixties, and her lack of an heir meant that it was only a matter of time before, barring accidents, James would inherit the crown of England. He had married Anne of Denmark in 1589 and had a son and heir, Henry, born in February 1594, and a daughter, Elizabeth, in August 1596. Others would follow. No other king was so confident in his kingdom, and no other nation so expectant as Scotland. The news came on 26 March 1603 when a messenger arrived at Holyrood to inform the king that Elizabeth had died two days previously. Two days later another messenger arrived to say that the English Privy Council had decreed James as her successor. On 5 April James left Scotland for England. Although he promised to revisit it often he only returned once in the next twenty-two years. Scotland may have gained a kingdom but it had lost its king.

ENGLAND, WALES AND SCOTLAND: THE HOUSE OF STEWART (LATER STUART) (1603–1714)

The rule of the Stewarts, their banishment and restoration, would mark a time of tremendous social upheaval. Civil War devastated the country and split families, causing hardship and tragedy. Religious persecution would be a keynote, though the last burning of heretics at the stake would take place in 1612 under James I. And, under Cromwell, Jews would be readmitted into the country for the first time in almost 400 years.

This was also a time of great expansion. The daring explorations of the world, which had begun under Elizabeth's reign, took on an increasing momentum under the Stewarts and Cromwell. With new discoveries, Britain's first empire began to take shape. In 1609 Hudson explored the river and bay in Canada; some fifty years later the Hudson Bay Company, chartered by Charles II, would have a monopoly on fur trading and become virtually a sovereign power in the region. In 1620 the Pilgrim Fathers set sail for America and founded the Plymouth Colony in New England.

A year later there were attempts to colonize Newfoundland and Nova Scotia; three years after that Virginia became a Crown colony, and a decade later the first settlers went to Maryland. In 1646 the Bahamas were colonized. New York was seized from the Dutch. In the 1670s and 80s Pennsylvania and the Carolinas were founded and the Niagara Falls discovered, and in 1684 the Bermudas became a Crown colony. Most significantly, thirty years earlier Jamaica had been captured. It had been a centre for buccaneers; in the 1680s it would become a centre for the slave trade and thus would begin an ignominious period in British history, on which much of Britain's wealth would be founded, for in 1713 Britain obtained sole rights to import slaves into America.

This was also a period when many of the everyday things we now take for granted in Britain appeared for the first time. Chocolate, tobacco and coffee became part of fashionable life, and potatoes by 1670 were part of everyone's diet; forks for eating were introduced from Italy. The Authorized version of the Bible, the first newspaper, the first insurance companies for property, logarithms, the slide-rule, the first patent laws and the first copyright laws, hackney coaches, postal services, calculating machines and the barometer, the first coke furnaces for smelting iron ore: all originated during this time.

There were still epidemics of the Plague in 1616, 1625 and 1665, but also a great flowering of art, culture and pleasure. Shakespeare continued to live and write for thirteen years after James I's accession; there was Restoration theatre, the work of Rubens, Inigo Jones, Van Dyck and Grinling Gibbons – and the first races at Ascot.

The population of Britain rose to 7 million, with some 675,000 people living in London by the beginning of the eighteenth century.

JAMES I
Crowned king of England: Westminster Abbey, 25 July 1603.

James was full of the joys of spring when he arrived in Westminster in April 1603. He had grand schemes to unite England and Scotland and establish a Great Britain. Unfortunately these plans failed. Although the Scottish Parliament, which had been left under the control of James's second cousin Louis Stuart (Esmé's son), passed an Act of Union in 1607, the English Parliament would have nothing to do with it, so that England and Scotland remained two discrete kingdoms. Nevertheless, to have two kingdoms ruled by one king meant that the border disputes that had cost so many lives for so many centuries became a thing of the past. James rapidly found that governing England was not like Scotland. They did things differently. Although the English statesmen welcomed him as their new king, and one with a considerable reputation, he was nevertheless a foreigner, and one who spoke in a strange accent and brought with him favourites of his court. After Elizabeth's final few years, which had become rather dour and constrained compared to the earlier glories, James was invigorating, but he was also pompous, full of considerable self-importance, and paranoid about his safety. The English found him difficult to understand, and James took a while to become accustomed to the English Parliament and way of life. In fact he and his Parliament usually disagreed so strongly after a while that he regularly dissolved it in order to find other ways to meet his needs, especially for money. James disliked having to acquire the approval of Parliament to raise money for foreign activities.

All this uncertainty about James added to his increasing unease, which was not helped by Robert Catesby's Gunpowder Plot of 1604/5, when extremist Catholics sought to destroy James and parliament. In this respect James was sorely misunderstood. Although he was not Catholic, he was not as fervent a Protestant as the members of the Scottish Kirk that he had left behind – even if the Gunpowder Plot made him appear a near martyr for Protestantism. James worked long and hard at moderating Presbyterianism. When he came south James delighted in the Church of England, which had retained an Episcopalian structure and gave James ultimate authority over it, whereas the Presbyterian Assembly treated James as an equal and denied him control. In England James had more opportunity to impose his will. In 1605 he outlawed the Assembly and those who objected he arrested on grounds of treason. Andrew Melville was summoned to England and imprisoned in the Tower of London for mocking the English church. He was not released until 1611, when he left England for France and did not return. James had broken the back of the General Assembly and was able to impose his own system of diocesan bishops over the Scottish church. He also imposed moderation on the English puritans, whom he attempted to force to conform to the Anglican church. As the final stroke in his reforms of the church, James introduced his own Authorised Edition of the Bible, usually known as the King James's Bible, in 1611.

In other English affairs James fared moderately well. Ruling Scotland from a distance enabled him to work through others to achieve ends he might never have done at home. In 1608, through the earl of Argyll, he arrested the leading clansmen in the Hebrides and forced them into submission. A subsequent rebellion by the MacDonalds in 1614, hoping to revive the lordship of the Isles, was soon quashed, as was the rebellious lifestyle of James's second cousin, Patrick Stewart, earl of Orkney, who was eventually executed in 1615. James also began the plantation of English and Scottish protestants into Ulster from 1611 on.

In foreign affairs James had mixed fortunes. Scotland's original friendship with Spain allowed him to curtail England's war with Spain expeditiously, though relationships were never again the same. In 1607 the first English colony in North America was established by John Smith at Jamestown in Virginia. James's 'kingdom' extended to Bermuda in 1609 and to New England in 1620 with the Pilgrim Fathers in the *Mayflower*. James endeavoured, through the marriages of his children, to establish a strong Protestant alliance throughout Europe. His crowning achievement was the marriage of his daughter Elizabeth to the Elector Palatine Frederick in February 1613 (from whom the

Hanoverian kings of England were descended). He also hoped to marry his sons into the Spanish royal family. This was never likely, but even the possibility was thwarted when his son-in-law Frederick became king of Bohemia in 1618 and found himself at war with the Hapsburg monarchy in Austria. Spain was the ally of Austria, and James came under pressure to support Bohemia against two of the greatest nations in Europe. He succeeded in maintaining his distance – mostly because the English Parliament would not vote him money for the enterprise – but his scheme of a Protestant alliance in Europe rapidly crumbled. By now premature senility was dulling his powers, and a series of poor decisions throughout the last fifteen years of his reign meant that this once ingenious and clever monarch became gradually more incompetent. It was not without good reason that he earned the reputation as 'the wisest fool in Christendom', a phrase coined some years earlier by Henri IV of France. Some of the scandals in his later years included the murder of Sir Thomas Overbury in 1613 and the subsequent pardoning of the earl of Somerset and Lady Essex who were convicted of masterminding the poisoning; the execution in 1618 of Sir Walter Ralegh, whom James had long believed was conspiring against him; and the arrest and imprisonment of Sir Francis Bacon on the grounds of bribery and corruption. Despite these darker spots James showed himself to be forward looking. He became interested in scientific development, especially where it might aid the defence of the realm. He was the patron of several inventors including the remarkable Dutch scientist Cornelius Drebbel, who presented him with a perpetual-motion machine. Drebbel is remembered for the development of the microscope and thermometer, but he should be better remembered for having developed the first submarine, which was really a submersible rowing-boat with the oarsmen breathing through a hollow mast. He demonstrated it in the Thames in 1620 and even took James I for a trip, making him the first king ever to travel underwater.

By the end of his reign, with his intellect fading, James found himself under the strong influence of George Villiers later Duke of

Buckingham, with whom James had become acquainted in 1614 and who rose rapidly to power. Villiers's schemes were often ill advised but James came wholly under his spell. James's final years thus saw him as a weak and dispirited monarch, a shadow of his former self. Nevertheless he had been an active king for over forty years, and in name had been a king almost all of his life. He had, in fact, ruled longer than any other Scottish king and had left a greater impact upon his nation of birth than any preceding him. Although it was only an accident of birth that caused him to become king of England, he nevertheless succeeded in governing both countries despite considerable handicaps and opposition, his ability to survive such trials and tribulations marks him down as one of the most remarkable and cunning of kings. He was succeeded by his son Charles.

CHARLES (I)
Ruled 27 March 1625–30 January 1649. Crowned king of England at Westminster Abbey, 2 February 1626, and king of Scotland at Holyrood Abbey, 8 June 1633.
Titles: king of England, Scotland and Ireland, prince of Wales (1616–25), duke of Albany, marquess of Ormonde, earl of Ross, baron of Ardmannoch, duke of York (from 1605), duke of Cornwall and Rothesay (from 1612) and earl of Chester (from 1616).
Born: Dunfermline Palace, Fife, 19 November 1600. **Died** (executed): Whitehall Palace, London, 30 January 1649, aged 48.
Buried: St George's Chapel, Windsor.
Married: 13 June 1625, at St Augustine's Church, Canterbury, Henrietta Maria (1609–69), dau. of Henri IV, king of France: 9 children.

Charles was the first king to succeed to the kingdoms of both England and Scotland. He had not become the heir apparent until 6 November 1612 when his elder brother Henry died of typhoid. Charles also had an elder sister, Elizabeth, who survived him and from whom the later kings of England from George I are descended, although all his other brothers and sisters died in infancy.

Charles himself was a weak child, backward and unable to walk or talk in infancy. He was left behind in Scotland when his father and family moved to London in 1603 and he followed a year later. He was nursed by Lady Carey who nurtured and strengthened him, so he could talk by the time he was four, though he never lost his stammer, and could walk by the age of seven. He was short (his final height was about five foot four inches), but grew into a more handsome figure than his father. He was devoted to his brother and sister and was much saddened at his brother's death and, a few months later, his sister married the Elector Palatine of the Rhine and went to live at Heidelberg. Charles's teens were lonely years during which he forced himself to become assertive, a trait important in a king but which was to become his downfall.

Charles was the first king to be raised within the Church of England. This religious divide made it impossible to marry the Infanta Maria of Spain, whom he visited incognito in 1623 with his friend George Villiers, who that year became the duke of Buckingham. Instead he married the French princess Henrietta Maria, but only on condition that she was allowed the free practice of the Catholic religion and to control the upbringing of their children. Their marriage happened two months after Charles succeeded to the throne. At first the marriage was unhappy: Henrietta was only fifteen and did not seem schooled in the art of courtship. She disliked Charles's childhood friend, the duke of Buckingham, and may have felt there was more than male bonding between them. Charles clashed with the large retinue that Henrietta had brought from France, which included a bishop, twenty-nine priests and over 400 attendants. Within a year he had despatched these back to France. In 1628, Buckingham was murdered and it seems, with both these barriers removed, that their relationship warmed, and their first child was born in May 1629 (but died the same day). Henrietta always managed to maintain a controlling hand over Charles and exerted an increasingly unwise influence.

For the first three years of his reign Charles had been heavily influenced by Buckingham whose exploits, which earlier might have seemed all a joke, became politically dangerous. Thanks to Buckingham, Charles found himself at war, first with Spain and then (in 1627) with France, with the intention of aiding the Huguenots. Buckingham led abortive and costly expeditions in both campaigns, and caused further international scandal by allegedly seducing the queen of France. Charles was also anxious to assist his brother-in-law Frederick to regain the Rhine Palatinate. Parliament did not like Buckingham and refused to grant Charles the finances for the wars. Charles consequently took what other avenues he could to raise money, including drawing on his wife's dowry and exacting loans from the wealthier peers. He also failed to pay soldiers. This attitude and his cavalier approach to Parliament, which he only called when he chose and then tended to ignore, incensed the Commons. In 1628 the Commons drew up a Petition of Right to control Charles's excesses. Although he accepted it, he chose largely to ignore it. Charles's clash with Parliament continued beyond the murder of Buckingham in August 1628. In the end, Charles adjourned Parliament in March 1629. He did not call another for eleven years, ruling in absolute authority and not seeking parliamentary sanction for his actions. He raised money through taxes and custom duties (known as 'tonnage and poundage') as he chose, and also imposed forced loans and purchased knighthoods upon his wealthier subjects. Although he saved much expenditure by bringing the pointless wars to a close, he frequently did not pay members of the royal household, even though he continued to live in great luxury.

He further upset his subjects, particularly those in Scotland, when he attempted to bring the Scottish church in line with the Church of England, imposing a new service book on Scotland, and introducing his own prejudices within the church, especially a tendency – known as Arminianism – to oppose strict Calvinist

From a portrait by Daniel Mytens, 1634

views of predestination. This was associated with high church practices, which echoed much of the Catholic service. Charles worked with William Laud, the new archbishop of Canterbury, and Thomas Wentworth, later earl of Strafford, who, in 1628, was created President of the North. Between the three they endeavoured to create an absolutism in church and state with Charles as the 'most absolute prince in Christendom', ruling by divine right.

In some actions Charles might almost be justified. Wentworth's activities in Ireland after 1633, where he was lord deputy, were remarkable compared to past campaigns. Whereas previously the expenditure on Ireland had always oustripped any revenues received, Wentworth made the island profitable through his imposition of taxes and custom dues, his elimination of piracy, the introduction of a sound agricultural programme relying on the cultivation of flax, and the transformation of the army into an orderly force. This was done with a heavy-handedness that did not endear Wentworth to the king's subjects, but it was effective.

Attempts to run roughshod over the Scottish church, however, did not work so well. The Scots rejected Laud's new service book and declared defiant loyalty to the old Kirk. They formed a National Covenant in 1638 in opposition to Charles's policies. Following Wentworth's suggestion, Charles decided to impose his intentions by force. He raised an army in the spring of 1639, only to discover how little loyalty he commanded from his troops. Many of the English defected, not expecting to be paid and regarding the Scots as oppressed. The planned force of 30,000 ended up as only 8,000. Charles was easily defeated by the determined Scots in what became known as the First Bishops' War. Charles was in a predicament. He did not have the finances for a second campaign and had no alternative but to summon Parliament in April 1639. This Parliament, known as 'the Short Parliament' because it was dissolved after only a few weeks, refused to grant Charles money unless he heard their grievances. Charles refused. Again he raised an army and again the Scots defeated him in the Second Bishops' War that August. Charles was again forced to call Parliament, and this time he was not allowed to dissolve it (hence it became known as 'the Long Parliament'). Parliament chose Wentworth as the scapegoat for Charles's rule of tyranny, treating the understanding that Wentworth had promised to summon the army from Ireland to subdue the Scots as evidence of treason. Charles was forced to sign Wentworth's death warrant, and he was executed on Tower Hill on 12 May 1641.

Charles conceded some of Parliament's wishes, particularly over the ship-taxes he had imposed, but he would not give way on his reform of the Church of England. Charles attempted to rally support in Scotland but without success. However, when he returned to London he believed some support amongst Parliament was swinging his way. When John Pym presented his list of grievances against the king, known as the Grand Remonstrance, in November 1641, it did not receive universal support. Charles, encouraged by his queen, believed he could swing the balance in Parliament by removing the main opposition. In January 1642 Charles entered the House of Commons with an armed guard intending to arrest the five primary offenders. The five Members, who included Pym, had already escaped. This was the final straw. There was much public opposition to Charles's actions, so he withdrew from London. Negotiations over the next seven months failed to reach any agreement, with the king totally intractable and Parliament increasing its demands. Civil war became inevitable and the king formally declared hostilities at Nottingham on 22 August 1642.

This was not the first civil war to divide England, and it was not the first to result in the deposition of a king, but because it was the first and only war in England to result in the abolition of the kingship, it has become known as *the* Civil War. The Royalists, or Cavaliers, generally had the upper hand in the early encounters, though they failed to strike decisively at the first main engagement at Edgehill on 23 October 1642 against the Parliamentarians, or Roundheads, under Robert Devereux, third earl of Essex (and son of Elizabeth's favourite). As the conflict continued, so the Roundheads began to take the offensive, especially when Thomas Fairfax and Oliver Cromwell took command with their specially trained cavalry and restructured New Model Army. They achieved victories at Marston Moor in 1644 and particularly at Naseby on 14 June 1645. With his defeat Charles deliberated about his position for nearly a year before surrendering to the Scots, expecting greater clemency. For their part, the Scots expected Charles to meet their terms over his church reform, but when Charles defiantly refused, the Scots handed him over to the English. While Charles was held by the Scots at Newcastle, the English Parliament issued a set of terms which became known as the Propositions of Newcastle in July 1646. These terms were to agree to the Covenant, abolish episcopacy, authorize Parliament's control over foreign policy and the army and amend his reforms of the Church. Charles refused. When handed over to the English, Charles was confined to Hampton Court, where Fairfax and Cromwell sought to come to terms with him over a formal written constitution. Again Charles refused. Escaping from Hampton Court, he sought refuge on the Isle of Wight, where he was immediately confined to Carisbroke Castle. Charles now intriguingly played one party against the other, negotiating at once with both the Parliamentarians and the Scots. The Scots reached an agreement with Charles which became known as the Engagement, signed on 26 December 1647. Under its terms the Scots would restore Charles as their king provided he would accept Presbyterianism for a trial period. This would be imposed upon the English and the two kingdoms united – though in fact it was a Scottish takeover of the English Parliament. Although not all Scots were united over this agreement, it was sufficient for an army to invade England in July 1648, only to be decisively defeated by Cromwell in three engagements in August at Preston, Wigan and Warrington. Fairfax's army also rapidly subdued a Royalist revolt in southern England.

In January 1649 Charles was brought to trial for treason, on the grounds that he had fought against his subjects. Charles refused to recognize the court as having any authority over him and thus offered no defence. He remained dignified but disdainful of the proceedings. When the court delivered its verdict the 135 judges were split almost evenly, 68 finding him guilty and 67 innocent. Thus by a majority of just one, Charles was condemned to death. He was executed at Whitehall on 30 January. He wore two shirts so as not to shiver from the cold and give the impression he was afraid. The Scots were vehemently opposed to the execution of their monarch by the English parliament but following their recent defeat they felt powerless to react. They nevertheless transferred their allegiance to Charles's son, Charles (II), while in England the kingship was abolished.

Charles had failed as a king in every respect except authority, and in that he presumed too much. He was an absolute dictator or autocrat who nevertheless, in practice, could not operate without the support of his Parliament. His dignity and defiance against the odds might make him a romantic figure were it not for his complete and utter intransigence and arrogance. Whilst he failed to pay his soldiers and supporters, he spent a small fortune on commissioning and acquiring works of art. Where Henry VIII and Elizabeth had the support of the people even though they acted in an almost similar way, Charles did not, because Charles worked against rather than for his subjects. It would be left to his son Charles to restore the humanity, if not the credibility, to the Crown.

CHARLES II

Ruled Scotland, 11 June 1650–3 September 1660 (fled into exile); restored 29 May 1660–6 February 1685. Crowned, Scone Abbey, 1 January 1651. Ruled England, 29 May 1660–6 February 1685. Crowned: Westminster Abbey, 23 April 1661.

Titles: *king of England, Scotland and Ireland; duke of Cornwall and Rothesay.*

Born: *St James's Palace, London, 29 May 1630.* **Died**: *Whitehall Palace, 6 February 1685, aged 54.* **Buried**: *Westminster Abbey.*

Married: *22 May 1662, in Portsmouth, Katherine Henrietta (1638–1705), dau. of John IV, duke of Braganza: 3 children (all stillborn). Charles had at least 16 illegitimate children by 8 mistresses.*

Charles was twelve when the Civil War had broken out. Until then he had been raised in the stately magnificence of Charles's royal palaces and had received a good if not extensive education. He rapidly became skilled in the arts of war, fighting alongside his father in the early engagements and being made commander of his troops in the West Country in March 1645, when only fourteen. As the tide of the war changed, however, Charles wisely left England, settling first (1646) in France and then (1648) Holland, where his sister, Maria, the Princess Royal, had married Prince William of Orange. Charles had at least two sexual encounters during these years, and probably more. Rumours persist that he had fathered a son, James, while in Jersey in 1646 but of more significance was a second son, also called James, born in the Hague on 9 April 1649. The mother was Lucy Walter. The son, who became the duke of Monmouth, later claimed his parents were married and that he was the legitimate heir to the throne.

It was while living in the Hague that Charles learned of his father's execution. On 16 February he was proclaimed king in Jersey. A few days later the Scottish Parliament proclaimed Charles their king, provided he was prepared to accept the Scottish Covenant. This widened the rift between Scotland and England, where the new Parliament abolished the monarchy in March 1649. Charles really wanted to be king of England, and accepting the Scottish Covenant would have barred that route completely. Charles learned early on, therefore, that he needed to be cautious and devious. He was a remarkably pragmatic individual whose main aim was to enjoy himself, but he was prepared to fight and prove himself. He felt that everyone should be allowed to lead their own life, and thus he would bend with the wind and take whatever options best served his purpose. He therefore bided his time, exploring what other avenues might exist. He found Ireland closed to him by Cromwell's army while, in April 1650, an unofficial advance guard under the command of James Graham, the marquess of Montrose was defeated and Montrose hanged. Charles had to act so, in June 1650, he signed a treaty which he managed to keep sufficiently ambiguous but which effectively made him a covenanted king of the Scots. Twelve days later he landed in Scotland, a stranger in his own land. He was dubiously accepted as king but not allowed to exert any authority. He was more a figurehead than a sovereign, but his very presence posed immense danger, not only from rival factions in Scotland but from the English. A month later Cromwell led an army into Scotland. It was not overtly an invasion force, rather a move to explore the relationships between the two countries, but it left little doubt that Cromwell meant business if he met any opposition. However, as many past campaigners had found, Scotland is a difficult land to conquer without a massive support infrastructure and Cromwell's was disrupted by weather and disease. Nevertheless he engaged and overwhelmingly defeated a Scottish force at Dunbar on 2 September 1650, taking possession of Edinburgh and Leith. This was the downfall of the government of Covenanters under Archibald Campbell, marquess of Argyll, and the chaos that followed saw an untrusting but necessary alliance between the extremist factions who overthrew the anti-Royalists (known as the Remonstrants) and proclaimed Charles their king. He was crowned at Scone on 1 January 1651.

Cromwell continued to stamp his authority on Scotland, and in July 1651 Charles led a hopeful army south into England. He was met by Cromwell's army at Worcester on 3 September 1651 and soundly defeated. Charles was lucky to escape with his life. He fled into Shropshire and sought refuge at Boscobel House, where he was helped by the yeoman Richard Penderel. It was at this time that the famous episode happened of Charles hiding in an oak tree whilst Cromwell's soldiers scoured the woods. Charles disguised himself as a servant and a few weeks later made his escape to France. It was difficult for Charles to disguise himself as he had a most distinctive physique. He was tall, at least six foot three inches, which is surprising considering the shortness of his parents. He probably inherited the genes through his Danish grandmother.

He spent the next eight years on the continent, wheeling-and-dealing with whatever power might assist him. He was well placed, as during the next few years England found itself at war with first the Dutch (1652–54) and then Spain (1656–9). Charles took advantage of both conflicts to gain support for his own cause. These hostilities brought the English closer to the French as allies, which further helped Charles because of his own close affinity with the French. An Anglo-French force defeated the Spanish in northern France in 1658, as a consequence of which the Spanish surrendered Dunkirk to the English, who once again held territory in France.

During this period Cromwell's hold on England and Scotland grew. The Commonwealth was declared and, in 1653 Cromwell was made 'Lord Protector'. Though he governed through a Parliament, he was granted almost absolute powers and, indeed, in May 1657 Cromwell was offered the title of king. He refused but accepted the right of succession, so that his son, Richard,

From a portrait by Samuel Cooper

would be Lord Protector after him. For a brief period religious tolerance was observed throughout England and the Jews were readmitted after their 365-year-long exile, but towards the end of Cromwell's government there was a backlash against puritanism and extremism, and a return to a more Catholic practice. Nevertheless civic marriages were allowed and the registration of birth, deaths and marriages enforced.

Cromwell died on 3 September 1658. His son, Richard Cromwell, did not want the role of Lord Protector, and neither was he the man for the job. Had his elder brothers survived, the Protectorate might have continued, but Richard was unable to enforce any authority or control Parliament or the military and in May 1659 he resigned. England came under military rule and it was thanks to the authority of George Monck, who had been made governor of Scotland by Cromwell in 1654, that order was restored. Monck marched on London in January 1660, entering the city without opposition. He soon whipped up enthusiasm for the restoration of the monarchy and paved the way for Charles to return to England on 23 May 1660. Charles entered London six days later on his thirtieth birthday. He was crowned eleven months later with new regalia, the former crown jewels having been broken up during the Commonwealth.

Charles's restoration was dependent upon his religious intentions. When he signed the Declaration of Breda in April 1660, which laid down the terms of his restoration, he acknowledged religious tolerance, though he had trouble gaining any form of acceptance among the clergy and, by 1661, within Parliament. Acts were passed against Jesuits and Quakers and Charles's efforts to reintroduce a modified form of the Church of England was rejected by an increasingly Puritanical parliament. A new English prayer book was introduced and Charles found most of his views ignored. The intolerance of the English Parliament pushed Charles back to his Catholic sympathies from his many years on the Continent. In 1662 he had married the Catholic Katherine of Braganza, the Portuguese Infanta. He negotiated in secret with Catholics and eventually, in 1672, he was able to carry through his Declaration of Indulgence, which suspended all penal laws against nonconformists and allowed private worship by Catholics. Charles himself was rumoured to be a secret Catholic and his brother, James, duke of York (later James II), openly professed his Catholicism. Feelings against Catholics continued to run strong resulting in the false Popish Plot of 1678. This was bumped up by Titus Oates, who spread rumours of an imminent rebellion by the Catholics to invade England from Ireland, over-throw the king and place James on the throne. The backlash against the Catholics was immense, with over thirty-five Catho-lics tried and executed on trumped-up charges. It was two years before Oates's hoax was uncovered.

Early in his reign Charles was guided by Edward Hyde, the Lord Chancellor and head of government, who was made earl of Clarendon in April 1661. Clarendon was a staunch Royalist, ultra-conservative and anti-Puritan, who would have set the country back twenty years. He ultimately became the scapegoat for all the problems that beset Charles's early reign. The sale of Dunkirk back to the French in October 1662 was an unpopular move, as was the outbreak of war with the Dutch in March 1665, although Clarendon spoke against this. It need never have hap-pened, and arose because of an impasse over merchant shipping routes and rights through the English Channel. As a precursor to this various Dutch trading posts and colonies were attacked and seized by the English, including New Amsterdam in the American colonies. This was captured by the distinguished sea captain, later admiral, Robert Holmes in August 1664 and renamed New York in honour of Charles's brother, the duke of York. Although the Dutch regained other territories, they never recovered New York. The war with the Dutch reached stalemate, because England suffered under the Great Plague which began to have its effects in London in April 1665 and was not assuaged until the Great Fire swept through London in September 1666. A treaty with the Dutch was eventually concluded in July 1667. Soon after Clarendon was dismissed and to avoid impeachment he fled to France, where he remained in exile. Clarendon's daughter, Anne, had married the duke of York secretly in 1659 and, through her, Clarendon became the grandfather of the future queens Mary II and Anne (though he did not live long enough to know it). Clarendon's son, Laurence, who was Charles's Master of the Robes and later became the First Lord of the Treasury (1679) was the man who nicknamed Charles 'the Merry Monarch'. He also made the famous quip about Charles that 'he never said a foolish thing and never did a wise one', to which Charles agreed, riposting 'my words are my own, and my actions are those of my ministers'.

Charles next came under the influence of a group of five advisers known from their initials as the Cabal: the Lords Clifford, Arlington, Buckingham, Ashley and Lauderdale. These advisers each looked after their own interests and so did not necessarily act in union. Indeed they had opposing religious views – Ashley (later earl of Shaftesbury) was an ardent Protestant, whilst Clifford was a Catholic. Clifford worked with Charles in his desire to wreak revenge upon the Dutch and helped negotiate a secret treaty with the French in May 1670, whereby the English would support the French against the Dutch in return for financial rewards and use of French ports. The treaty also provided that at some opportune time Charles would declare his reversion to Catholicism. Although Charles believed he was gaining ground, he effectively became a puppet of the French. A strong anti-French and anti-Catholic mood swept the country, aggravated in 1672 when the duke of York openly declared his conversion to Catholicism. Charles was forced to withdraw his Declaration of Indulgence and agree in 1673 to a Test Act, which excluded all Roman Catholics from official office. This excluded the duke of York from office, but did not stop James marrying the Catholic princess Mary of Modena. Parliament refused to sanction any finance to support the Dutch war, and Charles was compelled to act as mediator between the two countries which dragged on until the Peace of Nijmegen in 1678. One of the outcomes of this was that Charles's niece, the fifteen year old Mary, was married to William (III) of Orange in 1677.

The Popish Plot encouraged by Oates showed the strength of anti-Catholic feeling in England. There was a strong fear that personal liberties would be infringed by royal whim and in May 1679 Parliament passed the act of Habeas Corpus, one of this country's most important items of legislation which protects the individual's freedom from unlawful imprisonment. This same Whig Parliament, under the leadership of the earl of Shaftesbury, introduced an Exclusion Bill which would deny the duke of York succession to the throne. By then the queen had had several stillbirths and miscarriages and Charles believed he would have no legitimate son, for all that he had sired many illegitimate ones. Charles prevented the bill's enactment by using his authority in the Lords. When Parliament met the next year the bill was introduced again, and passed, but Charles dissolved Parliament. A third Parliament met in Oxford in 1681 and the bill passed through the Commons and the Lords, but again Charles dissolved Parliament. Charles brought military pressure upon the Whigs to moderate their actions, and the country was fearful of another civil war. Charles entered a secret treaty with the French for their support in the event of a rebellion. It was in this atmosphere that the Rye-House Plot was uncovered in June 1683. It was a scheme devised by Lord William Russell, Algernon Sidney, Lord Capel and others to assassinate Charles and James on their departure from the races at Newmarket in March, and raise Charles's eldest surviving illegitimate son, the duke of Monmouth, to the throne. The plot was thwarted when a fire caused them to leave early. Sidney became the first victim of the infamous Judge Jeffreys, who tried him with minimal evidence and consigned him to the execution block. Jeffreys became a willing tool in serving Charles who wreaked revenge upon any likely conspirator.

With his own private army, with the Whig opposition dispersed, and with Judge Jeffreys happy to execute anyone who dared oppose the king, Charles's final years were unsurprisingly peaceful. While this suggests he ruled like a despot, he was in reality an amusing and likeable man with a great sense of humour. He was really a loveable rogue, a kind of 'Chuck the Lad'. He enjoyed many sports and pursuits, including horse-racing. He established the race-course at Newmarket in 1667 and even raced there as a jockey in the Twelve-Stone Plate in 1675 and won. He loved the theatre, which he re-established and patronized after it was banned during the Commonwealth, and loved the actresses even more. Two actresses became his mistresses. The better known was Nell Gwynne, who bore him two children. The eldest, Charles Beauclerk, survived and married the daughter of the earl of Oxford, and their descendants survive today. By Moll Davies, Charles had Mary Tudor, who married the earl of Derwentwater. Nell Gwynne also had a great sense of humour and the episodes between Charles and Nell in London often caused much jollity. One such was when Nell tried to outdo Charles's other mistress, Louise, duchess of Portsmouth, by wearing a more outrageous hat which was so huge that it threatened to overwhelm her when she appeared on the stage in the King's presence. It was at Nell Gwynne's urging that Charles established the Royal Hospital at Chelsea for army pensioners.

Charles was also a great patron of the arts and sciences. He loved discussing scientific issues and conducted his own experiments. His primary interests were in clocks and watches (he had seven clocks in his bedroom each of which chimed at different times) and in navigation. He was the first monarch to have a royal yacht, the *Royal Escape*. Not surprisingly these two interests come together in his patronage of the Royal Observatory at Greenwich in 1675 under the first Astronomer-Royal, John Flamsteed. Charles established the Royal Society in London in 1660 with the view to 'improving Natural Knowledge'. This was the period when Isaac Newton formulated his theories on gravity; when Sir Christopher Wren undertook some of his greatest building works, including the present St Paul's Cathedral, on which work began in 1675; when Robert Boyle established the principles of scientific experimentation and developed modern chemistry out of ancient alchemy; when Richard Lower undertook the first blood transfusion between animals (1665); and when Edmund Halley correctly predicted the return of the comet now named after him (1682). Thanks to Charles's patronage, science received a boost which it had been denied under earlier rulers and saw the birth, in England, of a scientific reformation.

The first real newspapers appeared during Charles's reign, notably Roger L'Estrange's *The Public Intelligencer* in 1663 and the *London Gazette* in 1665. These were still controlled by royal licensing of the press and censorship of the press was reintroduced in 1680, lasting until 1695.

Some commentators on Charles's reign have called it 'the worst reign in English history', which is a considerable exaggeration. The criticism is that Charles followed whatever course he deemed best to save himself, even if it meant selling his country and his religion to the French. Charles cannot be regarded as a good king, but neither was he an especially bad one, since he was never vindictive, had no wish to cause anyone any harm or anguish provided everyone was moderate. It was the extremists about him who, frustrated at Charles's lack of firm direction, forced issues that caused Charles to react unfavourably. Nevertheless the monarchy survived under him and beyond him.

Charles died of a stroke while still comparatively young and was succeeded by his brother James.

JAMES II, also **JAMES VII** of Scotland.
Ruled 6 February 1685–11 December 1688 (deposed);
continued as king of Ireland until 1 July 1690. Crowned:
Westminster Abbey, 23 April 1685.
Titles: *king of England and Scotland; duke of York (from 1644),*
earl of Ulster (from 1659), duke of Normandy (from 1660).
Born: *St James's Palace, London, 14 October 1633.* **Died:** *St*
Germain-en-Laye, near Paris, 16 September 1701, aged 67.
Buried: *Church of the English Benedictines, Paris.*
Married: *(1) November/December 1659, at Breda, Holland,*
Anne (1637–71), dau. Edward Hyde, earl of Clarendon: 8
children; (2) 21 November 1673, at Dover, Kent: Mary (1658–
1718), dau. of Alfonso d'Este, duke of Modena: 12 children.
James also had at least seven illegitimate children by two
mistresses.

James was the younger brother of Charles II and the son of
Charles I. As the second son of the monarch he was granted the
title duke of York, though this was not formally bestowed until
January 1644. The English Civil War disrupted his education,
which always remained moderate. He was just nine when he
witnessed the battle of Edgehill (October 1642); he was then
removed for his protection to the Royalist headquarters at
Oxford where, apparently, he enjoyed the company of dwarfs.
When Oxford was captured by the Roundheads in 24 June 1646,
the young prince was taken prisoner and confined to St James's
Palace in London, where he remained for nearly two years. In
April 1648, disguised as a girl, and pretending to be playing hide-
and-seek, he effected his escape and fled to Holland, joining his
brother Charles with their sister Mary in the Hague. He frequently quarrelled with his brother and mother. Unlike Charles,
who was good-natured and happy-go-lucky, James was rather
dour and serious. This made him a better soldier than his brother
and, in 1652 he was commissioned into the French army, serving
under Turenne in the French wars in Spain and the Netherlands,

being promoted to lieutenant-general. He had to resign this commission when France and England reached an alliance, but he subsequently served with Spain against France and England in 1658, and was noted for his courage.

During this period James had entered protacted negotiations with the duke of Longueville to marry his daughter, but these came to nothing. His mistress at this time was Anne Hyde, daughter of Charles's chief minister Edward Hyde, and lady-in-waiting to James's sister Mary. He entered into a private marriage contract with her in Holland in November or December 1659. When news leaked out relatives were horrified. Most refused to acknowledge the marriage, and even James denied it for a while. However, with the Restoration of the monarchy in May 1660, and Anne now heavily pregnant, James went through a public ceremony on 3 September 1660 in London. It was some years, however, before there was any real family harmony.

With Charles installed as king, James had a number of titles bestowed upon him. In addition to duke of York, he became the duke of Albany and was made an honorary duke of Normandy by the French king, the last English monarch to hold that title. He also became Lord High Admiral. He commanded the navy during the Anglo-Dutch war, defeating the Dutch at the battle of Lowestoft in June 1665. In 1664 when the English captured New Amsterdam, it was presented to James and renamed New York after him.

In 1668 James and Anne converted to Catholicism but this was kept secret until Charles was able to force his Declaration of Indulgence through Parliament in March 1672. Anne died in 1671 and James was soon negotiating to marry the ardently Catholic Mary of Modena. The Whig government under the earl of Shaftesbury was horrified and in March 1673 forced the King to withdraw his Declaration of Indulgence and to pass the Test Act, which banned Catholics from holding public office. James, who had served bravely again in the third Anglo-Dutch War at Solebay in May 1672, had to step down as Lord High Admiral. The Government also tried to pass an Exclusion Bill which would have removed James from the succession. Charles was able to thwart this on three occasions between 1679 and 1681, but this and the Popish Plot of 1678 where rumour spread of a plan to assassinate Charles and instal James on the throne, caused a massive wave of anti-Catholic feeling. James prudently went into exile in Brussels, and thence to Scotland, in December 1679. He was greeted with considerable caution and trepidation. The Scots had been in upheaval over the last year against potential Catholic reform, and the presence of a Catholic heir in their midst did nothing to pacify them. James, however, remained the soul of discretion for the brief period he was there, and he was generally accepted. However on his return a year later, with the Exclusion Bills rejected, James became less moderate. In July 1681 he forced two bills through the Scottish Parliament. The Act of Succession made it clear that religious differences were no bar to the succession to the Scottish throne. The Test Act forced all those holding official posts to sign a document pledging their adherence to Presbyterianism, Episcopalianism and Catholicism. Few would comply and most resigned, James using this as an opportunity to purge government of any opposition. Over the next three years, even after he returned south, James continued to persecute the Covenanters and there are many stories (possibly not all true) of the atrocities committed by him and in his name.

These persecutions continued in Scotland after James became king in February 1685. Although he was proclaimed king, he never took the Scottish coronation oath and was the first king of Scotland not to be crowned in Scotland. In fact, he never visited it again. From the moment of his accession there was mounting opposition to James. Neither Scotland nor England wanted a Catholic monarch, especially one with such a cruel and vindictive streak. Two political exiles united with plans to invade their respective countries and oust the king. In Scotland this was Archibald Campbell, earl of Argyll, who invaded Scotland in May 1685, whilst in England it was James Scott, duke of Monmouth, Charles II's eldest illegitimate son, who arrived at Lyme Regis on 11 June 1685 and was proclaimed king at Taunton nine days later as the real James II. Both men were astonished that so little support rallied to their cause. Argyll was not joined by his clan. His small army was soon overpowered as it marched south. He was captured, imprisoned without trial and executed in Edinburgh on 30 June. Monmouth was defeated at Sedgemoor on 5 July and captured three days later. He was executed at Tower Hill in London on 15 July. The infamous Judge Jeffreys was sent on a Bloody Assizes circuit of the West Country, where many of Monmouth's followers were captured and executed.

James now imposed a reign of terror, determined to restore Catholicism in England and Scotland. He introduced a Declaration of Indulgence in April 1687 restoring rights to Catholics, and any protesters were imprisoned, including seven bishops, accused of seditious libel. His complete disregard for the wishes of Parliament and his evident intention to overthrow the Church of England at last galvanized his opponents into action. The last straw was the birth of a son, James (*see* James VIII) on 10 June 1688 after a succession of stillbirths and daughters who had died in infancy. Until then it was possible the church might have tolerated James, as his heir presumptives, Mary and Anne, were both Protestants, but the young James would be raised a Catholic and that prospect was too much. Rumours – false but declared in hope – that the new-born baby was a changeling and that James's child had died at birth, circulated rapidly and had sufficient credibility to allow the bishop of London and six supporters (known as the 'Immortal Seven') to invite James's son-in-law, William of Orange, to England to protect his wife's succession to the throne. William was himself alarmed at the return of England and Scotland to Catholicism, as it would confirm Britain as an ally of France against the Netherlands and in France's current mobilization against Germany. On 29 September William sent a declaration to the English Lords accepting their offer and laying out his terms for a 'free and lawful Parliament'. Delayed at first by bad weather, William's army landed at Brixham on 5 November 1688 and was welcomed at Exeter. Over the next two weeks most of the major cities and bishoprics in England declared their support for William. James's army was first based at Salisbury, but in the light of William's advance he retreated to Reading and called a war council. His commander-in-chief, John Churchill, and others defected to William on the same day, and the next day James discovered that his daughter, Anne, had also defected. Realizing he had been deserted, James called a Great Council and agreed to major concessions, including the dismissal of Catholics from office.

Negotiations, led by the marquis of Halifax, continued for a week, but they were little more than a delaying tactic. On 10 December James fled from London, discarding the Great Seal in the Thames. He was captured at Sheerness in Kent and returned to London, but William allowed him to escape again and he fled to France on 23 December. William accepted the government six days later.

James was installed at the château of Saint-Germain, near Paris and established a court-in-exile. (It was at this time that the spelling of Stewart was changed to Stuart, to imitate the French spelling, Steuart.) With James was his eldest surviving illegitimate son and chief agent and negotiator, James Fitzjames, duke of Berwick, son of Arabella Churchill, the sister of John Churchill. There were still pockets of support for James, especially amongst the Irish Catholics and the Scottish Jacobites. Following a rebellion amongst the Irish in January 1689, James landed at Kinsale in Ireland and in May 1689 held a Parliament in Dublin which still acknowledged his authority. James raised an army in Ireland, including support from France, and governed for a year, passing a number of acts in favour of the Catholics. In June 1690 William brought his army to Ireland and defeated James at the battle of the Boyne on 1 July 1690. James fled back to France three days later. He continued to plot and scheme for the next seven years, including a further attempted invasion in 1692 and another planned for but not executed in 1695. He eventually devoted himself to religious pursuits after 1697 and apparently suffered a mental decline. He succeeded in obtaining recognition from France that his legitimate son, James (the Old Pretender), should become king after the death of William III.

James's arrogance and viciousness cost him his crown, but surprisingly not his life. Continued support for him and his son amongst the Scots would result in two Jacobite rebellions over the next fifty years, and his descendants would remain pretenders to the Scottish and English thrones until 1807.

WILLIAM III, designated **WILLIAM II** of Scotland.
King of England and Scotland (jointly with MARY II), 13 February 1689–8 March 1702. Crowned: Westminster Abbey, 11 April 1689.
Full name and titles: king of England, Scotland and Ireland; Stadtholder of Holland, prince of Orange and count of Nassau-Dillenburg (from 1672).
Born: Binnenhof Palace, the Hague, Holland, 4 November 1650.
Died: Kensington Palace, 8 March 1702, aged 51. Buried: Westminster Abbey.
Married: 4 November 1677, at St James's Palace, London, Mary, dau. of James II of England: 3 children, all stillborn.

William III was descended from the ancient house of Nassau in Germany and was the great-grandson of William the Silent, prince of Orange, who became Stadtholder (or chief executive) of the Netherlands in 1572. His father, William II, died just eight days before William was born. His mother, Maria Henrietta, was Charles I's daughter, making him James II's nephew. He would marry James II's daughter Mary. William was deprived of his titles in Holland in his childhood because of his father's arguments with the regents of Holland, but he was restored in 1672 following the overthrow of the dictatorial John de Witt who had governed Holland, first in alliance with France and then, after war broke out with France in 1667, with England and Sweden. Young William led the Dutch against the French and succeeding in forcing a peace in 1678 in which all the Dutch terms were agreed. As a precursor to this, in his negotiations with his uncle, Charles II, who was acting as mediator between France and the

Netherlands, William secured a political marriage with England by marrying his cousin, Mary, in 1677.

When James had come to the throne and begun to pursue his active Catholic measures, William first distanced himself and then, afraid that James might actually tip the balance and secure a Catholic majority in Parliament, and thereby become an immediate ally of the French, decided to intervene. He responded to an invitation from seven English peers known as the 'Immortal Seven', invaded England in November 1688 and within eight weeks had succeeded in a bloodless *coup*. The English Parliament determined that by fleeing the country James had abdicated, whilst the Scots argued that he had forfeited the Crown by his pro-Catholic actions against the Scottish nation. Either way James was no longer recognized as king other than in Ireland. There was some support for a regency, but while James II was still active, and support grew in Ireland and Scotland, Parliament did not want an interminable interregnum. William, on his part, did not want to be seen solely as a king consort, and was prepared to return to Holland. The English did not want a vacant throne and Mary was uncomfortable about reigning alone, especially as it looked as if she had usurped her father's throne. As a consequence in February 1689 William was offered joint sovereignty with Mary. Although common in the time of the early Saxon rulers, there had been no joint rule in England for over 800 years, and none in Scotland since the eleventh century. A Declaration of Rights was issued which outlawed the way James II (and others) had exercised their royal prerogative. The next month a Mutiny Act was passed, to make the existence of an army in peacetime depend on the agreement of the House of Commons. The Commons also tightened the control over the royal expenditure with a Civil List Act. These measures restricted the royal authority considerably and because William needed the support of England for Holland he was prepared to accept these changes. They went a long way toward the modern form of constitutional monarchy.

William still needed to secure his authority across the realm. James II was causing problems in Ireland where he remained king and his army was besieging Derry. William sent troops into Ireland in August 1689 and followed himself in June 1690. He defeated James II at the battle of the Boyne on 1 July, which forced James to flee back to France. The Irish Catholics fought back but were defeated again, the following July, at Aughrim. Uprisings amongst the Scottish Highlanders were less easily dealt with, and the clansmen were given an ultimatum to swear their allegiance to the king by 1 January 1692 or face the consequences. When Alexander MacIan MacDonald failed to make the deadline, nearly forty members of his clan, including women, children and MacDonald himself, were massacred by the Campbells at Glencoe on 13 February. This was a deep stain on William's character and few Scots forgave him, even after he sought to acquit himself with a public enquiry three years later. This brought the perpetrators to justice but no sentence was enforced.

The action was not typical of William, but not surprising either. He was a deeply serious man, boringly so, who tolerated no nonsense, had no sense of humour, and had little interest in Scotland. He was short (Mary was five inches taller, and generally larger all round), bad-tempered – a tendency exacerbated by his asthma – and obsessive about his desire to keep the French out of Holland. Everything drove him towards that goal, and apart from consulting Parliament in order to raise finances for his foreign activities, William avoided government altogether, leaving this to his wife, Mary. Since Mary had no interest in government either, but merely followed her husband's wishes, Parliament had its own way much of the time.

There were two attempts by Jacobites to overthrow William. The Lancashire Plot in July 1694 failed virtually before it began, while Sir John Fenwick's conspiracy to assassinate William and restore James was uncovered in February 1696.

William's war with France dragged on until 1697. There were victories on both sides, none overwhelmingly decisive, but often involving severe losses. Although William was victorious in the naval battle of La Hogue on 19 May 1692, which curtailed James II's efforts to invade England, the English and Dutch suffered major losses at Neerwinden on 29 July 1693. The Treaty of Ryswick in September 1697 brought a temporary and uncertain end to the hostilities. One of the outcomes of this war was the establishment of the Bank of England in 1694 to help organize the finances required to support the war.

Mary had died of smallpox in December 1694. The couple had not been well matched. William was often accused of having homosexual tendencies, though it was also known that Elizabeth Villiers was his mistress. Mary was frigid and in her youth had had a lesbian relationship. They were also ill-matched physically, Mary being much larger than William, who was probably embarrassed by the whole procedure. Though they strove for an heir, they had a succession of stillbirths. The public had tolerated William because of their respect for Mary and, after her death, his popularity diminished further. This only drove him more into his foreign negotiations, in which he delighted. From 1698 till his death he became embroiled in the problems over the Spanish succession.

A succession crisis in England emerged in 1700 with the death of his nephew William, Anne's only surviving son. As a consequence an Act of Settlement was passed, which secured the Protestant succession to the throne, specifically the Hanoverian succession (*see* George I).

William died as the result of a riding accident. In February 1702 his horse stumbled on a mole hill and threw William, breaking his collarbone. A fever set in, followed by pleuresy and pneumonia from which he died. William may not have been a much-loved king, but he was more stable than James and, because of his general lack of interest in England, he allowed the strength of parliament to grow (even though he tried to by-pass it when he needed to). It was in his reign that parliamentary government began to emerge.

MARY II Queen of England and Scotland.
*Ruling jointly with WILLIAM III [II of Scotland], 13
February 1689–28 December 1694. Crowned: Westminster
Abbey, 11 April 1689.*
Born: St James's Palace, London, 30 April 1662. **Died:**
Kensington Palace, London, 28 December 1694, aged 32.
Buried: Westminster Abbey.
Married: 4 November 1677, at St James's Palace, William III,
prince of Orange: 3 children, all stillborn.

Mary was the eldest surviving child of James II and an heiress in
her own right, though the Exclusion Bills which Parliament
sought to introduce during 1679–81, which would have denied
her father's accession to the throne, could in turn have denied her.
Moreover when James did succeed, his fervent pro-Catholic acts
might have closed the succession completely to Protestants, which
would have denied Mary's accession again. It was James's Catholicism and his too close an alliance with France that caused
Mary's husband, William of Orange, to challenge and ultimately
overthrow James. William and Mary became joint sovereigns of
England (*see under* William III *for details*).

Mary remained forever in the shadow of her husband and
contributed little to government beyond her good humour. She
was the more loved sovereign of the two, and her gay demeanour
was much needed at court and in Parliament to lighten William's
surliness. Nevertheless Mary had not been raised for government,
and did not like it, preferring to defer to William except when he
was out of the country. Mary had not welcomed the match with
William. She had apparently wept when it was announced. The
two had three stillborn children in the first two years of their
marriage and nothing thereafter. From 1677 to 1689, she lived in
Holland where she was much loved by the Dutch.

Mary fell out with her sister (and eventual successor) Anne over
John Churchill, the Earl of Marlborough. It was Churchill's
defection to William in the rebellion of 1688 that had made

William's accession so easy, and Churchill had served him valiantly since, but did not feel he had been suitably rewarded. Rumours emerged that Churchill was starting to plot against William. Churchill's wife, Sarah, was a longtime friend of Anne's, having been her maid of honour and lady of the bedchamber. When Churchill was arrested and imprisoned in 1692, Mary expected Anne to dismiss Sarah, but Anne chose not to, and Mary regarded this as an affront. The two were never reconciled.

Mary was only thirty-two when she contracted smallpox and died in December 1694. The country mourned her passing far more than her husband's eight years later. Mary strove to improve the nation's morals, and instructed magistrates to be more active in enforcing the vice laws. She supported the Society for the Promotion of Christian Knowledge, which eventually took shape in 1698, and she had plans to build a hospital at Greenwich, which William carried through after her death.

ANNE
Ruled 8 March 1702–1 August 1714.
Crowned: Westminster Abbey, 23 April 1702.
Titles: *queen of England, Scotland, France and Ireland (became Great Britain, Ireland and France from 1 May 1707).*
Born: *St James's Palace, London, 6 February 1665;* **Died:** *Kensington Palace, London, 1 August 1714, aged 49.* **Buried:** *Westminster Abbey.*
Married: *28 July 1683, at St James's Palace, George (1653–1708), son of Frederik III, king of Denmark: 19 children, of which 14 were stillbirths or miscarriages.*

Anne was the second daughter of James, and through her mother, Anne, the grand-daughter of Edward Hyde, earl of Clarendon. She was comparatively poorly educated and preferred sport and riding to reading and art. In 1683, when she was eighteen, hot on the heels of a court scandal, when she was reputedly seduced by one of the courtiers, Lord Mulgrave, Anne was married to Prince George, brother of the Danish king Christian V. Whilst George had received a good education he seems to have absorbed remarkably little of it, as he was lacking in the most basic general knowledge and seemed to revel in being a nonentity. He was harmless, well-meaning and a good husband, and the pair made a pleasant couple, but no one wanted George as a possible future king. When Anne came to the throne in 1702, George was kept securely in the background. He certainly tried to do his duty in fathering an heir, but of nineteen children (including twins), fourteen were stillborn, and only one survived beyond infancy and he, William, died in July 1700, aged eleven, of hydrocephalus. Since each child arrived within scarcely a year of the previous one, Anne's body must have been exhausted – she was pregnant for at least thirteen of her twenty-five years of marriage. Anne was overweight, a condition that probably contributed to the lack of a healthy child, and she frequently needed to be carried in a chair (which may be why the sedan chair became so popular during her reign). She also suffered from gout and rheumatism, and must have been in constant pain. How she maintained her generally bright and kindhearted demeanour is a tribute to her stoicism and conscientiousness. She may not have wanted to be queen, she may have been ill equipped for it, but she nevertheless sought to do her duty. She relied heavily on Sidney Godolphin, the Lord High Treasurer and nearest equivalent of the day of the Prime Minister.

Early in her reign Anne demonstrated her interests in the Church and the needy by establishing a fund, known as Queen Anne's Bounty, which increased the stipends of poorer clergy. She also insisted upon the construction of more churches in London.

Anne's reign was dominated abroad by the War of the Spanish Succession. This had arisen because Louis XIV of France accepted the Spanish throne on behalf of his grandson Philip, instead of recognizing Charles of Austria as the successor, as had been agreed by the Partition Treaty of 1700. Britain, Austria, Portugal, Denmark and the Netherlands sided against France, Spain and Bavaria. War was declared in May 1702 and peace was not concluded until the Treaty of Utrecht in April 1713. England's hero in the war was John Churchill, whom Anne elevated to duke of Marlborough and gave a considerable income. His great victory was on 13 August 1704 at Blenheim, in Germany, where he stopped the French advance. When he came to establish his great estate at Woodstock, near Oxford, Churchill named it Blenheim Palace after his victory. Also of lasting consequence in the war was the capture by Admiral Sir George Rooke in July 1704 of Gibraltar, which has remained a British possession ever since.

Anne took an interest in the war but, like her subjects, grew tired of its inexorability. It forced her to take a stronger hand in her dealings with her government and even made her dismiss her chief ministers on more than one occasion. In this respect, while Parliament remained paramount and Anne had virtually become a constitutional monarch, she wielded sufficient authority to keep the government on its toes. She also believed that her actions reflected the mood of the nation as a whole. She wielded a similar authority against others in her life, eventually dismissing Sarah Churchill from her official duties in 1711, partly because the lady had become high and mighty, but mostly because she had been promoting Whig propaganda against Anne's own Tory preferences. Anne became lonely after the death of her husband in 1708, and her constant pain made her more moody and vindictive. Her closest friend was Lady Abigail Masham, the cousin of Sarah Churchill, who remained with her in her final years. During this period Anne endeavoured to negotiate with her half-brother James (the Old Pretender), imploring him to set aside his Catholic faith for the sake of the succession. The Act of Settlement of 1701 had conferred the succession on Anne's second cousin, Sophia, widow of the Elector of Hanover. She died six weeks before Anne, and the succession passed to her son, George I. By the time of her death in 1714 Anne had become so big she could not move and needed to go everywhere in a wheelchair. Her coffin was almost square.

The most significant change during Anne's reign was the Act of Union, effective from 1 May 1707, which united England and Scotland as one kingdom – Great Britain. This was personally encouraged by Anne who believed that the full economic and political union was the best development for both countries.

Anne's reign is often associated with the growth in tea and coffee houses, which themselves became the centres for developing businesses and commerce (the London Stock Exchange grew out of a coffee house). Trade grew considerably during this period, especially with the establishment of the South Sea Company in 1711, trading with South America, and the increased trade coming from India and the East. The new kingdom of Great Britain began to prosper as never before and the seeds of the British Empire were sprouting.

JAMES (VIII) *THE OLD PRETENDER*. Proclaimed king in France as James III of England and James VIII of Scotland on 16 September 1701.

Born: St James's Palace, London, 10 June 1688. *Died*: Rome, 1 January 1766, aged 78. *Buried*: St Peter's Basilica, Vatican. *Married*: 1 September 1719, at Montefiascone, Italy, Maria (1702–35) dau. Prince James Sobieski of Poland.

James Francis Edward Stuart, known commonly as the Old Pretender, was the only surviving legitimate son of James II and Mary of Modena. At his birth many believed that he was a chageling, introduced into the royal bed in a warming-pan. In the rebellion of 1688 he preceded his father in flight to France, where he was raised. He received the support of the French king as successor to the thrones of England and Scotland, and was declared king on the death of James. He made an abortive attempt to land in Scotland in 1708, but was defeated by the English. In the next few years he served with great courage in the French army in the War of the Spanish Succession. All this time he yearned to regain the English throne. His cousin Anne urged him to renounce his Catholicism and embrace the Church of England. He would then be the rightful heir. But James refused, sticking steadfastly to his faith. His next opportunity came in 1714, following Anne's death. By this time there were increasing Jacobite sympathies linked with concern over the Hanoverian succession (see George I). James's remoteness in France made it difficult for him to mobilize support. When rebellion broke out in Scotland on 26 August 1715, under John Erskine, earl of Mar, Louis XIV of France had just died, and James was indisposed. It took him months to cross France and gain a ship to Scotland, landing at Peterhead on December 22. The Jacobites were able to capture Perth, and James VIII held his court at Scone, but Edinburgh and Stirling resisted them. Over the next two weeks James's supporters at last got to know the man who had not set foot in Britain for twenty-seven years. Although he had the regal bearing of the Stewart monarchy, and appeared balanced and sincere, he did not rouse them to Jacobite fervour. Quite the opposite. He was a rather gloomy individual resigned to failure from years of ill luck. His support, which at most had not exceeded 12,000, rapidly dwindled. Six weeks after his arrival in Scotland, James departed, slipping quietly out of the country and returning to France. He remained a refugee in Europe for the rest of his life, finally settling in Rome where the pope awarded him an income and demanded he be known as the king of England. Only one other opportunity presented itself – in 1718 when Philip V of Spain agreed to support James. Another Spanish Armada set sail but, like the other two, it suffered in the bad weather and only a small force made it through to the Hebrides, without the Pretender. He retired to Rome where he took a bride, though it was far from a happy marriage. When the Jacobites rose again in 1745, James was too old and tired to bother and it was his son, Bonnie Prince Charlie who answered the call.

CHARLES (III) 'BONNIE PRINCE CHARLIE' or 'THE YOUNG PRETENDER'. Proclaimed prince regent, 12 August 1745; defeated 16 April 1746. Styled himself Charles III, 1 January 1766–31 January 1788.
Born: *Rome, 31 December 1720.* **Died:** *Rome 31 January 1788, aged 68.* **Buried:** *St Peter's, Rome.*
Married: *17 April 1772, at Marefischi, Ancona, Italy, Louise (1752–1824) dau. Gustavus Adolphus, Prince of Stolberg-Gedern (separated 1780): no children.*

Charles was the eldest son of James (see James VIII) and regarded himself as the rightful claimant to the throne of Scotland (and to a lesser degree England). Unlike his father he was not a staunch Catholic, but supported the Jacobite cause. Also, unlike his lugubrious father, he had a good sense of humour and was a dashing, sporting individual. He was involved in the siege of Gaeta in 1734 and served well at Dettingen in 1743 in battle against George II. He made himself available to Louis XV of France who sought to use the Jacobite resistance in an invasion of England during the War of the Austrian Succession. Louis's expedition was prevented by bad weather and, in the end, Charles went it alone, losing one ship en route, and arriving in Eriskay in the Hebrides on 23 July 1745 with just seven companions. His resolve, passion and optimism soon fostered support amongst the Highlanders and he was declared prince regent on 12 August. A week later he raised his father's standard at Glenfinnan. His army grew. He entered Edinburgh without opposition and established himself at Holyrood. An army sent against him under the command of Sir John Cope was rapidly despatched. After a brief pause Charles marched south, reaching as far as Derby on 4 December, without opposition. At this point it seemed that England was his for the taking. George II was preparing to flee to France. However, although there was no resistance, Charles did not find any support amongst the English and it was considered prudent to return to Edinburgh. Thereafter the army became dispirited. The duke of Cumberland followed in pursuit, regaining ground and establishing a base at Inverness in February. By now Charles's lack of ability as a leader was showing, as his army became weakened and ill. The showdown between the two forces happened at Culloden on 16 April 1746. The Jacobites were soundly defeated by Cumberland. This was the last battle fought on British soil. Charles escaped. Aided by Flora MacDonald, and disguised as a spinning-maid, Charles remained a fugitive throughout the Highlands for five months, during which period Cumberland took revenge on any Jacobite nests remaining in Scotland. Realizing his cause was lost Charles left Scotland in 18 September 1746 never to return. While in Scotland he had met the twenty-five-year-old Clementina Walkinshaw, who became his mistress and followed him to Europe. They had a daughter, Charlotte, born in 1753, who became duchess of Albany. Charles lost his verve and spirit and sank into drunkenness. He lost Clementine because of his cruelty, and had a short, unhappy and unfruitful marriage with Princess Louise of Stolberg-Gedern. His daughter, who was later legitimized, was his only companion in his final, sad years. He long regretted he had not died at Culloden with his supporters.

The Rise of Empire

THE HOUSE OF HANOVER
(1714–1901)

The rule of the House of Hanover would last almost 200 years, and would see the population of Britain rise from 7 million to 38 million. It would witness the end of its first empire – the loss of the American colonies and the collapse of the Slave Trade – and a mighty expansion of its second. In 1765 Robert Clive captured Bengal for the East India Trading Company and from then on the British spread across India. In the 1770s Australia was discovered and the first settlers (800 of whom were convicts) made their homes there. The Napoleonic Wars brought more colonial possessions: Trinidad, Tobago, St Lucia, Sri Lanka, Mauritius, Cape Colony and Malta. In the 1840s Britain further expanded in India, and began to settle in New Zealand. By 1850 Britain was the world's leading trading nation. Victoria would become Empress of India, and under her rule, Britain would gain control of Egypt, Sudan, The Gambia, Gold Coast (Ghana), Kenya, Uganda, Zambia, Zimbabwe, the Transvaal and Orange Free State.

There would be enormous social changes: the influence of the monarchy in government would decline as the power of Parliament, the Prime Minister and Cabinet increased. There would be a revolution in agriculture in the mid eighteenth century, and with greater yields from rotation of crops, new machines, scientific breeding, land reclamation, greater investment and enclosure of common lands, the population would double within fifty years. Only in Scotland would the population decline. From the mid eighteenth century onwards a steady stream of the poor and unemployed migrated to the colonies and to America: victims of the terrible Highland clearances where homesteads were destroyed to make way for sheep.

The Industrial Revolution, which began around 1760, would bring in its wake both good and evil. The rural poor of England and Wales moved *en masse* to the towns burgeoning near coal mines, for the newly invented steam engine required coal. New advances in spinning and weaving, and the making of iron encouraged a proliferation of smelting works and cotton mills, which had to be kept going day and night, while the poor packed into slums around these. In the first decades of the nineteenth century the first enlightened Acts of Parliament were passed to limit child labour to children over the age of nine and to no more than twelve hours a day. It would not be until 1847, under Queen Victoria, that the laws were changed to curtail daily working hours to ten and the age to thirteen and over. In the mid-nineteenth century, workhouses became compulsory for the poor without work. In the 1870s, primary education would become available for all children, and the first law permitting Trades Unions would be passed. Meanwhile canals, steamships and railways would open up the possibilities of travel and change the face of Britain.

GEORGE (I)
Ruled: 1 August 1714–11 June 1727. Crowned: Westminster Abbey, 20 October 1714.
Full name and titles: George Louis, king of Great Britain and Ireland, duke and elector of Hanover (from 1698).

Born: Osnabrück, Hanover, 28 May (7 June) 1660. **Died**:
Osnabrück, Hanover, 11 June 1727, aged 67. **Buried**:
Leinschloss Church, Hanover.
Married: 21 November 1682, at Celle Castle, Germany, Sophia
Dorothea (1666–1726), dau. George William, duke of
Brunswick-Lüneberg-Celle; marriage anulled 28 December 1694:
2 children. George also had at least three illegitimate children by
Ehrengard Melusine von Schulenburg (1667–1743), who may
subsequently have married George.

The Act of Settlement passed in 1701 formalized the succession to
exclude all Catholics, which was why James (the Old Pretender),
a legitimate son of James II was not allowed to rule. At the time
the act was concluded, the nearest living Protestant heir was
Sophia, the seventy-year-old daughter of Frederick, king of
Bohemia and Elector Palatine of the Rhine. Her mother, Elizabeth, was the eldest daughter of James I. Sophia died six weeks
before Queen Anne in the summer of 1714 and the succession
passed to her eldest son, George, who had succeeded his father,
Ernst August, as duke and elector of Hanover on 23 January
1698. When George came to the British throne he was fifty-four,
older than any previous English heir. Prior to 1701 there had been
little thought that he would become king of England, and even
during the last years of Queen Anne's reign efforts had been made
for James Stuart to convert to Protestantism, but the likelihood of
George's succession became increasingly inevitable in the last few
years. Whilst he had never learned English, he rapidly struggled to
master key sentences, but preferred to communicate in French,
the diplomatic language of the day. He also relied on his son,
George Augustus, to help translate.

Before his elevation to king of England, George had already led
an eventful life. He was the eldest child with five brothers and a
sister. He outlived them all except his youngest brother Ernst. He
had been a handsome youth, and still retained something of a
cherubic if fat face, though his seeming inability to smile made him

appear surly. He was not tall, but was fit and athletic, though he later became rather stout. He was well educated but delighted most in riding, hunting and military exercise. He first saw military service in 1675, and was involved in the Dutch and Turkish wars, distinguishing himself at Neerwinden in 1693. He developed a good relationship with John Churchill, the future duke of Marlborough, during the War of the Spanish Succession and commanded the Imperial Army on the Upper Rhine from 1707 to 1709.

He was elevated to the College of Electors of the Empire in 1708 and became arch-treasurer of the Empire in 1710. He was resourceful and much respected, but was also highly ambitious, vindictive and used to having his own way. He had already demonstrated this by his treatment of his wife, which had become something of a scandal in Europe.

He had married the beautiful sixteen-year-old Sophia Dorothea of Celle in 1682. The marriage was at first happy and they had two children: George Augustus and Sophia Dorothea. Sophia soon tired of her boorish husband, however, who seemed to have little respect for women, and she began an affair with Philip von Königsmark, a Swedish colonel of dragoons. When George discovered this in July 1694 he was furious. Sophia was imprisoned in the Castle of Ahlden for the rest of her life, forbidden to remarry and denied access to her children. Divorce proceedings were concluded in December 1694. Königsmark disappeared and it was widely believed that George had ordered his death. His body was supposed to have been discovered years later buried under the floorboards at the elector's palace. However, Königsmark had earlier had an affair with Clara, the Countess von Platten, and it was believed that she may have lured the Colonel to his death. This becomes even more sordid when we learn that Clara had also been the mistress of George's father, Ernst, and had borne him at least four children, one of whom, Sophia Charlotte, was rumoured to be George's mistress, even though she was his half-sister. It is more likely that the two simply enjoyed each other's company. Sophia Charlotte was not an attractive lady; in fact she grew to be excessively corpulent, so that when she and the king were seen together they were nick-named the Elephant and Castle. She became a naturalized British subject and was raised to the peerage as baroness of Brentford and countess of Darlington in 1722. George's one public mistress was Ehrengard Melusine von Schulenburg, an extremely thin lady whom the Germans called 'the scarecrow' and the British dubbed 'the Maypole'. There is a strong belief that George may have subsequently married Melusine in secret, especially as in later years she was created Princess von Eberstein by the Emperor Charles VI who would not have done so had she not had some royal status. Robert Walpole also regarded her 'as much queen of England as anyone ever was'. She was generally known by the title duchess of Kendal which she was given in March 1719. George had already had two children by her before he divorced his wife, which only emphasizes his hypocritical attitude when he discovered her affair. England's Queen Anne had taken a dislike to George when he visited her as far back as 1680 pursuing a possible marriage alliance, and from his subsequent sexual ad-ventures one can only imagine what the outcome might have been for Anne and England had they married.

The English and Scots did not warm to George either when he paraded through London in September 1714. He had already taken nearly eight weeks to come to Britain, revelling in his new found glory in a series of parties across Europe. He was jeered by Londoners, who never quite took him seriously. By this time the power of the king was waning against the growing power of Parliament and, while the authority of the king retained a certain mystical aura, this was not what it had been before the Civil War and the English were already starting to regard the monarch as a figurehead. While they had taken Mary and Anne to their hearts, they did not like these foreigners who kept turning up to claim the throne – first William of Orange and then George of Hanover. This seriously damaged the acceptability of the monarchy in the eyes of the public. The Scots liked this 'wee German laddie' even less. The Jacobite supporters of James II and his son James Edward Stuart grew in strength and in September 1715 the first Jacobite rebellion erupted at Braemar. It could have been far more serious than it was if the Old Pretender had not turned out to be such a discouraging pessimist. The rebellion fizzled out, but George still exacted a vicious penalty upon those who had taken part.

Despite what his amorous adventures might suggest (in fact they probably support it), George was shy and tended to keep out of the limelight when he could. He was not one for intellectual pursuits, though he did have a love for music and it was through George that the composer George Frederic Handel came to England. His *Water Music* was composed for a royal water-party on 22 August 1715, and George's love of Handel's work led to the foundation of the first Royal Academy of Music in 1720. George's shyness and inability to communicate well in English made him all the more blunt and short-tempered. He had been used to getting his own way in Hanover and could not adapt to the English parliamentary system where he needed to seek approval for his actions, especially when this affected his foreign policy and his wish to protect Hanover's interests. Because of the language problems, especially after the rift with his son in 1717 which meant the younger George no longer attended cabinet meetings to help translate, George needed another minister to represent him. This was the start of the post of Prime Minister, but it also reduced George's direct sphere of control.

George had previously allied himself with Peter the Great of Russia and was keen to ensure that he benefitted from Peter's war with Sweden. To do so he needed to have control over his foreign policy and he could not do this with the Whig government that had come to power under Robert Walpole in 1715 after the failure of the Jacobite rebellion. In 1716 the Septennial Act had been passed, which postponed the opportunity of the Tories to return to power for four years. George distrusted the strong-minded and exceedingly able Walpole who would not sanction the funds George needed for his new campaign against Russia. George, however, rapidly appreciated that he could influence who led the Whigs. George set one faction against another within the party and succeeded in aiding the weak and malleable earl of

Sunderland and Lord Stanhope to oust Walpole in 1717. George was now able to dictate his terms to Stanhope and gain an alliance with Holland and France against Russia. However in opposing Walpole he made a dangerous enemy.

Walpole allied himself with George's son, George Augustus (later George II), who served as regent on his father's many forays back to Hanover. George despised his father because of his treatment of his mother, and would have been only too happy to depose him. He established a clique, known as the Leicester House Set, with the sole intention of frustrating the king's plans, and Walpole became part of the group. Walpole also became friends with Prince George's wife, Caroline, princess of Wales, an intelligent and influential lady who gave Walpole her stolid support. King George soon realized that he could not prevail against such opposition and was forced to be reconciled with Walpole. This was precipitated by the economic distaster known as the South Sea Bubble. The South Sea Company had been established in 1711, trading with the Spanish colonies in South America in anticipation of benefits that would arise from success in the War of the Spanish Succession. King George was made governor of the company in 1718 and it became fashionable to invest, especially once the Company took over the management of the National Debt in 1720. Senior officials in the company began to issue false stock to meet the demand and in September 1720 this bubble burst. Thousands of speculators found that their investment was worthless, including most of the country's leading nobility. When it was found that cabinet ministers and court officials had been involved in the dirty dealings it became a national scandal, threatening the Hanoverian dynasty. George was forced to rely on Walpole's skill in resolving the affair and restoring order. From then on Walpole was in supreme power and dominated English affairs. George's relationship with his politicians and the general state of English religious and cultural society at this time was lampooned by Jonathan Swift in *Gulliver's Travels* (1726).

Because of the supremacy of Parliament, George removed himself further from public affairs. It made the king less of a target, although the Jacobites still wished to restore the Stuart Pretender.

In 1722 a plot was uncovered to do just that, known as the Atterbury Plot after one of its leading conspirators Francis Atterbury, bishop of Rochester. Where once he would have been executed, Atterbury was imprisoned and then banished, and all his possessions confiscated. Generally, though, plots against the king diminished because Walpole had him under control. George's excesses were by and large eradicated, although the relationship with Spain remained poor, resulting in a dispute over Gibraltar and a fruitless expedition against Spain's American colonies.

George liked to spend the summer and autumn in Hanover, and it was while travelling there in June 1727 that he died of a cerebral haemorrhage. His son and the British government were happy to leave him there and he was buried in the Leinschloss Church at Hanover. Although his brusqueness and pomposity caused him to be generally disliked, George had a considerable influence on the British parliamentary system and brought in (by default not design) the constitutional government that has dominated British politics ever since. He was succeeded by his only son.

GEORGE II
Ruled 28 May (11 June NS) 1727–25 October 1760.
Crowned: Westminster Abbey, 11 October 1727.
Full name and titles: George Augustus, king of Great Britain and Ireland, duke and elector of Hanover, duke and marquess of Cambridge (from 1706), earl of Milford Haven (from 1706), duke of Cornwall and Rothesay (from 1714), prince of Wales and earl of Chester (from 1714).
Born: Schloss Herrenhausen, Hanover, 30 October (9 November NS) 1683. **Died**: Kensington Palace, London, 25 October 1760, aged 76. **Buried**: Westminster Abbey.
Married: 22 August (2 September NS) 1705, at Schloss Herrenhausen, Hanover, Wilhelmina Charlotte Caroline (1683–1737) dau. of John Frederick, margrave of Brandenburg-Ansbach: 9 children (1 stillborn). George probably had one illegitimate child.

George had been born in Hanover before the Act of Settlement had nominated the Hanoverian line of succession, but after this was passed in 1701, when George was seventeen, the youth was tutored in both the English language and the English way of life. He became a naturalized British citizen in 1705 and received a flock of British titles. There was a considerable rift between George and his father after the imprisonment of his mother in 1694, and the elder George refused to grant his son any local responsibilities. Even though he proved his valour at the battle of Oudenarde in 1708 in the War of the Spanish Succession, his father failed to recognize his abilities. This drove George more towards his future British subjects, and in later years he would state that he regarded himself as more British than German, even if he said it in a strong German accent.

George had a passion for the strict rules of etiquette and probity which at times became obsessive and made him irritating at official functions, but at least it meant he strove to get things right, which made him a more acceptable monarch to the British than his father – at least at the outset.

In 1705, when twenty-one, George married Caroline of Ansbach, who was just seven months his elder. It was a good match. Caroline more than matched George in intelligence and canniness, and also softened his German preciseness. She had an earthy charm and was attractive in a beguiling way rather than in her looks. Both partners recognized the need to flirt: George simply because of his sexual desires; Caroline as a way of influencing men of power. It was Caroline who became the power behind the throne, first during the reign of her father-in-law when, in the absence of a Queen, she took on the role of first lady as princess of Wales; and certainly when George inherited the crown.

When George's father became king, George and Caroline accompanied him to England and took up residence in London. George aided his father in understanding English, often translating at meetings of the cabinet or the Privy Council, and serving as regent during his father's regular summer returns to Hanover. However at the close of 1717 an argument erupted between

George and his father over a misunderstanding that happened during the christening of the prince's latest son. The young George did not like the choice of the duke of Newcastle as godfather, and the duke misunderstood George's comments at the font as a threat. When the prince refused to apologize, the king first threatened to have the son imprisoned and then banished him from St James's Palace. George and Caroline set up home at Leicester House near St Martin-in-the-Fields and here established what became almost a rival court, often giving audience to the king's political enemies, most especially Robert Walpole. It was at Leicester House that Caroline used her wiles and influence to win over the men of authority whom she preferred. The consequences of this rift were significant. It meant that the king no longer felt comfortable at the cabinet meetings without his son and therefore handed over the management of them to his preferred minister, which was how the formal role of the Prime Minister emerged. It also meant that George and Caroline were able to have a trial run at their own cabinet meetings which were a solid grounding for the real thing.

What does seem surprising is that George, given the poor relationship with his father, should have been so hostile towards his own son, Frederick Louis. By all accounts he regarded Frederick as an imbecile, almost from birth, although Frederick was no such thing. George and Caroline left Frederick in Hanover when they came to England, and he was not allowed into England until 1728, when they did their best to ignore him. It rather irritated them both when they discovered that the young man, whom they reluctantly created prince of Wales in 1729, became something of a favourite among London society. With little parental control Frederick became a dandy and a man-about-town, often going on the razzle and ending up drunk. He frequently gambled and built up huge debts that his father refused to acknowledge, let alone pay. Frederick had all the qualities of being a cultured man if his father had paid him any attention: he had a love of sport, art and the theatre. But his father liked none of those things and regarded his son as a wastrel. When Frederick died of an aneurysm in March 1751, aged 44, his father rather callously remarked that he was glad. It is quite likely that George had hoped Frederick might have died younger and that his heir would have been his younger and favourite son, William Augustus, duke of Cumberland, who shared his father's Germanic ruthlessness. However Frederick lived long enough to marry and father nine legitimate children, amongst them the future GEORGE III. Frederick also lived long enough to become a major thorn in George's side, always opposing his father's plans and siding with the opposition in government. Had he become king, he would have settled down and been moderate and compassionate, but his father brought out the worst in him. It was a real-life example of 'like father, like son'.

When George became king in 1727, England was under the strong political control of Robert Walpole. George had little need to interfere, but that did not stop him wanting to give the impression of being in charge. He sought to change his ministers much like his father, but his preferred minister, Sir Spencer Compton, admitted he was not up to forming an administration. George was thus forced to continue with Sir Robert Walpole, who accommodated George by voting him a larger share of the Civil List.

Like his father, George had a passion for war and it was all that Walpole could do to stop George involving himself in a number of hostilities throughout Europe, particularly the War of the Polish Succession. Matters began to change after the death of Caroline in 1737. George genuinely loved his wife and sorely missed her. He never remarried, but he now lived more openly with his mistress, Amalia von Walmoden. With Caroline's influence and support gone, Walpole's star began to wane. George's desire for war was granted when hostilities broke out with Spain in September 1739 and then with France in 1742 in the War of the Austrian Succession. Even though nearing sixty, George took the opportunity to lead an army into the field at Dettingen on 16 June 1743. This was the last occasion that a British sovereign would command an army in battle. He served valiantly, fighting beside his men, and it gave his popularity a boost.

Interestingly also serving in the battle of Dettingen, on the side of the French, was Charles Edward Stuart, the Young Pretender. Charles's desire to win back the Scottish and English thrones caused him to invade Scotland in 1745 and on a wave of popularity brought an army as far south as Derby. It was as a consequence of the Jacobite rebellion that the first recorded singing of the National Anthem occurred at Drury Lane on 28 September 1745, in a patriotic reaction to the rebels. George sent his second son, William, against Charles. William, duke of Cumberland, defeated the Scots at Culloden in April 1746 and followed this with a vicious culling of the Jacobites, which earned him the name of 'Butcher Cumberland'. This did not endear the duke or the king to the Scots. William was not, in fact, an especially good commander. At the battle of Fontenoy in France, the previous May, Cumberland had suffered a humiliating defeat and heavy losses. He was defeated again by the French at Laffeldt in 1747 and in 1757, when Britain became unnecessarily involved in the Seven Years' War, Cumberland was forced to surrender the Hanoverian army at Klosterseven. George was so humiliated by this that he stripped his son of his military commands.

Walpole had stepped down as prime minister in 1742 and George's attempts to appoint a capable one proved uneven over the next few years. Control passed mostly to Henry Pelham, who sanctioned the funds for George's wars but who was not an especially gifted administrator. In the end George was forced to consider William Pitt (the elder), who had been a supporter of his son Frederick and had formed a clique known as the 'Patriot Boys', a kind of 'brat pack' of the 1740s.

The war against the French had other consequences. In India, the daring adventures of Robert Clive at Madras (in 1746) and at Arcot (in 1751) stirred the blood, and his subsequent achievements at Calcutta, Chandernagore and Plassey in 1756/7, saw the defeat of the French and the emergence of the British control of India. Soon afterwards, in Canada, General James Wolfe (who had served at Dettingen and Culloden) succeeded in capturing Quebec in September 1759 and fulfilling Pitt's plan to expel the

French from Canada. There were further territorial gains in the West Indies and Africa. Thus as George's reign drew to a close, the British Empire was expanding on both sides of the globe. Had George lived another eight years he would have seen Australia added to the map. The 1750s thus saw an increase in national pride and a restoration, to some degree, of George II in the national affection although, as with his father, the British found it difficult to take any Hanoverian to their hearts.

George's reign must ultimately be seen as a success, though a clouded one at that, but certainly better than the results of either the Old Stewart Pretender or Bonnie Prince Charlie gaining the throne. George's successes outweighed his failures, thanks mostly to his choice of prime ministers, and Britain became prosperous and an increasing world power. George himself died in a rather undignified fashion – he had a heart attack while sitting on the lavatory. He was succeeded by his grandson.

GEORGE III, 'FARMER GEORGE'
Ruled 25 October 1760–29 January 1820 (declared unfit to rule 5 February 1811). Crowned: Westminster Abbey, 22 September 1761.
Full name and titles: George William Frederick, king of Great Britain and Ireland (and nominally of France, a title relinquished in 1801), duke and elector of Hanover (king from 1814), duke of Cornwall and Rothesay, duke of Edinburgh, marquess of Ely, earl of Eltham, viscount of Launceston, baron of Snowdon, prince of Wales and earl of Chester (from 1751).
Born: Norfolk House, London, 24 May (4 June NS) 1738.
Died: Windsor Castle, 29 January 1820, aged 81. **Buried**: Windsor Castle.
Married: 8 September 1761, at St James's Palace, Sophia Charlotte (1744–1818), dau. Charles, duke of Mecklenburg-Strelitz: 15 children. It is alleged that George had previously married Hannah Lightfoot in secret on 17 April 1759, but this remains to be proven.

It seems that something of both George II and his son Frederick Louis whom he despised so much was passed on to the new king. He had a strain of obstinacy, like his grandfather, but in other matters he was flexible and conciliatory. He was the first of the Hanoverian kings to be born and raised in England and to speak English without a strong German accent, which helped the British warm to him. He had a binding sympathy with the English and never visited Hanover, even though he remained their ruler (and their king from 1814). He was good-hearted with a deep religious conviction, lacking, at least in his youth, the vicious streak that had been prominent in the first two Hanoverian kings. What George also lacked, however, was sound judgement, a fault inherited from his father. He was too trusting and was dominated by his mother. This contributed to some of the bad decisions that darkened his reign.

George was well educated and did not have the wayward streak of his father. The only skeleton in his youthful cupboard was his relationship with Hannah Lightfoot, the daughter of a shoemaker from Wapping. George allegedly married Hannah in secret in 1757 (or 1759, records vary) and she was supposed to have borne him three children. Although documentation exists which purportedly proves the marriage its authenticity is suspect. The likelihood of three children is also remote. Although Hannah may have been a momentary infatuation, George soon fell in love with Lady Sarah Lennox, a daughter of the duke of Richmond and great-granddaughter of Charles II by his mistress, the duchess of Portsmouth. George was advised that he should not marry a British subject but should look to the eligible German princesses. The final choice was the charming seventeen-year-old Charlotte of Mecklenburg. The coronation was delayed until after their wedding on 8 September 1761, so that a joint coronation could be held two weeks later.

George was twenty-two when he was proclaimed king. He was keen to do what was right and one of his first actions was to put out a proclamation against immorality. He also wanted to get

From a contemporary portrait

control back over the Government which had gradually leeched power from the monarch over the last sixty years. George did not like Pitt or the Whig philosophy. His preferred premier was John Stuart, earl of Bute, who had been a close friend of his mother's and had assisted in his education. Bute was a Whig, but being of Scottish descent, had Jacobite sympathies and was a staunch royalist. He was not a good administrator so that while George got his way, the country turned against Bute and he resigned in 1763. Bute remained in the king's confidence for two more years, but in the meantime the king suffered a long series of tedious prime ministers until he eventually found his man in Frederick, Lord North, who became premier in 1770.

The first ten years of George's reign were thus difficult ones for him in getting to grips with the reins of government. Issues which in hindsight seem positive, such as securing peace with France and Spain in 1763, at the time were seen in a darker light. Bute was accused of receiving bribes from France, and the king was accused of selling out to the enemy. The Stamp Act introduced in 1765 met with considerable opposition and had to be repealed the following year. Throughout this period the king was subjected to constant abuse and libel from the renegade politician John Wilkes who published material which in previous generations would have led to his execution for treason. The strain on the king told and in early 1765 he suffered a physical collapse which may have been a precursor of his later mental affliction. Though not as severe as the bout of 1788 or the final decline of 1810, it was sufficient for Parliament to rush through a Regency Act. It was further fodder to George's opponents to denigrate him, and so much stigma has attached to him as king that it becomes difficult to see the real man and his achievements.

Lord North has likewise been criticized and is regarded by some as the worst of all prime ministers. To his premiership belongs the American War of Independence. The American revolution had its roots before North's administration. The colonies had been free of taxation, but also had no parliamentary representation. When a tax was re-imposed on molasses in 1764 and the stamp duty on legal documents and newspapers in 1765 there was an outcry. Although both of these measures were subsequently repealed, a new tax on tea, introduced in 1773, sparked off more antagonism and led to the Boston Tea Party in December 1773, when tea held in Boston Harbour was thrown overboard. The British closed the port at Boston and sent in troops, with the inevitable consequence that hostilities broke out on 19 April 1775 with battles at Lexington and Concord. The US Congress issued its Declaration of Independence on 4 July 1776 and thereafter George III became the figurehead for American hostility. George was intent upon bringing America to its knees and approved any measure that would cause the Americans the utmost distress, though the allegation that he would make them all slaves is an exaggeration. The worst defeat for Britain came at Saratoga on 17 October 1777, when General John Burgoyne was forced to surrender his entire army. This action turned the balance of the war, as France now recognized the independence of the colonies and sent support. The last major battle was at Yorktown where George Washington, with the aid of the French, defeated Lord Cornwallis, who surrendered on 19 October 1781. The Treaty of Paris was signed on 3 September 1783. Whereas peace might have been concluded earlier and the colonies saved,

George insisted on fighting to the bitter end and took the consequences. George's reputation suffered irreparably while Lord North resigned. It was some years before George again found a minister with whom he could work, William Pitt the Younger.

George clashed with Pitt over Catholic Emancipation. Such measures had been the downfall of past kings, especially James II, and even the merest hint of equality had resulted in the Gordon Riots of June 1780 when the MP, Lord George Gordon, incited disorder throughout London, leading to widespread destruction of property and about 300 deaths. The king remained remarkably calm during the riots and through his own resoluteness restored order. The memory of the riots burned bright for many years so that when Pitt tried to issue a Catholic Emancipation Act in 1801, George violently opposed it and Pitt resigned. Pitt's measure had been his way of controlling the Irish rebellion which erupted in 1798, encouraged by the success of the French Revolution. There had been unrest generally throughout Britain since 1795 and the king's popularity declined. Pitt introduced several repressive measures, including suspending *habeas corpus*, and sought to negotiate with France in 1797, which angered George. Despite efforts by later ministers George refused to entertain any consideration of emancipation for Catholics. For an exceedingly pious and generally good-natured man, this obstinacy verged on bigotry. Pitt was, however, able to force through the Act of Union between Great Britain and Ireland which came into force on 1 January 1801. On the same day George relinquished the anachronistic title of king of France, which all English kings had maintained since 1340.

A measure of the times is reflected in the two assassination attempts upon George by the public. Margaret Nicholson, a house-maid, threatened him with a dessert-knife on 2 August 1786, while James Hadfield fired a shot at the king at Drury Lane on 15 May 1800. Both would-be assassins were pronounced insane. George's reign was not short of its scandals. There was the trial of Warren Hastings for corruption and cruelty in the Indian administration, which ran from 1788 to 1795. There was the private and illegal first marriage of his son (the future George IV) to a commoner in 1785, followed by the immoral conduct of his legal daughter-in-law, Caroline of Brunswick, the wife he had forced upon his son, who deserted her in 1796. A committee of enquiry was set up in 1806 to undertake the 'delicate investigation', as it was called, into Caroline's affairs. Caroline was eventually sent on a grand tour of Europe. There was the duel between the war secretary, viscount Castelreagh, and the foreign secretary, George Canning, in September 1809, in which Canning was wounded. Finally there was the assassination of the prime minister, Spencer Perceval, in May 1812, by John Bellingham. To set against this were the great victories of Horatio Nelson in the Napoleonic Wars, especially at Copenhagen in April 1801 and Trafalgar in October 1805, and the victories of Wellington in the Peninsular War, leading to the final defeat of Napoleon at Waterloo in June 1815. These victories abroad helped raise the morale of a country where the nobility and middle classes were clearly benefitting from the nation's commercial prosperity, but where the ordinary man and woman were discovering how repressed and neglected they were. Most of the angst, however, was aimed at the Government and not directly at George who, despite his obstinacy and occasional lapse of judgement, remained popular amongst his subjects. In fact he was often viewed, especially by the middle classes, as their champion against the Government. He gave the royal assent to William Wilberforce's act to abolish the slave trade, which became law in 1807 (though it was another twenty-six years before slaves in the British colonies were granted their freedom).

George was a man of wide interests and intellect. He became fascinated in agriculture and botany, giving some of the land at Windsor over to farming, hence his nickname of 'Farmer George'. It was an appropriate epithet since the name George means 'farmer' or 'landworker', so George genuinely lived up (or down!) to his name. He wrote pamphlets on agriculture under the pseudonym of Ralph Robinson. He became more tolerant in his later years about the moral state of the nation, especially in the

HENRY [IX] The last of the royal Stewarts, brother of Bonnie Prince Charlie. He was born in Rome on 6 March 1725. He never seriously pursued his title, although things may have been different had Charles succeeded in the rebellion of 1745. The Jacobites styled him the duke of York. After Charles's defeat, Henry became a cardinal in 1747 and, in 1761, bishop of Frascati. He received pensions from the Vatican and from Spain as well as income from two French abbeys. Although he styled himself Henry IX after his brother's death on 31 January 1788, it was only an honorific. He lost his fortune during the French Revolution, but was looked on kindly by George III who granted him a pension of £4000 in 1800. He died at Frascati on 13 July 1807, aged 82, and was buried at St Peter's Basilica in the Vatican.

theatre and literature, just as the most sensational literature emerged. The gothic horror novel *The Castle of Otranto* (1764) by Horace Walpole and the salacious *The Monk* (1795) by M.G. Lewis, could never have been published in earlier times. Literature flourished during George's reign – this was the era of the Romantics: William Wordsworth, Samuel Taylor Coleridge, Percy Shelley and Lord Byron. There were many scientific advances during this period, which was the dawn of the age of invention. The best remembered were James Watt's steam engine in 1769 and the use of the steam engine by Richard Arkwright to perfect his spinning machine in 1790. These inventions laid the foundations of the Industrial Revolution but also led to such outbursts as the Luddite riots of 1811, a culmination of considerable unrest amongst textile workers to the new machines which would rob them of their livelihood, but which also ushered in a new class of industralists.

George's last thirty years or so, however, were spent in sad decline. His recurrent bouts of 'madness' became more severe. In

November 1788 he suffered a particularly violent bout where he attacked the prince of Wales and began talking incessantly. He was forcibly restrained and removed to Kew where he underwent humiliating treatment by ignorant and not altogether well-meaning doctors. Remarkably he had recovered by April 1789, but there were further bouts in 1801 and 1804 and the final decline in November 1810, precipitated by the death of his youngest daughter Amelia. By then the king was also blind. His son was made 'Prince Regent' with powers of sovereignty from 5 February 1811. The old king was confined to Windsor Castle, where he was more or less neglected, his hair and beard growing long and white. Just what lucid moments he had during these years is not known. Recent assessments have judged that George was not mad in the psychological sense but suffered from porphyria, a blood disease which upsets the body's chemical balance and can produce symptoms akin to madness. It has been called 'the royal malady' and may have affected George's predecessors as far back as Charles VI of France. Charles's daughter, Katherine, married Henry V and through her it passed on to Henry VI. There are even suggestions that it may have afflicted the Saxon kings.

The two 'facts' that most people remember about King George are that he was mad and that he ruled longer than any other monarch besides Victoria. In fact neither are true, as George's reign effectively ended when his son was made regent. What fewer people recall was that he had a genuine desire to do the best for his country during an especially violent period. The fact that he remained king, while the French monarchy was abolished, is some testament to how he was regarded and that he had learned how to manipulate the system of government.

GEORGE IV
Ruled 29 January 1820–26 June 1830, with restricted powers as Prince Regent from 5 February 1811.
Crowned: Westminster Abbey, 19 July 1821.

Full name and titles: *George Augustus Frederick, king of the United Kingdom of Great Britain and Ireland, king of Hanover, duke of Cornwall and Rothesay, earl of Carrick, Baron Renfrew and lord of the Isles (from birth), prince of Wales and earl of Chester (from 1762).*

Born: *St James's Palace, 12 August 1762.* **Died**: *Windsor Castle, 26 June 1830, aged 67.* **Buried**: *Windsor Castle.*

Married: *(1) 15 December 1785, at Park Lane, Mayfair, London, Maria Anne Fitzherbert (1756–1837) dau. Walter Smythe of Brambridge: no children; marriage not recognized under British law; (2) 8 April 1795, at St James's Palace, London, Caroline Amelia Elizabeth (1768–1821) dau. of Charles II, duke of Brunswick: 1 daughter. George also had at least two illegitimate children that he acknowledged, and probably many more.*

George IV was the eldest son of George III, but in looks and manner he was more like his grandfather, Frederick, prince of Wales. He was tall and handsome in his youth, though became fat in middle age, and above all he was a spoilt child and a libertine. He had no care at all for his duties as prince of Wales or later as king, enjoying only the privileges and the money that came with them. His lifestyle resulted in many debts, which he managed to get the king and Parliament to pay. He had many mistresses and probably had more illegitimate children than he ever acknowledged. He was generally a profligate and ill-mannered man. Yet, like most such rascals, he could turn on the charm and dignity when he needed to, and he knew how to live and celebrate in style. London society therefore adored him, and today there is an idealized romantic view of the prince. The 'Regency', strictly the period between 1811 and 1820 when he served as Prince Regent during his father's final mental decline, has become a by-word today for a whole style of interior design, dress, dazzling society gatherings and exciting court intrigue. It was also the period of the Napoleonic Wars, and the height of fame for Richard Brinsley

Sheridan, Beau Brummell and the great poets and essayists of the day – Lord Byron, Robert Southey, John Keats, Percy Shelley, Wordsworth, and early novelists such as Jane Austin and Mary Shelley. The period holds much fascination and interest, and this has influenced our image of the Prince Regent. In simple terms, had Parliament not been there to run the country, it is almost certain that George IV, seeking to operate outside the rules, would have brought the country to ruin and would quite possibly have been assassinated or deposed.

Much of George's life story is a catalogue of his romantic affairs, at least one of which endangered his succession to the throne. All of the Hanoverian monarchs were highly sexed, but George IV was probably the most profligate. It is not entirely clear why this should have been so. Unlike the relationship between George II and his son, George IV was not despised from birth. Quite the opposite. George III doted on him, and was reluctant for him to grow up. He was certainly spoiled but had an excellent education and was a quick learner. Perhaps this precocity, mixed with his good looks, made him too assured and confident of himself with a total disregard for how others viewed him. He was only sixteen when he had his first affair with the actress Mary 'Perdita' Robinson whom he saw in Shakespeare's *The Winter's Tale* in 1779. They remained together for a short while before George fell in love with another, and found he had to pay Mary a princely sum to keep her quiet. He worked his way through at least a dozen other mistresses over the next seven years, of varying degrees of high and low birth, and all costing him or the king a small fortune, until he encountered a young widow, Maria Fitzherbert, who was six years his senior. She became the one true love of his life. She refused to be his mistress, however, and George, in a typical immature tantrum, threatened to stab himself if she did not return his love. She eventually agreed to marry him. George knew that this was not possible. Not only was she already a widow (twice over) and pretty much a commoner (the grand-daughter of a baronet), but worst of all she was a Roman Catholic. The Act of Settlement of 1701 barred any Catholic from inheriting the throne, and it would effectively have barred George's accession. Moreover the Royal Marriages Act, which George's father had introduced in 1772, made any marriage by members of the royal family aged under twenty-five void unless it had received the formal approval of the king and the Privy Council. George acquired no such approval, but went ahead with the marriage anyway in December 1785. Under English law, George's marriage to Maria was void. The pope, however, regarded it as valid. George continued to have many more affairs, the most torrid of which was with the countess of Jersey. George III made every effort to control his son's debaucheries, for the prince, who now drank and ate to excess, was also becoming violent. He had spent to excess in building his own home at Carlton House in London, and as part of the arrangement for helping finance the debt, the king and Parliament insisted that George marry a proper wife. The King selected his niece, Princess Caroline of Brunswick. He must have been blind to her reputation, for not only was she not that attractive, and took little heed for her own personal hygiene, she was already supposed to have had one affair during her youth and, like George, she had wild tantrums. When the two first met three days before their wedding in April 1795, George felt sick at the sight of her and asked for a brandy, and Caroline called him fat and unhandsome. The Prince was drunk throughout his wedding ceremony and spent most of the wedding night in a stupor by the fire, but he must have done his duty, for nine months later to the day the Princess gave birth to their one and only child, Charlotte Augusta. George and Caroline separated soon after the birth and George denied Caroline any involvement in the raising of her daughter. Caroline established an orphanage in Kent in August 1797, whilst George went back to his mistresses. Mrs Fitzherbert returned to live with George for a while after 1800, still regarding herself as his lawful wife.

With the outbreak of the Napoleonic War, George applied several times for military service, jealous of the commands held by his brothers, but he was always refused. This was realistic, because the heir to the throne would no longer be put at such risk, but it was also pragmatic, as George had no military training and the government were fearful of what damage he might cause. Frustrated, George became mischievous at home. A dispute arose in 1804 over the custody of his daughter with the result that Charlotte was handed over to George III. Annoyed at this, Prince George cast aspersions over the conduct of his estranged wife, alleging that one of the orphans in her care, William Austin, was her own son. This led to a 'delicate investigation' by Parliament in 1806 which, though it cleared Caroline of the charge, revealed that her conduct was far from becoming.

In 1810, when George III sank into his final decline George was made Prince Regent, with certain restricted powers. Nevertheless from 1811 he acted as if he were the sovereign. His extravagance, even though curtailed by Parliament, was still lavish. During this period the Royal Pavilion at Brighton was completely rebuilt on the mock-Oriental style designed by John Nash. Under instruction from the Prince, Nash also redesigned Central London, which is why Regent's Park and Regent Street are so named. The streets of the City of London were lit by gas from 1814. Waterloo Bridge was opened in 1817 and Southwark Bridge in 1819. The Prince Regent continued to entertain lavishly, especially after the victory of Wellington in the Napoleonic Wars, when England played host to the emperor of Russia and the king of Prussia in June 1814.

The Regency period however was not all glitter. Soldiers returning from war were not fully recompensed and did not find gainful employment. There was considerable unrest which found little sympathy from the government, especially from Lord Liverpool and Lord Sidmouth, who had previously dealt harshly with the Luddites. A gathering at Spa Fields in North London in December 1816, when manufacturers sought to present their views to the Prince Regent, turned ugly and was dealt with severely. Sidmouth used this as an opportunity to undertake what became called the Green-Bag inquiry in February 1817 when a series of secret committees looked into a number of alleged cases of sedition. As a result of this *habeas corpus* was suspended. A gathering in St Peter's Field in Manchester in August 1819 alarmed the authorities because of its size – the military dispersed the meeting, causing over 400 injuries and eleven deaths. This incident became known as Peterloo (after Waterloo) and led to even more repressive legislation outlawing public assemblies. The populace were not happy and within only a few weeks of the Prince Regent becoming king in January 1820, a plot was unearthed, known as the Cato Street Conspiracy, to assassinate the members of the Cabinet and overthrow the Government.

George had other things on his mind, however. He had been grief-stricken when his only daughter, Charlotte, who had married in May 1816, died due to complications after childbirth in November 1817. He now had no heir to the throne, and his wife, Caroline, now approaching fifty, was past child-bearing age. In fact George did everything to keep Caroline out of the country. She had gone on a grand tour of Europe after the end of the Napoleonic Wars and was by all accounts romantically involved with an Italian courtier, Bartolomeo Pergami. However, on George's accession to the throne Caroline was determined to return and take her place as queen. George offered her £50,000 a year to stay away, but she brushed this aside and returned to Britain in June 1820. George introduced a parliamentary bill, called the Bill of Pains and Penalties, which was an enquiry into Caroline's conduct. Since Caroline appeared in the House of Lords, the enquiry has come to be regarded as her trial, though she never spoke in her defence. The bill was dropped and Caroline exonerated with much public rejoicing. George still refused to admit her and went to great pains to exclude her from his coronation in July 1821. George had ensured no expense was spared over this event which he planned for over a year and it remains the most extravagant coronation ever held in England. To George's relief, but also his shame, Caroline died just three weeks later on 7 August 1821 of inflammation of the bowels. The public had always been very supportive of the queen and voiced strong opposition to the king. A few weeks later George went on a royal progress through the kingdom, visiting Ireland and, at the urging of Sir Walter Scott, Scotland (the first Hanoverian to do so). He put on all his charm and elegance and was remarkably well received. One might question how much the populace were celebrating the continuance of the monarchy as distinct from the individual. The institution of the monarchy suffered considerably under George IV, but survived sufficiently due to the fond memory of George III to enter a golden phase under Victoria.

George's reign as king lasted for just over ten years and it advanced the country but little. George had a succession of prime ministers, most of whom he tried to oppose, especially as regards their foreign policy. Both he and the duke of Wellington vigorously opposed any political reform and it was only with reluctance on their parts that, at last, in April 1829 the Catholic Emancipation Act became law, restoring to Catholics the right to public office. It did not meet with the riots accorded earlier attempts to do this. There were greater troubles besetting the nation than religion, and it required a much stronger government than George IV and his ministers to tackle them. George died on 26 June 1830 of respiratory problems, aged sixty-seven. For all his dandyism and extravagance he was at the end a sad and lonely man, who had damaged the stature of the monarchy and whose only lasting legacy is the Brighton Pavilion. He was succeeded by his brother, William IV.

WILLIAM IV 'THE SAILOR KING'
Ruled 26 June 1830–20 June 1837.
Crowned: Westminster Abbey, 8 September 1831.
Full name and titles: *William Henry, king of the United Kingdom of Great Britain and Ireland; duke of Clarence and St Andrews and earl of Munster (from 1789).*
Born: *Buckingham Palace, 21 August 1765.* **Died**: *Windsor Castle, 20 June 1837, aged 71.*
Married: *13 July 1818, at Kew Palace, Adelaide Louise Theresa Caroline Amelia (1792–1849), dau. George, duke of Saxe-Meiningen: 6 children (4 stillborn). William also had at least eleven illegitimate children, ten by Dorothea Bland (1761–1816).*

William was George III's third son and had not expected to become king. It was the death of George IV's daughter Charlotte in 1817, followed by the death of George's brother, Frederick (the 'Grand Old Duke of York' of the nursery rhyme), in 1827 that made William the heir presumptive. Until then he had led a life fairly distanced from the extravagant carousel of his brother. William entered the Navy in 1779 at the age of fourteen and served at the relief of Gibraltar. He received few concessions initially because of his status, but served first as an able seaman, rising to midshipman and then rising through the ranks. He served under Nelson during 1786/7 in the West Indies, and was given the command of his own frigate, the *Andromeda*, in 1788 and the next year was appointed the Rear Admiral of HMS *Valiant*. He was made duke of Clarence in 1789 and thereafter regularly attended the House of Lords. He was made Admiral of the Fleet in 1811 and delighted in the official duties that imposed.

Like his brothers, William was an inveterate womanizer. During a visit to Hanover in 1784 he was supposed to have seduced and even entered into a secret marriage with Caroline von Linsingen. The marriage was unlikely (though it seemed to be a tradition amongst the Hanoverians) but the seduction was very likely and she bore him a son called William, who drowned in 1807. A typical sailor, Prince William had a girl in every port, but in 1790 William fell in love with the actress Dorothea Bland, better known by her stage name Dorothea Jordan. Although they did not marry, they lived happily together for twenty years. She bore him ten children who adopted the surname Fitzclarence. Their descendants live to this day. William suddenly abandoned Dorothea in 1811, probably because she had become an alcoholic and was no longer attractive. She tried to return to the stage, without success, and died following a mental collapse in France in 1816. William's callous treatment of her was out of character with his past actions, but probably a true representation of the real man.

William did not marry until after the death of his brother's heiress, the Princess Charlotte. He was fifty-two when he married the twenty-five-year-old Princess Adelaide, but despite the age difference the two became devoted to each other and she became a devoted stepmother to William's illegitimate flock. Unfortunately none of their children survived infancy.

William was nearly sixty-five by the time he became king and by then he had become a bad-tempered, miserly old man who delighted in being obstinate. He refused to have an extravagant coronation like his brother's, but insisted that it be simple, and he thereby abandoned much of the tradition that had accompanied the ceremony. He felt rather that he was a caretaker monarch, holding the throne for his niece Victoria and determined to survive long enough to avoid her mother, the duchess of Kent, becoming regent. He had no interests in art, science or literature, though he did establish a Royal Library at Windsor because it seemed strange without one.

His single most significant contribution to the advance of the nation came in 1832 when, against his own personal judgement, he supported Earl Grey and encouraged the Tory peers to abstain from voting against the Reform Bill, securing its passage. This was the start of modern democracy in Britain, reforming the representation of the people. This opened up the opportunity for a series of reforms, most of which would come to fruition in Victoria's reign. Others of importance were passed in 1833 – the Factory Act, against child labour, and the Abolition Act, which emancipated slaves in the British colonies. The Poor Law of 1834 was a well-intentioned piece of legislation, institutionalizing the workhouse. Much of the administration of Britain was still at the level where it could transport the Tolpuddle Martyrs to Australia in 1834 for calling a trade union meeting of agricultural workers. Public reaction to their sentence added fuel to the growing Chartist movement for political and social reform. William found all this reform rather distressing, as if the whole moral structure of the nation was collapsing. He died of pneumonia and cirrhosis of the liver on 20 June 1837, the last of the Hanoverian kings. Little did he realize that his successor, Victoria, would rule for the rest of the century and rule over the greatest empire the world had seen.

VICTORIA
Ruled 20 June 1837–22 January 1901.
Crowned: Westminster Abbey, 28 June 1838.
*Full name and titles: Alexandrina Victoria, queen of the United
Kingdom of Great Britain and Ireland; empress of India (from
1 May 1876).*
Born: Kensington Palace, 24 May 1819. **Died:** *Osborne House,
Isle of Wight, 22 January 1901, aged 82.* **Buried:** *Frogmore,
Windsor.*
*Married: 10 February 1840, at St James's Palace, London,
Albert (1819–61) son of Ernst I, duke of Saxe-Coburg-Gotha:
9 children.*

Victoria might never have been born had not George IV's
daughter, Charlotte, died following childbirth in November
1817. At that time there was no legitimate heir to the throne
in the next generation amongst the descendants of George III.
This sent George IV's remaining unmarried brothers scurrying to
find wives and produce an heir. Edward Augustus, duke of Kent,
married Mary Louise Victoria, the daughter of Franz I, duke of
Saxe-Coburg-Saalfield on 29 May 1818. Edward was fifty years
old and had not previously been married, though he did have
several illegitimate children. Mary Louise (who was always
known as Victoria) was thirty-one and had recently been widowed following the death of her husband, the prince of Leiningen, in 1814. She already had two children, Karl (1804–56), who
became the next prince of Leiningen, and Anne (1807–72). Her
brother was Prince Leopold, the husband of George IV's ill-fated
daughter Charlotte. Leopold remained in London after his wife's
death to help support his sister. Victoria's father, the duke of
Kent, died on 23 January 1820 when she was only nine months
old, so she never knew him, which was probably all to the good as
he was a sadistic man with a vicious temper and no scruples.
Uncle Leopold thereby became the mainstay of the family, helping his sister and providing a father figure to the young Victoria.

She missed him tremendously when he became the king of the Belgians in 1831.

When George IV died in 1830, and her uncle, William IV became king, Victoria became the heir presumptive. When she was shown a genealogical chart, it brought home to her how close to the accession she was, and this occasioned her famous comment 'I will be good'. William IV died in the early hours of 20 June 1837, so that Victoria learned she was queen in the middle of the night. Under the Salic Law, women could not rule the kingdom of Hanover which passed to her Uncle Ernst, and thereafter (in 1851) to her cousin George, who was just three days younger than Victoria. Had Victoria not been born, then her uncle and cousin would have become the next two kings of England.

At the time that Victoria became queen, the monarchy was not popular. The post-Napoleonic period had seen considerable distress amongst the English working folk and the country was well in need of reform. The high and wild living of George IV and his brothers had not helped respect for the monarchy. There had been many riots across the country which had been put down with customary military zeal. The Whig government, with the reluctant aid of William IV, had succeeded in passing the Reform Act along with other much needed legislation, but it was still very early days and the Hanoverian dynasty, up until now, had shown little interest in such progress. There was a general attitude of 'Why bother?' amongst both the royal family and many leading politicians. All this would change under Victoria, though at the outset the public could never have anticipated the scale of change that would happen or, for that matter, the length of reign that Victoria would have, a reign that would change the face of Britain and, to a large extent, the globe. In the first few years of her reign Victoria, as the symbol of a corrupt and profligate monarchy, was as unpopular as her predecessors. There were three assassination attempts in the first four years, the first on 10 June 1840, by Edward Oxford, and then two within a few weeks of each other in May and July 1842, when shots were fired at the queen.

Victoria had to face a scandal within the first year of her reign.

During her youth she had always disliked Sir John Conroy, who was close to her mother (some felt too close) and who some believed wished to become the power behind the throne. When she became queen Victoria expelled Conroy, but believed that he continued to exert an influence through one of her mother's ladies-in-waiting, Lady Flora Hastings. She believed Conroy and Lady Flora had become lovers and that Lady Flora was pregnant with his child. In fact the poor woman had cancer of the liver and the tumour had swollen her stomach. Victoria subjected Lady Flora to an examination which proved she was still a virgin, though Victoria retained her doubts. Lady Flora died soon after. This episode caused her considerable unpopularity and she was heckled at Ascot races. She was jeeringly called Mrs Melbourne because of her close association with the Prime Minister.

Melbourne, who had himself been the subject of a scandal in 1836 over his friendship with the Honourable Mrs Caroline Norton (and had never really recovered from the association between his wife, Lady Caroline Lamb, and Lord Byron from twenty years earlier), was a close friend and adviser to Victoria in the first few years of her reign. He instructed her on political matters and provided an avuncular role in the absence of her Uncle Leopold. In 1839 Melbourne resigned and Victoria invited Robert Peel to form a government. As part of the arrangements Peel determined that the ladies in the royal household who had been Whig appointments should be replaced by Tory nominees. Victoria refused and Peel declined to form an administration. Melbourne returned. Victoria had flexed her muscles, albeit over a storm in a teacup and though she had won, she subsequently reconsidered the circumstances and allowed some changes when Peel was returned to power following the general election in 1841.

Victoria met her future husband, Prince Albert, in 1836 when his father (the brother of Victoria's Uncle Leopold) brought him to London. She was immediately attracted to him and on their second meeting in 1839 Victoria asked him to marry her. The marriage took place on 10 February 1840. They were both

From a painting by Winterhalter, 1846

twenty years old, with Victoria the senior by three months. Albert had not had a happy childhood. His parents had separated. Both his father and his brother were notorious womanizers, while Albert was the more studious, making the best use of his education. It was Albert and not Victoria who had the stronger moral values and he steadily impressed these upon her. Although they had nine children, Albert saw this more as his duty than as pleasure, whereas Victoria treasured the memory of their love-making.

Nevertheless Victoria was only too aware of the scandalous sexual adventures of her uncles as almost all her cousins were illegitimate, and many of her uncles' mistresses still held a place in society. Albert believed that the royal family should set an example. Although at the start of their marriage Victoria maintained her role as the queen with Albert as no more than her husband, and not the master of the house, she soon deferred to his judgement, and Albert's strong moral standpoint was forced upon the government of the day. Ministers soon knew that any unbecoming conduct would be severely criticized by the queen. The stern views of Albert and the queen began to change the moral climate of the country, at least on the surface, though it repressed much. Nevertheless the queen was not such a prude as she is often portrayed, since she was prepared to accept that men might have affairs. She denied ever using the phrase 'we are not amused', which was attributed to her late in life after seeing someone giving an impression of her.

Although they argued like any young couple, Victoria and Albert were ideally matched and intensely in love. Apart from their official residences in London and Windsor, the queen had Osborne House built for them on the Isle of Wight, which was completed in 1851. While it was under construction, the queen also purchased Balmoral House in Scotland in 1852. These became their two main country retreats.

Albert also took an interest in the social conditions of the country. It was his genuine concern for the condition of children and of workers that gave the reform movement a political acceptability that it had hitherto lacked. With the right ministers in place, especially Robert Peel at the outset, social reform gathered pace during the mid-nineteenth century. The extent of social and cultural reform during Victoria's reign was immense, much of it due to improved educational standards (especially after the Education Act of 1870), public health (with a series of acts in 1848, 1872 and 1875), and technology. In the last case it was Prince Albert's own initiative for Britain to hold a Great Exhibition in 1851, effectively the first World's Fair, for the display of technological knowledge and advances. The Exhibition was held in the famous Crystal Palace, designed and built by Joseph Paxton, which was later relocated to the park at Sydenham in South London. The Exhibition made a resounding profit which the Prince planned to spend on establishing the Victoria and Albert Museum in Kensington.

There is little doubt that the improvement in the working man's lot during the nineteenth century helped the monarchy by reducing social unrest. When Europe was racked by a wave of revolutions in 1848, the British monarchy remained intact, although the Chartists took advantage of the general unrest to stage a demonstration. Britain had become a more democratic country than others in Europe and this process was strongly supported by Albert and to a slightly lesser degree by Victoria. She maintained that the European monarchs (many of whom were relatives) should stand together in mutual support. To this end she encouraged royal visits between monarchs, undertaking several herself. Her first had been to Louis-Philippe of France in September 1843, the first visit between an English and French sovereign since Henry VIII visited François I in 1520. Her relationships with other European nations did much to stabilise Europe in the second half of the nineteenth century. Her involvement, for example, in keeping Prussia out of the war between Austria and Sardinia in 1857, and subsequently convincing her ministers to remain neutral, certainly stopped hostilities from escalating and brought a quick peace. She also strove to dampen down anti-Indian hysteria during the years of the Indian Mutiny (1857/8) and called for leniency in retribution in India. Victoria also urged neutrality in the American Civil War, although the incident over the British mailship *Trent*, which was boarded by the Federal Navy, taking prisoner two Confederate envoys on diplomatic business (later released), might have escalated into a British involvement in the war, had not Prince Albert intervened in a tactful rewording of the British government's despatch.

Albert was only ever 'Prince Consort', the title of which was confirmed in 1857, although Victoria would have liked to have made him king. The two were a formidable pair and, through Albert, the nation became endeared to the monarchy. The whole of Britain was devastated by the death of Albert (probably from typhoid) on 14 December 1861, and Victoria was racked by grief. She went so far as to consider suicide, and spent the rest of her life dressed in mourning. The Albert Hall and Albert Memorial were built in his memory.

After Albert's death, Victoria took a less prominent part in public affairs though she kept in touch with everything via her Prime Minister. Her relationship with her government had always been on a personal basis. Some prime ministers she could instinctively trust; and even though she did not like Robert Peel at first, she developed a high regard for him. She never trusted Lord Palmerston, although she eventually supported his action in the Crimean War of 1854/6. She instituted the Victoria Cross for valour in the Crimea; it was made from iron cast from the guns captured in the war. She never liked William Gladstone, whom she found patronizing and obstinate, but she had her best relationship with Benjamin Disraeli. Their views were similar and he knew how to flatter her. His greatest coup was making her empress of India in 1876. She sorely missed Disraeli when he died in 1881.

Throughout the second half of her reign, Victoria interceded in foreign affairs only in an effort to maintain peace and remain neutral. Generally she was successful, though at times this went to the brink as with the declaration of war between Russia and Turkey in 1877. Victoria and Disraeli's stand almost caused a war between Russia and Britain until terms were agreed at the Congress of Berlin in 1878. Victoria was horrified at the activities in the Sudan in 1883/4 and censured her ministers when they did not follow her orders and send relief to General Gordon in Khartoum in time to save him. Also throughout her reign there were continuing problems between Britain and Ireland. In 1886 Gladstone introduced a Home Rule Bill which would have restored the Irish parliament in Dublin and repealed the 1800 Act of Union. Victoria would have none of it and the discussion split Gladstone's Liberal Party, with the Unionists emerging on their own. A second attempt in 1893 was passed by the Commons but rejected in the Lords.

While there was every reason to hold Victoria in high respect for her abilities as a monarch, she came in for some criticism. The public believed her extended mourning for Albert was becoming unhealthy and affecting her judgement. She had found some consolation in a new shoulder to cry on, that of a Scottish estate worker and attendant John Brown, who was blunt and honest but caring. His concern for her welfare convinced Victoria that the working class often had better standards and morals than the aristocracy. This was not helped by the profligate behaviour of her son the Prince of Wales (*see* Edward VII). Her association with John Brown was interpreted as something more serious than it was, with newspapers referring to her as 'Mrs. Brown'. She was in danger of reducing respect once more for the monarchy and there was even some discussion in 1871 of abolishing the monarchy, but it came to nothing. Brown remained her faithful attendant and stalwart until his death in 1883.

Towards the end of her reign Victoria was seen as the grandmother of Europe, and with her Golden and Diamond Jubilees in 1887 and 1897 there was much celebration. Through her daughter Victoria, who had married the future Friedrich III of Prussia, she was the grandmother of the future Kaiser Wilhelm II. Through her second daughter, Alice, her granddaughter (also called Alice) married Tsar Nicholas II of Russia. Her second son, Prince Alfred, was elected king of Greece in 1862 but declined the throne. His daughter Marie married King Ferdinand of Romania. There was scarcely a royal family in Europe who did not have some matrimonial link with Victoria, and most of them were present at her Diamond Jubilee. At that time the British Empire was also at its greatest extent and it would have seemed to Victoria's subjects that Britain ruled the world. It was not true, as would soon be seen, but it was a great feeling to the British while it lasted and brought the nineteenth century to a magnificent close.

When the queen died at Osborne House on 22 January 1901, she had not only ruled longer than any previous British monarch, but she could count more people as her subjects than any ruler ever. On her own she was not as great a queen as she was in partnership with Prince Albert, or with a strong prime minister, so it is difficult to rank her as a greater monarch than Elizabeth I, but in terms of the changes that happened during her life, she must be accorded the most significant reign in British history.

Devolving Empire and Kingdom

THE HOUSE OF
SAXE-COBURG-GOTHA
(changed to WINDSOR) (1901–)

The twentieth century marked a period of enormous change. Scientific developments and inventions – telecommunications, radio, film, television, electronic media, air travel – would, more than in any other century, alter the United Kingdom's perception of itself and of other nations.

At the beginning of the twentieth century Britain, with its monarch as its titular head, ruled almost a third of the world's population, but this would not remain so.

In 1931 the Statute of Westminster would recognize Australia, Canada, Eire, New Zealand and South Africa as independent states within the Commonwealth of Nations. After the Second World War, Britain would find that it could no longer afford to maintain its remaining empire by force. India and Pakistan would become independent in 1947. In 1948, Palestine, a British mandate since 1920, would become the state of Israel. Also in 1948 Burma and Sri Lanka (Ceylon) would gain their freedom; in 1957 Malaya and the Gold Coast too, followed by all the remaining colonies of Africa, the Caribbean and the Pacific. In 1964 Malta would follow. In 1997 Hong Kong would be handed back to the Chinese. By the end of the century only a few colonies – such as Gibraltar and the Falklands – would remain, and British sovereignty of them would be constantly disputed by Spain and Argentina.

The twentieth-century's two world wars caused, worldwide, some 10 million deaths in the first, 55 million in the second, and changed irrevocably how the countries of Europe viewed one another. As a consequence the European Community was created to form closer economic and political ties in Europe, to try to prevent such devastating occurrences ever happening again. Britain joined in 1971. How far Britain will become involved, whether it can retain its autonomy, and whether there will still be a place for a British monarchy are questions it now asks itself.

EDWARD VII
Ruled 22 January 1901–6 May 1910. Crowned: Westminster Abbey, 9 August 1902.
Full name and titles: Albert Edward, king of Great Britain, Ireland and the British Dominions beyond the Seas, emperor of India, duke of Cornwall and Rothesay, earl of Carrick, lord of the Isles and Baron Renfrew (from birth), prince of Wales and earl of Chester (from 1841), duke of Saxe-Coburg-Gotha (1861–63).
Born: Buckingham Palace, 9 November 1841.
Died: Buckingham Palace, 6 May 1910, aged 68. *Buried*: Windsor Castle.
Married: 10 March 1863, at Windsor Castle, Alexandra Caroline Marie Charlotte Louise Julie (1844–1925), dau. of Christian IX, king of Denmark: 6 children.

Baptized Albert Edward, and always affectionately known as Bertie, he was the second child and eldest son of Victoria and Prince Albert of Saxe-Coburg. His parents were very strict with him as a child, determined that he would not become wayward and profligate like Victoria's father and uncles or Albert's father and brother, but it was to little avail. In fact they probably restricted him too much, as by his teens he had developed a cruel streak (which thankfully he lost), threw tantrums just as George IV did in his youth, and showed every tendency of rebelling against his parents. He grew out of this only because his good looks (he looked very much like his father and his maternal grandfather) allowed him to get his own way with women and he was able to enjoy himself as he pleased. His parents did not allow him to play any part in political affairs or undertake any state visits until much later in life, although he did tour Europe, Canada and America in his teens. Had they done so Edward might have taken his responsibilities more seriously because once he did become king, he became a skilled negotiator. Instead he suffered from the usual Hanoverian trait of parents not trusting their children and so, like his mother's great-grand-father, Frederick, prince of Wales, the new prince of Wales (which he was created when he was a month old) led the life of a playboy.

Although this made him a frustration to his parents, most people enjoyed his company and the nation took him to its heart, especially after the death of Prince Albert, when the queen went into mourning and became over sombre. Prince Edward main-tained a sense of humour and delighted in practical jokes and kept society bubbling. There was great national concern in 1871 when Edward became seriously ill with typhoid. The Queen, however, never forgave Edward for creating an incident in 1861 which she believed added to Prince Albert's stress and contributed to his early death. Prince Edward was in Ireland involved in army manoeuvres and as a joke a young actress was hidden in his tent. It caused a scandal. It was thought paramount that Edward should take a wife as soon as possible and on 10 March 1863 he married Princess Alexandra of Denmark. Edward had acquired a house and land at Sandringham in Norfolk in 1862, which became his and his wife's main country retreat. Alexandra was remarkably tolerant of her husband and her flexibility and good nature doubtless contributed to what is one of the longest marriages of any British monarch. They remained married for forty-seven years until Edward's death. Alexandra died on 20 November 1925 in her eighty-first year.

They had six children (though the last died after only a day in 1871). Edward, however, remained a philanderer and enjoyed the company of many women. Perhaps his best known mistress was the actress Lillie Langtry (real name Emilie Le Breton), but he was regularly seen in the company of many different society ladies. Generally Edward kept these affairs discreet, although most people in society knew about them. Occasionally though they became more public. In 1870 the MP Sir Charles Mordaunt brought a divorce suit against his wife on the grounds of adultery. In her statement, Lady Mordaunt cited the prince of Wales as one of the co-respondents. During the course of the trial, at which the prince appeared as a witness, it become known that he frequently visited her alone when her husband was in the House of Commons, though nothing more was proved. Prince Edward never acknowledged any illegitimate children, though rumours were rife. Sonia, the second daughter of Alice Keppel, born in May 1900, was widely believed to be the Prince's. She became the grandmother of Camilla Parker Bowles.

Perhaps the most notorious incident attached to Prince Edward was the baccarat scandal of 1890. The prince had attended a house party at Tranby Croft in Yorkshire where they played the then illegal game of baccarat. One of the party, Sir William Gordon-Cumming, was accused of cheating but the matter was kept quiet, provided Sir William did not play cards again. However word leaked out and Sir William sued others of the party for slander. Again the prince appeared in court as a witness, and the nation expressed its outrage that the prince should be involved in an illegal gambling game. Such is society that it should express more concern over this than over Prince Edward's affairs.

In fact Edward's activities set the fashion in society – how he dressed, where he went, what he did. Society life revolved about him. He was primarily responsible for making Monte Carlo a fashionable location for the elite; he went big-game hunting in India; he loved horse-racing and regularly attended major society meetings – three of his horses won the Derby and another the Grand National. Edward also took an interest in yacht racing – the racing yacht *Britannia* was built for him in 1892. The public followed everything that he did: even leaving the bottom button on the waistcoat undone (because of his increased corpulence) became the height of fashion.

Although Victoria denied Prince Edward involvement in political affairs, he still held his views. He caused sufficient family unrest in 1864 when the Schleswig-Holstein dispute erupted and Prussia declared war on Denmark. Victoria naturally supported Prussia, but Edward supported Denmark, his wife's country, and this view was shared by the Prime Minister. Edward further angered the queen when he welcomed the Italian revolutionary, Garibaldi, to England in April 1864, when he came to encourage further support for Denmark. In fact Edward proved himself far more tolerant and capable than ever his mother perceived. While she encouraged the nation to remain neutral when hostilities erupted elsewhere in Europe, Edward would, had he been allowed, have exerted his influence to resolve affairs. Instead the queen restricted him to state visits amongst peaceable nations and public ceremonies, such as the opening of the Thames Embankment in 1871, the Mersey Tunnel in 1886 and Tower Bridge in 1894. He performed his public duties with considerable energy and aplomb and applied himself to a number of charity organizations and public committees. In particular he had concern over the condition of housing in Britain and was a member of the Royal Commission on Housing established in 1884. Edward also enjoyed himself helping with the preparations for his mother's Golden Jubilee in 1887 and Diamond Jubilee in 1897.

In January 1892 his eldest son, Albert, died of pneumonia. Albert (known as 'Eddy' to the family) had always been an apathetic child and the prince believed him backward. It was later suspected that he suffered from syphilis of the brain.

Rumours attached themselves to 'Eddy' and his lifestyle – it was alleged that he had secretly married Annie Crook sometime in the mid-1880s and that the Jack the Ripper murders were committed to silence those in the know, though no evidence but hearsay supports this.

One other cloud cast a shadow over Edward and that was an assassination attempt on 4 April 1900, when the prince was fired at while travelling through Brussels on his way to Denmark. The prince was unhurt. The cause was related to the Boer War in South Africa, which had soured relationships between England and its European neighbours.

Edward was welcomed as king in January 1901. Edward's coronation was delayed by six weeks because he developed appendicitis. The food, which had already been prepared, was distributed among the poor of London. The eventual celebrations, held on 9 August, were magnificent. It may not have been the most expensive ceremony, but it was almost certainly the largest, with representatives from all over the world. Although he ruled for fewer than ten years, his lifestyle made sufficient impression for the first decade of this century to be known as the Edwardian period. It was a period of fun and enjoyment. It was a time of major advancement in the welfare of society – trades unions were recognized, old age pensions and national insurance were introduced.

Edward took little interest in this. His time was spent becoming what the French dubbed 'the uncle of Europe'. He undertook regular visits to European monarchs, most of whom were his relatives, and helped Europe maintain a steady peace. All his life Edward had been a Francophile and it was primarily through his relations with France that England was able to conclude the *Entente Cordiale* alliance in April 1904. Edward became a major symbol of British strength and authority and was highly respected through Europe and the Empire. He was far more of a humanist than any of his predecessors, something which he inherited from his father, and despite his reputation for the good life, was also charitable and philanthropic, sparing no energies in support of good causes. He upheld the best of the Victorian values and while not all his views would accord with today's values (for instance, he opposed women's suffrage) his wish that everyone should lead a good life shaped and influenced English society for fifty years and still remains the image of the 'good old days'.

He died on 6 May 1910 of bronchial complications. His funeral was the last time the monarchy of Europe assembled together, as four years later the Great War would rip Europe apart. Edward was succeeded by his only surviving son, George V.

GEORGE V
Ruled 6 May 1910–20 January 1936.
Crowned: Westminster Abbey, 22 June 1911.
Full name and titles: George Frederick Ernest Albert, king of Great Britain and Ireland (only Northern Ireland after 1920) and the British Dominions beyond the Seas, emperor of India, duke of York, earl of Inverness and Baron Killarney (from 1892), duke of Cornwall and Rothesay (from 1901), prince of Wales and earl of Chester (from 1901).
Born*: Marlborough House, London, 3 June 1865.* **Died***: Sandringham House, Norfolk, 20 January 1936, aged 70.*
Buried*: Windsor Castle.*
Married*: 6 July 1893, at St James's Palace, London, Mary Augusta Louise (1867–1953) dau. of Franz, duke of Teck: 6 children.*

George V was the second son of Edward VII. Until his elder brother, Prince Albert, died in 1892, George had not anticipated he would be the next in line to the throne after his father. He had opted for a career in the navy, like William IV, starting as a naval cadet at Dartmouth in 1877 and rising to the rank of commander in 1891. Unfortunately a bout of typhoid, followed by news of his brother's death, ended his naval career and he had to adjust to the prospect of becoming king. He had sufficient sense of duty to do this, though he did not welcome it, and neither did he like the additional political and language studies he had to do. He was not fond of intellectual pursuits, preferring, like his father, a sporting life. Unusually for the Hanoverian line, George was on very good terms with his father, but he did not copy him in any other way, especially the playboy role. George was rather shy, which he overcame by talking loudly in a booming voice, but he much preferred solitary pursuits and it was not unusual for him to hide away at Sandringham for periods of time, hunting, fishing and developing his collection of stamps of the British Empire. He was slightly below average height (about five foot seven inches) and had inherited his father's good looks and had captivating blue eyes.

George married his late brother's betrothed, Princess Mary of Teck, in 1893. He was twenty-eight; she was twenty-six. They had five sons and a daughter, Mary, who became the Princess Royal in 1932. Their two eldest sons became Edward VIII and George VI. Their third son, Henry, duke of Gloucester, lived until 1974. The fourth son, George, duke of Kent, was killed on active service in the Second World War, when his plane crashed into a Scottish hillside in August 1942. Their youngest son, John, was an epileptic and was kept out of the public gaze at Sandringham, where he died in 1919 aged thirteen. Their marriage was not a love match but by all accounts George was faithful. An early allegation that he had married the daughter of Admiral Culme-Seymour before his marriage to Mary was rapidly squashed and the perpetrator of the story prosecuted and imprisoned. There was never more than minor gossip about George's love life and he was the first king since Charles I not to have any sexual scandal attached to his name.

Although Edward VII did his best to prepare George for the monarchy, both in terms of becoming acquainted with the political process, and in visits to foreign courts, George felt ill equipped for the political crisis that he was plunged into after his father's death in May 1910. The Liberals' budget of 1909, which had included provision for a super-tax to cover the cost of old-age pensions, had been rejected by the House of Lords. Prime

The Royal Family

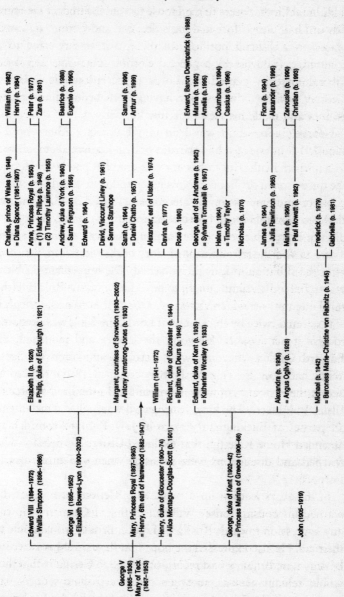

Minister Asquith had asked Edward VII to consider appointing additional Liberal peers to the House to vote the budget through. Edward had died before making a decision and George was now placed in a difficult position. In the end it was referred to a committee, followed by a general election where the increased Liberal majority caused the Lords to accept public opinion. George, however, did not like having been brought into party politics and made his views forcibly known.

George's coronation was held in Westminster Abbey on 22 June 1911, but he also had the idea of being crowned emperor in India, which neither his father nor grandmother had been. He and the queen sailed for India in November and were jointly crowned emperor and empress on 11 December 1911 at Delhi. It was on that occasion that Delhi became the country's capital. George VI did not repeat this second coronation, so it was a unique event.

It was also the last moment of glory of the old world, for soon after the situation in Europe worsened. The immediate problem was in Ireland. Asquith sought to introduce a Home Rule Bill (the third attempt; *see under* Victoria *for the first two*) and, though it was rejected twice by the House of Lords, the King was prepared to give it his support. However the lawyer and politician, Sir Edward Carson (the man whose cross-examination of Oscar Wilde had been the ruin of the playwright in 1895), refused to accept the provision of the Bill and in 1913 mobilized a force of Ulster Volunteers. The king, fearing civil war, called a meeting of all parties at Buckingham Palace in July 1914 to consider an amended Home Rule Bill that excluded Ulster. No decision was reached and discussions were set aside when war broke out in Europe.

In the years leading up to war, King George had repeatedly warned his cousin, Kaiser Wilhelm II, that if Germany showed any aggression towards Russia or France, Britain would come to their aid. He also expressed the hope that they would not have to be drawn in. Britain's past record suggested to Germany that they would remain neutral, so when the catastrophic sequence of events sparked off by the assassination of Archduke Ferdinand of Austria on 28 June 1914 escalated into war, Germany declared war on Russia and France and, to add to the problem, marched on France through Belgium. Britain, tied by its treaties to its allies, declared war on Germany on 4 August 1914. The King did what he could to keep morale high. He shared in the rationing, not wishing to be shown special treatment. He paid five visits to the Grand Fleet and seven visits to armies in France and Belgium. On one visit in 1915, he was thrown from his horse and fractured his pelvis. The King did what he could behind the scenes and the public seemed to accept his genuine patriotism, but when anti-German feeling became intense in 1917 he took the counsel of his government and changed his family name from Saxe-Coburg to Windsor. Even before the war had finished, there was revolution in Russia. George's cousin Alice had married Tsar Nicholas II and the couple, with all their children, were murdered on July 16th 1918. George was devastated by the news. The old Europe was crumbling and Victoria's descendants were being replaced. Kaiser Wilhelm survived the war but fled from Germany and spent the rest of his life in the Netherlands.

After the war, the matter of Ireland still needed to be resolved. The Easter Rising of April 1916 had done little to help the situation, the execution of the rebels Pearce, Connolly and others only shifted support to the nationalists. King George opted for a conciliatory approach. The Government of Ireland Act of 1920 proposed for separate parliaments in Dublin and Belfast. The king and queen opened the Ulster Parliament in June 1921. Sinn Fein rejected the proposal for southern Ireland and it was not until the Anglo-Irish Treaty of 6 December 1921 that all of Ireland, except for Ulster, was recognized as the Irish Free State.

To George the old order continued to fade away. In 1924 the first Labour government was formed under Prime Minister Ramsay MacDonald. George was surprised to find the ministers easy to operate with. Unfortunately the Zinoviev letter, allegedly written by the head of the Communist International, encouraged armed revolution. The Labour Party was tainted with Communism and the letter contributed to their downfall. The General

Strike of 1926 was further evidence of civil strife and potential revolution. The Baldwin government took a hard line with the strikers while the king had been prepared to be more conciliatory. It became evident as the years progressed and the strife grew that England was in the grip of a world depression. King George took a cut in his own pay via the Civil List. It was George who actively encouraged the idea of a National Government to tackle the problem, and this eventually came in under Ramsay MacDonald in 1931. It was this sense of needing to hold the nation together that caused George V to introduce two traditions in 1932. The first was his own personal distribution of Maundy Money on the Thursday before Easter. The tradition dated back to the time of Edward III in 1363, but since the Reformation had been conducted by the Lord High Almoner. His other innovation was to broadcast a Christmas Day message over the radio, which also continues to this day. These acts immediately brought the king to the hearts of people who otherwise had never seen him, let alone heard him, and it did more than any other action that he took to personalize the king. It undoubtedly contributed to his popularity, which he had never courted. He was overwhelmed at the enthusiasm and warmth accorded him at his silver jubilee in 1935.

In 1931 the Statute of Westminster made the change from the British Empire to the Commonwealth, with Parliament ceasing to control some of the overseas dominions directly. The King remained as Head of the Commonwealth and, in many cases, as head of state, but it was a further slide away from the old regime under which George had been reared and where he still felt most at home.

The king's health had declined in the last few years. In November 1928 he had suffered a near fatal bout of septicaemia, which weakened his constitution. He had been sent to Bognor Regis to recuperate. Thus, when he entered his final illness with a severe bronchial infection in January 1936, Queen Mary suggested he might again visit Bognor. This gave rise to his alleged but doubtless apocryphal last words, 'Bugger Bognor!'

George V succeeded more than he ever realized in moulding together the disciplinarian approach of Victoria and Albert with the homely geniality of Edward VII to produce a monarch who stood for the best standards and principles of the nation. Few of his contemporaries fully appreciated the lengths to which he went to understand the problems of Britain and to promote stability and understanding throughout Europe. He succeeded far more than he failed, and the love he received from the nation was the testament to that. He was succeeded by his son.

EDWARD VIII
Ruled 20 January–11 December 1936. Never crowned.
Full name and titles: Edward Albert Christian George Andrew Patrick David, king of Great Britain and Northern Ireland, emperor of India, duke of Cornwall and Rothesay, earl of Carrick, lord of the Isles and Baron Renfrew (from 1910), prince of Wales and earl of Chester (from 1910); duke of Windsor (from 1937).
Born: White Lodge, Richmond, Surrey, 23 June 1894. **Died**: Paris, France, 28 May 1972, aged 77. **Buried**: Frogmore, Windsor.
Married: 3 June 1937, at Château de Candé, Maine-et-Loire, France, Wallis Simpson (née Warfield) (1896–1986): no children.

Despite an abundant selection of Christian names (the last four being the four patron saints of Britain), the future Edward VIII was always known in the family as David. He inherited his family's handsome features, including the youthfulness of his mother and grandmother so that his face always had a boyish charm. Almost from the outset he reacted against the demands placed upon him. Like his distant predecessor Edward II he had little interest in state affairs, though unlike that same predecessor he also disliked the pomp and ceremony. He regarded his investiture as prince of Wales in 1911 as ridiculous and he rebelled against his father's discipline. He took after his grandfather, Edward VII, in preferring 'the good life' and though his father tried to curb these tendencies he only aggravated them by continually treating Edward like a child. He was refused active service during the Great War, something that would certainly have been the making of him had he survived, and after the war, the king refused to involve him in political affairs. Instead, in the same way that Victoria treated 'Bertie', so Edward was only entrusted with going on goodwill tours around the world. Edward enjoyed doing these, although they became exhausting, and over a period, throughout the 1920s, it came to look as if King George was doing all he could to keep Edward out of the country.

One side-effect of all of this that would later have significant consequences was that the prince became attracted to the United States. Here was a country that accepted him for what he was and allowed him to speak his mind. He felt trapped and censured in Britain but alive and free in America. Edward and his father grew further apart. The prince embarked upon a series of affairs. He showed no interest in marriage, but seemed to have a liking for older, married women. He was evidently seeking that affection denied him by his parents. There were allegations that the Prince was a repressed homosexual, although his many affairs would speak against this. Nevertheless he was attracted to more masculine looking women. In January 1931 he first met Mrs Wallis Simpson, an American divorcée who had recently married for a second time. Edward fell in love with her, though it was never that clear how much she loved him – it was more the attraction of power. Nevertheless the two drew closer together and it was evident by 1935 that Edward had made his mind up to marry her. He never found the right moment to tell his father, because of George's failing health.

In January 1936 the old king died and David became Edward VIII. Although he had no great desire to be king he was prepared to do his duty, but only if he could marry Mrs Simpson. Divorce proceedings were already going through between Mrs Simpson and her husband, and the decree *nisi* was granted on 27 October

1936. During this period Edward and Mrs Simpson were almost inseparable but the British press remained silent on the matter. The American and European press, however, covered the news with relish, and it was only a matter of time before it would break in Britain. The king continued to believe that the nation would happily accept an American as queen. The government, the archbishop of Canterbury, and Edward's mother did not agree, believing that a marriage with a woman twice divorced, especially with both past husbands still alive, would be unconstitutional and wholly unacceptable. Edward remained determined. Mrs Simpson's decree absolute was set for 27 April 1937, fifteen days before the day planned for the coronation. It was not until November that Mrs Simpson realized the import of the constitutional dilemma – known as the Abdication Crisis – in which Edward was caught, and she offered to step aside. Edward would have none of it. On 16 November he gave the Prime Minister, Stanley Baldwin, an ultimatum that either he be allowed to marry or he would abdicate. Edward was supported by such stalwarts as Winston Churchill and Lord Beaverbrook, who were prepared to rally the country behind Edward, but he wanted none of that. If anything, this was the escape he was looking for. Edward was not cut out to be king and, though he would have suffered it for the nation, he would not do it alone. On 5 December 1936, Edward confirmed his intention to abdicate. The necessary papers were prepared and signed on 10 December and the next day, after making a moving broadcast to the nation, Edward sailed away to exile in France. There he and Wallis Warfield (she reverted to her maiden name on 7 May 1937) were married on 3 June. A few months earlier, on 8 March, Edward had been made duke of Windsor, but the honorific of 'Royal Highness' was denied his wife, albeit legally she was entitled to be so addressed.

They remained living in France, mostly in Paris, for the rest of their lives, although they travelled extensively, mostly to the United States where they became the centre of high society. Edward wished to serve his nation during the Second World

War but the closest he got was as governor and commander-in-chief of the Bahamas from 1940 to 1945. After the war rumours became rife that he had Nazi sympathies, though in fact he had visited Germany in 1937 in an effort to help stop the inevitable. Edward had such a high opinion of himself that he was blinded to his use by the Nazi propaganda machine.

Edward and his younger brother, who succeeded him as George VI, remained at a distance, though there were efforts at reconciliation by Elizabeth II, who visited Edward just days before he died of cancer on 28 May 1972. His body was flown back to Britain and buried at Frogmore in Windsor. His widow survived for another fourteen years in a sorry state in their Paris home as senile dementia took hold. She died on 24 April 1986, in her ninetieth year, and was buried beside her husband at Frogmore.

Edward had let his heart rule his head, but since his heart was also telling him that kingship was not for him then he must have made the right decision. Although his reputation has suffered some brickbats over the years, he is still remembered as the king who sacrificed everything for love, and that romantic image will never fade.

GEORGE VI
Ruled 11 December 1936–6 February 1952. Crowned: Westminster Abbey, 12 May 1937.
Full name and titles: Albert Frederick Arthur George, king of Great Britain and Northern Ireland, emperor of India (until 22 June 1947), duke of York, earl of Inverness and Baron Killarney (from 1920).
Born: Sandringham, Norfolk, 14 December 1895. Died: 6 February 1952, aged 56. Buried: Windsor Castle.
Married: 26 April 1923, at Westminster Abbey, Elizabeth (1900–2002) dau. of Claude George Bowes-Lyon, earl of Strathmore and Kinghorne: 2 daughters.

Kings usually have many years to prepare for their role, unless they are usurpers, and even then they do it with intent. George VI had less than a week, and for much of that week he could not believe it was happening.

Albert Frederick Arthur George ('Bertie' to his family) was the second son of George V and had not expected to become king, certainly not within a few months of his brother, Edward VIII, succeeding to the throne. Edward's love for Mrs Wallis Simpson, however, which led to his abdication in December 1936, propelled George into the monarchy with scarcely a moment's notice.

Like his father, George VI had not been raised to be king. He was a rather delicate child who suffered from gastritis as a result of his nurse's neglect. It led to a duodenal ulcer in later years. He was shy and had a restricting stammer which he only overcame with hard work. He entered the Royal Navy in 1913, as a midshipman, and this was the making of him for, although he was sea-sick, he came to enjoy the naval life. He served with distinction during the First World War, being mentioned in despatches at the battle of Jutland. He served for a short period in the Royal Naval Air Service. He was created duke of York in 1920, of which he was excessively proud.

For all he was strait-laced and a stickler for protocol, George also had the common touch. In 1921 he set up the Duke of York's Boys' Camps which brought together working-class and public schoolboys in summer camps. They worked well and were held annually until 1939. He also became President of the Industrial Welfare Society and took a keen interest in workers' health and safety. He enjoyed sport, especially tennis, and made a brief appearance at Wimbledon in 1926 in the doubles with his wife.

He had met Lady Elizabeth Bowes-Lyon in 1922. She had originally been introduced to his brother Edward in the hope of making a match. Lady Elizabeth was attracted to the prince of Wales, but it was the duke of York who eventually won her hand, and the two were married in April 1923. Although not a member of a British or European royal family, Lady Elizabeth's family had a long and illustrious history, tracing its descent from John Lyon, secretary of David II of Scotland who was made Lord Glamis in 1372 and who married Jean, a daughter of Robert II, in 1376. On her mother's side, Lady Elizabeth could trace descent from the Welsh prince Owain Glyn Dwr. They were well matched and made a happy couple. They were blessed with two daughters, Elizabeth in 1926 and Margaret in 1930.

Following their marriage George and Elizabeth settled into the Royal Lodge in Windsor Great Park. Although he continued to undertake special visits on behalf of his father, George was not involved in any matters of government. On his accession he confessed that he had never seen a state paper and was at a complete loss as to what to do. His strong sense of duty carried him through. He wanted to emphasize the continuity of the monarchy and chose George as his regal name rather than Albert. The coronation already fixed for his brother went ahead as usual, but George simply stepped into his place. To the public it seemed as if George was well prepared, but it had been sheer pluck and determination that carried him through, along with the unstinting support of the queen.

One single affair dominated the world scene in 1937 and that was the growing menace of Nazi Germany. George supported his Prime Minister, Neville Chamberlain, in his policy of appeasement, not wishing to repeat another four years of war, but when all else failed to stop Hitler's intentions, George was also quick to show his support for the oppressed countries. No sooner was war declared on 3 September 1939 than the king broadcast a message to the Empire, encouraging them to show their allegiance. George's relationship with Winston Churchill, who became Prime Minister in May 1940, was initially remote, but they later became firm friends. The king and queen were determined to remain in residence in London, even during the dark period of the Blitz, and they both narrowly escaped with their lives when Buckingham Palace received a direct hit by six bombs in September 1940. The couple visited the worst hit areas in the East End and their genuine concern for the Londoners endeared them to the nation. He initiated the George Cross in 1940 as the highest award for heroism and gallantry shown by civilians, awarding it in 1942 to the island of Malta. The king kept a very public profile throughout the War, visiting factories and military sites, as well as the troops in North Africa in 1943. The victory celebrations on 8 May 1945 outside Buckingham Palace demonstrated just how much the royal family was the centre of Britain's hopes and aspirations.

George's affinity with his subjects made it easier to adapt to the Labour Government, which came to power in 1945 under Clement Attlee, than it had been for his father in 1924, even though he was not in total sympathy with their ideology. He advised caution in their policy of nationalization. The king continued a strenuous round of public duties, including a tour of South Africa and Rhodesia in 1947. 1947 also saw the withdrawal of the British from India and the establishment of the independent nations of India and Pakistan. In 1951 George opened the Festival of Britain, intended as a celebration of postwar Britain like the Great Exhibition of Prince Albert's exactly 100 years before.

The king's health continued to deteriorate. He had an operation for blocked arteries in his legs in 1948, and in September 1951 part of his left lung was removed because of lung cancer. Although he recovered, he died in his sleep in the early hours of 6 February 1952, aged only 56. For the man who did not want to be king he had achieved wonders in restoring the popularity of the monarchy after the abdication crisis and in helping sustain Britain's morale through the dark years of the War. He was a courageous and extremely dutiful king.

ELIZABETH II

Ruled 6 February 1952 to date. Crowned: Westminster Abbey, 2 June 1953.

Full name and titles: *Elizabeth Alexandra Mary, queen of the United Kingdom of Great Britain and Northern Ireland and of her other Realms and Territories; Head of the Commonwealth.*

Born: *17 Bruton Street, London, 21 April 1926.*

Married: *20 November 1947, at Westminster Abbey, Philip (b. 10 June 1921) son of Prince Andrew of Greece and Denmark.*

Elizabeth was the eldest of the two daughters of George VI. She became heir presumptive on the abdication of her uncle Edward VIII in 1936, when she was ten, and thereafter she was groomed for her future role. Her childhood, and that of her sister Margaret, was part of a close-knit family. There were none of the problems or fractures that had marred earlier generations and to the public the royal family became the epitome of family life. The family even remained together at Buckingham Palace throughout the Blitz, though they later moved out to Windsor. It is a sharp contrast to the way the royal family would come to be perceived in the 1980s and 1990s. Elizabeth was determined to play her part in the war effort and, after an initial refusal, her father eventually allowed her to join the ATS (Auxiliary Territorial Service) in 1945, where she learned how to handle and repair all manner of vehicles.

Princess Elizabeth first met her future husband in July 1939 during a visit to Dartmouth Naval College where he was a cadet. He was grandson of George, king of the Hellenes, and, through his mother, great-great grandson of Queen Victoria, and thereby Elizabeth's third cousin. His father had been banished from Greece during a military coup in 1922 and Philip was brought up by his uncle, Lord Mountbatten. Philip served with distinction in the Royal Navy during the Second World War, both with the Mediterranean Fleet and with the British Pacific Fleet in Southeast Asia and the Pacific. He was mentioned in despatches after the battle of Cape Matapan and received many decorations including the Greek War Cross, the Burma Star and the French Croix de Guerre.

When it became clear that Elizabeth and Philip would marry, it was necessary for Philip to renounce his rights to the Greek throne and he became a naturalized British subject as Philip Mountbatten, which was concluded on 28 February 1947. The couple were married on 20 November that year. He was created duke of Edinburgh on the same day. Their first son, Charles, was born on 14 November 1948. Princess Anne was born 15 August 1950, then, after a long gap, came Prince Andrew on 19 February 1960 and Prince Edward on 10 March 1964.

The descent of Elizabeth II from King Arthur

This chart shows the relationship of Elizabeth II to the two historic namesakes of King Arthur, Arthur of Dál Riata and Arthur of Dyfed.

Gábhran of dal Riata (d. 559)	Vortipor (*fl* 515–540)
Aidan mac Gabhran (d. 608)	Cyngar (*fl* 550s)
Eochaid mac Aidan (d. 630)	Pedr (*fl* 570s)
brother of **Arthur** mac Aidan	**Arthur** of Dyfed (*fl* 590s)
Domnall *Brecc* (d. 642)	Nowy (*fl* 610s)
Domangart (d. 673)	
Eochaid (d. 697)	
Eochaid (d. 733)	Sanan = Gwylog (*fl* 700s)
Aed *Find* (d. 778)	Elisedd (*fl* 720s)
Eochaid (d. 781)	Brochfael (*fl* 760s)
Alpin (d. 834)	Cadell (d. 808)
Kenneth macAlpin (d. 858)	Nest = Merfyn *Frych*
Constantine I (d. 820)	Rhodri Mawr (d. 878)
Donald II (d. 900)	Cadell (d. 909)
Malcolm I (d. 954)	Hywel Dda (d. 950)
Kenneth II (d. 995)	Owain (d. 988)
Malcolm II (*c*954–1034)	Einion (d. 984)
Bethoc = Crinan	Cadell (*fl* 1005–18)
Duncan I (*c*1001–40)	Tewdwr
Malcolm III (*c*1031–93)	Rhys (d. 1093)
David I (*c*1084-1153)	Gruffydd (*c*1090–1137)
Henry, earl of Huntingdon (*c*1114–52)	The Lord Rhys (*c*1133–97)
David, earl of Huntingdon (*c*1145–1219)	Gruffydd (d. 1201)
Isabella (1206–*c*1251) = Robert le Brus	Owain (d. 1235)
Robert le Brus, Lord of Annandale (d. 1295)	Maredudd (d. 1265)
Robert Bruce, earl of Carrick (1243–1304)	Owain (d. 1275)
Robert I (1274–1329)	Llywellyn (d. 1309)
Marjorie (*c*1297–1316) = Walter Stewart	Thomas (d. *c*1343)
Robert II (1316–90)	Margaret
Robert III (*c*1337–1406)	Maredudd ap Tudor
James I (1394–1437)	Owen Tudor (*c*1400–61)
James II (1430–60)	Edmund Tudor (*c*1430–56)
James III (1452–88)	Henry VII (1457–1509)
James IV (1473–1513) =	Margaret Tudor (1489–1541)
James V (1512–42)	

Elizabeth II (1926–)

George VI's health deteriorated over the next few years but he felt in sufficiently good health in 1952 for Elizabeth to agree to undertake a world tour. She was at the Treetops Hotel in Kenya when news came of her father's sudden death in February. She returned hurriedly to Britain and was crowned at Westminster Abbey on 2 June 1953. The whole event was televized. The queen was to make much use of television in popularizing the royal family and bringing her closer to the people. Her regular Christmas Day message was televized for the first time in 1957 and in 1969 she agreed to a television film being made about the daily routine of family life which displayed some remarkably rudimentary moments and also demonstrated the sense of humour Elizabeth inherited from her parents.

Elizabeth dedicated much of her time to establishing a closer bond to the Commonwealth of Nations. The independence of India in 1947 had seen the former Empire begin to crumble and its successor Commonwealth had a less clear identity. Elizabeth and the duke of Edinburgh undertook a number of state visits in order to foster stronger relationships. This was always difficult, especially during the 1950s and 1960s when much stronger national identities saw outbreaks of revolution and civil strife in many former colonies around the World. Problems and attitudes in Ghana, South Africa, Rhodesia, Canada and Australia, as examples, showed that Elizabeth's role as head of state was not always readily accepted and often criticized. Prince Philip's comments at the time of the Rhodesia crisis in 1963 caused friction with Parliament, and the prince needed to be reminded of his position. On balance, however, most of the Commonwealth countries respect the queen as a figurehead and recognize her constant efforts in striving to foster goodwill and harmony between fellow nations. It has been a demanding role, and possibly one that at times meant that the queen was becoming slightly removed from her own role towards her British subjects. Nevertheless, the constitutional role of the monarch had become so firmly established that despite a number of major foreign incidents, such as the Suez Crisis, Aden, and even the Falklands War in 1982, when her son Prince Andrew saw active service, they are seen as the responsibility of the government of the day and the queen's role, despite extensive consultation, is not seen by the public as paramount. Yet, despite this lack of association in Britain, other nations may use such events to praise or condemn the queen. This resurfaced in 1997 when the tour of India led to demonstrations seeking an apology from Britain for the massacre at Amritsar in 1919.

It was not until 22 February 1957 that the duke of Edinburgh was granted the title of 'Prince'. This followed a period of anguish when it was confirmed that the royal family would continue to use the surname Windsor, after Elizabeth's father, rather than Mountbatten. The Duke felt marginalized and, even though he respected his secondary role to the queen, he still strove to be recognized in his own right. It was as much Philip's desire as the queen's that the royal family be seen as contemporary and not as a curious British anachronism. He made considerable use of the public relations media and became known for his outspokenness. He also encouraged the children to mix freely with other children, and insisted upon their education at public schools rather than privately at the Palace. The duke initiated the Duke of Edinburgh's Award Scheme in 1956 to encourage young people to tackle a wide range of challenges or experiences.

The queen was admonished by Lord Altrincham in 1957 for being 'out of touch', a charge that has been levied by others in the intervening years despite the many measures the queen has taken to become closer to her subjects. The main problem is that society has moved on, particularly since the 1960s, so if the queen is out of touch, it is only because the monarchy is not designed to follow fashion. If it did it would be criticized for losing its traditional values and the balance between those and being part of society is a difficult one to assess, especially when there is a high level of hypocrisy amongst the media in their dealings with the royal family.

Although there have been scandals galore in all generations about the love life of the monarchy, it has only been in this generation that the queen and her immediate family has had to face censure and vilification from the press and certain factions of the public, even though they have striven to maintain high standards, and certainly far higher than any monarch between Charles I and Victoria. This judgement began in 1955 with the press criticism of the suggested marriage between Princess Margaret and Group Captain Peter Townsend, the queen's equerry, who had been divorced. Margaret followed the teachings of the church and decided not to marry him. In 1960 she married Antony Armstrong-Jones, who became Lord Snowdon in 1961. They had two children, but marital problems began to emerge in the 1960s and the couple were eventually divorced in May 1978. The problems with the marriages of the queen's children were blown out of all proportion by the press. Perhaps the least criticized was Princess Anne, whose charitable work has caused her to be more highly respected, but also because her formidable character means she is well equipped to handle herself in difficult situations. Her marriage to Mark Phillips in 1973 ended in divorce in April 1992, when it was leaked that the Princess had developed an attachment to another former equerry, Timothy Laurence, whom she subsequently married. Prince Andrew's marriage in July 1986 to Sarah Ferguson soon had its difficulties and the couple were separated in March 1992 and divorced in May 1996. Sarah Ferguson's vivacity and extravagance was itself something of a threat to the image of the royal family and she was later criticized for bringing them into disrepute as a consequence of such antics as a royal edition of the popular television programme *It's a Knockout* in 1987. 'Fergie', as she was popularly known, was not seen as acting with due decorum.

The major tragedy was the fairy-tale marriage with the unhappy ending between Prince Charles and Lady Diana Spencer. Charles had come under considerable pressure during the 1970s to marry, and his name had been duly linked to many famous people. His final choice of the twenty-year-old Diana, daughter of the eighth Earl Spencer, met with much enthusiasm, and the royal wedding on 29 July 1981 was a public holiday with street parties and great celebration. However over the ensuing years it became apparent that Diana was ill-suited to the pressure of life as a member of the Royal Family and her relationship with Charles, who became portrayed as an eccentric, 'New Age' prince, began to crack. The couple separated in 1992 and were divorced in August 1996.

The year 1992, with its rapid sequence of divorces and separations, brought a further decline in respect for the royal family, with a wave of support for abolishing the monarchy and establishing a republic. In the autumn of 1992, Windsor Castle was severely damaged by fire and there was increased criticism when it was learned that, because the castle and its priceless contents were not insured, the restoration work would have to be funded from the public purse. In response to the outcry the queen consented to pay income tax, and limited the scope of the Civil List. It was not surprising that in her annual speech at the Guildhall that year, the queen referred to 1992 as her 'annus horribilis'.

The queen and her relatives were not without personal threats and dangers. The most tragic of all was the murder of Lord Mountbatten by the IRA on 28 August 1979. In March 1974 a gunman named Ian Ball fired six shots at Princess Anne in his failed attempt to kidnap her. In June 1981 Marcus Sergeant fired six blanks at the queen while she was riding to the Trooping of the Colour, and in July 1982 there was the famous incident when Michael Fagan succeeding in breaching all security at Buckingham Palace and encountered the queen in her bedroom.

The tragic death of Diana, Princess of Wales in August 1997 saw such an upsurge in public sympathy, that it polarized attitudes between the traditional distant and stoic role of royalty and the apparently open and human approach adopted by Diana. The challenging encomium by Diana's brother Earl Spencer struck a chord with the public at large.

The Golden Jubilee year of 2002, anticipated as one for celebration, was tinged with sadness with the deaths of Princess Margaret and the Queen Mother. This went some way towards re-establishing sympathy and respect for Elizabeth as an individual, even if it has not necessarily resolved the split views towards the monarchy.

The role of the monarchy has become less appreciated than at any other time this century, and respect is given to individuals rather than to the institution as a whole, which many now regard

A Chronology of British Kings, Queens, Emperors and Rulers

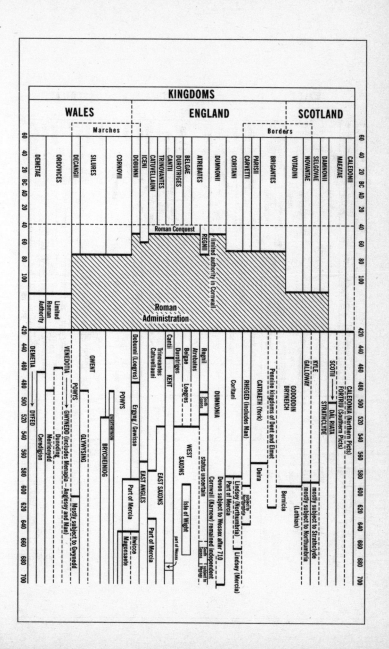

WALES　　　ENGLAND　　　SCOTLAND

700　720　740　760　780　800　820　840　860　880　900　920　940　960　980　1000　1020　1040　1060　1080　1100　1120　1140　1160　1180　1200

SCOTLAND

CALEDONIA (Northern Picts)
FORTRIU (Southern Picts)
DAL RIATA
STRATHCLYDE
(Kyle)
(Galloway)
(Lothian)
(Bernicia)
NORTHUMBRIA
(Deira)
(Rheged)
(Lindsey)
ALBA
Western Isles
Man and the Isles
SCOTLAND
sub-kingdom of Scotland
reclaimed by Scotland but in dispute for 140 yrs
Bernicia
Cumbria - sub-kingdom of Scotland
Earldom of Northumbria
JORVIK
in Danish/Norse hands
part of Earldom of Northumbria
ORKNEY
NORTH
Kingdom of the Isles
Kingdom of Man
SCOTLAND

ENGLAND

South Saxons
KENT
EAST SAXONS (Essex)
MERCIA
Hwicca (subject to Mercia)
WESSEX
KERNOW (Cornwall)
part of MERCIA
subject to Mercia
sub-kingdom of Wessex
part of Mercia
subject to Wessex
Danish kingdom
Earldom of East Anglia
Earldom of Mercia
Edwy crowned
King of the English
ENGLAND

WALES

Dunoding
Meirionydd
CEREDIGION / SEISYLLWG
RHEINWG / SEISYLLWG
RHEINWG / DYFED
CANTREF MAWR
BRYCHEINIOG
POWYS (Northern)
absorbed within Dyfed
GWENT
GLYWYSING
SEISYLLWG
GWYNEDD
BRYCHEINIOG
MORGANNWG
(Gwent)
(Glywysing)
Subject to Gwynedd
DEHEUBARTH
WALES
POWYS
Subject to England
Subject to England
Northern Powys
Southern Powys
Cantref Mawr
Deheubarth
Meirionydd

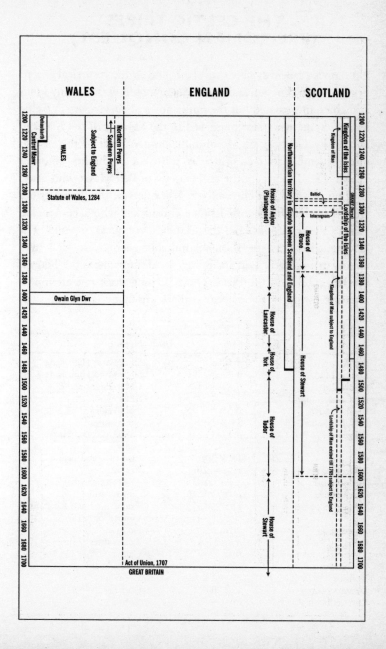

THE CELTIC TRIBES
(PRE-ROMAN CONQUEST)

No names of British kings will be found in the historical record prior to the Roman invasion of 55BC. We know that many kings and chieftains existed but the only names to survive are in Celtic legend. Some were also preserved in the *History of the Kings of Britain* by Geoffrey of Monmouth, though most of this is also more legend than fact. There is sufficient credibility amongst Welsh legend to accept the authenticity of Beli Mawr who is the starting point in this chronology. The rulers of the British tribes were first identified by the Roman chroniclers who accompanied Julius Caesar in 55BC and the Claudian conquest of AD43. The leading tribe was the Catuvellauni, but there were well over twenty tribes in Britain including the Trinovantes, the Silures, the Brigantes and the Picts. The following does not attempt a separate listing by tribe because there are many gaps and overlaps.

Ruler	Born	Reign	Died	Notes
Beli *Mawr*		*fl* 100BC		Silures and High King
Lud or Llud		*fl* 70BC–c60BC		Silures and High King
Caswallon (or Cassivelaunos)		*fl* 60BC–c48BC		Catuvellauni and High King;
Imanuentius		*fl* 55BC		Trinovantes
Mandubracius		54BC–c30BC		Trinovantes
Cingetorix		*fl* 55BC		Cantii; one of four co-rulers
Commius	c80BC	c50BC–c20BC		Atrebates and Belgae
Addedomaros		c30BC–c20BC		Trinovantes
Tincommius		c20BC–cAD5		Atrebates and Belgae
Tasciovanus		c20BC–cAD10		Catuvellauni
Dumnovellaunos		c20BC–cAD5		Trinovantes and Coritani; Cantii from c15BC
Antedrigos		c10BC		Dobunni
Diras		*fl* AD 1		Trinovantes
Vosenos		*fl* AD 5		Cantii
Andocomius		c5–c15		Catuvellauni
Volisios		c5–c20		Coritani
Dumnocoveros		c5–c20		Coritani
Cartivel(launos)		c5–c20		Coritani

Eppillus	c5–c10		Atrebates and Belgae; deposed but ruled the Cantii from c10–c25
Epatticus	fl 10		Atrebates and Belgae; deposed.
Verica (or Bericos)	c10–40		Atrebates and Belgae
Cunobelin (or Cymbeline)	c10–41		Catuvellauni; Trinovantes from c1 High King
Amminius	c25–c40		Cantii; deposed
Antedios	c25		Iceni
Togodumnus (or Teneuvan)	41–43		Catuvellauni
Caratacus	c40–51	c54	Cantii c40–43 then Catuvellauni; exiled in Rome High King
Cartimandua	43–69		Brigantes
Venutius	69–72		Brigantes
Arviragus (or Gweirydd)	fl 44–74	c74	Silures High King
Prasutagus	47–59	59	Iceni
Boudica (or Boadicea)	59–61	61	Iceni
Cogidubnus	43–75		Regnii
Marius	c74–c125	c125	Silures High King
Calgacus	fl 80		Caledonii
Coel (I)	fl c125–c150		Silures
Lleirwg Mawr or Lucius	fl c150–c180		Silures High King
Argentocoxos	fl 208		Caledonii. May be father of Ciniod of the Picts

THE ROMAN OCCUPATION
(AD43–AD410)

All Roman emperors whose authority extended to Britain
are listed. Very few visited Britain, and even fewer had any
interest in the island. This also covers all the governors who
were appointed directly by Rome and vested with imperial
authority. These were not hereditary monarchs. All existing
Celtic kingdoms became forfeit upon Roman occupation,
though Claudius and his successors allowed some client
kings to remain. These were soon abandoned and descendants
of the tribal nobility were treated as senior administrators
within the states or civitas established in Britain. Only in the

northernmost parts of Britain did the Celtic tribes remain independent.

ROMAN EMPERORS

Ruler	Born	Reign	Died	Notes
Claudius	10BC	41–54	54	probably poisoned
Nero	37	54–68	68	committed suicide
Galba	3BC	68–69	69	murdered after 7 months
Otho	AD32	Jan–Apr 69	69	committed suicide after 3 months
Vitellius	15?	Apr–Dec 69	69	murdered after 8 months
Vespasian	9	69–79	79	
Titus	39	79–81	81	
Domitian	51	81–96	96	murdered
Nerva	30	96–98	98	
Trajan	53	98–117	117	
Hadrian	76	117–138	138	
Antoninus Pius	86	138–161	161	
Marcus Aurelius	121	161–180	180	ruled jointly with Lucius Verus
Lucius Verus	130	161–169	169	ruled jointly with above
Commodus	161	180–192	192	murdered
Pertinax	126	Jan–Mar 193	193	murdered after 3 months
Didius Julianus	133	Mar–Jun 193	193	murdered after 66 days
Decimus Clodius Albinus		193–197	197	committed suicide
Pescennius Niger		193–194	194	murdered after a battle
Septimius Severus	145	193–211	211	
Caracalla	188	211–217	217	ruled with his brother; murdered
Geta	189	Feb–Dec 211	211	ruled with Caracalla; murdered
Macrinus	164	217–218	218	murdered
Elagabalus	203	218–222	222	murdered
Severus Alexander	208	222–235	235	murdered
Maximinus	172	235–238	238	murdered
Gordianus (I)	158	Jan 238	238	committed suicide after 20 days
Gordianus (II)	c192	Jan 238	238	ruled jointly with father; murdered
Pupienus	c164	Feb–May 238	238	ruled jointly with Balbinus; murdered
Balbinus		Feb–May 238	238	ruled jointly with Pupienus; murdered
Gordianus III	224	238–244	244	murdered
Philippus	c204	244–249	249	killed in battle

Decius	c190	249–251	251	killed in battle
Trebonianus Gallus	c206	251–253	253	murdered
Aemilius Aemilianus	c207	Aug–Oct 253	253	murdered after 88 days
Valerianus	c195	253–260	after 260	died in captivity
Gallienus	c213	253–268	268	emperor in the west; murdered

Valerianus and his son Gallienus split the empire between them with Gallienus ruling the West. Gallienus subsequently faced an uprising from Marcus Cassianus Postumus, governor of Lower Germany, who declared a separate Gallic Empire in 260. This covered all of the Roman empire west of the Rhine, including Britain. It shrank to cover only Gaul and Britain by 269 and was eventually reabsorbed into the Roman Empire in 274 under Aurelianus.

Gallic Empire

Postumus	260–269	269	murdered
Laelianus	Feb–Apr 269	269	usurper; killed in battle (?)
Aurelius Marius	Apr–Jul 269	269	murdered
Victorinus	269–271	271	murdered
Tetricus	271–274		abdicated authority back to Rome

Roman Empire *restored*

Aurelianus	214	270–275	275	murdered
Tacitus	c200	275–276	276	murdered after eight months
Florianus		Jul–Sep 276	276	murdered after 88 days
Probus	232	276–282	282	murdered
Carus	c224	282–283	283	purportedly killed by lightning!
Carinus	c250	283–285	285	emperor in the west; murdered
Diocletian	245	284–305	311	retired

Although Diocletian remained the senior emperor he divided the Empire into two in 286 (East and West) delegating authority in the west to Maximian.

Maximian	c250	286–305	310	retired; tried to regain the imperial throne and was killed

During Maximian's reign Britain declared independence under Carausius and Allectus.

Carausius		286–293	293	murdered
Allectus		293–295	296	deposed
Constantius (I) Chlorus (the Pale)	c250	305–306	306	emperor in the west
Severus (II)		306–307	307	emperor in the west; forced to abdicate then killed
Constantine (I)	272	306–337	337	declared emperor in Britain

Constantine was declared emperor in Britain before he was acknowledged as Augustus in the west in 307; he shared this with Licinius from 308 to 311, but thereafter Licinius gradually overpowered others to become emperor in the east. Constantine subsequently defeated and killed Licinius and from 324 was sole emperor.

Constantine II		337–340	340	emperor of Britain, Gaul and Spain; killed in battle
Constans		340–350	350	ruled Italy and eastern Europe until 340, then ruled all Europe; murdered
Magnentius		350–353	353	killed in battle
Constantius II		353–361	361	had been emperor in the east since 337
Julian *the Apostate*		360–363	363	died of battle wounds

Julian was appointed Caesar in the West from 355.

Jovian		363–364	364	accidentally gassed to death
Valentinian (I)		364–375	375	emperor in the west
Gratian	359	375–383	383	killed in battle

Britain declared its own emperor in 383 with Magnus Maximus.

Magnus Maximus[b]	c300	383–388	388	Britain and Gaul; killed in battle
Valentinian II	370	388–392	392	killed; nominal co-emperor with Gratian from 375
Eugenius		392–394	394	killed in battle

After Eugenius's death Rome was briefly united under the eastern emperor Theodosius who died a few months later.

| Honorius | 384 | 395–423 | 423 | |

Stilicho was effectively ruler of Rome during Honorius' minority until his death in 408. The Western empire began to crumble and Britain declared several claimants to the throne:

Marcus		406	406	murdered
Gratian		407	407	deposed and murdered
Constantine (III)		407–411	411	legitimized emperor in 408

In AD410, Honorius withdrew his support from Britain leaving the island to defend itself. Thereafter Britain was no longer part of the Roman Empire.

ROMAN GOVERNORS OF BRITAIN

Ruler	Born	Reign	Died	Notes
Aulus Plautius		43–47		
Publius Ostorius Scapula		47–52		
Aulus Didius Gallus		52–57		
Quintus Veranius Nepos		57–59		

Gaius Suetonius Paulinus		59–61		
Publius Petronius Turpilianus		61–63		
Marcus Trebellius Maximus		63–69		
Marcus Vettius Bolanus		69–71		
Quintus Petillius Cerialis		71–74		
Sextus Julius Frontinus	c40	74–78	103	
Gnaeus Julius Agricola	37	78–85	93	
Sallustius Lucullus		85–c94	c94	executed
Publius Metilius Nepos		c95–c98		
Titus Avidius Quietus		c98–c101		
Lucius Neratius Marcellus		101–103		
Publius Pomponius Mammiliaus		103–109		
Marcus Appius Bradua		?115–118		first term?
Quintus Pompeius Falco		118–122		
Aulus Platorius Nepos		122–126		
Marcus Appius Bradua		126–129		
Sextus Julius Severus		129–133		
Publius Mummius Sisenna		133–138		
Quintus Lollius Urbicus		138–144		
Gnaeus Papirius Aelianus		144–155		
Gnaeus Julius Verus		155–158		
Longus or Longinus		?158–160?		name incomplete
Marcus Statius Priscus		160–161		
Sextus Calpurnius Agricola		161–166		
Caerellius Priscus		166–170		period uncertain
Lucius Ulpius Marcellus		170–174		first term
Quintus Antistius Adventus		174–177		period uncertain

Lucius Ulpius Marcellus		177–184		second term
Publius Helvius Pertinax	126	185–192	193	declared emperor
Decimus Clodius Albinus		192–197		declared emperor
Virius Lupus		197–202		
Marcus Antius Calpurnianus		202–203		acting governor only
Gaius Valerius Pudens		203–205		
Lucius Alfenus Senecio		205–211?		

Hereafter the province of Britannia was divided into Britannia Superior in the south, with its capital at London, and Britannia Inferior in the north with its capital at York.

Britannia Superior

Gaius Junius Faustinus	?211–222?
Titus Julius	?223–226
Pollienus Auspex Rufinus	?
Marcus Martiannius Pulcher	?
Titus Desticius Juba	c255–260

Britannia Inferior

Gaius Julius Marcus	?211–213?	probably executed
Marcus Antonius Gordianus	?215–218?	became emperor Gordinus I
Modius Julius	?218–219?	
Tiberius Claudius Paulinus	220	
Marius Valerianus	221–223?	
Claudius Xenephon	223	
Maximus	?224–225	
Claudius Apellinus	*between 222–235*	
Calvisius Rufus	*between 222–235*	
Valerius Crescens Fulvianus	*between 222–235*	
Tuccianus	?236–237?	
Maecilius Fuscus	*between 238–244*	
Egnatius Lucilianus	*between 238–244*	
Nonius Philippus	?241–242?	
Octavius Sabinus	*between 260–269*	

From 270 onwards records of Roman governors become sparse, whilst other information suggests that Britain was claiming increasingly greater independence. Over the next few years we see a succession of Romans who declared themselves as emperors within Britain, some moving on to claim the purple in Rome, others failing disastrously.

Governors and Vicarii

Britain was restored to the Empire after Allectus and a new governor installed. The administration was further complicated however by the creation of separate civil and military governors few of whose names are recorded. Britain was divided into four provinces, each with a provincial governor. The following are the few known remaining provincial governors who seemed to exercise control over parts of Britain.

Aurelius Arpagius	296–305	governor of Britannia Secunda
Flavius Sanctus	c350s	
Lucius Septimius	c360s	probably governor of Britannia Prima

There are no records of other governors and by 383 Magnus Maximus had declared himself emperor in Britain. For the remaining thirty years of Roman administration Britain become increasingly more independent.

THE BRITISH KINGDOMS (410–920)

NORTHERN BRITAIN
(from Yorkshire to the Clyde)

As Britain emerged from the Roman Empire it fell to the leading noblemen and generals to maintain law and order. A number of leaders began to establish themselves in various corners of Britain The first were along the northern frontier, where Coel the Old carved out a kingdom ruled by 'the Men of the North'. Their domain stretched from the northernmost Roman wall (that of Antoninus Pius) down to what is now Yorkshire. After Coel's death his kingdom was split between his descendants and it rapidly sub-divided, weakening the realm. The kingdoms were gradually reduced by the Saxons, although the British kingdom of Strathclyde (see p. 449) survived much longer as a unit. It is difficult to be clear about who ruled which kingdom so the following covers all the known Men of the North in as close chronological sequence as possible along with their likely territories.

Ruler	Born	Reign	Died	Notes
Coel *Hen* ('Old King Cole')	c380	c410–c430	c430	all of northern Britain
Tutagual		fl 400–c420s		Galloway and Kyle
Garbaniawn or Germanianus		c430s–c450s		southern Votadini (Bryneich)
Cunedda		c420–c450		northern Votadini (Gododdin); moved to North Wales
Ceneu or Cenen (also Keneu)		fl 450s–470s	c470s	Rheged and Catraeth (equal to Cumbria and York)
Ceretic		fl 450s–470s		Strathclyde
Lewdwn or Leudonus		fl 470s–490s		northern Votadini
Gurgust		fl 480s–500s	c500s	Rheged
Bran *Hen* (*the Old*)		fl 500s		Votadini (may be Gododdin and Bryneich)
Pabo or Pappo		fl 500s–c530	c530	central Yorkshire
Morcant *Bulc*		fl 510s–540s		Votadini
Cathen		fl 510s–540s		Galloway and Kyle
Merchiaun *Gul*		fl 510s–540s	c540s	Rheged
Eleuther or Elidyr		fl 530s–550s	c550s	Catraeth and York; murdered
Ceidiaw or Keidyaw		fl 540s–550s		Galloway or Rheged?
Rhun		fl 550s–560s		Galloway and Kyle; lost kingdom to rulers of Rheged
Outigern		fl 540s–550s		Votadini
Gwrgi or Gurci		fl 550s–580	580	Catraeth/York; killed in battle
Peredur		fl 550s–580	580	Catraeth/York; killed in battle
Elidyr		fl 540s–c560	c560	Rheged; killed on a raid
Cinmarc or Kynmarch		fl 560s–c570	c570	Rheged
Cinbelin or Kynvelin		fl 540s–570s		northern Votadini
Gwenddolau		fl 560s–570s	573	Galloway; killed in battle
Clinog or Clydno *Eitin*		fl 560s–580s		northern Votadini
Morcant		fl 580s–590s		Votadini?

Urien or Urbeg	c540	c570–c590	c590	Rheged
Gwallawg		fl 570s–590s	c595	Elmet; though this name may also apply to a ruler of Galloway and the Clyde
Dunaut		fl 570s–595	595	central Yorkshire
Owain		c590–c595	c595	Rheged
Llywarch *Hen*		c560–595	640	retired to Powys
Mynyddog or Mynydawc		580s–595		northern Votadini
Rhun		fl 600s	c630	Rheged; retired to the priesthood
Ceredig		c595–625	c625	Elmet; expelled
Rhoeth		fl 620s		Rheged

SOUTHERN BRITAIN
(England south of Yorkshire)

Southern Britain, the part which romantic legend has called Loegres, must also have divided into its former tribal status after the Roman departure, but it was less evident than in the north, where the defences were strongest against the Picts, Irish and Saxons. Southern Britain retained, to a degree, the heart of the former Roman administration and it is possible to see that there was an attempt, at least for a while, to maintain a more cohesive administration amongst the southern tribes probably based at the heart of the wealthiest Roman centres around Cirencester and Gloucester, where the tribes of the Dobunni, Silures and Cornovii mingled. It was probably from here that the primary leaders of southern Britain emerged in what would later be the British kingdoms of Gwent, Powys and the Gewisse. The following list is a close approximation of the high kings during the immediate post-Roman period before new kingdoms began to establish themselves. The Welsh Triads identify the first high king as Owain, though his existence is not otherwise recorded. The dates used are those most commonly associated with the rulers, but are in themselves dubious.

Ruler	Reign	Died	Notes
Owain	c411–c425	425	existence dubious
Vortigern (or Vitalinus)	c425–c466	c466	deposed 455–460; restored but deposed again and probably murdered

Vortimer (or Natalinus)	c466–c471	c471	poisoned or killed in battle
May be the same king as Natanleod			
Vortigern (*restored*)	c471–c480	c480	could be a different ruler using the same title of Vortigern; would have ruled in opposition to Ambrosius Aurelianus
Ambrosius Aurelianus	c466–c496	c496	
Tradition lists Uther Pendragon as the successor of Ambrosius but his existence is uncertain. Brychan was also High King at this time.			
Arthur	c496–c537	c537	
Constantine of Dumnonia	fl 530s	c540	
Hereafter the role of senior king passed to Maelgwyn of Gwynedd and continued in Wales.			

THE SOUTH-EAST AND SOUTH-WEST

The south-east was the first area to be dominated by the Saxons, especially Kent and Sussex. Within a century after Roman rule the British in what became England were forced further west into either Wales or Dumnonia (Devon and Cornwall), which became known as the West Welsh (the word Welsh being derived from the Saxon for foreigner). The Dumnonian king list is one of the hardest to reconcile. It is complicated by legend, the connection between its own kings and those in south Wales, and its relationship to Brittany in France, as some kings ruled both kingdoms. The British Dumnonia originally covered Cornwall, Devon, Dorset and Somerset, though by 710, only Cornwall (Kernow) remained. The post-Roman kings of Dumnonia may have been descended from the Cornovii who migrated from Wales in the early fifth century. There were probably several cases of kings ruling at the same time, and the following list is only indicative and not definitive.

Ruler	Reign	Died	Notes
Cantii (Kent)			
Gwyrangon	fl 450		
Dobunni (Severn Valley)			
This may also be the territory of the High Kings listed immediately above.			
Aurelius Caninus	fl 530		
Coinmail, Farinmail and Condidan	fl 577		defeated at Dyrham

Dumnonia

Cynan map Eudaf (Octavius)	fl 420s		
Gadeon map Cynan	fl 450s		
Docco	fl 470s	c473	
Gwrwawr map Gadeon	fl 480s		
Tudvawl map Gwrwawr	fl 500s		
Custennyn (Constantine) map Tudvawl	fl 530s	c540	
Erbin map Custennyn	fl 540s		
Geraint map Erbin	fl 550s		killed in battle
Hoel or Riwal	fl 550s–570s		also king in Brittany
Cunomor or Mark	fl 550s–570s		
Drust or Tristan	fl 570s		
Cador map Geraint	fl 580s		
Peredur map Cador	fl 600s		
Tewdwr or Theudo map Peredur	fl 620s		

Kingship at this point uncertain

Judhael	fl 650s		
Erbin	fl 690s		
Geraint	fl 700s	710	killed in battle

After 710 Dumnonia (except for Cornwall) was under the control of Wessex.

Kernow (Cornwall)

Kings of Cornwall between Geraint and Doniert are not known.

Doniert or Dungarth	fl 870s	875	drowned
Ricatus	fl 900?		
Hoel	fl 920s		
Cynan or Conan	fl 930s		

Probably the last native ruler of Cornwall, though his descendants survived as ealdormen, having probably married into local Saxon families. Cador (fl 1066) was one such and his son, Cadoc, had a daughter who married Henry I's illegitimate son Reginald, who became the first earl of Cornwall. Hereafter the kingdom became part of the Norman earldom of Cornwall.

THE SAXON KINGDOMS (455–933)

The Saxons began to settle in Britain in the second quarter of the fifth century. The *Anglo-Saxon Chronicle* proclaims the descent of all of the kings from Odin, but it is likely that many of the ancestral names are genuine. The earliest Saxon kingdom was in Kent, but elsewhere other roving bands of warriors gradually carved out territory for themselves, particularly in Wessex and Northumbria. The following are in order of the establishment of each kingdom. Some kingdoms, especially Mercia, had sub-kingdoms which, for a brief period, held a degree of autonomy.

KENT (455–933)

Kent was settled by the Jutes, who also settled on the Isle of Wight, although the two kingdoms are seldom linked or associated. Although the kingdom's origins are lost in legend, Kent was the first substantially independent kingdom to emerge and the first to introduce Christianity to the English. Kent was often ruled by two kings, one for East Kent and one for West Kent – divided by the river Medway.

Ruler	Born	Reign	Died	Notes
Hengest	c420	455?–?488	?488	
Oeric, Oisc (or Aesc)		?488–c516	c516	killed in battle (Badon?)
Octha		516–c40	c540	
Eormenric		c540–c80	c580	
Athelbert (I)	c552	c580–616	616	
Eadbald	c582	616–40	640	
Eorcenbert	c624	640–64	664	
Egbert (I)	c641	664–73	673	
Hlothhere	c644	673–85	685	killed in battle
Eadric	c663	685–6	686	killed during conquest by Caedwalla
Caedwalla of Wessex		686–7	688	Kent conquered by Wessex
Mul		686–7	687	burned to death
Sigehere of Essex		687–8	688	king of Essex
Oswine		688–90	?	
Swaefheard or Sweafred		689–692	c707	later king of Essex
Wihtred	c670	691–725	725	
Athelbert II		725–48		ruled jointly with Eadbert,
		c754–62	762	then retired; returned after Eardwulf's death
Eadbert (I)	c697	725–c62	c762	ruled with Athelbert II and then Eardwulf
Ealric		725– ?	?	ruled jointly with step-brothers

Eardwulf	c730	c748–54	754?	ruled jointly with father Eadbert
Sigered		759–63	after 778	
Ealhmund		762–4	784	deposed and later restored
Heaberht		764–c71	771?	
Egbert II		764–c84	c784	
Ealhmund (restored)		c784–c785	785	restored but then killed
Eadbert II Praen		796–8	after 811	deposed and imprisoned
Cuthred (of Mercia)		798–807		

Kent was ruled directly by Cenwulf and Ceolwulf of Mercia from 807 to 823.

Baldred		823–5	

Hereafter the kings of Kent were sub-kings to Wessex, a title usually offered to the heir presumptive.

Athelwolf	825–39	858
Athelstan	839–52?	852?
Athelbert	855–60	865

The title seems to have ceased after Athelbert, during the Danish wars, but was briefly restored for the son of Edward the Elder:

Edwin	c902	c920–33	933	drowned

ISLE OF WIGHT (534–687)

Although the *Anglo-Saxon Chronicles* would suggest Wight was occupied by the West Saxons it was, in fact, more closely associated with the Jutes who also occupied Kent. The full record of its kings does not survive.

Ruler	Reign	Died	Notes
Stuf	534– ?		joint rulers
Wihtgar	534–44?		joint rulers

The ruling house uncertain for the next century.

Arwald	? –687	687	killed by Caedwalla of Wessex

Wight thereafter came under Saxon rule. Part of the island was given to Beornwine, nephew of Wilfrid, the former Bishop of York, in order to convert the islanders to Christianity.

SOUTH SAXONS (491–791)

The original Saxon settlement was based around Pevensey and was contained on the north by the vast forest of the Weald. The first named rulers of the South Saxons were invading warlords who did not establish a kingdom. The kingdom of Sussex did not emerge until the early seventh century and the record of its first kings has not survived.

Ruler	Reign	Died	Notes
Aelle	491–c516	c516	killed in battle (Badon?)
Cissa	491–c516	c516	killed in battle (Badon?)
No further rulers are known between c516 and c660, when the kingdom became subject to Mercia.			
Athelwalh	c660–c85	685	killed in battle
Berthun	685–6	686	killed in battle
Overrun by Wessex; later kings are poorly documented and were all client kings of Wessex or Mercia.			
Nothhelm or Nunna	c692–c725	c725	
Wattus	fl 692		
Athelstan	fl 714		
Athelbert	c725–c50		possibly also ruler of Kent
Osmund	c758–c72		
After Osmund the status of kingship was demoted to the equivalent of duke.			
Oswald	fl 772		
Oslac	fl 772		
Ealdwulf	765–c91		may have ruled with Elfwald after 772
Elfwald	c772– ?		ruled with Ealdwulf
Hereafter the kings were relegated to 'dukes' and the kingdom became part of Mercia, and subsequently Wessex.			

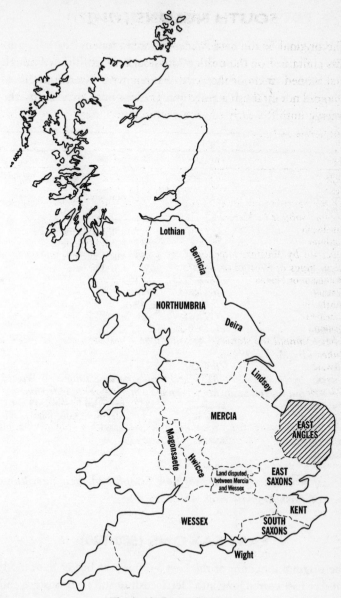

The Anglo-Saxon Kingdoms

EAST ANGLIA (571–799)

The kingdom of the East Angles covered modern Norfolk, Suffolk, and parts of Cambridgeshire and Bedfordshire. Although this kingdom acknowledged the sovereignty of Mercia at different times it remained fiercely independent until overrun by the Danes.

Ruler	Born	Reign	Died	Notes
Uffa		571–c8		
Tytila		c578–c99		
Redwald		c599–c625	c625	
Eorpwald		c625–c32	c632	murdered
Ricbert		c632–c34		
Sigebert		c634–c38	c641	retired to a monastery; killed in battle
Egric		c638–c41	c641	killed in battle
Anna		c641–c53	c653	killed in battle
Athelhere		c653–5	655	killed in battle
Athelwold		655–c63	c663	
Ealdwulf		c663–c713	c713	
Alfwald		c713–c49	c749	
Beonna		c749–c61		
Athelred		c761–90		
Athelbert		790–4	794	beheaded

Overrun by Mercia 794–6.

Eadwald		c796–c9?		

Overrun by Mercia c799–823? Technically became subject to Wessex after 829 but the following kings retained a high degree of independence.

Athelstan		c823–37	?852	may also have ruled Kent
Athelweard		837–50?		may have ruled jointly with below
Beorhtric		852–4		
Edmund	c841	854–69	869	killed in battle
Oswald		c870		

Hereafter colonized by Danes who established their own kingdom of East Anglia (see p. 439).

EAST SAXONS (580–820)

The original kingdom of the East Saxons was bigger than modern-day Essex stretching into Hertfordshire and Bedfordshire and even into parts of Middlesex and Berkshire. London was part of the kingdom. The East Saxons were initially subordinate to Kent, but subsequently gained their independence and for a brief period ruled Kent, before becoming subject to Mercia and later Wessex. Aescwine is usually identified as their first king, but he was in all probability a governor imposed by Eormenric or Athelbert of Kent.

Ruler	Reign	Died	Notes
Sledda	c580s–c600		
Saebert	c600–c616		
Sexred	c616–23	623	killed in battle
Saeward	c616–23	623	killed in battle
Saexbald	c616–23	623	killed in battle
Sigebert (I) *Parvus* (*the Little*)	623–c50		
Sigebert II *Sanctus* (*the Good*)	c650–c3	c653	murdered
Swithhelm	c653–63	663	
Sigehere	663–88	688	also king of Kent
Sebbi	663–c93	693	abdicated and retired to a monastery
Sigeheard	693–c707		
Swaefred or Swaefheard	693–c707		earlier king of Kent
Offa	707–9	c710	abdicated and became a monk
Saelred	709?–46	746	
Swebert	709–38	738	
Swithred	746–59		
Sigeric	759–98		
Sigered	798–825		

Thereafter Essex became part of the kingdom of Wessex.

MERCIA (585–919)
(including Hwicce, Lindsey and the Magonsæte)

Mercia was one of the three major kingdoms of Anglo-Saxon England. Its kings were Angles. Its earliest rulers almost certainly ruled a much smaller territory around Tamworth and Lichfield. At its greatest extent Mercia covered all central England south of the Humber and north of the Thames, and held authority over territories south of the Thames, especially Sussex and Kent. Its ruler Offa was the greatest of all English kings before Alfred the Great.

Ruler	Born	Reign	Died	Notes
Creoda or Crida		c585–c93		see also Critta of Lindsey
Pybba		c593–c606		
Ceorl		c606–c26		
Penda	c604	c626–55	655	may have shared rule for a period; killed in battle
Eowa		c635–42	642	co-ruler and possible rival claimant
Peada	c629	c653–6	656	murdered

Peada was sub-king of the Middle Angles and briefly sub-king of Southern Mercia after 655, Oswy of Northumbria held authority over Mercia between 655 and 658.

Ruler	Born	Reign	Died	Notes
Wulfhere	c640	658–75	675	
Athelred	c642	675–704	716	abdicated and retired to a monastery
Cenred		704–9		abdicated and went to Rome as a monk
Ceolred		709–16		died of madness (or possibly poisoned)
Athelbald		716–57	757	murdered by his own soldiers
Beornred		757		
Offa		757–96	796	
Egfrith		Jul–Dec 796	796	ruled jointly with his father from 782
Cenwulf		796–821	821	
Ceolwulf (I)		821–3		deposed
Beornwulf		823–6	826	killed during a revolt
Ludeca		826–7	827	killed during a revolt
Wiglaf		827–9		expelled by Egbert of Mercia
		830–9	839	regained the kingdom
Wigmund		c839–40?	840	may have been only sub-king
Beorhtwulf		840–52		
Burgred		852–74?		expelled and retired to Rome
Ceolwulf II		874–c83	c883	

Hereafter Mercia came under the control of Wessex. Alfred established the title of 'Lord of the Mercians' whose holders ruled with sub-regnal authority.

Ruler	Born	Reign	Died	Notes
Athelred		c883–911	911	
Athelflaed	c869	911–18	918	
Elfwynn	c898	918–19?		deprived of her lands

In 919 Edward the Elder of Wessex took control of Mercia. He installed his son Athelstan as king of Mercia in 924, but after his brother's death, Athelstan united Mercia and Wessex (see p. 439).

HWICCE

Although a Mercian sub-kingdom, roughly equivalent to the territory of Worcestershire, Hwicce seems to have been a much venerated territory. Its boundaries were roughly equal to the territory of the Dobunni at the Roman conquest, and was almost certainly the heartland of the British revival after the end of Roman authority and the home of Ambrosius Aurelianus and possibly Arthur. It may thus have held much greater historical and even religious significance in the seventh century than is remembered today.

Ruler	Reign	Died	Notes
Eanfrith	650s?–c74		
Eanhere	c674–5?		
Osric	c675–c85		
Oswald	c685–c90		
Oshere	c679–c99		
Athelbert	fl 700		
Athelweard	fl 710		
Athelric	fl 720		
Osred	fl 730s		
Eanbert	fl 759		brothers who ruled jointly
Uhtred	fl 759		brothers who ruled jointly
Ealdred	c759–c90		brothers who ruled jointly

Thereafter Hwicce came directly under Mercian rule.

LINDSEY

Roughly equivalent to Lincolnshire, the territory of the Coritani at the time of the Roman conquest. This kingdom is one of the least well documented and only the genealogy of Aldfrith provides any details on the Lindsey royal family. We cannot assume that all of his ancestors were kings and we do not know for certain their dates. Lindsey may once have been an independent kingdom, possibly Celtic, but it was subject to Northumbria from c620–58 (though may have been relatively independent from 642–51), to Mercia from c658–c75, to Northumbria c675–9, and Mercia again from 679, whereafter its kings were reduced in authority to 'dukes' or ealdormen.

Ruler	Reign	Died	Notes
Critta or Crida	fl 580s		may be same as first ruler of Mercia
Cueldgils	fl 600?		
Caedbaed	fl 625?		
Bubba	fl 650?		
Beda	fl 675?		
Biscop	fl 700?		

Eanfrith	*fl* 725?	
Eatta	*fl* 750?	
Aldfrith	*fl* 775?	

MAGONSÆTE

Roughly equivalent to northern Herefordshire and southern Shrop-shire, the territory of the Cornovii at the Roman conquest. The Magonsœte thus shared some of the territory of the Welsh Powys and certainly Ergyng. It is possible that the territory was once the homeland of the Gewisse, from whom some of the West Saxon kings were descended.

Ruler	Born	Reign	Died	Notes
Merewalh	*c*625	*c*650–685		
Merchhelm		685–?700		
Mildfrith		*fl* 700s		

The kingdom was probably overrun by Powys (see p. 473) around the year 710.

OTHER MERCIAN SUB-KINGDOMS

Ruler	Reign	Died	Notes
Chilterns			
Dida	*c*670–5		
Surrey			
Frithuwold	673–*c*5		

His son Frithuric may also have ruled briefly as a client king.

NORTHUMBRIA
(including BERNICIA and DEIRA) (557–913)

Some of the first Angles to reach Britain settled in Deira, in the lands south of the Tyne, and subsequently overran the British kingdom of Bernicia between the Tyne and the Tweed. Although the two kingdoms were united as Northumbria, the rivalries remained fierce throughout Northumbria's existence. At its greatest extent Northumbria stretched as far as the Forth and across all of northern England, absorbing Rheged, Strathclyde and Galloway.

Ruler	Born	Reign	Died	Notes
Bernicia				
Ida		c557–c69	c569	tradition cites reign as 547–59
Glappa or Clappa		c569–c574		
Adda		574?–81?		
Frithuwulf or Freothulf		c573–80?		
Theodulf		573?–74?		
Hussa		c580–c7		
Theodoric		584?–91?		
Athelric		587?–93?		killed in battle
Athelfrith		593–604		

In 604 Athelfrith drove Edwin of Deira into exile and united the two kingdoms.

Deira				
Aelle		569?–99?	599?	tradition cites reign as 559–89
Athelric		c599–c604	604?	murdered?

Northumbria				
Athelfrith		604–16	616	killed in battle
Edwin or Eadwine	c585	616–33?	633?	killed in battle
kingdom briefly split				
Eanfrith		633?–5?	635?	ruled Bernicia, killed
Osric of Deira		633?–4?	634?	killed in battle
kingdom reunited				
Oswald	c605	635?–42	642	killed in battle
Oswy	c611	642–70	670	
during Oswy's reign there were several sub-kings (●) of Deira				
● Oswine		643–51	651	murdered
● Athelwald		651–5	655?	killed in battle or fled
● Alfrith	c635	654–64?	?	killed, exiled or died of plague?
Egfrith	c645	664–85	685	king of Northumbria from 670; killed in battle
● Elfwine	661	670–9	679	sub-king of Deira; killed in battle
Aldfrith	c640	685–704	705	
Eadwulf		704–5	?	expelled after two months
Osred (I)	c696	705–16	716	murdered or killed in battle
Cenred		716–18	718	possibly murdered
Osric	c698?	718–29	729	slain
Ceolwulf		729–37	764	deposed and restored in 731; later retired to a monastery
Eadbert		737–58	768	abdicated to enter the church
Oswulf		758–9	759	murdered
Athelwold *Moll*		759–65	?	deposed

Alred	765–74	?	deposed
Athelred (I)	774–9		deposed and later restored
Elfwald (I)	779–88	788	murdered
Osred II	788–90	792	deposed
Athelred (I) restored	790–6	796	murdered
Osbald	Mar–Apr 796	799	deposed and later became a monk
Eardwulf	796–806		driven into exile
Elfwald II	806–8		deposed
Eardwulf restored	808–11	811	
Eanred	811–43	843	
Athelred II	843–9	849	briefly deposed in 844; restored but later murdered
Redwulf	c844	c844	killed in a Viking raid
Osbert	849–66	867	expelled; killed in the Viking invasion
Aelle (II)	862–7	867	initially ruled jointly with Osbert; killed in the Viking invasion

During Aelle's reign the Vikings settled in Northumbria establishing their kingdom at York (Jorvik) (see p. 438) which corresponded with Deira. The kingdom of Bernicia remained in Saxon hands though it was subservient to Danish overlords.

Bernicia

Egbert (I)	867–72	873	expelled
Ricsig	872–6	876?	
Egbert II	876–88?	?	may have been ejected by Scots
Eadulf or Eadwulf	888?–913	913	

After Eadulf's death the earldom of Bamburgh remained in his family's hands until 1041. The earls were Ealdred (913–30), Uhtred (930–49), Oswulf (949–63), Eadulf Evilcild (963–94), Waltheof (994–5), Uhtred II (995–1016), Eadulf Cudel (1016–19), Ealdred II (1019–38), Eadulf (1038–41). Thereafter it was absorbed into the earldom of Northumbria.

Dunbar or Lothian

After Oswy's death the Picts rebelled against the Northumbrian overlordship. Egfrith established an hereditary sub-kingdom in Lothian, similar to one of the Welsh Marcher lords.

Beornheth	670–85	685	killed in battle
Beorhtred	685–98	698	killed in battle
Beorhtfrith	698–after 711		

WEST SAXONS – Gewisse and Wessex (538–899)

It was not until the late seventh century that Wessex began to take on a unified shape. The West Saxons were a number of tribes who conquered territory across the south of Britain. The main concentration was in Wiltshire and Hampshire, but there was another core of settlers along the Berkshire Downs. There was considerable rivalry first with the British and then the Mercians for territory in Gloucestershire and the Severn valley. Later the West Saxons began to push further west into Somerset and Dorset. With territory fragmented and covering such a spread of ground there would have been several kings at any one time, not necessarily related, though later genealogists sought to contain them in a single family tree. In fact the West Saxons were a confederacy of tribes and adopted the name Gewisse, which means confederate but which originally related to a British tribe or tribes in the area known as Ergyng or Archenfield. It was not until the reign of Ine that these tribes became united. Under Egbert they would become the dominant kingdom, and the West Saxon dynasty became the rulers of England. This section traces these rulers down to the time of Alfred the Great and the Danish invasion.

Ruler	Born	Reign	Died	Notes
Cerdic		538?–54?	554?	
Cynric		554?–81?	581?	
Ceawlin		581?–8?	589?	ruled with Cutha; deposed
Cutha		fl 570s–80s		sub-king of the Gewisse
Ceol		588–94	594	
Ceolwulf		594–611	611	
Cynegils		611–43	643	ruled with Cwichelm
Cwichelm		c614–c36		sub-king of the West Saxons
Cenwealh		643–72	672	in exile 645–8
Cuthred I		645–8	661	Cuthred served as vassal king under Penda
Seaxburh (Queen)		672–3		the only recorded Saxon queen

Wessex was fragmented amongst many sub-kings during the period 672–82. These included Cenfus, Cenred and Baldred at the outset plus the following three kings in later years and almost certainly other claimants.

Aescwine		674–6	676	
Centwine		676–85	?	abdicated and became a monk
Caedwalla	c659	685–687	688	also ruled Kent and Sussex; died on pilgrimage in Rome
Ine		688–726	728	abdicated and retired to Rome
Athelheard		726–40	740	
Cuthred II		740–56	756	
Sigebert		756–7		expelled and murdered
Cynewulf		757–786	786	murdered
Beorhtric		786–802	802	
Egbert	771?	802–39	839	became bretwalda in 829
Athelwolf	c795	839–55	858	retired
Athelbald	c831	855–60	860	
Athelbert	c833	860–5	865	also sub-king of Kent
Athelred (I)	c837	865–71	871	died as a result of wounds in battle
Alfred (the Great)	849	871–99	899	

By the time of Alfred the West Saxons had imposed their authority over the rest of England, but the nation had again become riven by the Danish invasions and the fight for Britain began. *(continued on p. 440)*

THE DANISH KINGDOMS (866–954)

JORVIK (YORK)

Jorvik, the Danish kingdom of York, was essentially the same as the old Saxon kingdom of Deira in Northumbria. From 910 the kingdom was taken over by the Danish kings of Dublin.

Ruler	Born	Reign	Died	Notes
Ivarr *the Boneless*		866–73	873	also king of Dublin
Halfdan Ragnarson		873–7	877	also king of Dublin; killed in battle
Kingdom ruled from Bernicia				
Gothfrith		883–95	895	
Sigfrid		895–c9	c899	
Canute	c899–c900		c900	assassinated
Athelwold		899–902	902	killed in battle
Halfdan (II)		?902–10	910	co-ruler with Eowils; killed in battle
Eowils		?902–10	910	co-ruler with Halfdan; killed in battle

York was taken over by the expelled Danish kings of Dublin, some of whom later became joint rulers.

Ragnall		910–*c*21	*c*921	also ruled Man
Sitric *Caech*		921–7	927	previously king of Dublin

Kingdom conquered by Athelstan of Wessex and ruled by him till 939.

Erik *Bloodaxe*	*c*885	939?		this period as Athelstan's sub-king is spurious; restored in 947.
Olaf or Anlaf Gothfrithson	*c*919	939–41	941	also king of Dublin and of Danish Mercia ('the Five Boroughs')
Olaf or Anlaf Sitricson *Cuaran*	*c*920	941–3 949–52	981	also king of Dublin; expelled; expelled again; returned to Dublin.
Ragnall (II) Gothfrithson	*c*921	943–5	945	killed in battle

York back under control of kings of Wessex, 945–8.

Erik *Bloodaxe*	*c*885	947–8		expelled
		952–4	954	restored; expelled again and slain

Kingdom regained by the English.

DANISH EAST ANGLIA

This kingdom covered the same territory as the old kingdom of the Angles. The territory was awarded to Guthrum as part of the peace settlement with Alfred the Great.

Ruler	Reign	Died	Notes
Guthrum (baptized Athelstan)	879–90	890	
Eohric or Yorrik	890–902		
Guthrum II	902–16		

THE SAXON & DANISH KINGDOMS (899–1066)

The English and Normans (900–1284)

Although Alfred the Great held the Danes at bay and stopped a total conquest of England, they were granted land in East Anglia and Danish settlements rapidly grew. A foothold had been established. Danish and Norse raids continued and they were eventually victorious in 1013 when the English capitulated to Swein Forkbeard. After his death his son Canute became one of the great rulers of northern Europe. Even though Canute's sons were unable to sustain the scale of his empire, it was not the last England saw of the Northmen. Another branch of the ancient royal family, related to the earls of Orkney, had settled in Normandy, and their leader, William the Bastard, conquered England in 1066. The Northmen were ultimately victorious and drove the Saxons into serfdom. It was this generation of Northmen, William's sons and grandsons, that not only conquered England but dominated Wales and Scotland. Although Scotland was not quite conquered, Edward I died believing it was within his grasp, just like Wales, which he had dominated and absorbed into England in 1284. By the reign of Edward I Britain was fast becoming a united kingdom with the English king recognized as the soverign lord. This section covers the English kings from Alfred the Great to Edward I.

Ruler	Born	Reign	Died	Notes
Edward *the Elder*	*c*871	899–924	924	
Elfweard	*c*904	924	924	ruled only 16 days
Athelstan	*c*895	924–39	939	

Athelstan was the first true king of the English, and was acknowledged as overlord by the Welsh princes. He also defeated the Scots and Norse in 937.

Edmund I	*c*921	939–46	946	killed trying to stop a brawl
Eadred	*c*923	946–55	955	died after a long illness

From Eadred on, the kings are justifiably called kings of the English.

Edwy or Eadwig *the Fair*	*c*941	955–9	959	
Edgar	*c*943	959–75	975	king of Mercia from 957

Edgar was the first king to be crowned king of the English in 973.

Edward *the Martyr*	*c*962	975–8	978	murdered
Athelred II *the Unready*	*c*968	978–1013	1016	
Regent: Alfhere		978–83	983	ealdorman of Mercia

In 1013 the Danelaw submitted to Swein, king of Denmark.

Swein *Forkbeard*	*c*960	1013–14	1014	

Saxon rule restored.

Athelred II *the Unready*	c968	1014–16	1016	
Edmund II *Ironside*	c989	1016	1016	died of wounds received in battle, or possibly murdered

Danish rule restored.

Canute or Cnut	c995	1016–35	1035	also king of Denmark and Norway
Harold (I) *Harefoot*	c1016	1035–40	1040	made regent in 1035 but seized the kingdom in 1037
Harthacanute	c1018	1035–42	1042	in Denmark from 1035; deposed 1037; restored 1040 died of a fit or poisoned

Saxon rule restored.

Edward *the Confessor*	c1004	1042–66	1066	
Harold (II)	c1022	1066	1066	killed at the battle of Hastings
Edgar *the Atheling*	c1052	1066	1125	submitted to William the Conqueror

THE ENGLISH KINGDOMS

The House of Normandy (1066–1603)

William of Normandy gained the throne of England by conquest. The Saxon royal family was overthrown and a new regime, not simply a new dynasty, was imposed which changed England forever.

Ruler	Born	Reign	Died	Notes
William (I) *the Conqueror*	c1027	1066–87	1087	William II of Normandy
William II *Rufus*	c1057	1087–1100	1100	killed in a hunting accident; possibly murdered
Henry I	c1068	1100–35	1135	
Stephen	c1097	1135–54	1154	briefly deposed Apr–Nov 1141
Eustace	c1131	1152–3	1153	crowned by his father but never acknowledged
Matilda	1102	Apr–Nov 1141	1167	not crowned

The House of Anjou,
commonly known as Plantagenet (1154–1399)

Henry II	1133	1154–89	1189	
Henry (III) *the Young King*	1155	1170–83	1183	crowned as Henry's successor
Richard I *Lionheart*	1157	1189–99	1199	
John *Lackland*	1167	1199–1216	1216	
Henry III	1207	1216–72	1272	minority until Jan 1227

Regents during minority: William Marshal (1216–19) Hubert de Burgh (1219–27)

Edward I	1239	1272–1307	1307	
Edward II	1284	1307–27	1327	deposed and later murdered
Edward III	1312	1327–77	1377	assumed direct authority from October 1330
Richard II	1367	1377–99	1400	deposed and possibly murdered

House of Lancaster (1300–1461; 1470–1)

Henry IV *Bolingbroke*	1367?	1399–1413	1413	
Henry V	1387	1413–22	1422	
Henry VI	1421	1422–61		declared of age November 1437; deposed March 1461
(restored)		1470–1	1471	restored October 1470; deposed again April 1471; murdered

Protector during minority: John, duke of Bedford 1422–29.

House of York (1461–70; 1471–85)

Edward IV	1442	1461–70		deposed October 1470;
(restored)		1471–83	1483	restored April 1471
Edward V	1470	Apr–Jun 1483	1483	deposed; one of the Princes in the Tower
Richard III *Crookback*	1452	1483–85	1485	killed in battle

House of Tudor (1485–1603)

Henry VII	1457	1485–1509	1509	
Henry VIII	1491	1509–47	1547	
Edward VI	1537	1547–53	1553	

Protector during minority: Edward Seymour, earl of Hertford, 1547–9.

Jane	1537	10–19 Jul 1553 1554	deposed after nine days; executed
Mary (I)	1516	1553–8	1558
Elizabeth (I)	1533	1558–1603	1603

ENGLAND AND SCOTLAND

House of Stewart (1604–49; 1660–1714)

| James (I) | 1566 | 1603–25 | 1625 | James VI of Scotland |
| Charles (I) | 1600 | 1625–49 | 1649 | deposed and executed |

Commonwealth declared 19 May 1649 under rule of a Lord Protector.

| Oliver Cromwell | 1599 | 1653–8 | 1658 | |
| Richard Cromwell | 1626 | 1658–9 | 1712 | abdicated |

Commonwealth nullified May 1659; monarchy restored May 1660.

| Charles II | 1630 | 1660–85 | 1685 | |
| James II | 1633 | 1685–8 | 1701 | abdicated |

Interregnum 11 Dec 1688–12 Feb 1689 when government assumed by the Peers.

| William III | 1650 | 1689–1702 | 1702 | joint ruler with Mary II |
| Mary II | 1662 | 1689–94 | 1694 | joint ruler with William III |

GREAT BRITAIN
after Act of Union 1 May 1707

| Anne | 1665 | 1702–14 | 1714 |

House of Hanover (1714–1901)

George I	1660	1714–27	1727
George II	1683	1727–60	1760
George III	1738	1760–1820	1820

From 5 Feb 1811 the prince of Wales (future George IV) became 'Prince Regent'.

George IV	1762	1820–30	1830
William IV	1765	1830–7	1837
Victoria	1819	1837–1901	1901

House of Saxe-Coburg-Gotha,
(changed to Windsor from 1917) (1901–)

Edward VII	1841	1901–10	1910
George V	1865	1910–36	1936
Edward VIII	1894	Jan–Dec 1936	1972 abdicated
George VI	1895	1936–52	1952
Elizabeth II	1926	1952–	

THE PICTS AND SCOTS
(Pre-Roman–847)

PICTS

Pict is a generic name created by the Romans for the tribes of the northern most part of Britain. They were from an older wave of Celtic settlers, and not the same as the Belgic tribes of southern Britain who had moved across from the continent in the first or seventh century BC. The early history of the Picts is lost in legend. The king-lists usually start with a legendary ancestor called Cruithne. He and his sons came from Ireland and settled in Alba (Scotland) probably in the seventh century BC. The various provinces of Scotland are named after his seven sons. These, with their later names, were Círech (Angus and Mearns), Fótla (Atholl and Gowrie), Fortriu (Strathearn and Menteith), Fíobh (Fife), Cé (Mar and Buchan), Moireabh (Moray) and Cat (Caithness). Cat remained in Scotland whilst his brothers went to France. It was from Cat that the line of Pictish high-kings descends. Another legend states that Gub, king of the Picts, was banished from Ireland and his son, Cathluan (who is probably the same as Cat), became the first high-king of the Picts. The king-lists vary, and it is highly probable that some of the kings ruled concurrently in different provinces rather than in succession. The Picts were not a single unit. Over time two strong divisions emerged. The Southern Picts or Maetae (where the kingdom became called Fortrenn or Fortriu) based around Forteviot, and the Northern Picts, or Caledonii, with their capital at Inverness. The following list contains rulers from both territories, and begins with the first semi-historical rulers.

Ruler	Reign	Died	Notes
Legendary or Semi-historical rulers			
Gede or Gilgidi	reigned 50 years		son of Cathluan
Tharan or Tarain	reigned 100 years		
Merleo	reigned 15 years		not present in all lists
Deocillimon or Duchil	reigned 40 years		
Ciniod mac Artcois	reigned 7 years		not in all lists
Deort or Duordegel	reigned either 50 or 20 years		
Blieblith	reigned 5 years		*fl. c*220BC
Deototreic or Tethothrect	reigned 40 years		
Conbust or Usconbust	reigned 20 years		
Crautreic or Karanochrect	reigned 40 years		
Deordiuois	reigned 20 years		not in all lists
Uist	reigned 30 years		not in all lists
Caruorst	reigned 40 years		not in all lists
Gartnait *Bolgh*	reigned either 4 or 9 years		*fl. c*AD165

One list suggests that after Gartnait Bolgh had reigned 4 years he was succeeded by four further kings, each called Gartnait, who reigned for 9 years in total.

Breth or Brude mac Muthut[b]	reigned 7 years		*fl. c*AD170
Vipoig Namet also called Poponeuet or Vipoguenech	reigned 30 years		
Fiachu or Fyahor *Albus*	reigned 30 years		

Some lists merge the previous two kings into one king who reigned for 30 years.

Canatumel or Canutulachama	reigned 6 years		some lists say reigned 5 years or 1 year; also called Tonaculmel
Donarmahl or Douernach *Uetalec*	reigned 2 years		
Feradach or Feodak *Finlegh*	reigned 2 years		probably same as king called Wradechuecla
Gartnait or Gauiach Diuberr	c335		reigned 40 or 60 years
Talorc map Achiuir	reigned 25 years		also called Balarg

Historical rulers

Drust	424–53		
Talorc	453–7		
Nechtan *Morbet*	457–68		
Drest *Gurthinmoch*	468–98		
Galanan (or Galam I) *Erilich*	498–513		see also Caw of Strathclyde
Drest	513–33		deposed between 521–9
Drest	513–29		ruled jointly with above
Gartnait	533–40		
Cailtram	533–41		
Talorg	541–52		
Drest	552–3		
Cennalath (or Galam II)	553–7	579	
Brude (I)	556–84	584	possibly killed in battle
Gartnait	584–602		
Nechtan (II)	602–21	621	
Cinioch or Ciniath	621–31		
Gartnait	631–5		
Brude (II)	635–41		
Talorc	641–53		
Talorcen	653–7		
Gartnait	657–63		
Drust	663–72		expelled
Brude (III)	672–93		
Taran	693–7		expelled
Brude (IV)	697–706		
Nechtan (III)	706–24	732	abdicated
Drust	724–6	729	driven out; killed in battle
Alpin	726–8	736	driven out; became king of Dál Riata in 733; possibly killed
Nechtan (III) (*restored*)	728–9	732	
Angus (Oengus)	729–61	761	King of Dál Riata from 736
Brude (V)	761–3	763	
Ciniod	763–75	775	
Alpin	775–9		
Talorgen or Talorcen	779–81	781	
Drust	780–2		
Talorcen	782–5		
Conall	785–9	807	deposed; became King of Dál Riata in 805
Constantine	789–820	820	King of Dál Riata from 811
Angus or Oengus II	820–34	834	also king of Dál Riata
Drust	834–7		ruled jointly with Talorc
Talorc	834–7		ruled jointly with Drust VIII
Eoganan (or Ewen)	*c*837–9	839	king of Dál Riata killed in battle
Ferat or Uurad	839–42		
Brude (VI)	842	842	

Kineth	842–3		
Brude (VII)	843–5		
Drust	845–7	847	killed in battle

Thereafter the Southern Picts were absorbed into the kingdom of Alba under Kenneth macAlpin. For a period the Viking Thorstein established a kingdom in the northern Pict territory of Caithness and Sutherland. It is likely that a Pictish kingdom continued in the north in Moray.

DÁL RIATA SCOTS

The original 'Scots' were the Irish who came from the Dál Riatan homeland in northern Ireland and settled in Argyll. They gradually took over most of Argyll, Galloway and the southern Hebrides until the Viking invasions pushed them inland to conquer the kingdom of the Picts. The Scots developed a genealogy taking their pedigree back to 330BC, based on their Irish ancestry. These earlier kings almost certainly existed but probably as no more than chieftains amongst the Scottish islands and coastal fringes.

Ruler	Born	Reign	Died	Notes
Fergus (I) *Mor (the Great)*	c440	c498–501	501	
Domangart		501–7	507	
Comgall		507–38	538	
Gabhrán		538–58	558	
Conall		558–74	574	
Aedán	c533	574–608	608	first king to be anointed
Eochaid *Buide*	c583	608–29	629	
Connad *Cerr*		629	629	killed in battle after reign of 3 months
Domnall *Brecc*		629–42	642	killed in battle
Ferchar		637–50	650	shared kingdom with Domnall
Dúnchad		650–4	654	killed in battle
Conall *Crandomna*		650–60	660	ruled jointly with Dúnchad
Domangart (II)		660–73	673	
Maelduin		673–88	688	
Domnall Donn		688–95		killed (in battle?)
Ferchar *Fota* of Loarn		695–7	697	usurped the throne
Eochaid (II)		697	697	murdered after a brief reign
Ainbcellach of Loarn		697–8	719	usurper; expelled within a year.

Fiannamail	698–700	700	killed in battle
Selbach of Loarn	700–23	730	abdicated in favour of his son
Dúngal	723–26	after 736	expelled
Eochaid (III)	726–33	733	
Alpin	733–6	736	king of the Picts; possibly killed
Muiredach	733–6	736	
Eogan	736–9		
Angus or Oengus (I)	736–50	761	king of the Picts
Aed *Find* (*the Fair*)	750–78	778	
Fergus mac Eochaid	778–81	781	
Donncorci	?781–91	791	possibly shared kingdom
Domnall	781–805		possibly shared kingdom
Eochaid (IV) *the Poisonous*	781– ?		possibly shared kingdom
Conall mac Tarl'a (or Tagd)	805–7	807	king of the Picts killed in battle
Conall mac Aedán	807–11		
Constantine	811–20	820	king of the Picts
Angus (II)	820–34	834	king of the Picts
Aed mac Boanta	834–9		
Alpin	834	834	sub-king of Galloway; killed in battle
Eoganan (or Uen)	c837–839	839	king of the Picts killed in battle

With the death of Eoganan, Kenneth macAlpin would unite the Picts and the Scots and the infant kingdom of Scotland (at first known as Alba) would emerge (see p. 449).

STRATHCLYDE (c.450–890)

This kingdom was based on the British tribal division of the Damnonii around Alclud, or Dumbarton. At its greatest extent it included Kyle, Galloway and northern Rheged.

Ruler	Reign	Died	Notes
Ceretic or Coroticus	fl 450s–70s		

After Ceretic's death the kingdom was subdivided between his sons and grandsons.

Erbin	fl 470s–80s		probably inherited Alclud and Galloway

Cinuit	fl 470s–80s		probably Manau Gododdin
Geraint	fl 480s–90s		probably Alclud
Tutagual	fl 490s–500s		probably Galloway and Kyle
Caw map Geraint	fl c490s		abdicated; may be same as Galam of Picts
Dyfnwal or Dumnagual (I) Hen	fl 510s–30s		initially Manau, but reunited Strathclyde
Clydno or Clinoch	fl 530s–40s		probably Alclud and Manau
Tutagual	c559–80		reunited Strathclyde
Rhydderch Hen (the Old)	c580–612	612	may have ruled as early as 560
Nechtan	612–21	621	
Bili (I)	621–33		
Owen or Eugene (I)	633–c45		
Gwraid or Gureit	c645–58		
Dumnagual (II) or Dyfnwal	658–94		
Bili II	694–722		
Teudebur	722–52		
Dumnagual (II) or Dyfnwal	752–60		
Owen or Eugene (II)	760–c80		
Rhydderch II	fl 790s		
Cynan	? –816	816	
Dumnagual (IV)	816– ?		
Artgal	? –872		
Rhun	872–?7		
Eochaid	?877–89	?890	also king of Alba; deposed

Hereafter Strathclyde was merged with the kingdom of the Scots. It was initially ruled by Donald II but, under Constantine, Strathclyde became a sub-kingdom governed by a member of the royal family, usually the heir.

THE SCOTTISH KINGDOMS (908–1130)

STRATHCLYDE and CUMBRIA (908–1045)

In 889 the once British kingdom of Strathclyde was merged with the kingdom of the Scots. It retained a degree of autonomy and it later became the practice that the heir to the Scottish throne was made king or prince of Strathclyde. This practice was not always

consistent and there remained a few rulers of Strathclyde who
were not subsequently elevated to the Scottish throne.

Ruler	Born	Reign	Died	Notes
Donald mac Aed		908–c25	934	retired
Owen *Caesarius*		c925–37	937	probably killed in battle
Probably ruled directly by the Scottish kings Constantine and Malcolm, 937–45.				
Donald mac Donald		937–45	?	deposed and blinded
Indulf		945–54	962	became king of the Scots 954
Dub or Duff		954–62	966	became king of the Scots 962
Donald mac Owen		962–73	975	abdicated in favour of his son
Malcolm mac Donald		973–97	997	
Malcolm mac Kenneth	c954	990–5		deposed
(*restored*)		997–1005	1034	became Malcolm II of Scotland
Owen *the Bald*		1005–18	1018?	
Duncan		c1018–34	1040	became king of Scotland 1034
Malcolm mac Duncan	c1031	1034–58	1093	became Malcolm III of Scotland
Maldred mac Duncan	c1003	1034–45	1045	Regent; probably killed in battle

*When Malcolm inherited the Scottish throne Strathclyde was fully
integrated into his kingdom. Malcolm seems to have styled his
son Edmund as prince of Cumbria, though his cousin's son
Dolfin was earl of Cumberland before 1092 when he was
expelled by William II of England, and Cumbria was taken from
Scotland.*

SCOTLAND (840–1298)

In 848 Kenneth macAlpin united the kingdoms of the Picts and
the Scots which later became known as Scotland. At this stage the
kingdom was centred at Forteviot in southern Scotland and
Kenneth and his successors held little authority over the Highlands which were still dominated by the Cenél Loarn and the Picts

who later emerged as the separate 'kingdom' of Moray. Further north the Vikings settled in Orkney and their authority spilled over into Caithness.

It was centuries before Scotland became united. Only in 1265 did Norway cede the sovereignty of the Western Isles and Man to Scotland and, though the earldom of Orkney passed into the hands of a Scottish family it remained Norwegian territory for another two centuries. It was ironic, therefore, that at the time that Scotland began to feel it had control over its affairs, Alexander III should die with only an infant successor and her death left the country with a succession crisis. The country fell into the hands of the English king Edward I. This section therefore follows the Scottish kingship through from the creation of Alba under Kenneth macAlpin to its fight for freedom at the time of John Balliol and William Wallace.

The House of Alpin

Ruler	Born	Reign	Died	Notes
Kenneth (I) macAlpin		840–58	858	
Donald (I)		858–63	863	murdered or killed in battle
Constantine (I)		863–77	877	killed in battle
Olaf *the White*		866–71	872	also king of Dublin; overlord of Picts and Scots
Aed		877–78	878	killed in battle
Giric		878–89	?	deposed; ruled jointly with Eochaid
Eochaid		878–89	889	also king of Strathclyde; deposed

Hereafter the kingdoms of the Picts, Dál Riata and Strathclyde were united under one monarch, the first to be honoured as **king of Scotland***.*

Ruler	Born	Reign	Died	Notes
Donald II		889–900	900	killed in battle
Constantine II		900–43	952	abdicated to become a monk
Malcolm (I)		943–54	954	killed in battle
Indulf		954–62	962	abdicated to become a monk; slain by Vikings soon after
Duff or Dub		962–*c*66	*c*966	driven into exile and slain
Cuilean *Ring* (or Colin)		*c*967–71	971	killed in battle
Kenneth II		971–95	995	murdered

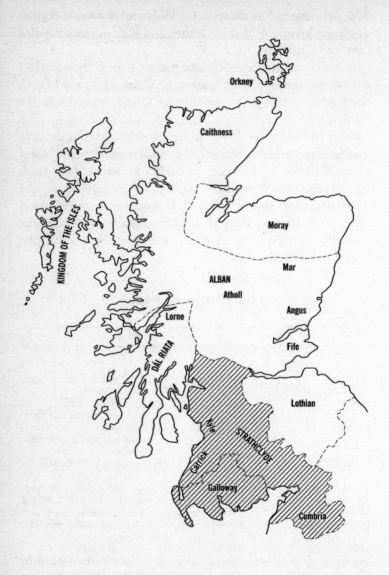

Scotland 500–1200

Name	Born	Reign	Died	Notes
Olaf		971–7	977	rival claimant; killed in battle
Constantine III the Bald		995–7	997	killed in battle
Kenneth III		997–1005	1005	killed in battle
Giric II		997–1005	1005	sub-king ruled with above; killed in battle
Malcolm II	c954	1005–34	1034	
Duncan	c1001	1034–40	1040	murdered
Macbeth	c1005	1040–57	1057	killed in battle
Lulach the Fool	c1031	1057–8	1058	killed in battle
Malcolm III Canmore (Bighead)	c1031	1058–93	1093	killed in an ambush
Donald III Bane	c1033	1093–4		deposed, but later restored
Duncan II	c1060	May–Nov 1094	1094	killed in battle
Donald III Bane (restored)	c1033	1094–7	1099	ruled northern Scotland; deposed again, blinded and imprisoned
Edmund		1094–7	?	ruled southern Scotland; deposed and retired to a monastery
Edgar	c1074	1097–1107	1107	
Alexander (I) the Fierce	c1077	1107–24	1124	
David (I) the Saint	c1084	1124–53	1153	
Malcolm IV the Maiden	1141	1153–65	1165	
William (I) the Lyon	c1143	1165–1214	1214	William submitted to English under Henry II from 1174–1189.
Alexander II the Peaceful	1198	1214–49	1249	
Alexander III the Glorious	1241	1249–86	1286	killed in riding accident
Margaret, Maid of Norway	1283	1286–90	1290	died at sea

Interregnum from 26 Sep 1290–17 Nov 1292 during which Edward I served as overlord.

Name	Born	Reign	Died	Notes
John (Balliol)	c1250	1292–6	1313	abdicated

Second interregnum from 10 Jul 1296–25 Mar 1306 during which period Edward I claimed the throne. The kingdom was governed by several regents and for a while wrested from the English by William Wallace.

Name	Born	Reign	Died	Notes
William Wallace	c1274	1297–8	1305	Governor: briefly held control

The year after William Wallace's death Robert the Bruce would lay claim to the throne of Scotland and began a new chapter in the country's history. This is continued on page 461.

MORAY (980–1130)

One of seven sub-kingdoms of the Picts. By the ninth century it was ruled by a *mórmaer*, or earl, who was sometimes referred to as a king. The Cenél Loarn, a collateral dynasty of the kings of Dál Riata who believed they had equal right to the kingship, had migrated along the Great Glen away from the Viking raids. At the head of the dynasty were the descendants of Ainbcellach who joined with the northern Picts in opposing the Scottish kingdom established by Kenneth macAlpin in the 840s. Usually referred to in the chronicles as the 'men of Moray' this kingdom remained almost autonomous for three centuries and two of its rulers, Macbeth and Lulach, also ruled Scotland. The full list of rulers is not known. A Maelbrigte is mentioned as having been killed by Sigurd I of Orkney in 892, whilst a Donnchad mac Morgain was involved in a raid in Northern Ireland in 976. The following is incomplete and covers only the rulers after Donnchad mac Morgain.

Ruler	Born	Reign	Died	Notes
Ruairaidh or Rory		*fl* 980s		
Ruairaidh may have been succeeded by his elder son Maelbrigte.				
Findlaech or Finlay		990?–1020	1020	murdered?
Malcolm macMaelbrigte		1020–29		
Gillecomgain		1029–32	1032	murdered
Macbeth	*c*1005	1032–57	1057	killed in battle
Lulach	*c*1031	1057–8	1058	killed in battle
Mael Snechta	*c*1051/2	1058–78	1085	deposed; retired to a monastery
Aed or Heth		1078– ?	?	ancestry unknown; married Mael Snechta's sister
Angus mac Heth	*c*1080	? –1130	1130	killed in battle

After 1130 Moray was formally absorbed into Scotland although factions continued to rebel including Malcolm macHeth (whose ancestry is much disputed but may have been Angus's brother or son but who is also believed to be related to Alexander I), who was the earl of Ross and was defeated and imprisoned in 1134 and not released until 1157. Malcolm's great-grandson, Kenneth, belonged to the last generation of rebels, being defeated in 1215. The MacHeths were the ancestors of the Clan Mackay.

THE DANISH and NORSE KINGDOMS
(560–1471)

Danish and Norse raids began in Britain at the end of the eighth century but it was fifty years before they established their own kingdoms. This included lands in Ireland (the kingdom of Dublin) and Normandy. Some kingdoms grew out of existing Scottish or English kingdoms as identified below.

WESTERN ISLES – HEBRIDES and THE ISLE OF MAN (560–1265)

The Hebrides and the Isle of Man formed a kingdom known as the Western Isles to the Scots and the Southern Isles (or Sudreys) to the Norse. Identifying sovereignty over them is complicated. The islands were occupied by both the Irish and British during the various waves of invasion around the first centuries BC and AD. Legend attributes names to four early Celtic rulers of Man who may have some basis in fact – Dalboeth, Elathan, Alladh or Athas and Manannán. Manannán's name is most closely associated with the island. During the fifth century Man came under the control of the rulers of Rheged. It was conquered by Edwin of Northumbria in 620, but its rulership remained with the descendents of Llywarch Hen until it passed briefly to Wales and was then conquered by the Danes.

Ruler	Born	Reign	Died	Notes
Llywarch Hen		c560–95		
Man was conquered by Báetán mac Cairill of Ireland in 577 and then by Aedán mac Gabhrán of Dál Riata in 582. It may have remained under Scottish domination until conquered by Edwin of Northumbria in 620.				
Diwg		fl 600s		
Gwyar		fl 630s		Man overrun by Edwin of Northumbria

Tegid	fl 670s		
Algwn	fl 700s		
Sandde	fl 730s		
Elidr	fl 760s		
Gwriad	fl 800s		

Gwriad's son, Merfyn Frych, became king of Gwynedd and Man in 825, but Man soon slipped out of his hands. By the 830s the Western Isles were being settled by Vikings and the Hiberno-Norse Gael-Gaedhil.

Godred mac Fergus	fl 836–53	853	lord of the Hebrides
Ketil *Flatnose* or Caitill *Find*	c853–c66	c870	

Olaf the White of Norway who became king of Dublin in 853 brought a degree of control to the Hebrides and Man and established his own jarls over the islands. Ketil Flatnose was the first, though he ruled more like a king. Others were Tryggvi (in the 870s) and Asbjorn Skerjablesi in the 880s. Asbjorn was slain by the children of Ketil Flatnose in around 899 and thereafter Man and the Western Isles were disputed between the Norwegian kings of Dublin and the Danish kings of York, until Ragnall established his authority across the North.

Ragnall of York	c914–c21	c921	

Ruled by kings of Dublin and York, 920–940, who appointed sub-kings to the Isles. The only ones known are:

Gebeachan or Gibhleachán	? –937	937	killed in battle
Mac Ragnall	?937–42	942	killed

Probably came under authority of Olaf Sitricson of Dublin until 972 or so.

Magnus Haraldsson	c972–7	977	killed
Godred Haraldsson	977–89	989	killed in battle
Ragnald Godredson	fl 1000	1005	
Kenneth Godredson	1005– ?		
Swein	? –1034	1034	

Authority on the Western Isles was imposed by Sigurd the Stout of Orkney from 989–1014, but was regained by the kings of Dublin under Sitric Olafson from 1014–35. During this period Ragnald's brother Kenneth and Kenneth's son Swein continued to claim the title of king of Man until Swein's death in 1034. Thorfinn the Mighty of Orkney reconquered the Isles around 1038 and demanded tribute from Man if not directly administering it. Man and the Isles continued to be governed from Dublin subject to Orkney until soon after 1065.

Margad Ragnallson of Dublin	1052–c61	1065	deposed
Murchaid mac Diarmit of Dublin	1061–70	?	former king of Dublin
Fingal Godredsson	1070–9		ejected by Godred Crovan

With the arrival of Godred Crovan the formal kingdom of Man and the Isles was created.

Man and the Isles

Godred *Crovan*	?1040	1079–95	1095	also king of Dublin
Lagman		1095–9	?1111	deposed; later went to Jerusalem
Sigurd (I of Norway)	c1089	1099–1103	1130	

Sigurd was installed as king of Orkney and the Southern Isles by his father Magnus III of Norway.

Domnall mac Teige		1103–14?	1115	expelled and later killed
Olaf (I) *the Red*	?1085	?1114–53	1153	murdered
Godred II *the Black*		1153–58		expelled by Somerled

In 1156 Somerled established the separate lordship of the Isles, and he ruled the full kingdom of Man and the Isles from 1158–64. Thereafter Man included the Outer Hebrides under its jurisdiction until 1266.

Godred II (restored)		1164–87	1187	
Ragnald		1164	1164	usurper, overthrown after 4 days
Ragnald (I)		1187–1226	1229	killed in battle
Olaf II *the Black*	1177	1226–37	1237	
Godred *Donn* (the Brown-Haired)		1230	1230	shared kingdom; slain
Harald (I)	1223	1237–48	1248	shipwrecked and drowned
Ragnald II		6–30 May 1249	1249	murdered
Harald II		1249–50		deposed
Ivar		1250–2		
Magnus		1252–65	1265	submitted to Alexander III in 1264

Alexander III governed Man via a bailiff after 1265 until the island was seized by Edward I of England in 1290. There was a brief rebellion in September 1275 when Magnus's son, Godred, seized the island and was declared prince by the Manxmen, but Alexander's forces soon quelled the uprising.

KINGS OF THE ISLES (1164–1545)

This kingdom was created by Somerled from the kingdom of Man and the Isles. It consisted of the eight island groupings centred on Mull and Islay. The holders were variously known as king or lord of the Isles.

Ruler	Born	Reign	Died	Notes
Somerled	c1105	1156–64	1164	murdered

After Somerled's death the kingdom was divided amongst three of his sons. The kingdom of the Isles was vested in his second son, Ragnald of Islay, but each son and grandson could style himself as king and often did. The following details the senior claimants only, who were the descendants of Ragnald and his brother Dugald.

Ruler	Born	Reign	Died	Notes
Ragnald		1164–c1210	c1210	
Dugald		1164–c92	c1192	lord of Lorne and Argyll
Donald (I)		c1210–30	1247?	
Duncan Mac Dougall	c1170	c1210–c47	c1247	
Dugald *Screech*	c1210–35?		1235?	joint claimant with Duncan
Uspak or Gillespie	1230		1230	died of wounds
Ewen Mac Dougall		c1248–66	c1270	strictly only held kingship 1247–9, but continued as vassal to Alexander III
Dugald Mac Ruari (MacRory)	1249–66		1268	was appointed by Norse king over Ewen

Ewen submitted to Alexander III and his lands passed to the Scottish crown. Alexander later invested the titled Lord of the Isles in the MacDonald family, who held it for the next two hundred years.

Ruler	Born	Reign	Died	Notes
Angus *Mór* (*the Great*) MacDonald		c1266–96	1296	
Alexander (I)		1296–99	1308?	deposed
Angus *Og* (*the Younger*)		1299–1330	1330	
John (I)		1330–87	1387	
Donald II		1387–23	1423	
Alexander II		1423–49	1449	
John II		1449–93	1503	imprisoned
Angus (III)		1480–90	1490	usurped power; assassinated
Donald *Dubh*		1545	1545	unsuccessful claimant

Title and lands were forfeited to the Scottish crown in 1493.

ORKNEY (874–1480)

The earldom of the Orkneys was created by Harald king of Norway in the ninth century. Although its earls, or jarls, remained subordinate to Norway, they had considerable autonomy in Britain. Their territory included the northern (and sometimes the southern) Hebrides, known as the Sudreys, and usually included Caithness (and sometimes Sutherland) in mainland Scotland.

Ruler	Born	Reign	Died	Notes
Ragnald (I) or Rögnvaldur *the Wise*		c874–c5	894	returned to Norway; murdered
Sigurd (I) *Riki (the Mighty)*		c875–92	892	died from bites from a dead head
Thorstein *Raudr (the Red)*		c875–900	900	established as king of Caithness and Sutherland; killed in battle
Guthorm		c892–3	893	
Hallad		c893–4		abdicated

Orkneys occupied by Danish pirates under Thori Treebeard and Kalf Skurfa.

Ruler	Born	Reign	Died	Notes
Einar (I)		894–?920	?920	known as *Torf*-Einar
Arnkel		?920–54	954	ruled jointly and became subordinate to Erik; both killed
Erlend (I)		?920–54	954	in battle
Erik *Bloodaxe*	c885	c937–54	954	also king of Jorvik at different times between 939? and 954; killed in battle
Gunnhildr (*returned*)		954–5 976–7		widow of Erik *Bloodaxe*; ruled with her sons Ragnfred and Godred
Thorfinn (I) *Hausakljúfr (Skull-splitter)*	c910	c947–77	977	
Arnfinn	c942	977–?9	?979	murdered
Havard	c944	?979–?81	?981	murdered
Liot	c948	?981–?4		killed in battle
Hlodvir	c946	?984–?7	c988	
Sigurd II		?987–1014	1014	killed in battle
Somerled		1014–15	1015	shared earldom
Einar II		1014–20	1020	murdered
Brúsi		1014–c30	c1031	handed his share to Einar 1018–20
Thorfinn II *the Mighty*	c1007	c1018–c60	c1060	became primary earl from 1028
Ragnald II	1011	1038–46	1046	murdered
Paul (I)	c1038	c1060–98	1099	deposed and died in prison
Erlend II	c1040	c1060–98	1099	deposed and died in prison
Sigurd III	c1089	1099–1105	1130	

Ruled as king of Orkney and the Isles, subject to his father Magnus III of Norway.

Ruler	Born	Reign	Died	Notes
Haakon	c1071	1105–26	1126	previously Regent 1099–1105; co-ruled with Magnus
Magnus (I)	c1075	1108–17	1117	executed
Paul II *the Silent*		1126–37	?1138	deposed and probably murdered
Harald (I)		1126–31	1131	allegedly poisoned

Slettmali (Smoothtalker)

Ragnald III	*c*1100	1137–58	1158	murdered
Harald II *Gamli*	1133	1139–1206	1206	
(*the Old*)				
Erlend III		1154–6	1156	killed in battle
Harald III *Ungi*	*c*1156	?1195–8	1198	killed in battle
(*the Young*)				
David		1206–14	1214	
John (I)		1206–31	1231	murdered

John was the last earl of the house of Möre. With his death the earldom passed to a distant cousin and descendant of the earls of Angus.

House of Angus

Magnus II		1231–9	1239	
Gilbert		1239–56	1256	
Magnus III		1256–73	1273	
Magnus IV		1276–84	1284	
John II	*c*1259	1284–1311	1311	
Magnus V		1311–*c*29	*c*1329	
Malise		*c*1329–?53	?1353	
Erengisl		1353–60	1392	may have lost the title in 1357

The title was in dispute after 1360. It was claimed by Erengisl's nephew Alexander de l'Arde but was removed from him and confirmed upon Henry St. Clair in 1363, though it was not formally granted until 1379. Although the islands remained nominally Norwegian until 1469, the loyalty of the earls was increasingly to the Scottish king.

House of St Clair

Henry	1345	1379–1400	1400	murdered; noted navigator who also ruled the Faeroes and Greenland; may have colonized north-eastern America in 1398
Henry	*c*1375	1400–20	1420	died of the plague
William	*c*1404	1420–71	1480	resigned earldom to the Scottish crown

SCOTLAND (1306–1807)

After two interregna, during which time Edward I sought to gain control over Scotland, Robert the Bruce declared himself king of Scotland, soundly defeated the English at Bannockburn and obtained sovereign status for Scotland. His descendants ruled Scotland for the next three hundred years until James VI became James I of England and paved the way for the final union of Scotland and England.

House of Bruce

Ruler	Born	Reign	Died	Notes
Robert (I) the Bruce	1274	1306–29	1329	
David II	1324	1329–32		deposed by Edward Balliol
		1332–3		restored but again deposed
		1336–71	1371	restored, most of 1334–1357 in captivity in England
Edward (Balliol)	c1282	Aug–Dec 1332		deposed and expelled
		1333–4		restored but again deposed
		1335–6	c1364	restored and deposed again

House of Stewart

Robert II	1316	1371–90	1390	
Robert III	c1337	1390–1406	1406	

Lieutenant of the Realm: David, duke of Rothesay (his son), 1398–1401.

James (I)	1394	1406–37	1437	captive in England 1406–24; assassinated

Governor during imprisonment: Robert, duke of Albany, 1406–20; Murdoch, duke of Albany, 1420–4.

James II	1430	1437–60	1460	killed during siege of Roxburgh

Regents during infancy: Joan (his mother), 1437–9; *Lieutenant:* Alexander Livingston, 1439–49.

James III	1452	1460–88	1488	assassinated

Regents during infancy: Mary (his mother), 1460–3; Bishop James Kennedy, 1463–5; Alexander Boyd, 1466–9.

James IV	1473	1488–1513	1513	killed in battle
James V	1512	1513–42	1542	

Regents during infancy: Margaret (his mother), 1513–4; John, duke of Albany, governor, 1515–24; James, earl of Arran, chancellor, 1524–5; Archibald, earl of Angus, governor, 1525–8.

Mary	1542	1542–67	1587	assumed authority in 1561; abdicated, imprisoned and executed

Regents during infancy: James, earl of Arran as governor, 1542–54; Mary, the queen mother, 1554–60.

James VI	1566	1567–1625	1625	assumed authority 1580; became James I of England

Regents during infancy: James, earl of Moray, 1567–70; Matthew, earl of Lennox, 1570–1; John, earl of Mar, 1571–2; James, earl of Morton, 1572–80.

Charles (I)	1600	1625–49	1649	deposed and executed; also king of England

Council of State existed 14 Feb 1649–16 Dec 1653, during which period the Commonwealth of England was not recognized and Charles II was elected king.

Charles II	1630	1650–85	1685	also king of England
James VII	1633	1685–8	1701	deposed; see James II of England

Interregnum from Dec 1688–Feb 1689 when William and Mary were recognized as monarchs.

William II	1650	1689–1702	1702	also William III of England; ruled jointly with Mary II
Mary II	1662	1689–94	1694	also Queen of England; ruled jointly with William III
Anne	1665	1702–14	1714	

With the Act of Union in 1707, Scotland and England were formerly united as Great Britain.

Stewart Pretenders

James (VIII) the Old Pretender	1688	1701–16	1766	never reigned but was acknowledged rightful heir by the Jacobites
Charles (III) the Young Pretender	1720	1745–6	1788	acknowledged by a few supporters
Henry (IX)	1725	1788–1807	1807	never seriously pursued the claim

KINGDOM OF MAN (1333–1765)

In 1290 Edward I took possession of the island for England, placing it under the governorship of Richard de Burgh, earl of Ulster. John Balliol briefly reclaimed the island for Scotland from 1293–96; otherwise it remained under English control. During this period the most stable period of governorship was under Antony Bek, bishop of Durham, from 1298 to 1311. Robert the Bruce claimed Man again for Scotland in 1313. In 1316 the Irish ravaged the island and it remained a battlefield plundered and claimed by Ireland, Scotland and England until the powerful reign of Edward III. In 1333 Edward granted the island to William de Montacute in full possession, so that he became the first restored sovereign lord of Man for nearly seventy years.

Ruler	Born	Reign	Died	Notes
William de Montacute (i.e. Montague)		1333–44	1344	also created earl of Salisbury in 1337
William Montague (II)		1344–92	1397	sold the island to William le Scrope
William le Scrope		1393–9	1399	beheaded
Henry Percy, earl of Northumberland		1399–1405	1408	deprived of lordship

House of Stanley

Ruler	Born	Reign	Died	Notes
John	c1350	1405–14	1414	
John II		1414–37	1437	
Thomas	c1405	1437–59	1459	
Thomas II	c1435	1459–1504	1504	created earl of Derby in 1485

On the death of Thomas II, his successor gave up the title of king and became lord of Man.

Ruler	Born	Reign	Died	Notes
Thomas III	c1481	1504–21	1521	
Edward	1509	1521–72	1572	
Henry	1531	1572–93	1593	
Ferdinando	c1559	1593–4	1594	

Succession in dispute 1594–1612; meanwhile Man returned to Elizabeth I and James I of England.

Ruler	Born	Reign	Died	Notes
William I	c1561	1610–12	1647	Although the lawful ruler, William left governorship with his wife Elizabeth, and then his son James
Elizabeth, countess of Derby	1575	1612–27	1627	
James, Lord Strange	1607	1627–51	1651	executed

After the earl of Derby's death his wife briefly controlled the island, though she was deposed in a rebellion. Governorship passed to Lord Fairfax from 1651–60 until the restoration of the English monarchy, restored the Stanleys to the lordship of Man.

Ruler	Born	Reign	Died	Notes
Charles	1628	1660–72	1672	
William II	c1655	1672–1702	1702	
James II	1664	1702–36	1736	

House of Murray

Ruler	Born	Reign	Died	Notes
James Murray	c1690	1736–64	1764	2nd duke of Atholl
John Murray	1729	1764–5	1774	

Murray sold the lordship to the British Crown in 1765 and the island came under British sovereignty.

THE WELSH KINGDOMS (400–1291)

The native British retained a degree of autonomy in Wales throughout the Roman occupation. Little is recorded about them that can be established as firm historical fact though it is possible that the Silures, Ordovices and Demetae continued to be ruled by tribal chieftains within the Roman administration. Towards the end of this period an influx of Irish from the west and British from the east began to test these tribal boundaries and new ones emerged based, initially, on the old tribes, but subsequently developing into four main kingdoms – Gwent, Gwynedd, Powys and Deheubarth. The following lists all of the main kingdoms and most of the sub-kingdoms.

GWENT and GLYWYSING (420–950)

The rulership of south-east Wales is complicated by the many sub-divisions of the land due to partible succession. Essentially there were two main kingdoms: Gwent and Glywysing, both descended from the Silures. Petty chieftains responded to the stronger rulers, sometimes from Gwent and sometimes from Glywysing but it was not until the tenth century that the two kingdoms effectively united under the name Morgannwg. The following lists the primary rulers. In almost all cases lands were sub-divided between sons and brothers, resulting in many sub-kings who are not listed here.

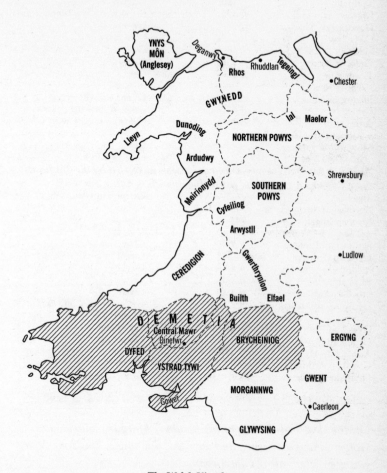

The Welsh Kingdoms

Ruler	Reign	Died	Notes
Erb	fl 420s		Gwent
Nynniaw	fl 450s		Gwent
Teithfallt	fl 480s		Gwent
Glywys	fl 490s		founder of Glywysing
Honorius or Ynyr	fl 510s		Gwent
Gwynllyw	fl 520s		Glywysing
Iddon	fl 540s		Gwent
Cadoc or Cadog	fl 550s		Glywysing
Tewdrig or Theodosius	fl 550s	?584	Gwent; abdicated but killed in battle
Meurig or Mouric	c580–c615	c615	Gwent and Glywysing
Cynfeddw	fl 610s		possibly sub-king in Gwent
Arthwyr or Athrwys ap Meurig	c615–c630		probably ruled Gwent
Morgan Mwynfawr (the Generous)	c630–c665	665	Gwent and Glywysing; may have died in battle

Although Morgan is reckoned to have been succeeded by his son Ithael, there remains a gap in the chronology which is difficult to fill.

Ruler	Reign	Died	Notes
Ithael	c715–c745		Gwent and Glywysing
Ffernfael ap Ithael	745–775	775	Gwent
Rhys ab Ithael	745– ?		Glywysing
Arthwyr ap Ffernfael	775– ?		Gwent
Arthfael ap Rhys	fl 800		Glywysing
Ithael ab Arthwyr	? –848		Gwent
Meurig ab Arthfael	fl 830s		Gwent
Rhys ab Arthfael	fl 830s		Glywysing
Brochwael ab Meurig	fl 880s		Gwent
Ffernwael ab Meurig	fl 880s		Gwent; ruled jointly with above
Hywel ap Rhys	c840–c885	885	Glywysing
Owain ap Hywel	c885–c930	930	Glywysing
Arthfael ap Hywel	fl 920s		Gwent
Cadell ap Arthfael	fl 930s	942	Gwent
Gruffydd ap Owain	930–934	934	Glywysing; Gower from 928; killed in battle
Cadwgan ap Owain	930–950	950	West Glywysing; killed in battle

On the death of Cadwgan his brother, Morgan, united Gwent, Gower and Glywysing and created the single kingdom Morgannwg, later called Glamorgan.

MORGANNWG and GLAMORGAN (930–1091)

The individual kingdoms retained their identity to some degree and Morgannwg continued to be fragmented under successor kings, although there was now more propensity to unity, especially in facing the advance of the Danes and later the Normans.

Ruler	Reign	Died	Notes
Morgan *Hen* (*the Old*) ab Owain	930–74	974	Morgannwg
Nowy ap Gwriad	*fl* 950s		Gwent
Owain ap Morgan	974– ?		Glywysing
Arthfael ap Nowy	*fl* 970s	*c*983	Gwent; probably murdered
Rhys ab Owain	*fl* 990s		Glywysing (part)
Iestyn ab Owain	*fl* 990s	*c*1015	Glywysing (part)
Hywel ab Owain	*c*990s–*c*1043	1043	Glywysing (part)
Rhodri ap Elisedd	983–*c*1015	*c*1015	Gwent
Gruffydd ap Elisedd	983–*c*1015	*c*1015	Gwent
Edwyn ap Gwriad	1015–45		Gwent; imprisoned and blinded by Meurig
Rhydderch ab Iestyn	*c*1015–33	1033	Glywysing and Deheubarth killed in battle
Gruffydd ap Rhydderch	1033–55	1055	Glywysing and Deheubarth killed in battle
Meurig ap Hywel	1045–55		Gwent

Morgannwg and Gwent were taken over by Gruffydd ap Llywelyn of Gwynedd, 1055–63.

Ruler	Reign	Died	Notes
Cadwgan ap Meurig	1063–74		Morgannwg
Caradog ap Gruffydd	1075–81	1081	Gwent 1063–74; usurped Morgannwg; killed in battle
Iestyn ap Gwrgan	1081–91	?1093	deposed; died in a priory

Glamorgan (Morgannwg) and Gwent were taken over by the Normans in 1091 under the control of Robert Fitzhamon. The descendants of Caradog ap Gruffydd became lords of Caerleon until they were deprived of their lands in 1270; the descendants of Iestyn ap Gwrgan became lords of Afan until deprived of their lands in 1282.

CEREDIGION and SEISYLLWG (470–920)

Ceredigion was one of the sub-kingdoms allegedly established by Cunedda's son Ceredig. It probably formed around a previous Ordovician kingdom. Its early history may be indistinguishable from Gwynedd in the north whilst in the south it originally formed part of the kingdom of Dyfed. Its independence did not start to emerge until the reign of Seisyll ap Clydog.

Ruler	Reign	Died	Notes
Ceredig	*fl* 470s		
Iusay	*fl* 500s		
Serguil	*fl* 530s		
Bodgu ap Serguil	*fl* 560s		
Artbodgu ap Bodgu	*fl* 600s		
Artglys ap Artbodgu	*fl* 640s		
Kingship during this period is uncertain.			
Clydog ap Artglys	*fl* 730s		
Seisyll ap Clydog	*fl* 770s		

Seisyllwg

Ruler	Reign	Died	Notes
Arthgen ap Seisyll	? –807		
Dyfnwallon ap Arthgen	807– ?		
Meurig ap Dyfnwallon	*fl* 850s		
Gwgon ap Meurig	? –871	871	drowned

After Gwgon's death Rhodri the Great annexed Seisyllwg to the kingdoms of Gwynedd and Powys. After his death his kingdom was split and Seisyllwg passed to his son Cadell.

Cadell ap Rhodri	878–909	909	
Clydog	909–920	920	

After Clydog's death his brother Hywel, who had inherited Dyfed after his father's conquests in 904, combined Seisyllwg and Dyfed to form the new kingdom of Deheubarth which occupied most of South Wales except for Glamorgan. Hywel also annexed Gwynedd in 942 making him the ruler of all West Wales.

DEMETIA and DYFED (400–950)

The kingdom of Dyfed, in the far south-west of Wales, was originally the tribal territory of the Demetae, and the kingdom was first known as Demetia. When Roman authority waned it was settled by the Irish, who traced their descent from Artchorp in the fourth century, who was descended from the Irish High Kings. Details of the kings and their reigns are sparse. The Demetian rulers are distantly related to the Scottish settlers of Dál Riata.

Ruler	Born	Reign	Died	Notes
Eochaid		*fl* 400		son of Artchorp
Corath		*fl* 420s		

Aed	*fl* 450s		
Tryffin	*fl* 480s		
Aircol *Lawhir* (*Longhand*)	*fl* 500		
Gwrthefyr, or Vortepor	*c*515–*c*540		
Cyngar	*fl* 550s		
Pedr	*fl* 570s		
Arthwyr	*fl* 590s		
Nowy	*fl* 610s		
Gwlyddien	*fl* 640s		
Cathen	*fl* 670s		
Cadwgan	*fl* 700s		
Rhain	*fl* 730s		

Rhain's kingdom was severely diminished by conquest by Seisyll of Ceredigion and the remnant became the smaller kingdom of Rheinwg.

Rheinwg

Tewdws or Tewdwr		*fl* 770s	
Maredudd	*c*745	? –*c*797	*c*797
Rhain (II)	*c*767	*c*797–808	808
Owain ap Maredudd	*c*770	808–811	811
Tryffin ap Rhain		811–814	814

Details of Dyfed's rulers vanish at this time, possibly as the result of Viking raids. No more rulers are recorded until the time of Owain's grandson, Hyfaidd.

Hyfaidd ap Bledri		*fl* 880s–893	893	
Llywarch ap Hyfaidd		? –904	904	drowned
Rhodri ap Hyfaidd		904–905	905	beheaded
Hywel *Dda* (the Good)		905–950	950	

Hywel Dda inherited Seisyllwg after his brother's death and combined the two kingdoms as Deheubarth.

DEHEUBARTH (920–1291)

Deheubarth came into existence in 920 when Hywel Dda combined the former kingdoms of Dyfed and Seisyllwg. Occasionally rulers of Deheubarth gained control over Gwynedd and vice versa. The Normans conquered Deheubarth in 1093, though descendants of the ruling family were allowed to hold authority over Cantref Mawr ('the Great Cantref...') and Ystrad Tywi and from this base the former kingdom of Deheubarth briefly re-emerged in the twelfth century under Maredudd ap Gruffydd and the Lord Rhys. Thereafter Norman control was re-exerted and Deheubarth ceased to exist as a kingdom after 1234.

Ruler	Born	Reign	Died	Notes
Hywel *Dda* (*the Good*)	c882	920–50	950	also ruled Gwynedd and Powys, 942–50

After Hywel's death Gwynedd regained its independence. Hywel's three sons split the kingdom of Deheubarth, but after Rhodri died in 953 and Edwin in 954, Owain was able to reconsolidate it.

Owain ap Hywel		954–86	988	retired
Maredudd ab Owain		986–99	999	also annexed Gwynedd from 986

After Maredudd's death the combined kingdoms of Gwynedd and Deheubarth were ruled from Gwynedd by Cynan ap Hywel from 999–1005.

Edwin ab Einion		1005–18		
Cadell ab Einion		1005–18		

In 1018, Llywelyn ap Seisyll of Gwynedd, who married into the Deheubarth royal family, laid claim to Deheubarth and ruled until his death in 1023. Gwynedd and Deheubarth were then overrun by Rhydderch ab Iestyn of Gwent, who styled himself king of Deheubarth.

Rhydderch ab Iestyn		1023–33	1033	also ruled Gwent; killed in battle
Hywel ab Edwin		1033–44	1044	killed in battle

Hywel was overthrown by Gruffydd ap Llywelyn of Gwynedd in 1044 and, in the ensuing power struggle, Rhydderch's son Gruffydd laid claim to Deheubarth.

Gruffydd ab Rhydderch		1047–55	1055	also ruled Gwent; killed in battle

Conquered by Gruffydd ap Llywelyn of Gwynedd from 1055–63.

Maredudd ab Owain ab Edwin		1063–72	1072	killed in battle
Rhys ab Owain ab Edwin		1072–78	1078	killed in battle
Rhys ap Tewdwr		1078–93	1093	briefly overthrown in 1081 and 1088; killed in battle

Deheubarth was overrun by the Normans in 1093, remaining in their possession until 1155. Territory was granted to Rhys's son Gruffydd in 1116, and further land was progressively regained after the grand revolt of 1136/37.

Gruffydd ap Rhys	c1090	1116–37	1137	ruled only Cantref Mawr; killed in battle
Anarawd ap Gruffydd	c1116	1136–43	1143	murdered
Cadell ap Gruffydd		1143–51	c1175	seriously injured and incapacitated

Maredudd ap Gruffydd	*c*1130	1151–5	1155	rebuilt old kingdom of Deheubarth
Rhys ap Gruffydd	*c*1133	1155–97	1197	in 1158 submitted to Henry II and dropped title of king, being known as The Lord Rhys
Gruffydd ap Rhys		1197–1201	1201	
Maelgwyn ap Rhys	*c*1170	1199–1230	1230	gained control of Ceredigion, though lost the northern part in 1207
Rhys *Gryg* (*the Hoarse*)		1216–34	1234	ruled Cantref Mawr (from 1204) and neighbouring territory; died of wounds

After the deaths of Maelgwyn and Rhys the princes of Deheubarth were effectively minor lords subject to Gwynedd and ruling small commotes and cantrefs in Ystrad Tywi and Ceredigion with no real authority. Rhys ap Maredudd below was the last to make a stand in the South and was briefly proclaimed lord of Ystrad Tywi.

Rhys *Mechyll*	1234–44	1244	ruled Cantref Mawr only
Maredudd	1244–71	1271	ruled Cantref Mawr only
Rhys ap Maredudd	1271–83	1291	ruled Cantraf Mawr only; executed for treason

VENEDOTIA and GWYNEDD (450–844)

Gwynedd covered the territory of the Ordovices, but the kingdom established by Cunedda brought together migratory British from elsewhere in Britain. The territory was originally known as Venedotia, a name which mutated to Gwynedd over the next two centuries. The heart of Gwynedd was originally at Deganwy, but shifted to Anglesey and at one time included the Isle of Man. It became the most powerful kingdom of Wales.

Ruler	Born	Reign	Died	Notes
House of Cunedda				
Cunedda		*c*450s–*c*460s		
Einion		*c*470s–*c*480s		
Cadwallon *Lawhir* (*Longhand*)		*c*500–*c*534	*c*534	
Maelgwn *Hir* (*the Tall*)	*c*497	*c*520s–*c*549	*c*549	died in a plague
Rhun *Hir*	*c*520	*c*549–?580s		
Beli		580s–*c*599	*c*599	

Iago		c599–c613	c613	
Cadfan		c615–c620	c625	

Edwin of Northumbria overran Gwynedd between 620 and 627.

Ruler	Born	Reign	Died	Notes
Cadwallon	c590s	c620–634	634	in exile 620–627; killed in battle
Cadfael		634–c655		usurper; later deposed
Cadwaladr		c655–c682	c682	died in a plague
Idwal		c682–?720	?720	
Rhodri *Molwynog*		c720–c754	c754	
Caradog		c754–c798	c798	killed
Cynan		c798–816	816	may have ruled from 813 only
Hywel		814–825	825	
Merfyn *Frych* (the Freckled)		825–844	844	son of Gwriad of Man

Merfyn's son, Rhodri, succeeded to the kingdoms of Powys in 855 and that of Seisyllwg in 872, becoming king of all North Wales.

GWYNEDD (844–1283)

Gwynedd was always the primary kingdom of Wales, even though it had moments when it was dominated by rulers from the south. It had several great rulers during its early years but the first to earn the title 'the Great' was Rhodri ap Merfyn who by 871 had inherited Powys and Seisyllwg, in addition to Gwynedd, and was effectively ruler of all northern and western Wales.

Ruler	Born	Reign	Died	Notes
Rhodri *Mawr* (the Great)		844–78	878	driven out by Vikings; killed in battle
Anarawd ap Rhodri		878–916	916	
Idwal *Foel* (the Bald)		916–42	942	killed in battle

Idwal submitted to Edward the Elder of England from 918–37. Gwynedd was ruled by Hywel Dda of Deheubarth from 942–50.

Iago ab Idwal		950–79	?	deposed
Ieuaf ab Idwal		950–69	988	deposed and imprisoned
Hywel ap Ieuaf		974–85	985	killed
Cadwallon ap Ieuaf		985–6	986	slain

Gwynedd was ruled by Maredudd ap Owain of Deheubarth from 986–999.

Cynan ap Hywel		999–1005	1005	

Llywelyn ap Seisyll		1005–23	1023	also ruled Deheubarth from 1018
Iago ap Idwal ap Meurig		1023–39	1039	murdered
Gruffydd ap Llywelyn		1039–63	1063	ruled Deheubarth from 1055; recognized as sovereign ruler of all Wales; murdered.
Bleddyn ap Cynfyn	c1025	1063–75	1075	murdered
Rhiwallon ap Cynfyn		1063–70	1070	co-ruler with Bleddyn; killed in battle
Trahern ap Caradog		1075–81	1081	killed in battle
Gruffydd ap Cynan	c1055	1081–1137	1137	regained territory briefly in 1075
Owain Gwynedd	c1100	1137–70	1170	styled Prince of Gwynedd from 1157

Upon Owain's death his lands were divided between his sons, of whom Maelgwyn inherited Anglesey. Civil war broke out from 1170–4, from which emerged two victors who eventually divided the kingdom between them. Another son, Cynan, succeeded in retaining his land at Merioneth and briefly re-established a ruling dynasty there.

Maelgwyn ab Owain		1170–3	?	fled to Ireland; returned but imprisoned.
Dafydd ab Owain Gwynedd	c1135	1170–95	1203	East Gwynedd; ruled all of Gwynedd 1174–5; deposed
Rhodri ab Owain Gwynedd		1170–90	1195	West Gwynedd; deposed, though temporarily regained Anglesey in 1193
Llywelyn *the Great*	1173	1195–1240	1240	acceded to East Gwynedd in 1195 and gradually rebuilt the kingdom; became effective ruler of Wales from 1216
Dafydd ap Llywelyn	c1208	1240–6	1246	styled himself 'Prince of Wales'
Llywelyn (II) *the Last* ap Gruffydd	c1225	1246–82	1282	killed
Owain *Goch* ap Gruffydd		1246–55	1282?	deposed by his brother; later reinstated by Edward I as co-ruler, 1277–1282?
Dafydd ap Gruffydd		1282–3	1283	deposed and executed for treason.

POWYS AND THE MARCHES (450–855)

The kingdom of Powys was carved out of the lands of the Cornovii and Decangii in eastern and north-eastern Wales. At the height of its power, during the late sixth century, its boundaries stretched beyond the current border of Wales into Cheshire, Shropshire and Herefordshire, the territory known today as the Marches. It struggled to retain its independence since it was under threat from the might of Gwynedd to the west and the encroachment of the Mercians to the east. The identity of its early rulers is uncertain because there were almost certainly several tribes along the borders of Wales with no single dominant ruler. For related kingdoms see Gwerthrynion and Brycheiniog.

Ruler	Reign	Died	Notes
Cadell or Catel(lus)	fl 450		

Powys was partitioned between Cadell's sons and the sons of Cunedda and Vortigern. Rulers probably included Owain ap Einion, Cattegirn, Brittu and Pascent, but precise details are uncertain.

Cynlas ab Owain, or Cuneglasus	fl 530s		
Cyngen	fl 550s		
Brochfael *Ysgythrog* (of the Tusks)	fl 570s		
Cynan *Garwyn* (the Cruel)	fl c600		
Selyf ap Cynan	? –615	615	killed in battle
Eiludd ap Cynan	615– ?		

At this stage Powys fragmented into North and South.

Southern Powys (Shropshire) – Pengwern

Cyndrwyn *the Stubborn*	fl 620s		
Cynddylan	c640–c655	c655	killed in battle

Northern Powys (Chester, Clwyd)

Beli ap Eiludd	fl 630s		

Rulers between Beli and Gwylog are uncertain.

Gwylog ap Beli	fl 700s		
Elisedd ap Gwylog	c725– ?		
Brochfael ap Elisedd	fl 760s		
Cadell ap Brochfael	? –808	808	
Cyngen ap Cadell	c808–c853	855	died in Rome

After Cyngen's death Powys passed to his nephew Rhodri Mawr and formed part of the kingdom of Gwynedd.

MEDIEVAL POWYS (1075–1416)

For over two hundred years Powys formed part of the kingdom of Gwynedd. It was re-established as a separate kingdom by the sons of Bleddyn ap Cynfyn soon after 1075 and although it was later divided into Northern and Southern Powys it remained independent for two centuries until eventually possessed by England.

Ruler	Born	Reign	Died	Notes
House of Bleddyn				
Madog ap Bleddyn		1075–88	1088	
Iorweth ap Bleddyn		1088–1103	1111	imprisoned; restored 1110, but murdered
Cadwgan ap Bleddyn		1088–1111	1111	murdered
Owain ap Cadwgan		1111–16	1116	captured 1114–15; murdered
Maredudd ap Bleddyn		1116–32	1132	
Madog ap Maredudd		1132–60	1160	

After Madog's death the kingdom was divided into North and South.

Ruler	Born	Reign	Died	Notes
Northern Powys				
Gruffydd Maelor (I)		1160–91	1191	Powys was shared with Owain Fychan (to 1187) and Owain Brogynton (to 1188)
Owain		1191–97	1197	ruled jointly with his brother Madog
Madog ap Gruffyd		1191–1236	1236	initially ruled jointly with his brother
Gruffydd Maelor II		1236–69	1269	

After Gruffydd Maelor's death his lands were partitioned amongst his sons, and Powys was never again reunited. His youngest son, Gruffydd Fychan (d.1289) had a son called Madog Crippil (d. c.1304) whose grandson, Gruffydd Fychan, was the father of Owain Glyn Dwr (see below).

Ruler	Born	Reign	Died	Notes
Southern Powys				
Owain Cyfeiliog	c1125	1160–95	1197	retired to a monastery
Gwenwynwyn		1195–1216	1216	dispossessed and died in exile

Lands came under the rule of Llywelyn the Great of Gwynedd, 1216–40.

Ruler	Born	Reign	Died	Notes
Gruffydd ap Gwenwynwyn	c1215	1240–86	1286	in exile 1257–63 and 1274–7

After Gruffydd's death Powys came under the sovereignty of England. Gruffydd had already given up his title as king to become a lord of the Marches, a title maintained by his family until 1421.

Wales

Owain Glyn Dwr (Glendower)	*c*1354	1400–12	*c*1416 declared Prince of Wales

BRYCHEINIOG (520–925)

Brycheiniog's origins are lost in legend and are also associated with Vortigern. The territory was initially part of southern Powys but later formed part of northern Gwent. It was named after its first and most famous ruler, Brychan.

Ruler	Reign	Died	Notes
Brychan	*fl* 520s		
Rhun *Dremrudd* (*the Red-Eyed*)	*fl* 550s		
Awst	*fl* 580s		
Here the king list becomes corrupt. Brycheiniog may have been overrun by Dyfed and remained part of that kingdom until the time of the second Awst.			
Awst	*fl* 750s		
Elwystl ap Awst	*fl* 770s		murdered
Tewdwr or Tewdws ap Rhain	*fl* 770s		
Brycheiniog may have been ruled from Dyfed for the next century.			
Tewdwr	*fl* 870s		
Elise ap Tewdwr	*fl* 890s		
Tewdwr ap Elise	*fl* 925		may be the last ruler

MEIRIONYDD (490–880)

Meironydd was a small *cantref* on the western seaboard of Wales. It was never a fully autonomous kingdom, existing as a vassal state to Gwynedd. The rulers were reputedly descended from Meirion, the grandson of Cunedda.

Ruler	Reign	Died	Notes
Meirion	*fl* 490s		
Catgualart	*fl* 510s		
Gwrin *Farfdrwch* (*of the Ragged Beard*)	*fl* 530s		
Glitnoth	*fl* 570s		
Gueinoth	*fl* 600s		
Idris or Iudric	? –632	632	killed in battle

Sualda	*fl* 640s		
Brochmael	? –662	662	killed in battle
Egeniud or Owein	662– ?		
Iutnimet	*fl* 690s		
Brochmael (II)	*fl* 710s		

Although the genealogies show Brochmael as the father of Cynan the next four or five generations are not known.

Cynan	*fl* 870s	880	killed in battle

Merioneth was absorbed into Gwynedd; the territory often inherited by younger sons of the king.

List of Royal Consorts

In pre-Norman times the wife of a monarch was seldom recognized as holding any authority, and they were seldom crowned or anointed as queen. Indeed, the West Saxons outlawed the crowning of the king's wife because of the wickedness of Beorhtric's wife Eadburh. Nevertheless some of the earlier queens were highly influential, especially in the rise of Christianity amongst the Saxons, starting with Bertha, the wife of Athelbert. The connection between the queen and the church gradually gave them a special status, which developed in the tenth century. By the time of some of the queens of the Middle Ages the king's wife had come to be regarded as a lady of power and authority. The queen ceases to be the queen when the king dies. If they are the mother of the successor they become the 'Queen Mother'; otherwise they are known as the 'Queen Dowager'. The following lists all of the known Saxon queens, plus the later Queens of England and Scotland. By the nature of the role, few of the titles, especially in the early years, are continuous.

Ruler	Born	Reign	Died	Notes

Queens of Kent

Bertha	post 561	c580–c601	c601	wife of Athelbert (I)

The name of Athelbert's second wife, who subsequently married Eadbald, is not known.

Emma	c603	c618–40	post 640	wife of Eadbald
Seaxburh		c640–64	c700	wife of Eorcenbert

Nothing is known of the later queens of Kent, except for the three wives of Wihtred, and it is not recorded whether they were consecrated as queens.

Queens of Mercia

Cynewise		fl630–55		wife of Penda

Cynewise appears to be Penda's only wife, and a sufficiently strong woman that she was left in charge of the kingdom when Penda undertook campaigns away.

Eormenhild		c660–75	c700	wife of Wulfhere
Osthryth		675–97	697	wife of Athelred; murdered

Identities of the next few queens are not known.

Cynethryth		c769–96		wife of Offa; may be regarded as the first queen of the English
Aelthryth		c796–821		wife of Cenwulf

Identities of the next few queens are not known.

Saethryth		c840–52		wife of Beohrtwulf
Athelswith		853–74	888	wife of Burgred, and daughter of Athelwulf of Wessex

Queens of Northumbria

Bebba		c595–c603	c603?	first wife of Athelfrith
Acha	c586	c604–?	?	second wife of Athelfrith; it is not certain whether she pre-deceased him
Athelburh	c595	625–33	647	wife of Edwin, and daughter of Athelbert (I) of Kent

Eanfrith had married a Pictish princess whose name is not recorded.

Cyneburh		c640–2	?	wife of Oswald, and daughter of Cynegils of Wessex
Enfleda or Eanfled	c626	642–70	c704	wife of Oswy
Etheldreda	c630	664–74	679	first wife of Egfrith; retired to monastery
Eormenburh		679–85	after 685	second wife of Egfrith
Cuthburh	c670	c695–c700	c725	wife of Aldfrith; retired to a monastery

Nothing is recorded of the subsequent wives of the Northumbrian kings or their status as queen.

Queens of Wessex

The West Saxons or Gewisse did not usually recognize the king's wife as having any status until the reign of Ine.

Athelburh	?688–?726		wife of Ine
Frithugyth	?726–?40		wife of Athelheard

Subsequent wives are not recorded until the reign of Beorhtric.

Eadburh	789–802	after 814	

Due to Eadburh's reputation, the title of queen was banned by the West Saxons.

Judith	c843	856–8	after 870	second wife of Athelwolf and briefly wife of Athelbald

The title of queen again lapsed until the reign of Edgar. Even Alfred the Great's wife, Ealhswith, was never apparently consecrated queen. Their details however are provided here for completeness.

Ealhswith	871–99	902	wife of Alfred
Elfleda	c901–20	920	second wife of Edward the Elder
Edgiva	c920–4	968	third wife of Edward the Elder
Elgiva or Elfgiva	c940–c5	c945	wife of Edmund (I)
Elgiva or Elfgiva	c957–8	959	wife of Edwy; marriage annulled; died in suspicious circumstances
Athelfleda	c961–c4	c964?	first wife of Edgar

The Queens of England

Elfrida	c945	c964–75	c1002	second wife of Edgar

Elfrida was the first woman to be crowned queen of England, on 11 May 973 at Bath.

Elfgiva or Elgiva	c963	c985–1002	1002	first wife of Athelred II
Emma (changed name to Elfgiva)	c985	1002–16	1052	second wife of Athelred II; subsequently married Canute
Edith or Eadgyth		Apr–Nov 1016		wife of Edmund II
Emma	c985	1017–1035	1052	wife of Canute and widow of Athelred II (*see above*)
Edith	c1020	1045–1066	1075	wife of Edward the Confessor
Edith	c1042	Jan–Oct 1066		wife of Harold II

Following the Norman Conquest the wife of the king was usually formally crowned as Queen Consort and these are the dates listed below. Where the marriage date is different it is included in the final column.

Matilda	c1031	1068–83	1083	wife of William I, married 1053
Edith (changed name to Matilda)	c1080	1100–18	1118	first wife of Henry I
Adeliza (or Adela or Alice)	c1105	1121–35	1151	second wife of Henry I
Matilda	c1103	1136–52	1152	wife of Stephen, married c1125
Eleanor of Aquitaine	c1122	1154–89	1204	wife of Henry II, married 1152
Berengaria of Navarre	c1163	1191–9	c1231	wife of Richard I
Isabella of Angoulême	c1187	1200–16	1246	second wife of John
Eleanor of Provence	c1223	1236–72	1291	wife of Henry III
Eleanor of Castile	1241	1274–90	1290	first wife of Edward I, married 1254

Edward I's second wife, Margaret of France (1279–1318), whom he married in 1299, was never crowned queen.

Isabella of France	c1292	1308–27	1358	wife of Edward II
Philippa of Hainault	1311	1328–69	1369	wife of Edward III
Anne of Bohemia	1366	1382–94	1394	first wife of Richard II
Isabella of France	1389	1397–9	1409	second wife of Richard II
Joan of Navarre	c1370	1403–13	1437	second wife of Henry IV
Katherine of France	1401	1420–2	1437	wife of Henry V
Margaret of Anjou	1429	1445–61	1482	wife of Henry VI, who was deposed in 1461 and briefly restored in 1471
Elizabeth Wydville	c1437	1465–83	1492	wife of Edward IV
Anne Nevill	1456	1483–5	1485	wife of Richard III, married 1472
Elizabeth of York	1466	1487–1503	1503	wife of Henry VII
Katherine of Aragon	1485	1509–33	1536	first wife of Henry VIII; divorced
Anne Boleyn	c1500	1533–6	1536	second wife of Henry VIII; marriage annulled; executed

None of Henry VIII's remaining wives were crowned, although plans were in hand for Jane's coronation before she died. They are all listed below, however, for completeness.

Jane Seymour	c1506	1536–7	1537	third wife of Henry VIII; not crowned; died after childbirth

Anne of Cleves	1515	Jan-Jul 1540	1557	fourth wife of Henry VIII; divorced
Katherine Howard	c1520	1540–2	1542	fifth wife of Henry VIII; executed
Katherine Parr	c1512	1543–7	1548	sixth wife of Henry VIII
Philip of Spain	1527	1554–8	1598	husband of Mary I; the only king consort of England; also king of Spain from 1556

The Queens of Scotland

Records of the wives of the early Scottish rulers are virtually non-existent, and this includes the wives of the Pictish kings through whom inheritance passed. No queen consort was officially crowned until the reign of David II, but earlier queens are listed here, where known, for completeness.

Ruler	Born	Reign	Died	Notes
Sybilla		1034–?	?	wife of Duncan I; it is not known whether she predeceased him
Gruoch	c1015	1040–?	?	wife of Macbeth; it is not known whether she predeceased him
Ingibiorg		c1060–c9	c1069	first wife of Malcolm III
Margaret	1046	1069–93	1093	second wife of Malcolm III
Ethelreda		1094–?	?	wife of Duncan II; it is not known whether she predeceased him
Sybilla	c1092	1107–22	1122	wife of Alexander I
Matilda	c1072	1124–c30	c1130	wife of David I
Ermengarde		1186–1214	1234	wife of William the Lyon
Joan	1210	1221–38	1238	first wife of Alexander II
Marie de Coucy		1239–49	?	second wife of Alexander II
Margaret	1240	1251–75	1275	first wife of Alexander III
Yolande of Dreux		1285–6	1323	second wife of Alexander III
Isabella de Warrenne	1253	1292–6	?	wife of John Balliol, married 1281
Elizabeth de Burgh		1306–27	1329	second wife of Robert I
Joanna	1321	1329–62	1362	first wife of David II

Joanna was the first queen consort of Scotland to be anointed and crowned, on 24 November 1331.

Margaret Drummond		1364–70	1375	second wife of David II; divorced
Euphemia Ross	c1330	1371–87	1387	second wife of Robert II, married 1355; crowned 1372

Annabella Drummond	c1350	1390–1401	1401 wife of Robert III, married 1366
Joan Beaufort		1424–37	1445 wife of James I
Mary of Gueldres	1433	1449–60	1463 wife of James II
Margaret of Denmark	1456	1469–86	1486 wife of James III
Margaret Tudor	1489	1503–13	1541 wife of James IV
Madeleine of France	1520	Jan–Jul 1537	1537 first wife of James V; not crowned
Mary of Guise	1515	1538–42	1560 second wife of James V; crowned 1540
Henry Stuart (Lord Darnley)	1545	1565–7	1567 Mary's second husband, the only king consort to be proclaimed king of Scotland

Queens of England and Scotland (Great Britain from 1701)

Anne of Denmark	1574	1590–1619	1619 wife of James VI (I); crowned queen consort of England in 1603
Henrietta Maria	1609	1625–49	1669 wife of Charles I; not crowned
Katherine of Braganza	1638	1662–85	1705 wife of Charles II; not crowned
Mary of Modena	1658	1685–8	1718 wife of James II
George of Denmark	1653	1702–8	1708 husband of Anne; not officially created prince consort
Caroline of Ansbach	1683	1727–37	1737 wife of George II, married 1705
Charlotte	1744	1761–1818	1818 wife of George III
Caroline of Brunswick	1768	1820–1	1821 wife of George IV; not crowned
Adelaide	1792	1830–7	1849 wife of William IV, married 1818; crowned 1831
Albert	1819	1840–61	1861 husband of Victoria; created Prince Consort 26 June 1857
Alexandra	1844	1901–10	1925 wife of Edward VII; married 1863, crowned 1902
Mary of Teck	1867	1910–36	1953 wife of George V; married 1893, crowned 1911; also crowned empress of India
Elizabeth Bowes-Lyon	1900	1936–52	2002 wife of George VI; married 1923, crowned 1937; also crowned empress of India, relinquished 1947
Philip Mountbatten	1921	1952–	husband of Elizabeth II; married 1947; created Prince Philip 1957

Royal Family Trees

The direct descent of Elizabeth II

73 generations from Beli Mawr to Elizabeth II

Beli Mawr (*fl* 100BC)
Caswallon (*fl* 55BC)
Llyr (*fl* 20BC)
Bran *the Blessed* (*fl* AD1)
Beli (*fl* AD 20)
Amalech (*fl* AD 50s)
Eugein (*fl* AD 70s)
Brithguein (*fl* 100)
Dyfwn (*fl* 120s)
Oumun (*fl* 150s)
Anguerit (*fl* 170s)
Amgualoyt (*fl* 200)
Gurdumn (*fl* 220s)
Dyfwn (*fl* 250s)
Guordoli (*fl* 270s)
Doli (*fl* 300)
Guorcein (*fl* 320s)
Cein (*fl* 350s)
Tacit (*fl* 370s)
Paternus (*fl* 400)
Edern (*fl* 430s)
Cunedda (*fl* 450–460)
Einion (*fl* 470–480)
Cadwallon *Lawhir* (*fl* 500–520)
Maelgwn (d. *c*549)
Rhun (*fl* 560s)
Beli (*fl* 590s)
Iago (d. *c*615)
Cadfan (d. *c*625)
Cadwallon (d. 634)
Cadwaladr (d. 682)
Idwal (d. *c*720)
Rhodri *Molwynog* (*fl* 754)
Cynan (d. 816)
Essyllt
Merfyn *Frych* (d. 844)
Rhodri *Mawr* (d. 878)

Cadell (d. 909)
Hywel *Dda* (d. 950)
Owain (d. 988)
Einion (d. 984)
Cadell (*fl* 1005–18)
Tewdwr
Rhys (d. 1093)
Gruffydd (*c*1090–1137)
The Lord Rhys (*c*1133–97)
Gruffydd (d. 1201)
Owain (d. 1235)
Maredudd (d. 1265)
Owain (d. 1275)
Llywellyn (d. 1309)
Thomas (d. *c*1343)
Margaret
Maredudd ap Tudor
Owen Tudor (c1400–61)
Edmund Tudor (c1430–56)
Henry VII (1457–1509)
Margaret Tudor (1489–1541) = James IV
James V of Scotland (1512–42)
Mary, Queen of Scots (1542–87)
James VI [James I] (1566–1625)
Elizabeth of Bohemia (1596–1662)
Sophia, Electress of Hanover (1630–1714)
George I (1660–1727)
George II (1683–1760)
Frederick, Prince of Wales (1707–51)
George III (1738–1820)
Edward, Duke of Kent (1767–1820)
Victoria (1819–1901)
Edward VII (1841–1910)
George V (1865–1936)
George VI (1895–1952)
Elizabeth II (1926–)

The Saxon Kings of the English

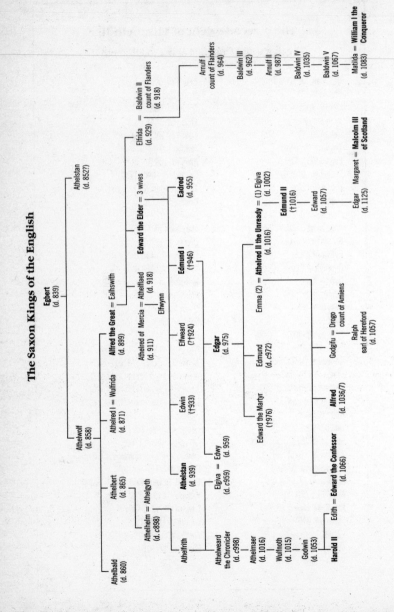

Egbert
(d. 839)

Athelstan
(d. 852?)

Athelwolf
(d. 858)

Athelbald
(d. 860)

Athelbert
(d. 865)

Athelhelm
(d. c898)

Athelfrith

Athelweard
the Chronicler
(d. c998)

Athelmaer
(d. 1016)

Wulfnoth
(d. 1015)

Godwin
(d. 1053)

Harold II

Athelred I = Wulfrida
(d. 871)

Athelgyth

Elgiva = Edwy
(d. c959) (d. 959)

Athelstan
(d. 939)

Alfred the Great = Ealhswith
(d. 899)

Athelred of Mercia = Athelflaed
(d. 911)   (d. 918)

Elfwynn

Edwin
(†933)

Elfweard
(†924)

Edward the Elder = 3 wives

Edmund I
(†946)

Eadred
(d. 955)

Edgar
(d. 975)

Elfrida = Baldwin II
(d. 929)   count of Flanders
           (d. 918)

Arnulf I
count of Flanders
(d. 964)

Baldwin III
(d. 962)

Arnulf II
(d. 987)

Baldwin IV
(d. 1035)

Baldwin V
(d. 1067)

Matilda = **William I the
(d. 1083)   Conqueror**

Edmund
(d. c972)

Edward the Martyr
(†976)

Emma (2) = **Athelred II the Unready** = (1) Elgiva
                (d. 1016)   (d. 1002)

Edmund II
(†1016)

Edward
(d. 1057)

Edgar   Margaret = **Malcolm III
(d. 1125)   of Scotland**

Godgifu = Drogo
           count of Amiens

Ralph
earl of Hereford
(d. 1057)

Alfred
(d. 1036/7)

Edith = **Edward the Confessor**
        (d. 1066)

The House of Normandy

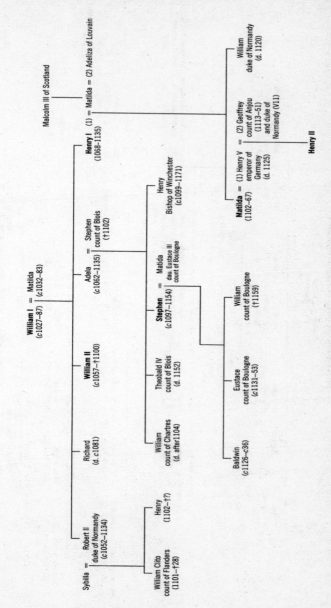

The House of Anjou / Plantagenet

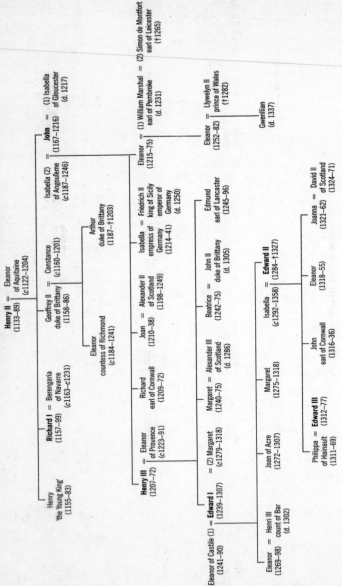

The Houses of York and Lancaster

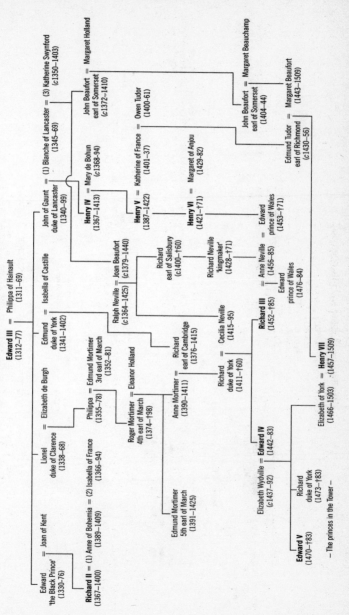

The Tudor and Stewart Succession

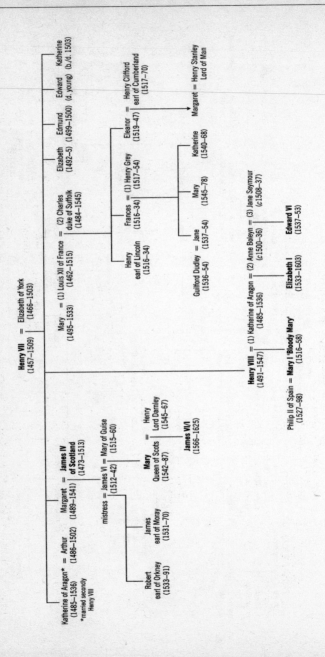

The House of Stewart

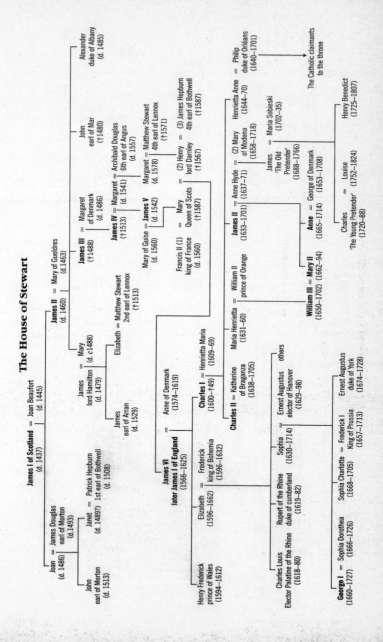

The House of Hanover

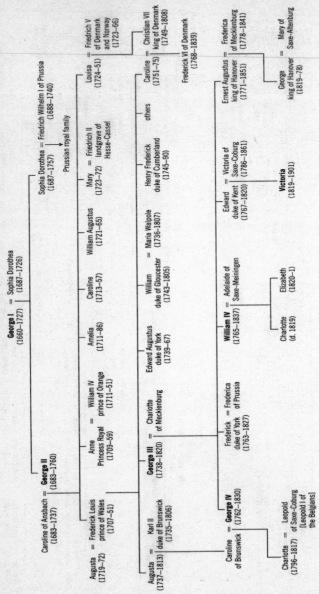

The Houses of Saxe-Coburg-Gotha (changed to Windsor)

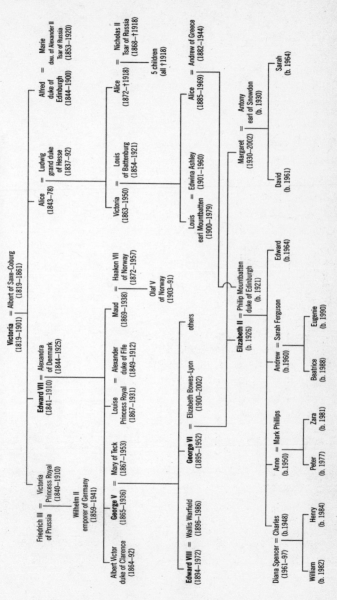

BIBLIOGRAPHY AND ACKNOWLEDGEMENTS

In the thirty years or more that I have been fascinated with British and European monarchy, particularly the period before 1066, I have read and taken notes from more books about the subject than I can remember, and certainly many more than I have collected and consulted in compiling this present volume. The following is nevertheless as representative a list as I can produce of books that I have consulted in whole or in part in researching this book, in addition to the many specialist magazines and papers as well as countless visits to castles and royal homes over the years. I would also like to acknowledge the special help of Peter Berresford Ellis on Celtic matters and Julian Lock for his invaluable historical knowledge and perception. This *Brief History* has been abridged from my *Mammoth Book of British Kings and Queens* by Elfreda Powell, who has also written some of the introductory material.

Adam, Frank, *The Clans, Septs, and Regiments of the Scottish Highlands*, Edinburgh: Johnston & Bacon, 1960 (6th edition, revised by Sir Thomas Innes).

Anderson, Marjorie O., *Kings & Kingship in Early Scotland*, Edinburgh: Scottish Academic Press, 1973.

Ashbee, Paul, *The Ancient British: A Social-Archaeological Narrative*, Norwich: University of East Anglia, 1978.

Ashdown, Dulcie M., *Queen Victoria's Family*, London: Robert Hale, 1975.

Ashdown, Dulcie M., *Royal Children*, London: Robert Hale, 1979.

Ashe, Geoffrey, *Kings and Queens of Early Britain*, London: Methuen, 1982.

Ashley, Maurice, *King John*, London: Weidenfeld and Nicolson, 1972.

Barber, Richard, *Henry Plantagenet*, Woodbridge: Boydell Press, 1972.

Barlow, Frank, *Edward the Confessor*, London: Eyre Methuen, 1970; revised New Haven: Yale University Press, 1997.

Barlow, Frank, *William Rufus*, London: Methuen, 1983.

Barnwell, P.S., *Emperor, Prefects and Kings: The Roman West, 395–565*, London: Duckworth, 1992.

Barnwell, P.S., *Kings, Courtiers & Imperium: The Barbarian West, 565–725*, London: Duckworth, 1997.

Barrow, G. W. S., *Kingship and Unity: Scotland 1000–1306*, London: Edward Arnold, 1981; revised, Edinburgh University Press, 1989.

Barrow, G.W.S., *Robert Bruce and the Community of the Realm of Scotland*, London: Eyre and Spottiswoode, 1965.

Bassett, Steven (ed), *The Origins of Anglo-Saxon Kingdoms*, Leicester University Press, 1989.

Bede, *Ecclesiastical History of the English People* trs. Leo Sherley-Price, rev R.E. Latham: Harmondsworth: Penguin, 1990.

Bellenden, John (translator), *The History and Chronicles of Scotland* by Hector Boece, Edinburgh, 1821.

Bingham, Caroline, *The Crowned Lions: The Early Plantagenet Kings*, Newton Abbot: David & Charles, 1978.

Bingham, Caroline, *Edward II*, London: Weidenfeld and Nicolson, 1973.

Bingham, Caroline, *James V, King of Scots*, London: William Collins, 1971.

Bingham, Caroline, *The Kings and Queens of Scotland*, London: Weidenfeld & Nicolson, 1976.

Birley, Anthony, *The People of Roman Britain*, London: B.T. Batsford, 1979.

Blackett, A.T. and Wilson, Alan, *Arthur and the Charters of the Kings*, Cardiff: M.T. Byrd, 1981.

Blackett, A.T. and Wilson, Alan, *King Arthur: King of Glamorgan and Gwent*, Cardiff: M.T. Byrd, 1981.

Blakeley, Brian L. and Collins, Jacquelin, *Documents in English History*, London and New York: John Wiley, 1975.

Bradbury, Jim, *Stephen and Matilda: The Civil War of 1139–53*, Stroud: Alan Sutton, 1996.

Branigan, Keith, *Prehistoric Britain, An Illustrated Survey*, Bourne End, Buckinghamshire: Spurbooks, 1976.

Breeze, David J., *The Northern Frontiers of Roman Britain*, London: B.T. Batsford, 1982.

Breeze, David J. and Dobson, Brian, *Hadrian's Wall*, London: Allen Lane, 1976.

Brooke, Christopher, *The Saxon and Norman Kings*, London: B.T. Batsford, 1963.

Brown, P. Hume, *History of Scotland*, Cambridge University Press, 1912 (3 volumes).

Bushell, T.A., *Barracuda Guide to County History, Volume I – Kent*, Chesham: Barracuda Books, 1976.

Casey, P.J., *Carausius and Allectus: The British Usurpers*, London: B.T. Batsford, 1994.

Chadwick, Nora K. (editor). *Celt and Saxon: Studies in the Early British Border*, Cambridge University Press, 1963.

Chadwick, Nora K. *The Celts*, London: Pelican Books, 1971.

Chapman, Hester W., *Lady Jane Grey*, London: Jonathan Cape, 1962.

Clarke, John, *The Life and Times of George III*, London: Weidenfeld & Nicolson, 1972.

Cleary, A.S. Esmonde, *The Ending of Roman Britain*, London: B.T. Batsford, 1989.

Clive, Mary, *This Sun of York*, London: Macmillan, 1973.

Collingwood, W.G., *Scandinavian Britain*, 1908; reprinted by Llanerch Publishers, 1993.

Crawford, Barbara E., *Scandinavian Scotland*, Leicester University Press, 1987.

Dark, K.R., *Civitas to Kingdom, British Political Continuity 300–800*, Leicester University Press, 1994.

Davies, John, *A History of Wales*, London: Allen Lane, 1993.

Davies, R.R., *Conquest, Coexistence, and Change: Wales 1063–1415* (History of Wales, Volume II), University of Wales Press in association with Clarendon Press, Oxford: 1987.

Davies, R.R., *The Revolt of Owain Glyn Dwr*, Oxford University Press, 1995.

Davies, Wendy, *Wales in the Early Middle Ages*, Leicester University Press, 1982.

Donaldson, Frances, *Edward VIII*, London: Weidenfeld & Nicolson, 1974.

Donaldson, Gordon, *Scottish Kings*, London: B.T. Batsford, 1967.

Donaldson, Gordon & Morpeth, Robert S., *A Dictionary of Scottish History*, Edinburgh: John Donald, 1977.

Douglas, D.C., *William the Conqueror*, London: Eyre and Spottiswoode, 1964.

Dudley, Donald R. & Webster, Graham, *The Rebellion of Boudicca*, London: Routledge & Kegan Paul, 1962.

Duncan, Archibald A.M., *Scotland: The Making of the Kingdom*, Edinburgh: Oliver & Boyd, 1975.

Earle, Peter, *Henry V*, London: Weidenfeld & Nicolson, 1972.

Edwards, Nancy and Lane, Alan, *The Early Church in Wales and the West*, Oxford: Oxbow Books, 1992.

Ellis, Peter Berresford, *Celt and Saxon: The Struggle for Britain*, London: Constable, 1993.

Ellis, Peter Berresford, *The Celtic Empire: The First Millenium of Celtic History*, London: Constable, 1990.

Ellis, Peter Berresford, *Macbeth, High King of Scotland 1040–57*, London: Frederick Muller, 1980.

Eluère, Christiane, *The Celts: First Masters of Europe* London: Thames & Hudson, 1993.

Falkus, Christopher, *Charles II*, London: Weidenfeld & Nicolson, 1972.

Falkus, Malcolm and Gillingham, John (eds), *Historical Atlas of Britain*, Book Club Associates by arrangement with Grisewood & Dempsey, 1981.

Farmer, David Hugh, *The Oxford Dictionary of Saints*, Oxford: University Press, 1992 (third edition).

Finberg, H.P.R., *The Formation of England 550–1042*, London: Hart-Davis, MacGibbon, 1974.

Fletcher, Richard, *Who's Who in Roman Britain and Anglo-Saxon England*, London: Shepheard-Walwyn, 1989.

Foster, Sally M., *Picts, Gaels and Scots*, London: Batsford, 1996.

Fraser, Antonia (editor), *The Lives of the Kings & Queens of England*, London: Weidenfeld & Nicolson, 1975.

Fraser, Antonia, *King Charles II*, London: Weidenfeld & Nicolson, 1979.

Fraser, Antonia, *The Life and Times of King James*, London: Weidenfeld & Nicolson, 1973.

Fraser, Antonia, *Mary, Queen of Scots*, London: Weidenfeld & Nicolson, 1969.

Fraser, Flora, *The Unruly Queen*, London: Macmillan, 1996.

Frazer, N.L. *English History Illustrated from Original Sources 1485–1603*, London, A.&C. Black, 1908.

Galliou, Patrick and Jones, Michael, *The Bretons*, Oxford: Basil Blackwell, 1991.

Gardner, Laurence, *Bloodline of the Holy Grail*, Shaftesbury: Element, 1996.

Garmonsway, G.N. (translator and editor), *The Anglo-Saxon Chronicle*, London: J.M. Dent, 1953.

Gelling, Margaret, *The West Midlands in the Early Middle Ages*, Leicester University Press, 1992.

Gillingham, John, *Richard I*, London: Weidenfeld & Nicolson, 1973.

Grimble, Ian, *Scottish Islands*, London: BBC, 1985.

Grinnell-Milne, Duncan, *The Killing of William Rufus*, Newton Abbot: David & Charles, 1968.

Hadfield, John, *The New Shell Guide to England*, London: Michael Joseph in association with Rainbird Publishing, 1981.

Hartley, Brian and Fitts, Leon, *The Brigantes*, Gloucester: Alan Sutton, 1988.

Hatton, Ragnald, *George I, Elector and King*, London: Thames and Hudson, 1978.

Haywood, John, *The Penguin Historical Atlas of the Vikings*, London: Penguin Books, 1995.

Head, Victor, *Hereward*, Stroud: Alan Sutton, 1995.

Hibbert, Christopher, *Edward VII*, London: Allen Lane, 1976.

Hibbert, Christopher, *George IV, Prince of Wales*, London: Longmans, 1972.

Hibbert, Christopher, *George IV, Regent and King*, London: Longmans, 1973.

Higham, Nicholas, *Rome, Britain and the Anglo-Saxons*, London: Seaby, 1992.

Higham, Nicholas, *The Northern Counties to AD 1000*, London, Longman, 1986.

Higham, Nicholas, *The Kingdom of Northumbria, AD350–1100*, Stroud: Alan Sutton, 1993.

Hill, David, *An Atlas of Anglo-Saxon England*, Oxford: Basil Blackwell, 1981.

Hood, A.B.E., *St. Patrick, His Writings and Muirchu's Life*, London and Chichester: Phillimore, 1978.

Hooke, Della, *The Anglo-Saxon Landscape: The Kingdom of the Hwicce*, Manchester University Press, 1985.

Howarth, Patrick, *George VI*, London: Hutchinson, 1987.

Ireland, S., *Roman Britain, A Sourcebook*, New York: St. Martin's Press, 1986.

Keynes, Simon and Lapidge, Michael, *Alfred the Great: Asser's Life of King Alfred and Other Contemporary Sources*, London: Penguin Classics, 1983.

Kightly, Charles, *Folk Heroes of Britain*, London: Thames and Hudson, 1982.

Kinvig, R.H., *The Isle of Man* (3rd ed., revised), Liverpool University Press, 1975.

Kirby, D.P., *The Earliest English Kings*, London: Unwin Hyman, 1991.

Kirby, J.L., *Henry IV of England*, London: Constable, 1970.

Lacey, Robert, *The Life and Times of Henry VIII*, London: Weidenfeld & Nicolson, 1972.

Lacey, Robert, *Majesty*, London: Hutchinson, 1977.

Laing, Lloyd, *The Archaeology of Late Celtic Britain and Ireland c.400–1200 AD*, London: Methuen, 1975.

Lambert, David and Gray, Randal, *Kings and Queens*, Glasgow: HarperCollins, 1991.

Lapidge, Michael and Dumville, David (eds), *Gildas: New Approaches*, Woodbridge: The Boydell Press, 1984.

Lawson, M.K., *Cnut: the Danes in England in the Early Eleventh Century*, London: Longman, 1993.

Lloyd, Sir John Edward, *A History of Wales*, London: Longmans, Green, 1939 (2 vols; third edition).

Lloyd, Sir John Edward and Jenkins, R.T. (eds), *The Dictionary of Welsh Biography, down to 1940*, Oxford: Basil Blackwell, 1959.

Lofts, Norah, *Queens of Britain*, London: Hodder & Stoughton, 1977.

Longford, Elizabeth, *Elizabeth R*, London: Weidenfeld & Nicolson, 1983.

Longford, Elizabeth, *Victoria R.I.*, London: Weidenfeld & Nicolson, 1964.

McClure, Judith and Collins, Roger (eds), Bede's *The Ecclesiastical History of the English People*, Oxford University Press, 1969.

Macdonald, Donald, *Lewis: A History of the Island*, Edinburgh: Gordon Wright, 1978.

McDonald, R. Andrew, *The Kingdom of the Isles*, East Linton: Tuckwell Press, 1997.

MacManus, Seamus, *The Story of the Irish Race*, 1921.

Mac Niocaill, Gearóid, *Ireland before the Vikings*, Dublin: Gill and Macmillan, 1972.

Maier, Bernhard, *Dictionary of Celtic Religion and Culture*, Woodbridge: Boydell Press, 1997.

Marsden, John, *Alba of the Ravens*, London: Constable, 1997.

Marsden, John, *The Fury of the Northmen*, London: Kyle Cathie, 1996.

Marsden, John, *Northanhymbre Saga: The History of the Anglo-Saxon Kings of Northumbria*, London: Kyle Cathie, 1992.

Marsden, John, *Sea-Road of the Saints*, Edinburgh, Floris Books, 1995.

Marsden, John, *The Tombs of the Kings: An Iona Book of the Dead*, Felinfach: Llanerch Publishers, 1994.

Middlemas, Keith, *The Life and Times of Edward VII*, London: Weidenfeld & Nicolson, 1972.

Mitchell, Stephen and Reeds, Brian, *Coins of England and the United Kingdom* (30th Edition), London: Seaby, 1995.

Mongan, Norman, *The Menapia Quest*, Dublin: The Herodotus Press, 1995.

Montgomery-Massingberd, Hugh (Editorial Director), *Burke's Guide to the Royal Family*, London: Burke's Peerage, 1973.

Moody, T.W., Martin, F.X., Byrne, F.J. (eds), *A New History of Ireland, Vol. IX: Maps, Genealogies, Lists*, Oxford University Press, 1984.

Morris, John, *The Age of Arthur*, 3 volumes, London & Chichester: Phillimore, 1977.

Morris, John, *Arthurian Sources Volume 2: Annals and Charters*, Chichester: Phillimore, 1995.

Morris, John, *Arthurian Sources Volume 3: Persons*, Chichester: Phillimore, 1995.

Morris, John, *Arthurian Sources Volume 4: Places & Peoples, & Saxon Archaeology*, Chichester: Phillimore, 1995.

Morris, John, *Arthurian Sources Volume 5: Genealogies and Texts*, Chichester: Phillimore, 1995.

Morris, John, *Arthurian Sources Volume 6: Studies in Dark-Age History*, Chichester: Phillimore, 1995.

Morris, John, *Nennius: British History and the Welsh Annals*, Chichester: Phillimore, 1980.

Myres, J.N.L., *The English Settlements*, Oxford University Press, 1986.

Nicolson, Harold, *George V: His Life and Reign*, London: Constable, 1952.

O Corráin, Donncha, *Ireland Before the Normans*, Dublin: Gill and Macmillan, 1972.

O Cróinín, Dáibhí, *Early Medieval Ireland 400–1200*, Harlow: Longman, 1995.

Oakley, Stewart, *The Story of Denmark*, London: Faber & Faber, 1972.

Packe, M., *King Edward III*, London: Routledge and Kegan Paul, 1983.

Palmer, Alan, *The Life and Times of George IV*, London: Weidenfeld & Nicolson, 1972.

Pálsson, Hermann and Edwards, Paul, *Orkneyinga Saga, The History of the Earls of Orkney*, London: Hogarth Press, 1978.

Pearce, Susan M., *The Kingdom of Dumnonia*, Padstow, Cornwall: Lodenek Press, 1978.

Powicke, Sir F. Maurice and Fryde, E.B., *Handbook of British Chronology*, London: Royal Historical Society, 1961 (3rd edition, 1986).

Richardson, Joanna, *Victoria and Albert*, London: J.M. Dent, 1977.

Ridley, Jasper, *Elizabeth I*, London: Constable, 1987.

Ridley, Jasper, *Henry VIII*, London: Constable, 1984.

Ridley, Jasper, *Mary Tudor*, London: Weidenfeld & Nicolson, 1973.

Roberts, John L., *Lost Kingdoms*, Edinburgh: University Press, 1997.

Rollinson, William, *A History of Cumberland and Westmorland*, Chichester: Phillimore, 1978.

Ross, Charles, *Edward IV*, London: Eyre Methuen, 1974.

Ross, Stewart, *Monarchs of Scotland*, Moffat: Lochar Publishing, 1990.

Salway, Peter, *Roman Britain*, Oxford University Press, 1981.

Saul, Nigel (ed), *Historical Atlas of Britain: Prehistoric and Medieval*, Stroud: Alan Sutton for the National Trust, 1994.

Sawyer, P.H., *Kings and Vikings*, London: Methuen, 1982.

Scarre, Chris, *Chronicle of the Roman Emperors*, London: Thames and Hudson, 1995.

Simons, Eric N., *Henry VII: The First Tudor King*, London: Muller, 1968.

Sinclair, Andrew, *The Sword and the Grail*, London: Random House, 1993.

Smout, T.A. *A History of the Scottish People 1560–1830*, London: Fontana, 1985.

Smurthwaite, David. *Complete Guide to the Battlefields of Britain*, Exeter: Webb & Bower, 1984.

Smyth, Alfred P., *King Alfred the Great*, Oxford University Press, 1995.

Smyth, Alfred P., *Warlords and Holy Men*, London: Edward Arnold, 1984.

Somerset, Anne, *Elizabeth I*, London: Weidenfeld & Nicolson, 1991.

Stafford, Pauline, *The East Midlands in the Early Middle Ages*, Leicester University Press, 1985.

Stenton, Sir Frank, *Anglo-Saxon England*, Oxford University Press, 3rd edition, 1971.

Swanton, Michael (translator and editor). *The Anglo-Saxon Chronicles*, London: J.M. Dent, 1996.

Tacitus, *The Agricola and the Germania*, trans H. Mattingly rev S.A. Handford, Harmondsworth: Penguin, 1970.

Tapsell, R.F., *Monarchs, Rulers, Dynasties and Kingdoms of the World*, London: Thames and Hudson, 1983.

Taylor, Alexander Burt (trans). *The Orkneyinga Saga*, London and Edinburgh: Oliver and Boyd, 1938.

Thomas, Charles, *Christianity in Roman Britain to AD 500*, London: B.T. Batsford, 1981.

Thorpe, Lewis (translator and editor), *The History of the Kings of Britain* by Geoffrey of Monmouth, Harmondsworth: Penguin Books, 1966.

Todd, Malcolm, *The Coritani*, Stroud: Alan Sutton, 1991 (revised).

Treharne, R.F. and Fullard, Harold (eds), *Muir's Historical Atlas, Ancient and Classical*, London: George Phillip, 1963 (sixth edition).

Vince, Alan, *Pre-Viking Lindsey*, Lincoln: City of Lincoln Archeological Unit, 1993.

Walker, Ian W., *Harold, the Last Anglo-Saxon King*, Stroud: Sutton Publishing, 1997.

Watson, D.R., *The Life and Times of Charles I*, London: Weidenfeld & Nicolson, 1972.

Webster, Graham, *Boudica*, London: B.T. Batsford, 1978, revised 1993.

Wedeck, H. (ed.), *Putnam's Dark and Middle Ages Reader*, New York: Putnam, 1964.

Weir, Alison, *Britain's Royal Families: The Complete Genealogy*, London: The Bodley Head, 1989; revised edition, London: Pimlico, 1996.

Weir, Alison, *Children of England*, London: Jonathan Cape, 1996.

Weir, Alison, *Lancaster and York*, London: Jonathan Cape, 1995.

Weir, Alison, *The Princes in the Tower*, London: The Bodley Head, 1992.

Weir, Alison, *The Six Wives of Henry VIII*, London: The Bodley Head, 1991.

Whitelock, Dorothy, *English Historical Documents, Volume 1: c500–1042*, London: Eyre Methuen, 1979.

Whitlock, Ralph, *The Warrior Kings of Saxon England*, London: Moonraker Press, 1977.

Williams, Ann, Smyth, Alfred P., Kirby, D.P., *A Biographical Dictionary of Dark Age Britain*, London: Seaby, 1991.

Williams, Neville, *The Life and Times of Elizabeth I*, London: Weidenfeld & Nicolson, 1972.

Williamson, David, *Brewer's British Royalty*, London: Cassell, 1996.

Williamson, David, *Kings & Queens of Britain*, London: Webb & Bower, 1991.

Winterbottom, Michael (translator and editor), *Gildas: The Ruin of Britain and other documents*, London and Chichester: Phillimore, 1978.

Witney, K.P., *The Kingdom of Kent*, London and Chichester: Phillimore, 1982.

Woodruff, Douglas, *The Life and Times of Alfred the Great*, London: Weidenfeld & Nicolson, 1984.

Wroughton, John. *The Longman Companion to the Stuart Age, 1603–1714*, Harlow, Essex: Longman, 1997.

Yorke, Barbara, *Kings and Kingdoms of Early Anglo-Saxon England*, London: Seaby, 1990.

Yorke, Barbara, *Wessex in the Early Middle Ages*, London: Cassell on behalf of Leicester University Press, 1995.

Young, A.J., *The Swords of the Britons: A Military Review*, London: Regency Press, 1984.

INDEX

This index provides page references for all kings and queens as well as the majority of other individuals whose lives intermeshed with royalty. Primary entries for each ruler are indicated in bold and illustrations in italic. All other individuals are listed with their dates (if known) and a brief description of their identity, e.g. Becket, Thomas (c1118–70), archbishop of Canterbury. Where individuals share a common name the entries are in chronological order. However, for convenience, rulers of a common name within a kingdom are grouped together. All kings, queens, princes and princesses are listed by their best known first name (e.g. Anne Boleyn, not Boleyn, Anne). All dukes and earls are listed by their family name and only exceptionally by their title.